THE GREAT WALK

BY THE SAME AUTHOR

The Selsey Tram
Six Of The Best!
The Jennings Companion
Financial Penalties
Around Chichester In Old Photographs
Here's A Pretty Mess!
Magisterial Lore
The Beaten Track (republished as The Big Walks Of Great Britain and subsequently Best Walks Of The North and Best Walks Of The South)
Poetic Justice
Walking The Coastline Of Sussex
Best Sussex Walks
That's My Girl (a play)
Let's Take It From The Top
Walking The Disused Railways Of Sussex (republished as Walking The Disused Railways Of Sussex And Surrey)
Once More From The Top
Sussex Top Tens
Walking The Kent Coast From End To End
Walking The Riversides Of Sussex
Walking The South Coast Of England
Anyone For Tenors?
Walking The Triangulation Points Of Sussex
Walking The Disused Railways Of Kent
Walking The Sussex Border Path
Walking The County High Points Of England
Sussex Station Walks
The Joy Of Walking (republished as Walk)
The Walker's Year
Stumbling On Mountains
The Muddlesfield Messiah

Cover illustration: The spectacular approach to Beachy Head on the South Downs Way and England Coast Path

THE GREAT WALKS OF SUSSEX

by David Bathurst

[signature]

with very best
wishes

October 2018

First published in 2018 by

Walk & Write Publications
41 Park Road
Yapton
Arundel
West Sussex BN18 0JE

Cover and typesetting by The Better Book Company,
5 Lime Close, Chichester, West Sussex PO19 6SW

Printed in the UK by Imprint Digital, Seychelles Farm,
Upton Pyne, Devon EX5 5HY

British Library Cataloguing-in-Publication Data.
A catalogue record for this book is available from the British
Library.

ISBN 978-0-9933241-2-3

CONTENTS

ACKNOWLEDGEMENTS

I would like to acknowledge the great generosity of Kathy Gore, Chair of Friends of Sussex Hospices, in contributing to the costs of publishing this book. I would also like to acknowledge the kindness and expertise of Michael Walsh in preparing this book for publication, and to thank my wife Sue and daughter Jenny for their constant love, forbearance and support.

ABOUT ME

I have lived in Sussex for over 30 years but have loved walking all my adult life. I was inspired to write this book by the beautiful scenery and wealth of interesting features in Sussex and the opportunities given to the walker by the number of great walking routes across it. By profession I am a solicitor and for over 24 years was legal adviser to magistrates in West Sussex. When I'm not writing or walking I love singing, vintage sitcom and crosswords.

TO JANE

I would like to dedicate this book to my professional colleague Jane Macdougall, another walking enthusiast, who has been immensely helpful and kind to me in so many ways.

ABOUT THE FRIENDS OF SUSSEX HOSPICES (FSH)

Friends of Sussex Hospices is a registered charity run entirely by volunteers. It raises funds, through a variety of activities, to support the running costs of the twelve hospice care providers that serve the adults and children of Sussex. FSH works alongside the hospices, promoting awareness of the invaluable services provided by them to our community. All proceeds of sale of this book will be donated to FSH.

INTRODUCTION

Sussex (that is, for the purposes of this book, the combined areas of East Sussex, West Sussex and Brighton & Hove) is hugely blessed with countryside of great, often spectacular, beauty and diversity, numerous fine towns and villages, a wealth of magnificent architecture and many attractions of immense interest to the visitor.

By far the best way of appreciating all that Sussex has to offer is by exploring on foot. A glance at an Ordnance Survey (OS) map covering any part of Sussex will reveal the impressive network of public footpaths, bridleways and other rights of way that are available to the foot traveller, and indeed a walk along any one of the footpaths and bridleways will be an enjoyable and rewarding experience. However, more enjoyable still is to tackle a "name" long-distance trail through part of Sussex. Each of these trails, all but the most recent of which are symbolised by the green diamond on the OS Explorer maps, will be waymarked with that trail's distinctive logo, will usually be themed, will invariably pass through fine and varied scenery, and will visit or go close to many features of great historical or scenic interest. Several of the routes pass through the South Downs National Park. Completion of one or more of these trails is an immensely satisfying achievement for a walker.

This book provides an overview of the nineteen trails which in my view qualify as Great Walks of Sussex. My criteria for such a qualification are as follows. Firstly, the trail concerned must be named; secondly, the trail concerned must be at least partially waymarked; and thirdly, more than 12 miles of the trail concerned must pass through Sussex. A number of the trails start or finish in, and/or pass through, other counties beside Sussex – in one or two cases, the Sussex section will be only a small part of its overall journey – but if more than 12 miles are in Sussex, it may be included in this book. There are other name trails in Sussex which are not included, either because they are not waymarked (eg Midhurst Way), they are no more than 12 miles in length (eg Seahaven Coastal Trail), and/or insufficient passes through Sussex (eg Harold's Way). You may also notice, on OS maps, reference to the E9 European Coastal Path. This simply overlaps with the South Downs Way, 1066 Country Walk and Saxon Shore Way (all covered in this book) throughout its time in Sussex, and in any case isn't waymarked as such at all. As for the England Coast Path, it is true that at the time of writing only a minute proportion of the Sussex section of this path, which I have included in this book, has been waymarked, but it is envisaged that waymarking for this route will be complete by 2020, and this book would not be complete without a description of the Sussex coastal route which is a worthy and fascinating undertaking for any walker.

Given the amount of information available online, why this book? The answer is there is no single tool either in the form of a traditional paper book or an online facility that provides a complete overview of this very distinctive "family" of Great Walks of Sussex. I hope that this book will appeal to two kinds of reader. The first is the aspiring walker who wants to tackle something a bit meatier than s/he has been used to, and/or is wanting to enjoy the wonderfully rewarding walking offered by these trails. The second is the armchair traveller who may for various reasons be unable to tackle any of the walks but who will enjoy a virtual journey along them and in doing so get to know a great deal about the history, geology, scenery and architecture of Sussex.

This is a "Sussex" book intended for the explorer of Sussex, and in the descriptions below I have confined myself to the Sussex sections of each of the trails. There are two exceptions, the High Weald Landscape Trail and Sussex Border Path, which start and finish in Sussex but where on the course of their journeys there are incursions into other counties. In these cases I have provided route descriptions of these incursions for the sake of continuity but I have kept to a minimum the background information on places visited in the other counties and they are not contained in the index.

The book is divided into 19 sections, each section devoted to one of the 19 Great Walks, the walks described alphabetically. With the exception of the England Coast Path, where the definitive route hasn't yet been finalised, the descriptions don't pretend to provide a full route guide. There are numerous online facilities for accessing these, and with the exception of the England Coast Path (which is still effectively work in progress), Greenwich Meridian Trail and Sussex Hospices Trail (both of which are recent additions to the family of Great Walks of Sussex) all are represented on the OS Explorer maps. What the descriptions will do, however, is provide a summary of the routes, highlighting features of particular interest either on or close by the route, and providing full descriptions of detours and route variations to enable you to find your way to features of interest just off the route. Sometimes I will unashamedly recommend a variation rather than the actual mapped route, if I think it is better! A detour, which always returns to the point at the route at which you left it (give or take a few yards sometimes), is denoted by a D and then a number, the description being given at the end of the section. A route variation, which picks up the route further on, is denoted by a V and then a number, with the description again given at the end of the section. (Very minor/straightforward detours and variations are covered in the body of each section.) Of course there's no reason why if you want to stick exclusively to the mapped route you can't return at a later date to walk the detours and route variations! The great thing about the routes, plus detours and variations, taken together is that walking them in full will enable you to get to see all of the scenic, historic and architectural highlights of Sussex, as well as many less well known gems that non-walkers might miss. The index section at the end lists features of interest under category to assist in locating them on your walks. It's not possible, for practical reasons, to include every single feature of interest for the Sussex explorer; churches are a particular issue, as there are so many historic churches in Sussex. To try and include them all would make this book, and your walks, really too long! My criteria for inclusion of churches are set out in the pre-amble to the index section.

I have deliberately tried to let the descriptions flow in order to create a sense of progress and purpose, saving to the end of each section not only the descriptions of the more intricate detours and route variations but a Good To Know paragraph which provides all the practical information you will need. An explanatory note in relation to the Good To Know paragraphs will follow this Introduction. I am very conscious that some would-be walkers will be daunted by the total length of some of the trails. However by breaking down each Great Walk into bite-sized chunks, using the cumulative mileage "stages" guide in the Good To Know paragraph, you'll find that even the biggest walks become manageable. This book does not presuppose any particular level of walking ability. Some readers may regard say 6 miles a day as their maximum, while others may only be satisfied if they've covered upwards of three times that. This book caters for all walking abilities and aspirations, from the weekend stroller to the marathon hiker.

It is important to observe basic safety precautions when tackling one of the walks, particularly those stated in the Good To Know paragraph as strenuous for any part. Never try and tackle more miles than you know you're reasonably capable of in one day, and always have your phone with you in case you find you can't complete your day's walk for any reason and need help. None of the walks contain climbs or descents that are excessively steep or dangerous, but minor injuries can occur in even the most benign terrain so have with you some basic first aid just in case. It's vitally important to get footwear right. Heavy walking boots aren't necessary: light leather or fabric boots, stout outdoor shoes, or even trainers will be fine, and I've walked many of these trails in Converses or even wellies, which are particularly good in mud! Always have with you a supply of slow-release energy food such as bananas, and (non-alcoholic) liquid refreshment, with water and/or a thermos hot drink being the best. It's vital to stay properly hydrated, drinking water regularly and often throughout your walk, to avoid thirst. And be prepared to change your plans and postpone if the weather turns nasty. Heavy rain is no fun at all to be out in and spoils the views, so wait for an improvement. Sussex enjoys lots of sunshine, and really bad days are comparatively few, so you won't have to wait long!

Good luck and happy walking.

GOOD TO KNOW

Start and Finish: The Start and Finish won't necessarily be the official start and finish of the trail – don't forget either may be outside Sussex! – but they'll be where I recommend you start and finish for the purpose of your Great Walk, having regard to public transport and ease of access. The cumulative mileage is calculated from/to these points. The official start and/or finish points, where these occur in Sussex, will be stated in the body of the text.

Total Mileage: This is the total for the basic route, from recommended start to recommended finish, and does not include any additional mileage for detours, route variations or accessing off-route amenities. Please note that I have given all distances in miles, in keeping with normal road signage in Great Britain, rather than kilometres. To convert miles into kilometres, multiply by 8 and divide by 5.

Difficulty: This is of course subjective. What for some walkers will be easy and straightforward will for others be demanding and challenging. Even an adverse wind direction can make an ostensibly easy walk feel very tough. I have tried to be as objective as possible having regard to the nature of the terrain and overall length of the journey, but weather conditions, which can't be predicted when planning a walk several days, weeks or months ahead, will play their part.

Stages: This section is designed to assist in planning. Each stage offers opportunity for one or more of the following: refreshment, public transport, accommodation and/or a convenient place for pick-up or drop-off by car (though not necessarily parking facilities).

Each stage is given a location name (stage name) which could be a town or village or just a road crossing, e.g. A27, B2139. The stage names are emboldened in the route description. An asterisk against a stage name indicates a convenient railway station is situated in or close to that place, and the description will tell you how you may access it. An R indicates that refreshments in the form of a shop, pub or café should be available at the place concerned, an A indicates the availability of accommodation close by, and a B indicates regular buses serve the place in question. However, things do change: establishments may shut down and bus services may be withdrawn so check before you set out, or at least have phone numbers you can call in case you find yourself in difficulties. I have generally avoided providing specific information about amenities such as names of establishments, not only because as stated they may have shut down but also to avoid any accusations of favouritism or free advertising!

The figure given against each stage name is the CUMULATIVE mileage for the walk as a whole up to that point, so to work out the distance between one stage and the next, simply subtract the smaller figure from the larger! With a handful of unavoidable exceptions there are never more than 6 miles between each stage – I work on the basis that practical users of this book will have the capacity to walk at least that distance in one go – and sometimes the distances between stages will be much less.

NOTE: Extra mileages for detours and route variations are stated at the end of the detour/variation descriptions but are not included for the purpose of the cumulative mileage. This means that if they're followed, the distance between some stages may exceed 6 miles, so make sure you take this into account when planning. The detour/variation descriptions incorporate information as to amenities available in the course of those extra pieces of walking. Where extra mileage is required to access amenities just off route, that is shown in the text but again NOT included for purpose of the cumulative mileage. The fact that there may be a (possibly substantial) detour to reach a place offering amenities is denoted by the use of the word "for" against a stage name, e.g. "Upper Station Road for Henfield."

OS: Numbers here denote the OS Explorer maps you'll need for the walk in question, that is if you're relying on old-fashioned paper maps. Those using GPS, ifootpath or other apps won't necessarily want this information but it may be useful as back-up in the event of a technological failure.

SKETCH MAPS

The sketch maps in this book are intended simply to show the location of each trail within Sussex and the principal places visited on that trail. The scale on all maps is 1:500,000, ie one twentieth of the scale of OS Explorer maps.

1 CUCKOO TRAIL

The Cuckoo Trail (CT) is inspired by a railway line which used to link Heathfield with Polegate via Hailsham. The line, opening in two sections (Hailsham to Polegate in 1849 and Heathfield to Hailsham in 1880), was actually part of a rail link going all the way between Eastbourne and Tunbridge Wells, and was affectionately known as the Cuckoo Line because of the Cuckoo Fair held at Heathfield on 14th April each year, with many fairgoers arriving by train. A 1924 timetable shows 9 daily return journeys on weekdays. Journeys were exceedingly slow, the 30 miles from Tunbridge Wells to Eastbourne liable to take an hour and a half or more, so there was certainly plenty of opportunity to enjoy the scenery! The line became a victim of British Rail chairman Dr Beeching and his notorious programme of railway closures, with the section between Heathfield and Hailsham shutting in June 1965 and that between Hailsham and Polegate closing in September 1968. It was in 1990 that the old line was reopened as a walking/ cycling trail, and today's Cuckoo Trail consists of a walk along virtually all of its length and then a short walk along another stretch of old railway; the trail ends with a link path to Hampden Park on the outskirts of Eastbourne. For those who've experienced fiddly field walking on other paths in Sussex, with sometimes less than adequate signage, this feels like a dream. Almost at once, from its beginning, you can see how much time and effort has been invested into the project by the local council, with excellent signposting throughout including very helpful mileposts, firm concrete surfacing, and lineside benches with most artistic wood carvings. It all makes for an easy, relaxing and enjoyable walk, although it has to be said that the section south of the A27 is a good deal less scenically rewarding.

To reach the start of the CT from **Heathfield High Street**, simply walk southwards away from that street down Station Road, soon veering left with the road, and then bearing right into Newnham Way, almost immediately then bearing left to join the route of the CT and embark on your journey along the course of the old line. Look out, very early, for the old Pevensey level crossing gate and red signal! There's a suburban feel to this early part of the walk which

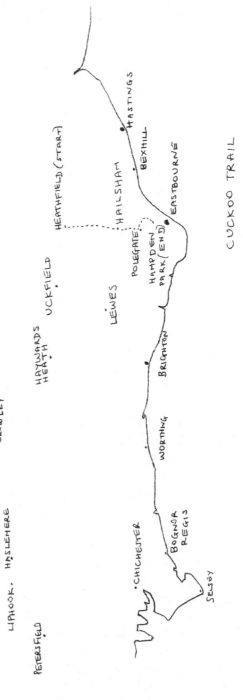

continues as far as your crossing of Ghyll Road which you follow briefly before striking out just west of south. Thus far you've been overlapping with the Sussex Hospices Trail but this now darts off to the right and you proceed most enjoyably southwards, away from the suburbs of Heathfield and roughly parallel with the B2203 which is to your left. There is a contrasting scene between left and right: to the right, delightful rolling fields and woods, and to the left, the busy B2203 road, the noise from which can seem quite intrusive. Shortly you arrive at **Horam**, passing the site of the station and in fact going under the B2203 – if you wish to detour to the village, the detour is well signed and just a few steps away – then you continue through a modern estate, with a separate route signed for horse riders. The next section, as far as Hellingly, is the loveliest on the whole of this walk. Veering now just east of south from Horam, beyond Horebeech Lane, you're able to leave the traffic noise as well as housing behind, and enjoy quite beautiful scenery from the comfort of your immaculate path. You pass through a lovely area of refreshing woodland which provides glorious colours in spring, then after crossing the quaintly named Cattle Creep Bridge and going under the fine triple-arched Woodhams Bridge, you find you're joined by the pretty Cuckmere river which is to your left. You veer gently from just east of south to just west of south and pass under Shawpits Bridge, then shortly cross over the Cuckmere, enjoying delightful scenery around the river crossing. You drop down to cross Mill Lane then soon pass under Station Road and you'll immediately see the very well preserved old station building at Hellingly to your right. By joining Station Road, heading westwards for 250 yards and then south along the Wealdway you'll reach, in 100 yards, the splendid Horselunges Manor, described in the Wealdway section.

The walk from Hellingly to Hailsham is pleasant but you have lost the lovely rural feel you enjoyed north of Hellingly; initially there is countryside on both sides but beyond the very busy Upper Horsebridge Road the walking takes on a more suburban feel as the CT approaches the centre of Hailsham, passing under a number of bridges and emerging in a car park. The trail turns sharp left and then right (A) to continue southwards down Station Road but by turning left at (A) instead of right, and immediately right into George Street and left up the High Street, you reach the centre of

Hailsham. In fact you can create a nice circular walk by following the church path roughly parallel with and to the right of the High Street to view the impressive part-flint church of St Mary, arriving at the High Street and then walking back down the High Street and George Street to return to Station Road. The total detour is half a mile. Hailsham is nowhere near the prettiest town in Sussex – I searched the town's main newsagent's shop for postcards of it and found none! – but it boasts some attractive buildings in its centre, including Town House and Old Manor House in Market Street (this being the south-eastward continuation of High Street beyond George Street), and the splendid Pavilion cinema in George Street, dating from 1921.

After proceeding southwards down Station Road the CT rejoins the course of the old line and the walk becomes very pleasantly rural once again. You swing from southwards to just west of south to cross two roads in close succession, and proceed through pleasant countryside with now excellent views ahead to the South Downs. The calm is somewhat rudely disturbed by the A27 Polegate bypass, crossed thankfully by a footbridge, and very soon you reach the outskirts of Polegate, arriving at a **path junction (B)**. By taking the path immediately parallel with and to the right of the old line, going forward along School Lane then right along Station Road, you reach the top of Polegate High Street which you can follow southwards to reach its shops and railway station, this detour roughly half a mile each way. However at (B) the CT leaves the course of the old railway and is signed eastwards, using cycle route 21, following the northern edge of suburban development then turning south-westwards along Levett Road to reach Pevensey Road. The CT follows this eastwards briefly, then strikes south-eastwards away from it through further areas of suburban housing around Aberdale Road and Bramley Road to reach an excellent path/cycle track that is the course of another old railway. Opening in 1846 and shutting in 1969, this provided a direct rail link between Polegate and Pevensey, bypassing Eastbourne. The CT follows this just south of east, as far as the A22 bypass, meeting the 1066 Country Walk; according to OS maps (signage on the ground would seem to suggest the CT actually ends here!) it then turns right, just east of south, to run parallel with and to the right of the A22. It's hardly inspiring walking although there are good views to Butts Brow above Eastbourne. OS maps suggest that at a signed path T-junction (C) just short of the A22/B2191 roundabout, the CT branches left under the A22 to end at the B2191 just outside Langney. However this particular spot is a pretty nondescript place to end such a good walk. Therefore, I suggest that having branched left at (C), you don't continue under the A22 but bear very shortly right along a signed path that follows beside a road leading past the hotel and arrives at the B2191 south-west of the roundabout. By turning right here alongside the B2191, right at the roundabout up Lottbridge Drove and left at the next roundabout along Mountfield Road you soon reach **Hampden Park Station** with regular train services to Eastbourne, Lewes and Hastings.

GOOD TO KNOW
Start: Heathfield High Street. Finish: Hampden Park Station.
Total mileage: 14.5.
Difficulty: Easy.
Stages: Horam (RAB) 3, Hailsham (RAB) 8, Path junction (B) for Polegate (*RB) 10.5, Hampden Park Station (*RAB) 14.5.
OS: OL25.

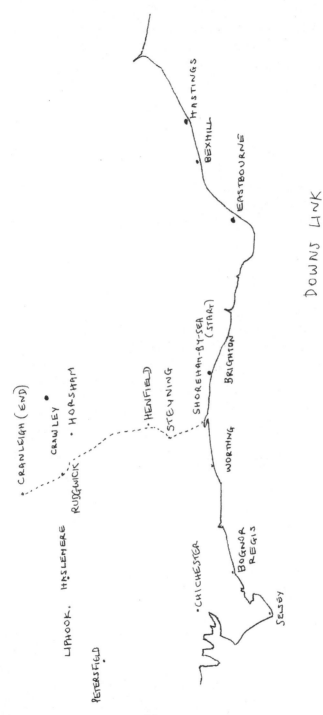

2 DOWNS LINK

The Downs Link is one of the easiest of the Great Walks of Sussex, following, for most of its course, two old railway lines, one connecting Shoreham with Itchingfield Junction on the still extant Arun Valley line, the other connecting Itchingfield Junction with Guildford. The Shoreham-Itchingfield section opened in 1861 with station stops at Bramber, Steyning, Partridge Green, West Grinstead (over a mile from the village it purported to serve) and Southwater where an adjacent brickworks brought some traffic onto the line. Itchingfield Junction was just two miles beyond Southwater, with all trains going forward into Horsham along the pre-existing line. An additional station, Christ's Hospital (named after the famous nearby school), was built just beyond Itchingfield Junction in 1902. Train times between Shoreham and Christ's Hospital in 1948 were about 45 minutes. The line enjoyed an excellent service for much of its life: in 1922 there were 10 journeys each way each weekday, and this figure had risen to 17 by 1960. However passenger numbers were in decline by the early 1960's, and the line was an inevitable victim of Dr Beeching's axe. Most freight services were withdrawn in 1962/63, and the final passenger services ran in March 1966, although some freight trains continued to run to the Beeding cement works for a time afterwards. The line north of Itchingfield Junction towards Guildford opened in 1865 with station stops at Slinfold, Rudgwick, Baynards, Cranleigh and Bramley & Wonersh. The total journey time from Horsham to Guildford was just under an hour. In 1922 there were 7 weekday journeys each day between Horsham and Guildford, rising to 9 by 1939. Generally, however, connections between this line and that linking Horsham with Shoreham were poor. Notwithstanding its scenic beauty – indeed it was used as the setting for a 1950's dramatisation of the film *The Railway Children* – it was another obvious target for Dr Beeching, and the last train ran on 14th June 1965.

It is indeed great to see old railways being put to such positive use rather than allowing them to become victims to unforgiving Mother Nature or even more unforgiving fly-tippers. Some walkers may find this kind of path uninspiring, as it is mostly straight level going, without the excitement of hill climbing and great views. However it is ideal for any walker who finds navigation difficult, it's an especially effective antidote for the foot traveller who strayed five miles off course last time out and was forced to abandon the expedition, and it's also a good wet-weather walk when low cloud or mist blot out the views from the hills. It's exceedingly well signposted and the course of the route will, for the most part, be very obvious; if you were wishing to do a sponsored walk in Sussex with sponsorship based on number of miles completed, this would be an ideal choice. One thing you as a walker will need to be aware of is cyclists. A good many Lycra-clad 2-wheeled enthusiasts use the route, and it does often seem that those cyclists who are the fastest and most apparently oblivious to other path users are the ones whose approaches from behind are the hardest to hear. Anyway, if you're not put off, the walk "proper" starts just outside Shoreham-by-Sea, the town itself more fully described in the England Coast Path section, and our route begins at **Shoreham-by-Sea Station**. The suggested signed route from the station – a more picturesque option is set out in route variation V1 – exits onto Brunswick Road and crosses straight over into the road opposite the station's north entrance, signed as Queen's Place. Follow this road to a crossroads junction, going straight over into Hebe Road and following this to its junction with Victoria Road. Cross straight over into Swiss Gardens and go forward along Connaught Avenue; at the end, bear left to reach Old Shoreham Road. Before crossing it's worth visiting the immediately adjacent lovely mid-Norman (and part Saxon) church of St Nicholas. Among its highlights are its long narrow Saxon nave and superb carved arches in every type of Norman ornament. Now cross Old Shoreham Road and walk up the slipway. Immediately beyond is Old Shoreham Bridge, a pedestrian footbridge which became a focus for mourners and wreath-layers following the Shoreham Airshow disaster in August 2015 when a Hawker Hunter plane crashed onto the A27 hereabouts, killing 11 people. By crossing the footbridge and following the Worthing-Shoreham route variation in the England Coast Path section in reverse, you can detour to Lancing College Chapel, adding 1.5 miles to the journey, but your continuous route turns right, northwards, along the bank, now officially on the DL and joined by V1. Already this is fascinating stuff: you can enjoy views across the Adur estuary to the magnificent Lancing College Chapel, while ahead of you is the A27 flyover, and although some might regard it as an eyesore it is a fine piece of road engineering nonetheless.

Beyond the flyover the DL continues on north-westwards through pleasant but unspectacular countryside to the old and currently abandoned Beeding cement works. This really *is* an eyesore, one of the ghastliest to deface the Sussex landscape, crying out to be redeveloped or done away with altogether, and it's a relief to leave it behind and arrive at, then cross, the river Adur. Beyond the bridge crossing you forsake the course of the old railway for a short while, and briefly overlap with the South Downs Way, first alongside the river then westwards away from it. Very shortly after leaving the river you reach a path junction, the South Downs Way going straight on and the DL going right. However a <u>detour D1</u> is possible here to visit the picturesque churches of Botolphs with its 13th century tower and fragments of wall paintings, and Coombes, of Norman origin and with further wall paintings that date back to the 11th century. Beyond the path junction, the DL rejoins the old line, following an excellent tree-shaded path north-westwards as far as the crossing of the A283, and beyond this crossing, it's a short walk to the roundabout junction where the A283 meets roads coming from Steyning and Bramber. **Bramber** is described more fully in the chapter devoted to the Monarch's Way, but it's easy enough to detour right from the DL at the roundabout along the Street to visit it; see the Monarch's Way section regarding how to access Bramber Castle and adjacent church. As far as visiting **Steyning** is concerned, a <u>route variation V2</u> which takes you through the heart of Steyning is not only possible here but recommended. Among the highlights of Steyning are the old Grammar School in Church Street, founded in 1614 but housed in a 15th century building, and further along the same street, the church of St Andrew, which boasts a late Norman nave with 12th century arcades and clerestories, decorated with magnificent carvings depicting the heads of humans and animals; the altar boasts 48 carved panels, one of which bears the coat of arms of Henry VIII. The lovely High Street is dominated by the tile-hung Old Market House and its very prominent clock tower and all along this street there are 14th and 15th century hall houses, and many examples of tile-hanging, timber-framing and weatherboarding. The mapped DL eschews both Bramber and Steyning, but from the roundabout follows various residential roads including Roman Road then King's Stone Avenue (at the top of which you're rejoined by V2) and King's Barn Lane north-eastwards past Steyning; it's a long and rather tedious tarmac tramp, although the surroundings become more agreeably rural as you proceed. You cross the old railway line by a sturdy brick bridge, going forward along Wyckham Lane, a rougher stony track. Beyond the buildings of Wyckham Farm you rise quite sharply – this ascent is one of the very few of any significance on the DL – to be rewarded at the top of the rise by a lovely view to the South Downs escarpment towards Devil's Dyke. Here you turn eastwards and descend on a wide track with a lovely open feel, in due course rejoining the course of the old line and veering north-eastwards.

The going is now really enjoyable as you follow the old line to Henfield; the surrounding scenery is most attractive with beautiful meadows bordering the old line and fine views to the South Downs. There is one particularly scenic spot, at the point where the old line goes over the river Adur, with the beautiful grounds of the tile-hung and timbered Stretham Manor immediately beyond. (While Stretham is the OS spelling, Nikolaus Pevsner spells it Streatham!) This was the original main manor house of Henfield, although even by Elizabeth's time it was already deserted. In times of very wet weather the fields hereabouts may flood, adding to the charm of the surroundings for walkers (but not for farmers!). In roughly a third of a mile beyond the Adur crossing, there's a signed footpath going to the right and by detouring along it all the way along the left bank of the stream, ignoring turnings right and left, you reach the A2037; by turning left alongside the A2037 and then first right into Horn Lane you immediately arrive at Woods Mill, the home of the Sussex Wildlife Trust. A mapped nature trail here takes you through a mixed landscape of meadows, hedgerows, waters and woodland hosting a huge variety of birds including sandpipers, egrets, herons, barn owls, sparrow hawks and buzzards, as well as roe deer, badgers, foxes, toads, frogs, water shrews, newts and even sea trout. Return the same way to rejoin the DL. The total detour is 2 miles.

Back on the DL you continue along the course of the old line, veering north-westwards, and in roughly 2 miles beyond Stretham you reach the outskirts of **Henfield**. Here the DL leaves the old line to go up Station Road, and it's when you reach the Cat & Canary on **Upper Station Road** that you could detour to Henfield's centre, a good three quarters of a mile eastwards along this road which becomes Church Street. Henfield, arguably too big to be called a village and too small to be called a town, is summed up by Pevsner thus: "Many pleasant buildings in Henfield, few notable." The church of St Peter, just off Church Street along Church Lane to the right, is one of the more notable ones with its 13th century nave walls and impressive windows. Just before the church is the pretty tile-hung Hacketts Cottage and to the right of the church is the fine timber-framed Apple Tree Cottage with some dazzling topiary work. The main street through Henfield does boast some good buildings too including the 17th century White Hart and red-brick Norton House. Meanwhile a detour D2 takes you from Henfield's centre to Sussex Prairies Garden, an 8-acre site crammed with summer-flowering perennials and grasses 8ft high; described in *The Rough Guide To Kent, Sussex & Surrey* as a "riot of colour," it has, since its establishment in 2009, become one of the best-loved gardens in Sussex. Back on the DL beyond Upper Station Road, easy walking along the old railway, north-westwards, takes you away from Henfield towards Partridge Green. Initially the path is in the shade of vegetation, but does open out; shortly after it does so, there is another crossing of the Adur at Betley Bridge. You'll notice how much narrower it is here than when you started at Shoreham, and indeed it's not far from Betley Bridge to its sources (plural, as the Adur has more than one). Beyond Betley Bridge, which sounds more like a North Yorkshire market town than just an isolated river crossing, there's a short section of field walking and, shortly, another departure from the old line as you approach the undistinguished village of **Partridge Green**. You veer away westwards to join the B2135 at the village's south end. The DL turns right alongside the B2135, northwards into the village, but by turning left, southwards away from the village beside this road, you can embark on a detour D3 to the pretty village of Ashurst with its flint church (which contains a "vamping horn" once used to accompany church singing), superb half-timbered Fountain pub and fine cottages of brick and timber. Otherwise head north up the B2135 as stated; the DL soon forks away left, north-westwards, from the village, but to access the amenities of Partridge Green, including excellent bus links and refreshment possibilities, keep alongside the B2135 to reach the village centre.

The walk between Partridge Green and West Grinstead is delightfully rural and unspoilt. By turning left at the first bridleway crossroads after leaving the B2135, about half a mile beyond Partridge Green, there is the possibility of a route variation V3 to visit West Grinstead Church, Knepp and Shipley, each with their own historic or architectural highlight. West Grinstead boasts a beautiful church dedicated to St George and dominated by its 13th century tower, and inside there is a part 11th century nave, some fragments of wall painting, pews whose backs have local farm names inscribed upon them, and some large monuments including one whose ghost is said to haunt a nearby forest. Nearby, and also visited on this route variation, is West Grinstead's Roman Catholic church where the writer Hilaire Belloc is buried. Shipley's windmill, a smock mill built in 1879 and also known as King's Mill, is arguably the most impressive windmill in Sussex, famed for its associations with Belloc who lived very close by. Knepp, meanwhile, has two castles. The original was built by William de Braose, a trusted lieutenant of William the Conqueror; used as a hunting lodge, it was the favourite residence of King John, but having remained a residence until the end of the 13th century it became a ruin and all that's left today is a portion of wall on a grassy mound, surrounded by a moat. A more recent castle was built nearby in 1809 by John Nash, with large circular tower and turrets, and having been burnt down in 1904 was rebuilt with Nash's details reproduced exactly. The DL itself bypasses all these features but, being rejoined by the V3 alternative from the RC church after about a mile, follows a straightforward northward course with pleasant pasture on both sides although, as you approach West Grinstead, there is the very pretty Furzefield Wood to the right. It is just after passing under a substantial bridge carrying the A272 – there used to be a most useful Little Chef beside the A272 here, sadly now long since defunct, so no break for Olympic Breakfasts possible! – that you arrive at the site of West Grinstead Station (here rejoined by the shorter V3 route from RC church) which is one of the highlights of the walk. It has been restored to look very much as it would have done when the old line was still functioning, with platform, signal and station board, and even an old railway carriage on a piece of old railway line; there is a seat on the platform where you can sit, enjoy a snack or a picnic, and pretend to be waiting for a train!

Beyond the old station the DL veers north-westwards, a direction it will continue to follow virtually the whole of the rest of the way to Cranleigh. Initially the surroundings remain very rural, with rather more woodland than previously, although there are few landmarks and the surroundings are pleasant rather than spectacular. It's such easy going that you can indulge your imagination a little, perhaps to the extent of visualising yourself driving a train along this stretch, enjoying views "real" drivers would have had for roughly a century. Though the trains were hardly speedy, to travel nowadays from Shoreham-by-Sea to Horsham by train, involving a change at Barnham, is liable to take about twice the time trains took to do the direct journey! You pass the little village of Copsale beyond which there follows a quite beautiful stretch which is best seen in the spring where the surrounding woodland is crammed with bluebells and wild garlic. Slight anticlimax follows with the negotiation of the A24 by means of a modern underpass, beyond which you pass Southwater Country Park and go forward to pass the centre of **Southwater** which is just a few yards away to the right. Although Southwater is a rather sprawling place, having been transformed from little more than a hamlet in the mid-20th century to a modern dormitory village for Horsham, its centre has been rejuvenated in recent years, and even if you don't want to take advantage of the excellent range of shops and eateries there, it's worth detouring the very short distance to view the magnificent modern iguanadon sculpture, created by local sculptor Hannah Stewart and completed in 2006.

Once beyond the centre of Southwater and its railway bridge, which looks somewhat incongruous and almost too bold in relation to its surroundings, you'll find things soon become pleasantly rural again, the DL rising gently then descending to proceed once more along the course of the old line with the bonus of a path-side pub, Bax Castle, to your right. There's no castle and the pub derives the name Bax from a weaver who lived locally. Soon you will be aware of the existing Arun Valley railway line coming in from the left, and after walking briefly parallel with it you approach the buildings of **Christ's Hospital**, reaching a T-junction with Christ's Hospital Road. The DL bears left onto this road but to access the station turn right along what is King Edward Road, soon forking left down Station Road to reach the station (500 yards from the DL); by remaining on King Edward Road, veering right with the road, you reach, in 400 yards or so, Christ's Hospital School, described more fully in the Sussex Hospices Trail section. Returning to the DL, you face a rather dull interlude, the route constrained to follow Christ's Hospital Road westwards and Weston's Hill northwards, before joining the course of the old line linking Itchingfield Junction and Guildford. Once you're on it, it is plain sailing north-westwards for several miles, as you proceed along or immediately adjacent to the old line on an excellent well-signed path past Slinfold and Rudgwick. Initially the surroundings are pleasantly rural, but even when after a mile and a half you pass the housing and industrial development of Slinfold – there was a station here, with a private siding to brickworks – the walking remains agreeable and very easy. The DL, keeping to the old line, stays to the south of the centre of **Slinfold**; the village centre is in fact visited by the West Sussex Literary Trail but is easily accessible from the DL in roughly 400 yards via **Hayes Lane**. The section between Slinfold and Rudgwick is in my opinion the most beautiful of the entire walk, passing lovely unspoilt woodland interspersed with fine stretches of open pasture, perhaps the climax coming with the impressive underbridge crossing of the river Arun. This bridge is quite iconic in DL terms, as it forms the motif that appears on many of the DL signposts, but you need to drop down the steps (actually signed "View Point!") to see it properly. It is a double bridge, the original brick bridge not acceptable to the Board of Trade because the gradient required for the line to drop down to it would have been too great, hence the additional metal bridge built above the brick one. The scene is extremely picturesque, particularly if the Arun is swollen during times of heavy rain. Sadly, not far beyond the double bridge, the tranquillity is broken with the crossing of the busy A281, and having crossed you'll notice the surroundings become more suburban as you approach **Rudgwick**. The large overbridge you reach a few hundred yards beyond the A281 carries the village street. There is very easy access to Rudgwick from the old line: look out for the Medical Centre car park to your right just beyond the overbridge, and follow the road leading from the car park a few steps up to the village street with its attractive tile-hung cottages. The church of the Holy Trinity is roughly half a mile further up this street (Church Street) and is passed by the Sussex Border Path.

The walking immediately beyond Rudgwick is predominantly wooded and initially straightforward, but soon a further detour away from the old line is necessary in order to negotiate the now closed Baynards Tunnel. The clear track veers slightly left, and quite steeply uphill in the shade of trees, overlapping briefly with the Sussex Border Path heading west, but then turns northwards and descends steeply through attractive woodland to reach a road and rejoin the old line. Baynards Tunnel was 381 yards long and coincided with the highest point of the railway line at 250ft above sea level, as well as being the point where the old line moved from Sussex into Surrey. You continue forward to within sight of the old Baynards Station, named after the nearby Baynards Park; access to the station is fenced round so when you reach the fence you need to bear left then almost immediately right. You pass just to the left of the private but beautifully preserved station complex, its buildings and advertising hoardings looking very much as they would have done when the line was last operational in June 1965, and there is also a nicely sited pub just here. The need for a station here appears puzzling today, it being apparently in the middle of nowhere and little more than a mile from the bustling village of Rudgwick which had its own station. The explanation is that a goods yard was sited here and there was also a private rail system serving a fuller's earth plant.

The remainder of the DL is all in Surrey but it makes sense to continue to Cranleigh rather than retrace to Rudgwick; it's a very straightforward walk which sticks to the old line throughout. Though the beautiful woodland around Rudgwick has been left behind, the countryside remains unspoilt and attractive, with pleasant wooded walking in Lodge Copse and some particularly pleasant parkland in the vicinity of Vachery House and Vachery Pond, with a fine backdrop of wooded hills, to your right. At length, a build-up of housing to your right and playing fields to your left signifies your approach to Cranleigh; shortly beyond the well-signed Snoxhall Playing Fields you pass an M & S foodstore which is to your right, and you reach Knowle Lane. By turning right up this street you very shortly reach **Cranleigh High Street** which is well served by buses, has a remarkably good range of shops and eateries for a place of its size, and is a perfect place to end your DL walk, although as stated above you could continue to follow the DL to its end at St Martha's Hill via Bramley and Chilworth. You will then have truly linked the South Downs and North Downs!

GOOD TO KNOW

Start: Shoreham-by-Sea Station. Finish: Cranleigh High Street.
Total mileage: 27.5.
Difficulty: Easy.
Stages: Bramber (RAB) for Steyning (RAB) 5, Upper Station Road for Henfield (RAB) 9, Partridge Green (RB) 11, Southwater (RAB) 16, Christ's Hospital (*) 18, Hayes Lane for Slinfold (RAB) 21, Rudgwick (RAB) 23.5, Cranleigh High Street (RAB) 27.5.
OS: OL11, OL34.

D1 Instead of turning right at the path junction with the DL, go straight on with the South Downs Way, shortly reaching a road. Turn left along it, soon reaching the church at Botolphs which is to the left. To reach Coombes, continue along the road southwards for about three quarters of a mile, then at the Church Farm sign at the bottom of the hill, turn right up the farm lane and go forward uphill along a signed bridleway via a gate which is to the left. You soon reach the church which is to the right. Return the same way. (Total detour 2 miles)

D2 From the centre of Henfield follow the main street (A281) northwards past the White Hart and past Furners Lane. Some 275 yards beyond this lane kink right and left to walk up Manor Way parallel with the A281, then veer sharp right with the road and proceed briefly eastwards along Charlwood Drive. You veer sharp left with this road, and in roughly 140 yards reach a signed crossing footpath. Turn right along the path, going forward between the houses and then veering left, north-eastwards, across two fields as clearly signed. You're signed diagonally over a third field but in practice you may need to follow the right-hand field edge round, before resuming your north-easterly course, signage taking you down to cross a stream by a footbridge and follow a field beyond. This field can get very soggy! At the top left corner of the field veer left, northwards, aiming just to the right of the trees. Cross a stile and pass the trees, then veer sharp right with the path and head eastwards to a driveway for Woolfly Wood. Turn left up the driveway, going straight ahead across the grass as the driveway bends left, and arrive at the B2116. Turn right alongside this road for half a mile to reach Sussex Prairies Garden which is on the right. Return the same way. (Total detour 3.5 miles)

D3 *Follow the B2135 southwards from Partridge Green, the road soon bending right and crossing Bines Bridge over the river Adur. You continue beside the B2135 through the hamlet of Bines Green, and just at the top of a small rise, 1.25 miles from the start of this detour, bear right along Golden Lane, kinking right and left, rising and then veering sharp left downhill, the road now Church Lane. You pass the pretty flint church of St James then continue along Church Lane to its end, bearing left along School Lane to return to the B2135, now in the centre of Ashurst. Turn left to pass (or perhaps visit!) the lovely Fountain inn, and continue past the 16th century half-timbered Blocques. Then follow the B2135 back to the start of the detour. (Total detour 3 miles)*

V1 *Exit the station onto Brunswick Road on which the level crossing is situated. Now bear left, seawards, down Brunswick Road, shortly bearing right along St Mary's Road, left along East Street past the church of St Mary de Haura and, at the end, right along the A259 High Street to the Ropetackle at the bottom end beyond the A283/ A259 roundabout junction. Walk immediately past the right-hand side of the Ropetackle along Little High Street then turn right to follow the riverside walkway, soon passing under the railway and going forward to the official start of the DL by Old Shoreham Bridge. Note and perhaps detour to the church of St Nicholas across the road here to the right. (Extra quarter of a mile)*

V2 *Follow the roundabout round anticlockwise, crossing the A283 exit then using the metalled path to cut to Clays Hill (the next exit round); follow this uphill, then go straight on along Bramber Road, dropping then rising to a crossroads junction in Steyning's town centre. To make progress (although you may of course want to detour to the High Street beyond to see Old Market House and many attractive shops and houses besides) turn right here along Church Street past the Grammar School on the right and then the church of St Andrew on the left. Go straight on along Vicarage Lane which becomes Cripps Lane, and then in turn Jarvis Lane. From here you bear left to cross* over the bypass and continue to rejoin the DL at the end of King's Stone Avenue. (Extra half a mile)

V3 (PLEASE NOTE – THIS IS A LENGTHY VARIATION WITH NO AMENITIES) Turn left at the bridleway crossroads. Follow the signed path over fields, in due course picking up a left-hand field edge and reaching the bottom left corner. Go forward through a wood, dropping down sharply; beyond the trees cross the meadow as far as a bridge over the Adur. Don't cross the bridge but turn right to follow the Adur upstream on its right bank, negotiating a number of field boundaries. Just beyond a double stile at a farm lane crossing, within sight of the church at West Grinstead, you turn right and walk up to enter the churchyard. You reach a signed path junction (A), here turning left; you pass the church entrance and continue in a straight line, exiting the churchyard. Immediately beyond the churchyard turn right and walk up to a path T-junction, here turning left. Follow the left-hand field edges steadily downhill, all the way to the very bottom left corner where there's a stile and fingerpost just inside the woodland. Turn right as signed through the trees, then shortly left, again as signed; emerging from the trees you go forward to the A24. Cross with great care, then turn right and almost immediately left along a footpath-signed driveway past the ancient Knepp Castle ruin. You pass a large lake – at one time the largest body of fresh water in south-east England – and just beyond, you reach Trollards Barn to the left. Immediately beyond this barn turn left as signed along a left-hand field-edge path, veering right and descending to cross a number of footbridges in close succession and reaching a path T-junction. Turn right along the right-hand field edge then shortly left as signed, crossing the field and reaching a road. Turn right along the road, then as it bends right, northwards, go straight on westwards along a narrower road. Ignore the first signed path for Church Farm South, but then turn right along the signed bridleway a little way beyond, following this to King's Mill. Shortly beyond the mill, turn right along a road that takes you to the centre of Shipley, 3 miles from the start of the variation. Follow the main street on, round to the left, perhaps detouring right (at the left bend) to visit the fine Norman church of St Mary, in the churchyard of which the composer John Ireland is buried. Then, just beyond the last building on the right you turn right, eastwards along a signed path, shortly entering woodland and then emerging to follow a field. You arrive at a road, crossing more or less straight over and following the path on into the Knepp Castle Estate, continuing in the same easterly direction. You arrive at an estate road, turning right to follow it, but shortly you're signed off it again, bearing right over the grass to reach another estate road, the impressive turreted "new" Knepp Castle buildings visible to your left. Turn right and follow this estate road, keeping the splendid Knepp Pond to your left, and then passing the ruin of the ancient Knepp Castle which is in a field to your right. There is no right of access to the ruin. Go forward to reach the A24 and cross it, again taking great care. Almost immediately opposite on the other side is a footpath heading just south of east; take this path which descends through a field, crosses a stream and turns sharp right, then shortly turns left and rises, following a right-hand field edge. The path is rough and not always clear on the ground. In due course you lose the boundary to your right. At this point you'll see the spire of the church at West Grinstead you visited earlier in front of you, and you reach a path junction. Don't continue along the right-hand field edge but fork right here, almost immediately being signed left to enter the churchyard and pass immediately to the left of the front door of the church. Just past the church you reach the footpath junction at (A) above, here turning left as signed, and going forward along a lane which takes you to the B2135. Turn right to walk beside it, using the wide verge, as far as the RC church just beyond the Park Lane turning on the left. Having visited the church, you have a choice. You could follow Park Lane north-eastwards for just under a mile to the A272, crossing straight over and walking down the slip road to rejoin the DL at West Grinstead Station. Alternatively (at a cost of an extra 650 yards) keep alongside the B2135; the verge peters out, so be careful especially as you negotiate a left bend. Just beyond the bend the road rises a little and bends right, but before the right bend turn left along the Black Barn driveway. Immediately beyond the first gate, turn right as path-signed up a right-hand field-edge path which returns you to the DL. (Extra 5.5 miles)

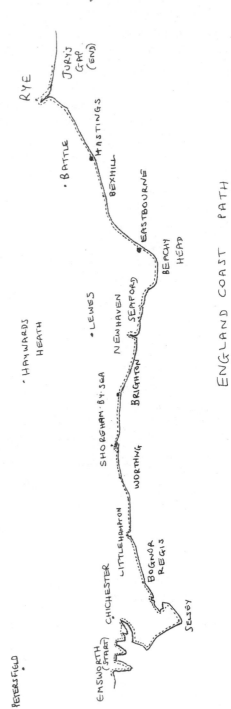

3 ENGLAND COAST PATH

The England Coast Path (ECP) is the newest National Trail, and this walk, which follows the entire coastline of England, is scheduled to open in full, with waymarking throughout, in 2020. The Sussex section of the coastline is not yet fully waymarked, albeit some waymarking is in place at the time of writing. However, although it may seem premature, I have decided to include the Sussex section in this book, accepting that there may be some variations when the Sussex section is fully open. The Sussex section of the ECP is full of variety, with much that is of really great interest to the walker, including some superb cliff scenery, beautiful beaches, many lovely towns and villages, and ample refreshment opportunities. There is in total far more to see than on any other Great Walk described in this book, and because of the lack of waymarking the description below is necessarily more thorough than for other routes – hence the length of this section.

Your walk along the ECP through Sussex will require a good deal of planning and you're advised to read the whole section below before starting out, for a number of reasons. Firstly, and of particular note, is the fact that some segments of the path flood at high tide, and you'll either need to use alternatives, which are described in the text, or simply sit it out and wait for the tide to recede. Tide tables are readily available online. Secondly, the opening stage of this walk is necessarily 8 miles long, and there is no chance of breaking it up. And thirdly, right at the very end of the walk, the final half mile between Jury's Gap and the Kent border is closed when firing is taking place on Lydd Ranges. If the purist in you wants to walk that last stretch (not that there is anything in particular to recommend it) you need to plan to do it on a non-firing day.

Anyway, back to the very start! Beginning from **Emsworth Station**, you turn right onto North Street and follow it (possibly detouring right at the left bend to visit the fine flint-built church of St James) to arrive at a roundabout junction with the A259; cross straight over along the attractive High Street – a 200-yard each way detour right down South Street takes you to the town's lovely waterfront – then just beyond the central square turn left down Queen Street towards the A259. There's a splendidly-converted late

19th century red-brick flour mill on the left down this road. Just beyond the Lord Raglan pub turn right along a Sussex Border Path-signed footpath going forward past houses then along a causeway. Bear left to reach Slipper Road and turn right along it, passing the impressively renovated Slipper Mill of 1760. The road soon peters out but you continue in the same direction through a gap in the boundary fence, arriving at **Emsworth Marina** and Yacht Harbour. Keep straight ahead, entering the marina complex, the basin of the marina to your right. Kink left and right by the red-brick Yacht Harbour building (which incorporates a café), continuing along a wide gravelled driveway, and keeping houses on stilts to your left; at the end, take the path signed half-right and then in a few yards turn right again along a driveway between the boats, arriving at the waters of Chichester Harbour and a path junction. Here bear left to begin your walk beside Chichester Harbour, keeping it close by to your right. Chichester Harbour was formed after the last Ice Age by rivers of snowmelt and thawing permafrost; the gravel and stone carried by the rivers scoured out the harbour bed and as the sea level rose, the harbour was created. You will follow the harbour all the way round to its south-eastern end at East Head, starting now as you join the waterside path. As you proceed beside the harbour, you will for a while at least enjoy lovely views across the harbour to Hayling Island and the causeway linking the island with the mainland. The going is simple and straightforward along an excellent path which reaches a gate signifying your arrival at Thorney Island and its military base. To progress, you will need either to press a button, or phone 01243 388269, and the gate should automatically click open for you. Thorney Island once really was an island, separated from the mainland by a channel that is marked on maps as the Great Deep. In 1870, 178 acres of land were reclaimed from the sea and a small area of land across the Great Deep channel was "created," joining Thorney to the mainland. In 1937 the RAF moved in, and remained until 1976; thereafter the island became an Army base. There are no difficulties in following the coastline around Thorney, as long as you keep to the path on the water's edge, and you should look out for a fine variety of plants including glasswort, sea purslane, sea lavender, poppy and sea holly. There is a very pronounced swing eastwards at Marker Point, and as you proceed eastwards and then south-eastwards it really feels like a coastal walk for the first time. The path temporarily leaves the water's edge, going round the landward side of an area of quite dense vegetation, but soon returns to the water and duly arrives within sight of the south-eastern tip of Thorney at Longmere Point, with Pilsey Island Nature Reserve (not open to walkers) immediately ahead. The harbour waters are visible beyond.

Moving northwards from Longmere Point, sticking (not literally, one would hope!) to a potentially very muddy path, you pass the old runway, a reminder of the RAF presence here, then go forward to pass the island's sailing club. At low tide you can walk down steps onto the beach and follow the beach, while at high tide you'll need to bear left then right, passing along a road to the landward side of the club buildings. Either way, you'll shortly reach the impressive 12th century church of St Nicholas with Norman windows still remaining and also a cylindrical Norman font, raised on two layers of stone. The church is noteworthy for its unusual length (120ft by 20ft) and its massive west tower. Beyond the church you can enjoy quite beautiful harbourside walking, although at the very start you may have to be careful at high tide as there may not be much path to play with. Having negotiated Stanbury Point you arrive at another secure gate, and again you need to press a button (or telephone 01243 388269) and wait for the click! Having "escaped" from the secure area, use a bridge to pass over the Great Deep out of Thorney Island, and continue to enjoy beautiful walking past Thornham Point and Prinsted Point. You pass through the popular Thornham Marina, and then along a clear embankment path, going forward to Prinsted, where there's a small car park, seating area and a meeting with the clearly signed Sussex Border Path that comes in from the left. The ECP veers right to continue on the embankment but by dropping down past the car park and detouring north up Prinsted Lane for roughly 300 yards you reach the charming centre of **Prinsted** with its delightful central square and impressive houses of brick and thatch; by forking right at the square along Prinsted Lane you will in another 300 yards reach the A259 at **Southbourne** with regular buses on the Chichester-Havant-Portsmouth route. And by turning right along the A259 then left up Stein Road you reach Southbourne Station. This will add a further 600 yards.

Beyond Prinsted the going remains easy and straightforward, your solid embankment path proceeding on round an inlet between the Thorney and Chidham peninsulas, and there are fine views towards Bosham and Chichester. The path swings a little to the left as it approaches the far corner of the inlet; at the top of this swing you can join a **path** taking you to the A259 at **Nutbourne**, and by turning right alongside the A259 then left up Broad Road you reach Nutbourne Station, just under a mile from the ECP. However the ECP veers gently right at the far corner of the inlet to embark on the Chidham peninsula. Hereabouts is the site of the old port of Nutbourne; the port has long gone and the marshes separating the sea from "new" Nutbourne are now designated as a local bird sanctuary and nature reserve. From here you follow the Chidham peninsula towards its foot at Cobnor Point, soon passing round Chidham Point and then keeping to the obvious path. The path is clear but often rough. In due course, about a mile and a half from Chidham Point, you arrive at a patch of trees where the path gives out and you need to continue along the shore. At high tide, however, this may not be possible and you'll need to veer left along the edge of the trees, then scramble through a gap in the hedge beyond the trees and follow a succession of right-hand field edges, dropping down to the shore at the bottom corner of the last one. In due course you reach another flight of steps which takes you back up to a proper, wheelchair-friendly path and, keeping Chichester Harbour to your right, you now go forward along a clear metalled waterside path, rounding Cobnor Point. Your excellent path incorporates beautifully crafted bridges, adding to the charm. You now swing north-eastwards, slightly away from the water as you pass the buildings of Cobnor and its Activities Centre, but are soon reunited with the water's edge, and go forward along what is a quite superb embankment path. There are gorgeous views across the water to Bosham and its church, and also north to the wooded Kingley Vale.

The coast path, remaining on an embankment, now becomes rather rougher; you're forced to the land side of houses and briefly follow a section of road, Harbour Way, reaching a T-junction of roads. The ECP turns right here along Chidham Lane, and you can soon switch to the (unsigned) parallel embankment. Shortly the embankment, as it strikes out eastwards of Chidham Lane before veering northwards, becomes overgrown and you're forced to use a parallel path on its landward side. You go forward to a footbridge over a little stream and shortly arrive at the **A259**. For **Nutbourne** Station turn left along it then right up Broad Road, the station just under a mile from the ECP. However the ECP turns right very briefly alongside the A259 – for Bosham Station, 0.75 miles from the ECP, continue beside it then bear left at the roundabout up Station Road – then almost immediately bears right again, just before the driveway leading to the house Snow Goose, along a rough path. You follow it past Snow Goose then shortly beyond the house use a slipway to climb onto an embankment, continuing seawards along a right-hand field edge. (If the path past Snow Goose is flooded, follow the A259 for a few yards, then immediately beyond the adjacent house turn right and follow the right-hand field edge to meet the slipway.) You veer left with the field edge to reach a junction with a signed path, and you continue straight on along an excellent field-edge path heading southwards for Bosham. This is superb walking, with great views both ahead and across the serene waters of the harbour.

Your trusty field-edge path comes to an end at a signed path junction (A) where you have low tide and high tide options. The mileage is the same for each.

LOW TIDE: It's a straightforward walk from (A) onto and then along the shore beside the creek, as it is known. Soon you could scramble up onto an embankment path to pass a modern red-brick and flint house; beyond this house, continue along the shore to a house which seems to protrude right out onto the shore. Pass to its shore side, now aiming just to the left of the black weatherboarded boathouse, but soon, just beyond the PRIVATE HOUSE plate, bear left as signed away from the foreshore along a gravelled path. Turn right at the end along the top side of a green known as Quay Meadow and at the far corner turn right to the end of Shore Road by the boatyard. Here you bear left along Shore Road to the bottom end of Bosham Lane, which provides easy access to the centre of **Bosham**.

HIGH TIDE: Fork left at (A), passing beside the back of houses, reaching a tarmac strip and then a path crossroads. Go straight over, taking care to follow the path just to the left of the gravel drive leading to Windrift, and emerge onto Moreton Road at a signed footpath junction. Go straight on along Moreton Road past the back of the Millstream Hotel, turning right onto Bosham Lane and following it down to its end.

Bosham is a delightful village with a part-Saxon church depicted in the Bayeux Tapestry, it being in this church that King Harold worshipped before going to meet William the Conqueror in battle. The church, in which the daughter of King Canute is buried, is easily reached by detouring across Quay Meadow (if you're following the low tide route) or High Street to the right off Bosham Lane just past the Bosham Walk craft centre (if you're following the high tide route) .The village boasts many attractive cottages of red brick, stone and flint, some dating back to the 17th and 18th centuries. Bosham used to be a thriving fishing port but is now primarily a sailing centre and a magnet for tourists many of whom have rued leaving their cars in Shore Road at the mercy of the high tides.

Beyond the bottom of Bosham Lane continue along the road beside the harbour or, at high tide, the embankment path. At low tide you may use a causeway to take a short cut to continue your waterside walk but at high tide you'll need to follow Shore Road right round, ignoring the Stumps Lane turning at the south-east corner. Short cut or no, you then stick to Shore Road heading south-westwards, passing some beautiful houses and enjoying great views across the inlet to Bosham. In due course the road bends left, away from the shore; just beyond the left turn, look to your left at the very impressive fir trees on the lawn in front of a private house. Just beyond here, fork right onto a signed footpath which proceeds along the shore all the way to the departure point for the seasonal Itchenor ferry. Signs indicate access along the path may be restricted at high tide and I really recommend you plan in advance to ensure you can walk it without such problems as it's a lovely walk with beautiful views especially to Itchenor across the harbour. The alternative is sticking to the road – not a good option and not recommended! At the ferry point, the path veers sharp left and returns to the road, now Smugglers Lane, and you turn right to follow it for about a mile. At the entrance to Bosham Hoe the lane bends sharply left; continue on it beyond this point for about half a mile then turn right into Old Park Lane, reaching a T-junction by Church Farm. Bear right here along the metalled lane which after half a mile veers sharp right, but you turn left as signed along a track. You arrive at open fields and a path junction; turn right here along a right-hand field edge, now heading back to the harbour and soon walking beside it. It becomes a proper embankment path, with stunning views across to

Dell Quay and beyond Chichester to the South Downs. You come off the embankment and veer right, dropping down to the marshes and crossing a number of bridges which enable you to negotiate the marshes even at high tide, and you soon arrive at the bottom of Mill Lane in **Fishbourne**. Here there's the option of a detour (just under half a mile each way) to the remains of the Roman Palace, dating back to 75 AD, now incorporated into a superb exhibition with particularly fine mosaic floors: to do this, simply go up Mill Lane to its end, turn left beside the A259, then bear right up Salthill Road and right as signed along Roman Way. Fishbourne Station is a little further up Salthill Road on the left. By turning right alongside the A259 at the top of Mill Lane and following it to the sharp right bend then continuing east along Fishbourne Road East, over the railway and straight on, going forward along Westgate and West Street, you reach **Chichester** (1.5 miles from the ECP); please refer to the Sussex Hospices Trail section for more information about the city. The station is reached by following South Street from the Cross at the end of West Street.

The ECP goes straight on eastwards beyond the Mill Lane crossing in the shade of trees, keeping a narrow channel to the left, and arriving at a footpath junction. Don't continue eastwards here but fork right, soon crossing a footbridge and continuing along an excellent harbourside path. There are lovely views in all directions as you proceed along the clear path which does veer sharply right along an embankment. When the embankment peters out go straight on as shown by the footpath sign, enjoying good views to the pretty village of Appledram, also spelt Apuldram – nobody seems to know which is correct! – to the left. A signed path provides a 250-yard-each-way detour to the pretty 13th century church of St Mary, Appledram. If you do detour, instead of returning to the coast path you could turn right to exit the churchyard southwards and go forward along a lane to a T-junction, turning left to reach Appledram Lane. A left turn here brings you immediately to a fine 15th century stone manor house, Rymans. As an alternative to backtracking to the coast path which proceeds on to Dell Quay, you could turn southwards down Appledram Lane to meet Dell Quay Road. A left turn brings you immediately to the A286 with regular buses into Chichester while a right turn brings you to Dell Quay. The total variation is an extra two thirds of a mile.

Dell Quay was formerly a very busy port and ranked in the 8th century as the most important town in Sussex. Throughout the 18th century there was a flourishing trade in grain, and other cargoes would include bacon, butter, cheese, salt, fish, oysters, canvas, leather, lead, iron, timber and stone. A fleet of fishing boats also operated from the port, which is now a haven for the sailing fraternity. Turn left (inland) along the road past the Crown and Anchor, and up to Apuldram Cottage, the last house on the right. Immediately beyond it you bear right along a permissive path which follows a right-hand field edge then veers right to return you to the waterside. You now follow the waterside past Copperas Point. This is stunning walking, with beautiful views back to Dell Quay and up the harbour back towards Chichester. You go forward through a patch of woodland known as Salterns Copse, arriving at a path junction; go straight on to arrive at the lock gates, noting to your left the huge Chichester Yacht Basin and marina, which is crammed with luxury craft. Assuming the lights aren't against you – this is the exit channel for boats coming out of the Yacht Basin into the harbour, so expect to have to wait awhile at summer weekends – cross straight over the lock gates and continue walking through the car park of Chichester Yacht Club, shortly arriving at another set of lock gates. This is Salterns Lock which you use to cross Chichester Canal. The canal is described more fully in the section devoted to the New Lipchis Way, with which you'll now overlap as far as Snow Hill.

Cross the lock gates and continue along the path, ignoring a right path fork by some modern houses, but then bearing right as signed and shortly left along a road leading to Birdham Pool, crossing over the pool along the causeway. This is the pool of the former tide mill, built in 1767 and remaining operational until 1935; the pool became a marina in 1937 and was thus one of the earliest marinas in the country. It was hereabouts that the painter J.M.W. Turner discovered the beauty of Chichester Harbour, and his painting of it is on view in Petworth House. Beyond the causeway you continue briefly along the lane which rises slightly, and just beyond a left-hand bend in the road, now Court Barn Lane (which will lead to the unremarkable Birdham village in half a mile), you bear right onto a signed path, in fact a metalled drive signed Harbour Meadow. You soon fork left off the road along a path which skirts the right-hand edge of a large field; you in turn skirt a small area of woodland that lies to your right, and arrive back at the water's edge at Westlands, following a narrow path between large houses to your left and the harbour to your right. I recall walking this section on a classic summer morning, with clear blue skies and hot sunshine, but thundery downpours were forecast and every glance to the build-up of white cloud to the south brought a tinge of apprehension that the weather would break. Fortunately the worst deluges waited till after nightfall. You enjoy an all too brief waterside walk, with splendid views, but you are soon forced left, away from the water and up to a metalled drive. Turn right onto it, and follow it round to the left to arrive at a T-junction with a metalled lane, bearing right along it for a few hundred yards to reach the buildings of Westlands Farm. Just before the farm buildings, however, a signpost directs you along a path which passes round the left-hand side of the farm. Once round the farm you reach a path junction; go straight ahead along a right-hand field edge, then to the left of a small area of trees, to arrive at Spinney Lane. Turn left onto it then in 300 yards or so bear right onto a path that returns you to the waterfront, and from here it's a really delightful waterside walk for about a quarter of a mile to the lovely village of **Itchenor.** Immediately before the Itchenor Sailing Club building, swing left and make your way up the path to Itchenor's village street, arriving opposite the Ship inn. Turn right to follow the street down to the waterside again. Itchenor is historically best known for its association with shipbuilding, its heyday being in the 18th and early 19th centuries. Now virtually all the boats you'll find being built and sailed here are pleasure craft.

At the waterside turn left along the road then just past Haines Boatyard go forward along a clearly marked footpath. Initially you're walking beside the harbour, and it's really lovely walking, with magnificent views to Bosham Church, Cobnor Point, Thorney Island and Hayling Island. Roughly 2 miles from Itchenor, the path swings inland to reach a metalled drive; turn right onto it then continue forward as signed along a stony area to just before Bricket Cottage, bearing right here to return to the waterside and resume your walk beside the harbour. Look immediately to your left here at the fine red-brick Rookwood House, the setting of which could hardly be more idyllic. Continue along the harbourside and shortly veer left to reach the end of Ella Nore Lane; don't follow the lane, but turn immediately right through a gate onto a good path, with views on your right to a spit of land known as Ella Nore which provides a habitat for plants that include sea kale, sea campion, and yellow horned-poppy. Easy harbourside walking from here brings you to **Snow Hill** and its green, where the New Lipchis Way leaves you and proceeds to **West Wittering** just under half a mile away, as follows: at a 4-way signed footpath junction at the front edge of Snow Hill, bear left, just south of east, along a metalled lane then a grassy footpath between fences, then another metalled lane, bearing right at a T-junction, almost immediately reaching a T-junction with Pound Road. Turn left along it to shortly arrive at the main village street. There's more about West Wittering in the New Lipchis Way section.

The ECP follows the right side of the Snow Hill green then continues along the excellent raised harbourside path to reach the neck of the sand spit of East Head with its magnificent dunes supporting a wide range of bird life and plant life, and stunning views from its top end. The dunes, among which you'll find marram grass and grasswort, provide an important habitat for certain birds including the lapwing, snipe and black-tailed godwit. The continuous route turns left at the top end of the neck of the spit (B) to continue along a good – and massively popular – path past a big car park; this, and the road coming down to it from Chichester, can get ridiculously busy on hot summer weekends, so be warned! If you've time, I recommend you turn right at (B) and walk to the far end of the spit (this walk adding up to an extra mile and a half to your ECP walk) either via the sands or the dunes to enjoy a superb view, including not only Bosham Church (again!) but Kingley Vale Nature Reserve, The Trundle and the buildings of Goodwood racecourse. Then return to (B) and join the continuous route as described above. You've now reached the open sea at last! Beyond the car park you have the option of following the clear green path along the foreshore or proceeding along the beach, depending on the tide; when the taller breakwaters start, you can return to the path which continues all the way to East Wittering. Watch out to your left for the distinctive hexagonal red-brick Cakeham Tower, a useful navigation point for seamen, built in the 16th century. The green carpet you've been following does give way to a stonier surface and for a short while shingle, this providing a foretaste of harder work to come. You're by the shore most of the way to East Wittering but become separated from it by houses in places, the path threading its way past them but very clear throughout, the shingle easing and the surface becoming firmer. An ice-cream café by a road signals where you can access **East Wittering** village centre, but otherwise proceed as path-signed. The going starts to get tougher, with a shingle tramp for a few hundred yards until a concrete area just to your left signifies your arrival at Bracklesham. The shore at Bracklesham is renowned for its fossils including the remains of turtles, crocodiles, snakes and large sharks, some over 40 million years old. Beyond the concrete area the shingle resumes and it's a long slog south-eastwards along the shore away from the built-up area.

A few hundred yards beyond the end of the houses on your left, you get almost level with an embankment to the left and you'll see a sign telling you there's no access to Selsey via the beach. Here you must leave the shore and bear left onto a signed path, shortly forking right onto a permissive footpath, and following it for its entire length along the embankment as it rounds the new RSPB Medmerry Nature Reserve with its profusion of bird life. It curls right in a north-easterly direction; don't be tempted off it, but keep on it until just before a gate barring further progress along it, where you're forced to veer left to join a path below and continue straight on to cross Ham Road by Wilsons Farm. Having crossed, you immediately reach a path junction, and here you take a right turn and follow the path south-eastwards to a lane. Turn right along it past Little Ham Barn and Great Ham Cottages then immediately beyond these cottages, turn left at a signed path junction, rising to an embankment. Turn left along the embankment. It would appear that the aim is for there to be a continuous embankment path all the way back to the beach (and there may well be by the time you read this – be guided by the signage!) but at the time of writing the necessary work hadn't been completed and you may be signed along a path immediately below and to the left of the embankment. However the final section of embankment is certainly available, with seats and a plaque commemorating the opening of Medmerry sea defences. The views to those defences and the surroundings are superb. You then arrive at the beach and turn decisively left, south-eastwards, to follow the shingle, passing a caravan park. Look out on the left, roughly three quarters of a mile from where you joined the beach, for the imposing and impressive Medmerry Windmill, a tower mill dating from 1820. As you get level with it, there's a choice. The true coastal route goes forward to follow the top of a low line of cliffs, beyond which you proceed to West Street, turning left along it then first right along Clayton Road which you follow all the way to a T-junction with Hillfield Road at the south end of Selsey, turning right along this road to arrive at the beach. However owing to erosion the low cliff path is vulnerable and this alternative is recommended which takes in both the windmill and the centre of Selsey. Turn left along a path that aims just to the right of the windmill and arrives at the west end of Mill Lane immediately beside the mill. Having admired the mill – there's a little shop/café beside it – turn right along Mill Lane, then right at the T-junction along Crablands and, at the end, left along West Street bringing you to Selsey's main street. **Selsey**, the southernmost town in Sussex, once stood on an island known as Seal Island, and for centuries it was only accessible by ferry. Even today only one road properly links it with the outside world. It was in 681 AD that St Wilfrid arrived at Selsey, and he subsequently built both a cathedral and a monastery here, neither of which survived. In World War 2 Selsey became a minor naval base with many sections of Mulberry Harbour, which played a key role in the D-day landings, kept here. The town has had, and still has, a prosperous fishing industry, but it has never enjoyed the popularity of other south coast resorts. That said, its centre has a certain charm, with several attractive houses, some thatched; one particularly impressive building is the brick-and-timbered Old Malt House opposite School Lane just up the High Street on the right. The 19th century church of St Peter just beyond contains all but the chancel of the original St Wilfrid's Chapel which you'll see a little further on. Having enjoyed the amenities the town has to offer, walk seawards down the High Street and forward along Hillfield Road to the beach, joining up with the shorter route described above.

At the beach turn left onto a clear path along the foreshore. You arrive at a green, at the far bottom corner of which you have a choice, again depending on the tide. If the tide permits – you should be okay 2.5 hours or more outside high tide – drop down to the beach then walk round, negotiating the fences/breakwaters in turn, using the concrete steps and walkways provided. You've reached Selsey Bill, the southernmost point in Sussex. Having got round, use the stone ramp to rise to and turn right onto the coast path continuing up the east side of the peninsula. If the tide renders the negotiation of Selsey Bill impossible, veer left at the far corner of the green, away from the sea, and then turn right at the top corner, going forward along the coast path. Suddenly a brand new vista opens up with excellent views ahead to Pagham Harbour, Aldwick and Bognor Regis. The going is very pleasant and easy for a while, along an excellent path. Soon you pass the magnificent new RNLI building – the old one was on a now demolished structure over the sea immediately adjacent – and continue making good fast progress, in due course reaching the memorial plaque to Eric Coates who was inspired by the view from here to write *By The Sleepy Lagoon*, the theme tune to *Desert Island Discs*. Here the concrete path ends and you continue either along the shingle bank or, if you prefer, a parallel driveway. In any case you need to join the driveway by the last house. You then go forward along a firm path initially, then plough on along the shingle, ignoring a footpath signed left. Keep in a straight line all the way to the point at which the waters of Pagham Harbour come in on your left. You've now reached the neck of a large shingle spit. The continuous route turns left down over some wooden sleepers to follow a clear shingle path along the near side of the harbour waters, but if you wish you could go straight on and follow the shingle spit to its end, keeping out of fenced areas which protect the rich bird life on the spit. Initially there's a good path but then it gets more arduous. The views from the top end of the spit are stunning in every direction. Simply return to the sleepers to rejoin the continuous route. This detour will add a mile and a quarter to your journey.

You now embark on the circuit of Pagham Harbour, initially on a good path alongside the harbour waters. The harbour, with its surrounding shingle, saltmarsh and fields, is a designated nature reserve; it's perhaps most noteworthy for being a visiting place and breeding ground for the little tern, one of Britain's rarest breeding sea birds, but there are many other feathered visitors including the shoveler, wigeon, curlew, lapwing and golden plover. Soon, by an information board, turn left onto a path leading away from the water's edge, passing the Mound, an earthwork believed to be a Roman coastal defence fort, with a castle being built within the earthwork in Norman times. You then immediately reach St Wilfrid's Chapel, turning right to walk through the churchyard. The chapel, originally built in the 12th and 13th centuries and well worth visiting, was once much larger than it is today, but in 1864 all save the chancel of the building was removed and incorporated into St Peter's, Selsey. The chancel, which by ecclesiastical law could not be removed, remains and is immortalised by Rudyard Kipling in his poem *Eddi's Service*. Continue on through the churchyard, turning right at the end along a path which soon veers left and proceeds along an embankment; ignore the steps dropping down to the shore but keep to the path along the embankment. Shortly your path veers down to the shore and proceeds along it then veers left to join the embankment again! It's then a very pleasant easy embankment walk, overlooking Pagham Harbour, to just short of the Chichester-Selsey road. Just before the road (easily accessible from here, with regular buses from the nearby stop to both Selsey and Chichester) you veer right and cross the harbour waters, then immediately after the crossing, bear right to follow the inlet round, shortly getting level with a bridge over the water. Here you turn left to follow a permissive path along the course of the former Chichester-Selsey railway: known as the Selsey Tramway, it opened in 1897 and closed in 1935, and was known for its multiplicity of stations and antiquated rolling stock. At the top end your path emerges at Mill Lane. To access the village of **Sidlesham** and its excellent bus service to Chichester, simply turn left along it as far as the B2145 Chichester-Selsey road (roughly a quarter of a mile away). However the ECP turns right along Mill Lane towards the **Crab & Lobster** pub, a most popular and beautifully situated watering hole.

You're now at the mercy of the tides. You're advised to stick to the high tide route 2 hours either side of high tide – Pagham Harbour tide times are posted on the Internet – but be prepared to turn back and follow it outside those hours if necessary. Mileages are the same for both routes.

LOW TIDE: Having turned right into Mill Lane you follow it briefly, but just before the road bends left (and before the Crab & Lobster), join a signed path (C) leading off to the right, keeping the harbour waters to your right and an embankment immediately to the left. The path can be very slippery and isn't always well defined but by hugging the embankment you won't go wrong. However you come to a point where the embankment veers sharply away to the left; simply follow the obvious harbourside path onwards, away from the embankment, soon crossing a channel using stepping stones and arriving at the raised sea defence known as Pagham Wall. Follow the excellent path along the top of the wall which ends at the thatched **Salt House**. Pass the house then turn immediately right down a slipway to proceed beside the shore. Before joining the slipway you've the option of a visit to the fine church of St Thomas a Becket, **Pagham**. To do this, continue along the track beyond the Salt House, shortly veering left and then right before bearing left along Church Lane. In 600 yards or so you reach the church which contains a reconstructed Saxon jar in the south aisle, a Norman font, a part 13th century chancel, 13th century nave arcades, and a rose window at the west end which was erected in thanksgiving for the recovery of George V from illness in 1928. Note that the amenities of Pagham are a further mile up this road. If you've detoured, return to the Salt House, and now, whether you've detoured or not, use the slipway and continue along the shoreside path – which can be wet and slippery in places – keeping a line of vegetation to your left. Just beyond a jutting-out area of trees, you veer left to arrive at a signed path junction; turn right here onto a good clear path that continues alongside the harbour with caravans/chalets and then the waters of Pagham Lagoon to your left. For a couple of hundred yards there's a parallel raised boardwalk available. Beyond this you're then able to fork right onto a path that dips down to harbour level then rises to a shingle spit. Turn right to follow the spit towards its far end.

HIGH TIDE: Continue along Mill Lane past path (C) and the Crab & Lobster. Ignore a footpath signed right a little beyond the pub, but continue to the next path signed to the right, being the clearly marked driveway for Halsey's Farm House, just under a quarter of a mile beyond the Crab & Lobster. Turn right along this driveway then just before the gate leading to the house, turn right along an obvious path, leading to a field. Follow the right-hand field edge then proceed straight on through the next field, again along the right-hand edge, then climb onto the embankment, here reunited with the low tide route. Turn left to follow Pagham Wall as far as the Salt House. Assuming the slipway path is submerged, go straight on along the track which bends left, then right, then left again, here becoming a metalled road. A detour to Pagham Church, described above, is possible up this road. Very shortly turn right through a gap in the hedge along a path through a field, parallel with the harbourside. The path, staying parallel with a fence, veers to the right and heads for the harbour, but then veers left again by a gate to proceed above the shoreline, shielded from it by trees for much of the way. As you reach the chalets at a path T-junction, turn right to continue along the path above the shore; for a couple of hundred yards there's a parallel raised boardwalk available. Beyond this remain on what is a shingle path, keeping a lagoon to the left, now reunited with the low tide route.

Now continue to and round the far end of the spit, here getting superb views across to St Wilfrid's Chapel. I suggest that having rounded the far end of the spit and begun heading north-eastwards again, you keep to the highest ground for the best views, keeping the fence and lagoon immediately to your left, then when the fence goes away left, turn right down a shingle path to the far side of the spit nearest the harbour. Now turn left and simply continue along the spit towards the houses, passing the narrow harbour mouth, the buildings of Bognor Regis clearly visible ahead. You continue along the bank past the houses and begin your walk along the sand/shingle of Aldwick Bay, where in 1793 a gun battery was erected to guard against the threat of French invasion. Outside high tide you can follow the sands which provide reasonably firm walking, but at high tide you may have to stick to the shingle bank, thereby making much slower progress. The houses you can see to your left, built between the two World Wars, are part of Aldwick, regarded as the "posher" end of Bognor Regis. In the spring of 1929 King George V and Queen Mary stayed at the now demolished early 19th century Craigweil House in Aldwick while the King was convalescing from illness, and it was as a result of their visit that Bognor had the accolade of "Regis" being added to its title. Whether the King really did say "Bugger Bognor" on his deathbed has to remain the subject of speculation! At length you reach a succession of breakwaters, and immediately beyond these, there is a nasty little sting, in the form of a huge wall of large rocks which you can't climb over. The shingle beach is blocked by private development and the only way through is a narrow concrete way interspersed with steps. At high tide the concrete way and steps could be submerged and this time there is no alternative – you will have to sit it out. DON'T TRY AND CLIMB OVER THE ROCKS. Your hard work is still not done beyond the rocks, with more shingle tramping likely to be necessary, until you reach a line of beach huts and are able to pick up a concrete path running behind them. Beyond the huts you continue along the concrete walkway known as The Esplanade, past the Bognor Yacht Club, Rock Gardens, the gracious 1830 Royal Norfolk Hotel and Waterloo Square, immediately beyond which is the pier. From the pier continue along the wide promenade beside The Esplanade. Access to **Bognor Regis** town centre is available by turning left off the promenade just before the brick-built and very conspicuous Regis Centre/Alexandra Theatre; cross The Esplanade and follow the near (west) side of the Regis Centre buildings, going forward to cross more or less straight over Belmont Street and follow The Arcade to the High Street. Cross straight over into London Road to access Bognor's main shopping area, going straight on from there along Station Road to reach the station. It was Sir Richard Hotham, a wealthy Southwark hatter, who in the 1780's made it his mission to convert Bognor into an elegant seaside resort and encourage Royalty to visit. However it was only with the arrival of the railway in 1864 that the town expanded significantly and became a much more popular destination. A pier was built the very next year, boasting a 1000ft jetty, and early in the 20th century, two huge entertainment centres were built: the Kursaal, which opened in 1910 and included shops, a theatre, skating rink and tearoom, and also the Pavilion which opened in the summer of 1922, and was used for dances, plays and exhibitions, but which was demolished in 1949. The Kursaal was demolished in 1975, to be succeeded by the Regis Centre (incorporating the Alexandra Theatre) which is still flourishing. Bognor's best-known visitor attraction is Butlins, which arrived in 1960. The town has continued to host a number of events of national interest including the Clowns' Convention, the Birdman Rally, where competitors see how high and how far they can fly off the pier with the aid of all manner of ingenious devices, and the Rox music festival.

The coast path continues along the seafront past Butlins with its unmistakeable frothy white roof. Beyond Butlins the concrete promenade bends to the left, then right, passing the Beachcroft Hotel; beyond the right bend you pass some boats and a line of blue and yellow beach huts behind a green. You're now in **Felpham** (pronounced "Felfam!"). Immediately beyond the huts and greensward you can detour left up Blakes Road; near the far end on the right is the flint and thatched Blake's Cottage where the poet, artist and mystic William Blake lived between 1800 and 1803. By going straight on from there across Vicarage Lane you can follow Waterloo Road as far as the Fox inn, rebuilt in 1949 after a fire – it was at the entrance to the original Fox inn that Blake was arrested after allegedly making seditious remarks to a soldier billeted here. Return the same way to rejoin the prom. The total detour is just under half a mile. The surroundings now become more genteel with trim suburban houses and gardens along the left-hand side of your route; at length the concrete promenade ends, being replaced by a dirt track and then a stonier path, followed by a green. Follow the green and then reasonably firm path to the end of Sea Lane at Middleton-on-Sea. To continue along the shore you are forced down to the sands, there being nothing between sand and the high stone walls protecting the shoreside houses. At low tide the going is very easy, as you can simply follow the sands, or if necessary pass round the edge of the walls using steps to negotiate the breakwaters, albeit care is needed on these in places. At high tide neither of these may be possible and you'll need to turn left up Sea Lane to a T-junction with Middleton Road. Turn right along this road then at the mini-roundabout go straight over into Elmer Road, following it past the 19th century church of St Nicholas. Immediately beyond the church, turn right down Southdean Drive, going forward from there along a footpath returning you to the beach. The detour will add 500 yards to your walk. Now continue beside (or along) Elmer Sands, soon passing a succession of rock-built groynes which separate you from the sea, and are part of a coastal defence scheme that opened in 1993; if the tide is too high, you may be forced to stick to the shingle bank. From here there are excellent views back towards Selsey Bill and, on a clear day, the Isle of Wight. At last you're leaving suburbia behind to proceed through a precious countryside gap between the sprawls of Bognor Regis and Littlehampton.

Between here and Climping Beach you're at the mercy of the tides. At lower tide you can enjoy walking along the sands but when the tide is higher, you may be forced to stick to the back of the beach, where firmer sections are interspersed with some tough shingle walking. There are a number of escape routes to the parallel road which you can then follow via Elmer Road and Manor Way, passing the (private) slipway and going forward alongside a green to the right, taking the signed footpath forking opposite No.2 just beyond the green. This leads to a firmer broader bank where you rejoin the shore route. The going's good as you veer slightly left at Poole Place, but you're then forced down to the beach and have to negotiate a careful path between large rocks before proceeding along the sands. At low tide you'll have no problem but if the path between the rocks is submerged at high tide you'll have to sit it out – you should be ok more than an hour either side! Depending on the tide, you'll then be able to proceed either along the beach or the edge of the adjacent field before a proper shingle bank becomes available. Looking to your left as you walk, you'll see the buildings of Bailiffscourt, the centrepiece of which is a mock-medieval house of warm limestone built in 1935. You're then separated from these buildings by an area of thick vegetation and, passing a grassy picnic area (with café), you have the option of a narrow metalled walkway or the beach. You've arrived at Climping Beach, very popular with visitors in good weather although deserted when I visited one very wet Good Friday! As you get level with the car park (with barrier) you can detour off the beach to visit Bailiffscourt, dropping via the car park to the road, turning left along it and then left again in roughly 300 yards up the driveway to arrive at the complex. The village of Climping (or Clymping – nobody seems to know which is correct!) and its pub is further up the road, some half a mile from the beach.

Back on the beach beyond the car park you have a choice. There's a route variation V1 from here which visits the magnificent church of St Mary, Climping, the main part of which is pure Early English, dating from the early 13th century; the tower was built in 1170, and the main door is carved with Norman ornament. The variation continues on an inland route towards Littlehampton. If however you prefer to continue along the coast, then at low tide you can stick to the beach all the way to the breakwater marking the mouth of the Arun. At higher tide, continue along the back of the beach, having to veer slightly left and scramble a little higher up the shingle to make progress; it's tough going for a while but the consolation is a great view towards the South Downs and you may be able to identify the castle and cathedral at Arundel. Then veer slightly left onto a firmer green section, going forward to the dunes and following an excellent path immediately to the right (sea) side of the dunes, the sea coming into view in due course. The area is rich in bird life with visitors that include the kestrel, sanderling, finch, ringed plover and oystercatcher, and the sea offers crabs, whelks, cockles, shrimps and cuttlefish. Whichever shore route you've chosen, you arrive at the breakwater and now head inland to negotiate the crossing of the Arun, going forward alongside a road, keeping the Arun to your right. A parallel path becomes available as you pass a large assembly of boats separating you from the river. Soon you pass the golf clubhouse which is to your left, and here a concrete path forks right off the road; take this path, which provides a pleasant walk reasonably close to the riverbank. In due course the path is reunited with the road, named Rope Walk, and you follow the road in the same direction to arrive at a T-junction with Ferry Road, turning right towards a footbridge crossing over the river Arun and being met by V1.

You now cross the footbridge and enter **Littlehampton**. The footbridge was built in 1981, replacing a swing bridge that dated from 1908 and was floodlit by 1200 candle-powered lamps. Once over the bridge you turn immediately right into River Road. Follow this for a couple of hundred yards, then more or less opposite the garage of number 35 turn right up an alleyway and left to follow beside the Arun, this time downstream. For Littlehampton Station, just a couple of hundred yards away, take the first left alleyway, Mariners Quay, crossing and following Terminus Place to Terminus Road, the station straight ahead. Otherwise continue along the waterfront, soon reaching Look & Sea, the fine modern museum and café. The town centre is reached by bearing left up Surrey Street, arriving at High Street in barely 100 yards. The town was an important port in Saxon times, and in the Middle Ages was a landing place for Caen stone from Normandy which was used in churches and secular buildings throughout Sussex. The harbour was regularly visited by ships carrying coal from northern England and by vessels with cargoes of timber from the Baltic. At one time large quantities of both perishable and durable goods passed through the port to and from France, and the discovery of oyster beds off the shore of Littlehampton led to huge numbers of fishing boats congregating in the harbour. Gradually the importance of Littlehampton as a port declined, but it remains a base for pleasure cruises up the Arun, fishing and the dredging of marine aggregates. The town has also been an important base for shipbuilding. Leisure-wise, sea bathing began at Littlehampton in the 1750's, and amongst those who came here in the 19th century were Lord Byron, John Constable and Samuel Taylor Coleridge. The railway's arrival attracted many more visitors, and it has continued to prosper as a pleasant, if unsophisticated, resort ever since.

Beyond the museum/café continue along the promenade between Pier Road and the river to reach the river mouth, passing a huge fun park and the Windmill Entertainment Centre before turning sharp left to join the seafront promenade. The open sea is once again to your right and a broad expanse of green is to your left, separating you from the centre of the town; note particularly the remarkable Long Bench with its "rollercoaster" effects beneath a pair of shelters, the wooden slats bearing commemorations to loved ones. Carry on past the very distinctive modern East Beach Café, described as having a sculptural quality. By detouring 200 yards left down Norfolk Road just past the café, going straight over South Terrace, you reach, a few yards beyond that crossing, a convenience store on the wall of which is a sign commemorating the fact that the comedian Ronnie Barker lived in Littlehampton and got the inspiration for the sitcom *Open All Hours* from a corner shop in the street. Beyond East Beach Café the ECP follows the prom past Norfolk Gardens, Mewsbrook Park with its lovely lake and nature conservation area, and the red-brick Wren-style Rustington Convalescent Home with impressive clock tower, dating back to 1897. There are good views back to the dunes on the west side of the Arun, and you may see the dome of Butlins making a guest appearance on the horizon. The promenade ends but you are able to continue along the pavement beside Sea Road. This road swings sharply to the left to reach Rustington, sometime home of the composer Hubert Parry; however, the coast route continues straight on along a paved path. Note the plaque erected in 1996 to commemorate the attempt to break the world air speed record here on 7th September 1946 and again 7 years later. The path peters out and you then need to cross an area of shingle in order to pick up a further paved path which heads eastwards towards some beach huts. You're now embarking on a succession of greenswards – areas of smooth green for public and recreational use which run between the very exclusive properties to your left and the sea to your right. Between here and Sea Lane, which gives access to the useful amenities of Angmering, you can choose between firstly the comfort of the greenswards, sometimes separated from the sea by tall vegetation, or secondly the tougher shingle option. However, the tide may be low enough for a third option, namely to follow the sands. The last of the greenswards, if you've opted for these, is signed Willowhayne and has the feel of an avenue, with a line of vegetation to your right which means that views to the sea are restricted. It's probably still a better option than the shingle, though! At the end of the Willowhayne greensward you arrive at the bottom end of **Sea Lane** at East Preston. By turning left up this road, going forward up The Street, left at the end along Worthing Road and right along Station Road you reach **Angmering** Station, a mile from the ECP. Otherwise, the ECP continues perforce across the sands or shingle, passing a small boatyard.

No doubt to the relief of reluctant shingle walkers it's possible, beyond the boatyard and East Preston, to pick up another greensward with the houses of West Kingston and Kingston Gorse to your left. If the tide is out you've again the option of the magnificent sands punctuated by rocks, pools and channels; there is a small collection of black rocks, visible half a mile offshore at low tide, that are believed to contain the remains of Kingston Chapel which was submerged by the sea in the 17th century. If you stick to the greensward you will reach two gates in close succession and continue along the greensward beyond, then as you reach the end of the greensward you'll be confronted with more shingle. However it's not quite as difficult walking as the previous shingle tramp, and in any case you have a café immediately beside you to your left so you can break off from your labours. Continue past some beach huts to arrive at and follow the paved Pattersons Walk – for a short part of it there's the option of a raised promenade to the right, passing a pillbox. Beyond **Sea Lane**, which leads to the sprawling village of **Ferring**, you go forward onto a path which proceeds past the precious Goring Gap, a strategic countryside gap and a welcome break in the housing which has dominated the scene to your left virtually all the way here from Littlehampton; there's a particularly good view inland to Highdown Hill, site of a prehistoric hillfort, which is visited by the Sussex Hospices Trail.

Beyond Goring Gap, now overlapping in fact with the Sussex Hospices Trail, you follow a good path keeping a green to your left and the beach to your right, weaving between the trees. Across the green is **Goring-by-Sea**, its centre again well inland; it was at Goring-by-Sea that the naturalist Richard Jefferies died in 1887. As you move east of **Sea Lane**, from which there's a good view to the spire of the church of St Mary, Goring-by-Sea (and along which a walk of just under half a mile, turning right at the end, brings you to the A259 with ample amenities including buses; by turning left alongside the A259 you arrive in a further half a mile at Goring Station) your path becomes a proper concrete way. You pass another welcome café then proceed resolutely eastwards, the going remaining extremely easy with good views to the South Downs beyond the sprawl of Worthing. You pass the bottom of Sea Place; by following Sea Place inland to the A259, turning left then bearing shortly right down Shaftesbury Avenue you reach **Durrington-on-Sea** Station, three quarters of a mile from the ECP. Shortly beyond the bottom of Sea Place the walkway widens to become a proper seafront promenade with the coast road, West Parade, to your left, and it is very easy walking to the pier at Worthing, the largest town on the West Sussex coast. (**West Worthing** Station can be reached by, in a quarter of a mile, detouring inland up Grand Avenue, crossing the A259 and continuing along Grand Avenue then, at the very end, bearing right along Tarring Road; it's three quarters of a mile from the ECP.) To access **Worthing** town centre, turn left into Montague Place just before the pier, and you'll almost immediately reach Montague Street, Worthing's main shopping thoroughfare, with the fine Liverpool Terrace immediately beyond. (For the station, follow route variation V2 as described below.) It was during the 18th century that the increasing patronage of Brighton by Royalty began to influence adjacent areas and Worthing enjoyed a number of visits from Royalty and noblemen alike. Its population increased steadily in the 19th century when some fine building took place: public buildings of importance included the 1812 church of St Paul with its four-column Greek Doric portico, and the 1834 Grecian-style old Town Hall, and there was some fine housing built in Liverpool Terrace, Montague Place, Montague Street and The

Steyne. The late 19th and early 20th centuries saw the town developing as a traditional seaside resort, and a pier was opened in 1862. The town attracted a wide spectrum of visitors, including Oscar Wilde who wrote *The Importance Of Being Earnest* here in the 1890's whilst on holiday, and named the hero of the play, John Worthing, after the town. Worthing's long fishing traditions were maintained by the existence of a fish market on the beach, and even today you can find freshly caught fish being sold on the shore. At Easter 1910 the Dome Cinema was opened, and it remains a distinctive feature near the seafront to this day. The neo-Georgian Town Hall, which was built to replace the old Grecian-style hall and which opened in 1933, contains beautiful pastel-coloured mosaics with maritime themes, while the museum is particularly noteworthy for its fine Victorian watercolours. Worthing continued to expand during the 20th century and today enjoys a vibrant shopping centre and arts scene.

Between Worthing and Shoreham-by-Sea you have a choice of route from the pier: the coastal route or an inland route variation V2 via St Paul's Church, the museum, the Town Hall, the Art Deco-style Connaught Theatre, Broadwater Church, Sompting Church, Steep Down, and Lancing College Chapel. Broadwater Church is of Norman origin and boasts two late Norman arches carved with an exquisite variety of ornamentation. The church of St Mary, Sompting boasts England's finest Saxon steeple, built early in the 11th century, although the foundations can be traced back to 960. The Saxon carvings on the arches of the tower interior are among the earliest examples of English architectural carving, while the roof is made up of four diamond shaped surfaces meeting in a point; it is known as Rhenish helm, and is unique in England. Steep Down is a really superb viewpoint, with views which include the Weald, the South Downs to Truleigh Hill, the Adur valley, Lancing College Chapel, and a vast coastal strip from the cliffs east of Brighton to Butlins at Bognor and even beyond. Lancing College Chapel was begun in 1868 and built in early 14th century English Gothic style using Sussex sandstone; it boasts an internal height of 94ft and its foundations are in places 70ft deep. Its outstanding features are its painted ceiling, the 1978 stained-glass Rose Window at its west end, and, above the High Altar, massive tapestries, completed in 1933 and once the biggest in the country. The church of St Nicholas,

Old Shoreham, boasts some Saxon features but is predominantly Norman with quite superb intricate figure carvings and crossing arches. All of these places are well worth visiting. It's a tough call, but it's worth remembering that the Sussex Hospices Trail overlaps with the ECP almost all the way from Worthing to Shoreham-by-Sea so you could plump for the inland variation on one expedition and stick to the coast on the other. Just bear in mind that the Sussex Hospices Trail takes effectively a short cut into Shoreham-by-Sea from the church of the Good Shepherd just east of the Widewater Lagoon as described below, while the ECP, as again you'll see below, goes right out to the mouth of the river Adur then heads back – a much longer walk but a very good one. Another tough call!

If you stick to the coast route, then beyond the pier you continue past the Dome, The Steyne and the fine Steyne Gardens with its grand Boer War memorial and also, on the west side, the four-storeyed Chatsworth Hotel. A little further on, as you continue along the promenade, is a fine parade of white-painted residences and apartments; to your right are a number of impressively sculpted boulders, while across a green to the left is the opulent Beach House, where Edward VII once stayed. Continue along the prom, passing the impressive Splash Point leisure complex, then veer decisively to the left with the prom, running parallel with New Parade. At the far end of New Parade look for The Esplanade going away to the left; on the near side of Esplanade Court here is a blue plaque to Oscar Wilde who wrote *The Importance Of Being Earnest* on this site. The promenade becomes a narrower seafront walkway, soon joined by the busy A259 which is to your left. By turning inland up Ham Road as you reach the A259 you reach **East Worthing** Station in half a mile. Meanwhile, the ECP now simply follows the seafront walkway for roughly a mile to Lancing. As you draw level with Western Road, on arrival in **Lancing**, you get separated from the beach by houses including the pink timber-framed Boleyn, and shortly beyond these, you're signed back onto a seafront promenade. However, by continuing alongside the A259 and then bearing left up the A2025 South Street you'll reach the centre of Lancing, forking left up South Street by the Farmers pub to access its station. The coast route continues along the promenade, your view to the sea being impeded by a line of beach huts for a while; that said, there are good views to the South Downs and Lancing

College Chapel to the left, and shortly on your immediate left-hand side you'll see the Widewater Lagoon. Created by a combination of storms and longshore drift, it's a fine nature reserve with a wide variety of plants which include sea anemone, sea campion, sea kale, sea thrift and viper's bugloss, and birds which include redshank, pied wagtail, black-headed gull, swan, mallard, ringed plover, grey heron and kestrel. Continue along the south side of the lagoon; your path widens to become a road which you remain on as far as the delightful church of the Good Shepherd, built in 1913. Now (hereabouts losing the Sussex Hospices Trail which takes a short cut into Shoreham-by-Sea, albeit with a possible detour to Shoreham Airport – see the Sussex Hospices Trail section) climb up onto the shingle bank and follow it, embarking on your negotiation of what is in effect a mini-peninsula, known as Shoreham Beach, created by the Adur estuary. The peninsula is now little more than a glorified housing estate but it was very popular with film-makers in the 1920's, and celebrities of that era such as Hetty King and Marie Loftus spent time here. Your shingle walk is pretty tough going but in a few hundred yards you're able to join a proper boardwalk path through the shingle which takes you almost all the way to the mouth of the Adur, with a bearably short shingle walk on to the exit/entrance to Shoreham Harbour. There are fine views across the mouth of the Adur to the eastern arm of Shoreham Harbour although if you've time it's worth following West Breakwater to its end for the best views.

Having reached the harbour mouth you now need to follow the estuary back to Shoreham, effectively the western arm of the harbour. Proceed to the bank at the eastern end of the shingle and bear left to follow it round past Shoreham Fort, a brick-built fortification, completed in 1857 and rendered obsolete in 1870 by developments in artillery, though guns remained in service there until 1921. Continue through the fort car park along a road, Fort Haven, turning right at the end along Harbour Road. Veer left with it then just before Quay Court bear right along a signed path past the Harbour Club, passing through the car park and turning right onto Osprey Walk. This is a pedestrian walkway which passes round the side of the modern housing development to arrive at the waterfront, and you can then follow an excellent waterfront waterway, keeping the splendid new houses and flats to your left.

There's an inlet where you need to follow the walkway round, away from the river, but you're soon back by the river and you keep beside it till you're forced back to the road. You turn right to walk beside the road, then at the Waterside Inn you bear right, and go forward to cross the footbridge to reach the main street of **Shoreham-by-Sea**, the ECP here met by V2. The town was one of the leading ports of the medieval period, exporting wool, corn, salt and iron, and importing wine from France, and a large number of boats were engaged in fishing for mackerel and herring. The town also had an important association with shipbuilding, with reasonably priced timber easily obtained from the Weald by being floated down the Adur. The port itself dwindled in importance in the 16th century, but the fixing of the river mouth in 1818 and the opening of the eastern arm of the harbour in 1855 helped it to recover its prestige. A further positive development was the laying of oyster beds within the river mouth, bringing prosperity to fishermen and carriers who made daily journeys to the capital with the freshly caught delicacies. Over the 19th and into the 20th centuries the port was handling timber from the Baltic, oil from the refineries at Fawley, Canvey and Milford Haven, gravel dredged from the English Channel, sand, coal, stone and alcohol. In 1959 a bulk wine terminal was built, and in the 1980's one fifth of Spain's sherry exports passed through the port. By the turn of the millennium Shoreham was handling 3 million tons of cargo per annum. Architecturally, only two real historical gems remain despite the town's long history. The first is the church of St Mary de Haura ("of the harbour"), reached by crossing straight over the coast road from the footbridge and going on up East Street; the church dates back to 1130 and boasts magnificent choirstalls and tower which at 81ft high is visible for miles. The second building of interest, to the left along the High Street, is Marlipins. This is an unusual example of a surviving secular non-military Norman building with an exterior of very distinctive chequerboard flint and Caen stone; once the customs house from which harbour administration was conducted, it is now a museum. If you've detoured the short distance along the High Street to visit Marlipins, it's worth, on your return journey, detouring left up Church Street with its many fine flint-built cottages including one on the right that was inhabited by Captain Henry Roberts, who explored the South Seas with Captain Cook. Note that the station is reached in 400 yards or so off the High Street by walking up East Street past the church, bearing right at the end along St Mary's Road then immediately left up Brunswick Road.

Having joined the A259 from the footbridge, continue eastwards alongside this very busy road which you'll stick to as far as the Port Authority building. It's a pretty grim slog past various retail and industrial units – although you may be glad of the McDonald's on your left! – but at length the road does reach the water's edge, passing the lifeboat station, which is open to visitors, and lighthouse that dates back to 1846. The river veers seawards here, but you keep water to your right, this being the start of a lengthy inlet forming the eastern arm of Shoreham Harbour and extending all the way to Hove. The result is another strip of land beyond the inlet mirroring that of Shoreham Beach. Beyond the lighthouse there's some more rather dull pavement walking, but in a few hundred yards you pass the red-brick Shoreham Port Authority building opposite Grange Road; shortly beyond the Port Authority building turn right where indicated by a sign pointing you to the beach via the lock gates. By continuing briefly (barely 150 yards) along the A259 eastwards and turning first left you reach **Southwick** and its station. Back on the ECP, having turned right beyond the Port Authority building, follow the walkway to access and cross the lock gates over Shoreham Harbour. Note, however, that the gates frequently open to let harbour traffic through, so don't be surprised if you have to wait. The locks and other developments you see hereabouts are all legacies of the huge reconstruction works that were undertaken in the port in the 1950's. Having crossed over you've just a short walk to the seafront, with the conspicuous Shoreham Power Station, which opened in 2002, close by to your left. Having reached the seafront, you have a choice: if you're in a hurry, turn left here (D) and strike out eastwards towards Brighton. However I do recommend you turn right and, overlapping with a stretch of the Monarch's Way, follow the seafront for just over 500 yards back to the mouth of the Adur and, if you're feeling energetic, continue along East Breakwater to its very end. You'll get a superb view to the Adur estuary, Shoreham-by-Sea and its surrounding countryside, and you'll be able to enjoy the crash of the waves against the wall. Then retrace your steps to point (D) and continue, now overlapping with the Monarch's Way.

To begin with all is well: you have a pavement beside the beach with Basin Road South to your left, and behind that is the eastern arm of Shoreham Harbour separating you from the sprawling communities of Southwick, Fishersgate and Portslade. As you pass alongside Basin Road South, you leave West Sussex and enter Brighton & Hove. In due course, however, you lose the sea views from the road, though there is the possibility of following either the beach or, where it exists, a rough path at the top of the shingle bank. That said, I recommend you just stick to the road; in any case, by a mini-roundabout, you come to a section of private beach and are forced to follow the road, continuing along it on the landward side of industrial units at what is the very eastern end of Shoreham Harbour. The road swings sharp left, and as it does, you turn right onto a minor cul-de-sac to arrive at the start (or end) of Hove Western Esplanade. It's now plain sailing all the way to Brighton along a wide concrete promenade. Almost at once you pass the so-called Hove Lagoon, once a tidal reach of the Adur but during the 1930's transformed into a delightful area of water, used for model yachting events and also as a training ground in the run-up to D-day. Keeping the fine Western Lawns to your left, you then walk parallel with Kingsway, here within striking distance of the centre of **Hove**. Until the early 19th century Hove amounted to very little but as Brighton extended westwards, the period between 1824 and 1840 saw very extensive building work here, the quality of the building extremely good. During this period, the splendid Brunswick Square and Brunswick Terrace were developed, as well as the fine Adelaide Crescent, designed by Decimus Burton. Other buildings of merit dating from the 19th century were to be found in the Cliftonville area of Hove, between the present Kingsway and Church Road. These properties encompassed a variety of Victorian building styles, some Regency style, some with distinctive yellow brick fronts and some Italianate, but all meriting conservation area status. At the same time Hove became very popular as a seaside resort, with parks, lawns and promenades growing up around the town, and a continuous esplanade was completed towards the end of the 19th century. The locals loved the sea so much that seawater was stored in a reservoir and pumped into nearby houses so people could enjoy a seawater bath at home. Not surprisingly, Hove attracted a number of distinguished visitors, including Richard Jefferies the naturalist, General Booth who founded the Salvation

Army, and Winston Churchill who was educated at the Misses Thompson's Preparatory School at Hove between 1883 and 1885.

Excellent walking beside Kingsway takes you past King's Esplanade whose fine buildings, dating from 1892, extend right down to the promenade, and in fact at the end of King's Esplanade you could venture inland via Medina Terrace for route variation V3 to reach Hove Station and/or explore some of the best of Hove away from the seafront. Returning to the promenade, beyond King's Esplanade you pass some of the grandest streets in Hove including Brunswick Square, Brunswick Terrace and Adelaide Crescent, all adjoining or within sight of the coast road. You then enter **Brighton**. It's not clear when Hove ends and Brighton begins, but once beyond Montpelier Road (B2122) leading north-east from the A259, you can be said to have left Hove behind. The buildings are now taller, more impressive and more imposing, and there is the feeling of arriving not just in another town but a big city. You pass the Peace Memorial, dedicated to Edward VII and unveiled in October 1912, and soon after that, the ornate bandstand (now being rejoined by V3). Then comes the 2016 addition to Brighton's skyline, the tall thin I360 tower, with its covered viewing platform rising to provide potentially fantastic views along the coast. At this point you also pass level with the ruins of the West Pier out at sea, its doom effectively sealed by extensive storm damage in the early years of this century. Beyond West Pier you can't miss the luxurious Grand Hotel, designed in Italian Renaissance style and in 1864 regarded as the leading hotel of its day, and the bland Brighton Centre. At the junction of the coast road with West Street – by following West Street and then Queen's Road you reach Brighton Station in just over half a mile – you drop down the steps to the shore-level promenade and walk eastwards along it past the Fishing Museum and the Artists' Quarter with its little shops and galleries then, shortly before the (surviving!) pier, climb the slipway to follow beside the coast road. You'll soon reach Brighton Palace Pier and, just over the road from it, the Sea Life Centre, the world's oldest operating aquarium. It is at this point that a circular detour D1, visiting all the major sights of central Brighton, begins.

Brighton was originally a herring-fishing community and did not start to develop as we know it today until the latter part of the 18th century. The undisputed founder of modern Brighton was Dr

Richard Russell, who in 1750 was practising as a doctor in Lewes and sent patients to Brighton to try a seawater cure. He was one of a number of promoters of health to encourage people to Brighton and as a result many notable visitors were drawn to the town, including Royalty. In 1815 the Prince Regent appointed John Nash to build a palace to effectively replace the simple classical Marine Pavilion that Henry Holland had built some years before; the result was the remarkable Royal Pavilion which was completed in 1823 and which remains the most stunning building in Brighton, both inside and outside, the most notable rooms being the Music Room, the Great Kitchen and the Banqueting Room. Besides the Pavilion, a huge number of buildings were erected in Brighton in the early years of the 19th century, and the town was thus blessed with a rich legacy of Regency architecture. Two of the most notable buildings to be constructed in Brighton during the 19th century were the Grand Hotel (see above) and the church of St Bartholomew, Ann Street, then the biggest brick church in Europe, built to the same dimensions as Noah's Ark, magnificently decorated with oil paintings and Italian mosaics. 1841 saw the arrival of the railway, and the consequent increase in holiday traffic served as a catalyst for the town's future development as a resort. The first pier to be erected in Brighton was constructed in 1823, but destroyed by a storm in 1896. The West Pier followed in 1866 and the Palace Pier in 1899; the Brighton Palace Pier was to become Brighton's most popular attraction and is still flourishing today with its fattening snacks and stomach-churning rides. Two other significant attractions to arrive in Brighton in the 19th century were the aquarium (now the Sea Life Centre), which opened in August 1872, and Volk's Electric Railway which opened in 1883. Although Brighton suffered severe damage in World War 2, many wonderfully unspoilt Regency streets remain, and the character and ambience of former times are preserved in its splendid shopping area of narrow streets known as The Lanes, dating back mainly from the 19th century. Brighton is now designated, with Hove, as a city and unitary authority independent of East Sussex (although most people think of Brighton as part of Sussex). It is certainly the most cosmopolitan place you will visit on your coastal walk and indeed is known by some as "London by the Sea;" it is noteworthy for its gay scene which dates back over 100 years, and gay icons such as Noel Coward and Ivor Novello have both spent part of their lives in the town. A number of celebrities have made Brighton their home including the boxer Chris Eubank and the disc jockey Norman Cook (alias Fatboy Slim). It hosts a major arts festival in the spring, the huge Pride festival in August has become a massive community event, and it is the final destination for the veteran car run from London on the first Sunday in November as well as the popular London to Brighton Bike Ride in mid-June.

Beyond Brighton Palace Pier there's a choice: to stick to the coast or to visit Kemp Town, an opulent area of east Brighton created in the early 19th century by Thomas Kemp. For the latter there's a route variation V4. Otherwise continue along the promenade, soon separated from the shingle by Volk's Electric Railway, and follow it to just past the crazy golf course. You then fork left up the slip road, Duke's Mound, to reach Marine Parade, the A259 coast road. Follow the pedestrian walkway on the seaward side of the coast road, then just before it starts to drop away, use the pedestrian crossing to join and follow the clifftop cycle/footway, now rejoined by V4. Very soon, fork right onto a cliff-edge footpath running roughly parallel with the cycleway. A route variation V5 leaves the route here, going over the A259 at the crossing immediately level with the Marine Gate complex to visit the 11th century church at Ovingdean and then Rottingdean Windmill, a smock windmill dating from 1802; still boasting four sails, it was once used to store contraband goods and remains an important landmark for shipping. The ECP however continues on the cliff edge, now above the extensive Brighton Marina with its complex of houses and shops between the sailing boats on the harbour waters. This is your first proper clifftop walking on the route, and in fact you'll be following the cliffs for the majority of the way to Newhaven. There is the option of the undercliff path but after so many miles of coastal walking I think you deserve a proper clifftop march; in any case the undercliff path walk to Rottingdean is described in the Sussex Hospices Trail section. The views to the Marina are magnificent, as are the views to the sea beyond, and it's worth looking back for excellent views westwards to Brighton which you're now leaving behind. Looking to your left you'll see the Jacobean-style buildings of Roedean School, arguably the best known of all independent girls' schools, founded in 1885 and moved to its present site at the very end of the 19th century. Beyond the school you'll see Rottingdean Windmill referred to above. After passing the windmill you start to descend, and arrive in **Rottingdean**. You need to veer to the right just before the White Horse pub which you see on the right at the bottom of the hill, and having passed to the seaward side of the White Horse you come to the bottom of the High Street. Your way is right, but to detour to the village, turn left up the High Street and across the A259, continuing north-westwards up the High Street (being rejoined by V5) and following it up to the Green, then heading clockwise back down Vicarage Lane to return to the High Street. The total return trip is three quarters of a mile. By doing this you'll pass some very attractive old buildings, including a number built from flint, brick and timber, and a charming green and pond. The oldest complete secular building in the village is the early 16th century Black Horse, a popular meeting place for smugglers; in the late 18th century smuggling was rife, particularly in such commodities as tea, spirits, tobacco and lace. A number of most distinguished people have stayed or lived in Rottingdean including Rudyard Kipling who wrote some of his most famous work here including *Kim* and his *Stalky* stories. His house, The Elms, is on the village green and North End House, home of the artist Edward Burne-Jones – Kipling's uncle by marriage – is to the west of the green. Burne-Jones' plaque is actually on Prospect Cottage, adjoining North End House. On the east side, as you continue clockwise round, is the flint Saxon church of St Margaret and the imposing Grange, the former vicarage and now a museum with many Kipling-related exhibits.

Back on the coast route, you follow the High Street seawards and go straight on down the steep slipway which brings you to the undercliff path. Turn left to follow it. While the undercliff path was not the optimum route past Brighton Marina, it certainly is a much better option immediately beyond Rottingdean (though in very wild weather, it's advisable to stick to the A259 coast road, shortly branching off onto the adjacent coast path and following it first up and then down to the café at **Saltdean** referred to below). Just over half a mile from Rottingdean you reach a flight of steps, climb them and continue past the café, then turn left up steps to arrive at the A259 again. A bit further back (westwards) on the other side of the main road here is the recently restored Art Deco Saltdean Lido with open-air pool, and in fact by following the Sussex Hospices Trail from the Lido and detouring off Linchmere Avenue up Wicklands

Avenue – a detour of half a mile in all from the ECP – you'll reach Grand Ocean, another Art Deco construction. However the ECP turns right alongside the A259 briefly, before forking right to follow the cliff path uphill to a distinctive obelisk and weather vane. Beyond the obelisk you start to descend, and are signed away from the sea; follow carefully the clear path signs directing you over a tarmac road then on to a T-junction of paths just below the Smugglers Rest pub. Turn right at the T-junction along a path returning you to the cliff edge, then veer left to continue along the clifftops. It's now very easy and straightforward cliff walking, mostly over grass; it is great to have the sea below you to your right, but not so great to have the residential sprawl of Telscombe Cliffs to your left. At length, roughly 2 miles from Saltdean Lido, you reach the King George V Memorial, which is the start of the Greenwich Meridian Trail and described more fully in that section, and which also signifies your arrival at Peacehaven. You can conveniently access the town centre from any one of the numerous roads leading away from the cliff to the left hereabouts. Peacehaven was the brainchild of the wealthy businessman Charles Neville, and work duly began in 1915 to build on the 650 clifftop acres that Neville had bought here. Initially it was decided that the resort should be named New Anzac-on-Sea in honour of the Australians and New Zealanders who were stationed in the area at the start of the Great War and who took part in the hostilities. After the debacle at Gallipoli, however, it was felt that this name was insensitive and inappropriate, and Peacehaven was chosen instead as a result of a national competition. A massive advertising campaign was launched to persuade people to buy a house at Peacehaven, while the grand opening of the Peacehaven Hotel on 29 September 1922 was marked by a military band, fireworks and bonfire. Sadly the town now has a reputation for lacking, architecturally, any aesthetic merit whatsoever.

The ECP continues on beyond Peacehaven, the housing relents at last, and you're now able to enjoy a very fine cliff walk, here following part of the waymarked Seahaven Coastal Trail, with excellent views ahead to Newhaven and Seaford. Just take care not to stray too close to the cliff edge, and watch for one dip and slightly awkward crossing of a little stream using a bridge consisting of narrow metal strips. Generally, however, the going is easy and enjoyably rural, marred only by Newhaven Heights, a development of chalets which come up very close to the clifftop, but your path steers a clear course between the houses and the cliff edge. Beyond the chalets, you continue along the path onto Castle Hill, aiming for a mast. Pass to the right of the mast and carry on along the clifftop, but 150 yards or so beyond the mast you reach an area of bushes and a path junction. Pause and enjoy the superb views from here to the mouth of Newhaven Harbour then take the path swinging left through the bushes; it arrives at a gravelled path onto which you turn right and which you follow downhill. Go forward to a metalled road which descends, veering left and then right to arrive at a T-junction with Fort Road (E). Your way is left, but you could detour shortly right here to visit the adjacent Newhaven Fort. The original brick-built fort was constructed in the 1860's during one of the periodic 19th century French invasion scares. It was equipped with modern guns during World War 2 and bombed several times by the Germans, but it has now been restored as a museum, and you can relive the days when it was an active fort with its gun emplacements, mortar batteries, magazines and parade ground. Back on Fort Road, you've now reached the Ouse valley and are forced away from the coast to cross the river, so follow Fort Road inland from (E) above, passing a boatyard which is to your right. Just beyond the boats, turn right immediately before a small parade of shops/businesses to follow through the car parking area by the river, going forward into the metalled Riverside. You can now enjoy a pleasant waterside walk, at the top end of which you meet the A259 ring road (F). The ECP bears right and goes forward beside the A259 to cross the swing bridge over the Ouse; to explore **Newhaven** town, however, cross straight over the ring road at (F) and walk down Bridge Street to the old Bridge Hotel which dates back to 1623. Louis Philippe, deposed in the 1848 uprising in France, stayed there after fleeing across the Channel, booking in with Queen Mary Amelie as "Mr and Mrs Smith." By the hotel you could detour further, left, up the High Street, crossing the ring road again and continuing beyond it up Church Hill to reach the superbly situated early 12th century church of St Michael with an interior décor including shades of terracotta and a tiny east window beyond the intimate chancel and altar. The total detour will add 1 mile to your journey. If you've detoured, return via High Street and Bridge Street to recross the A259, then proceed to and cross the swing bridge to resume your coast route.

The bridge "opens" from time to time to allow boats through, so you may have a bit of a wait; opening times are usually advertised on local radio if you are anxious to plan your walk to avoid waiting. Newhaven was a port of considerable importance, standing as it does so close to the mouth of the Ouse. It was previously called Meeching, only changing its name when the Ouse's course changed to enter the sea there, and it is indeed as a harbour and a port that the town was to become principally known. During the 19th century a cross-Channel steamer service began linking Newhaven to Dieppe with a crossing time by 1891 of 3 hours 45 minutes. The port was used as a supply base during World War 1, and in World War 2 it became a base for hospital ships, motor gunboats, minesweepers and air/sea rescue missions, and was the base for the disastrous Dieppe Raid in August 1942. After the war, the cross-Channel service for civilian traffic resumed, with a car ferry service being introduced in 1964. Newhaven remains the only town on the Sussex coast offering a year-round cross-Channel ferry service, but even that may be in jeopardy thanks to the Channel Tunnel.

Having crossed the swing bridge you fork immediately right onto Drove Road which goes over a level crossing beside Newhaven Town Station; beyond the level crossing you go first right into Railway Road, the road becoming Clifton Road and then Beach Road, but not getting any prettier. In fact this is certainly the dullest bit of the walk between Brighton and Seaford. In just under half a mile you pass a right turn leading directly to **Newhaven Harbour Station**, then as Beach Road bends sharply to the left by the railway, look for a Vanguard Way-signed footpath which leads off to the right. You now follow this path (actually also overlapping with the Sussex Ouse Valley Way here), staying parallel with, and to the land side of, the railway briefly then crossing the railway by means of a footbridge. Once over the bridge keep walking along the Vanguard Way-signed path, keeping Mill Creek to your right. Follow the path all the way to a signed path junction, at a metalled road crossing at the far end of the creek. You're now on the site of the abandoned village of Tide Mills. The village consisted of a large tide mill and a number of workmen's cottages housing about a hundred workers; however, the mill stopped in around 1900 and the village was condemned as unfit for habitation in 1936, the last residents leaving in 1939. Cross straight over and continue past further ruins of Tide Mills, staying with the Vanguard Way and Sussex Ouse Valley Way, reaching a junction with the shore footpath. Turn left along it, shortly passing the sailing club building, immediately beyond which Marine Parade comes in from the left. At this point there's the possibility of a <u>detour D2</u> to Bishopstone Station and the old village of **Bishopstone** and its superb church, much of which predates the Norman Conquest; the porch boasts a Saxon sundial and under the tower there's a coffin lid decorated with 12th century carving. Whether or not you've detoured, continue on along the prom, in due course signed as the Bonningstedt Promenade, past the "new" Bishopstone and forward to the buildings of Seaford, keeping the coast road, Marine Parade, to the left (although for more elevated views you could walk beside the coast road if you prefer). As you arrive at the taller buildings immediately beside the seafront, and the coast road becomes Esplanade, you reach the bottom of Dane Road; the centre of **Seaford** is reachable in a few minutes up Dane Road and by using a <u>route variation V6</u> you can access the railway station and visit the most interesting parts of the town. Otherwise continue along the promenade. Back in the 13th century, Seaford was a busy port standing at the mouth of the Ouse, and in 1544 it was granted membership of the Cinque Ports Confederation. The Cinque Ports, originally Hastings, Romney, Hythe, Sandwich and Dover, were ports that were granted special privileges through their provision of men and ships for the defence of the Channel, and Seaford was one of a further 32 ports that were added subsequently. However towards the end of the 16th century the mouth of the river effectively transferred from Seaford to Meeching as described above, and poor Seaford was left high and dry! For the next three centuries Seaford could be said to be in limbo, of no practical use as a port, but yet to be developed as a resort. In 1806 the very real threat of French invasion prompted the building of 74 so-called Martello towers along the south coast, very distinctive round grey constructions of which the most westerly one was sited at Seaford, consisting of a gun platform, garrison and magazine. It was restored in the 1970's and is probably now the town's most interesting feature, housing a fine museum. Once the threat of invasion receded, the town again became something of a backwater, but despite the lack of success of the endeavours of a number of companies to turn Seaford into another Brighton, many Victorians did enjoy visiting the town; the railway arrived in 1864, and the town's popularity as a watering place inspired the building of the fine Esplanade Hotel which survived for 80 years, attracting Edward VII for a stay in 1905. However it was obvious that there was only limited demand for another resort between Brighton and Eastbourne, and today one is left with the impression of a seaside resort which never quite happened. Architecturally there are a number of buildings of interest in Seaford, arguably the most notable being the church of St Leonard, described by Pevsner as a "large and monumental medieval church;" of Norman origin, it boasts a number of Norman features and unusual pillar carvings.

Continue along the promenade beyond Dane Road past the very prominent redbrick Stratheden Court, being met in due course by V6. You pass the Martello tower, perhaps stopping to look in the museum housed inside it, and go forward to the car park at the end of the promenade, the cliffs of Seaford Head getting closer with each step. You'll feel as though you've been taxi-ing before take-off, but now you can put off the climbing no longer, and begin a steady climb up onto the cliffs, keeping the cliff edge to the right and the golf course to your left. There's no definitive path – just choose whichever way up you prefer! It's never intolerably steep, but it's certainly your most strenuous work so far on the ECP, so pause lots and enjoy the increasingly good views back to Seaford and Newhaven. Eventually you make it onto Seaford Head. The site of a triangular Iron Age hillfort, this headland provides not only the most spectacular walking so far but is of great interest to the naturalist and geologists. Plants hereabouts include thrift, ground ivy and kidney vetch, and the area is also popular with rabbits. You will note from information boards that an area of the plateau is known as "Buckle Church;" the Buckle is a reference to the coat of arms of the local aristocratic Pelham family, and the Church refers to a hermitage which is known to have existed here in 1372.

Continue along the clifftop enjoying superb views to the Seven Sisters cliffs ahead of you. All too soon, it seems, you begin to descend on a magnificent green path, eventually arriving at Hope Gap, a quite delightfully secluded spot in a valley between rising cliffs; you have the option of detouring down a flight of steps to the rocky pavements separating the cliffs from the sea. It is an area rich in fossils, the legacy of a complex marine environment dating back to the Late Cretaceous period some 89 million years ago. Back on the ECP, veering half-left, you rise again to get an excellent view of Cuckmere Haven, the valley between Seaford Head and the Seven Sisters through which the estuary of the Cuckmere river flows. Remaining on the cliff path you reach the coastguard cottages; pass to the left of them and arrive at a clear track running at right-angles to the one you've been following. Turn right onto the track, passing the cottages, and descend to the Cuckmere valley bottom, arriving at a gate. Don't bear left here as suggested by the Vanguard Way arrow, but go straight through the gate onto the shingle beach, and forward to the west bank of Cuckmere estuary itself, just as it arrives at the sea. Especially at low tide this will seem tantalisingly narrow but it's not possible to ford, and this means a bit of a tramp upstream. Enjoying a final terrific view ahead to the Seven Sisters, turn left to join a narrow but clear path up the west bank of the estuary, a new cut of the Cuckmere (about which more below). As you get within sight of the busy A259, the path kinks left away from the water, then veers right and goes forward to the A259 at the Cuckmere Inn, formerly the Golden Galleon. Turn right with the A259 and, immediately crossing over the Cuckmere, carry on beside this busy road – thankfully a pavement is provided – as far as the visitor centre and adjacent café/restaurant at **Exceat** a few hundred yards along the road. The hamlet of Exceat, where Edward the Confessor owned a manor, is not pronounced "Ex-seat" as one might suppose, but "Ex-sett" – having been recorded as Essete in the Domesday Book. More or less opposite the visitor centre, as the road bends left and begins to ascend, you turn right into the car park, but almost immediately bear left through a gate along a path which goes forward to a metalled track. You now follow it back towards the sea, admiring the extraordinary meanders of the "old" Cuckmere estuary to your right.

You're now walking through Cuckmere Haven, and as you do, you'll note the spectacular meanders of the Cuckmere itself. The mouth of the river has drifted east because of encroachments of the shingle beach, and in order to prevent flooding, the new cut referred to above was created in 1846, strengthened by automatic weir control. Although King Alfred is supposed to have founded a shipyard at Cuckmere Haven, the mouth of the Cuckmere is today blissfully devoid of any development and is by far the finest of the estuarine landscapes you will see on the whole walk, with a huge variety of bird life including cormorants, herons, dabchicks, curlews, peregrine falcons, hen harriers and Canada geese. The coastline hereabouts has seen several shipwrecks, and the area was also renowned in the 18th and 19th centuries as landing places for smuggled goods; a number of gangs operated from here, and there were some notorious encounters on the shore with customs officers. Some escapades were more successful than others. In 1923 an attempt was made to run a cargo of 91 cases of brandy aboard a French fishing boat from Dieppe, and at 9am on a Sunday morning the small craft left Dieppe intending to be met at Cuckmere Haven. Unfortunately the pilot suffered sea sickness and after a most uncomfortable night was forced to land at Newhaven where the boat was met by the customs men!

After roughly half a mile the path swings quite sharply left away from the valley, towards a group of farm buildings; don't swing left with the path, but fork right onto a path signposted Seven Sisters, pass through a gate, then after about 100 yards fork left. You're now on the course of the South Downs Way. Initially your path remains on the flat but then proceeds up a flight of steps, going forward to a fence; don't cross the gate in the fence that soon appears, but, keeping the fence to your right, press on uphill along a clearly marked path. This is quite a slog, but you can make it more enjoyable for yourself by pausing to look back at the superb views across Cuckmere Haven to Seaford Head. At length you arrive at the summit of the first of seven spectacular chalk clifftops known as the Seven Sisters. They form the eastern end of the South Downs and the climax of the South Downs Way, and owe their origin to geological activity between 50 and 100 million years ago. The depressions separating each "sister" are the valleys of ancient rivers, formed when the chalk extended further seawards, but later cut off when the sea pounded the chalk away. Each "sister" or clifftop has a name: in turn they are Haven Brow, Short Brow, Rough Brow, Brass Point, Flagstaff Point, Bailey's Hill and Went Hill Brow. The unspoilt chalk hills attract many birds, butterflies and rare plants. Now the going could not be more straightforward, although it's physically as demanding as anything you've done so far. There's no path as such: just take each "sister" in turn, enjoying the quite magnificent views back to Seaford Head and Cuckmere Haven, and forward towards the Belle Tout lighthouse and Beachy Head. The climbs are often steep and you need to be careful not to stray too close to the cliff edge as you ascend. The seventh "sister" having been conquered, you descend towards the assembly of houses and café at **Birling Gap**; note that as you come down off the final "sister" you'll need to veer a little left to a gate in the fence beyond which it's a simple walk down to the Gap, a freak cleft in the South Downs with steep steps to the sea that were used by smugglers. Note the houses at Birling Gap and how frighteningly vulnerable they are to the sea. By turning left up the road running inland from Birling Gap you reach, in one mile, the gorgeous village of **East Dean**, bearing left up Lower Street just before the church to reach the centre with its lovely green surrounded by flint cottages. If you head for the far top left corner of the green, pass through the car park and cross straight over Upper Street (leading to the main road where there are buses to Brighton and Eastbourne) and follow the footpath beyond you reach in another 400 yards or so the beautiful Norman church at Friston, with particularly fine monuments to the Selwyns of Friston Place. Just beyond the church there's a beautiful pond, the first in the country to be designated an ancient monument. Then retrace the same way to Birling Gap, perhaps availing yourself of refreshment at East Dean – there's plenty of choice!

Beyond Birling Gap, you press on; the way forward is obvious, with a choice of paths to take you back up to and along the clifftops. All the time you're aiming for the old Belle Tout lighthouse, and your path passes just to the left of it. It was built from Aberdeen granite by Thomas Stevenson in around 1830, and remained in use for the rest of the 19th century. Unfortunately it proved somewhat ineffective in the thick mists which crept in from the English Channel, and as a result, it was decided to build a replacement sea level lighthouse in 1902. It is that lighthouse, below the Beachy Head clifftop, which remains in use to this day; the Belle Tout became a dwelling although owing to cliff erosion it's had to be moved more than once. Beyond the old lighthouse you drop steeply to meet the road at a small car park, before beginning the assault on Beachy Head. It's a laborious climb, not helped by a big dip which sees you rapidly lose height you must then regain, but at least route finding is no problem, the grass is lovely to walk on, and the views just get better and better. Finally you arrive on **Beachy Head**. At the summit you are 535ft above the sea (the highest point on the Sussex coast) and it is a frighteningly long and steep drop to the water below. The name Beachy Head is thought to derive from the Middle Ages French "beau chef" meaning "beautiful headland" and on a clear day it certainly is beautiful, offering views which on a clear day can extend back to the Isle of Wight. Since 1990 it's become a breeding ground for falcons, it's one of the best places in Sussex to see the stone curlew, and plants include red valerian, sea radish, early gentian, harebell and orchid.

Getting off Beachy Head isn't straightforward, so follow the instructions carefully. Keep following the clifftop beyond the summit, but shortly look out for, and turn right onto, a South Downs Way-signed path. This is a narrow path which drops then rises again, crossing a metalled path and passing to the left of a fine war memorial; from beside the memorial itself there are superb views to the "new" lighthouse. Immediately beyond the memorial continue on as South Downs Way-signed, but in a few yards, just beyond a bench, look out carefully for steps to the right, and use these steps to descend to, and go forward along, an obvious wide green path heading for and reaching the edge of the cliff. You're now overlapping with the Wealdway. Having reached this point, veer left to walk along the clifftop, going forward through vegetation, ironically having to climb up some steps, and then climbing again to meet a wide stony track onto which you turn right. The track becomes a metalled road and drops down to a café, this being the end of the South Downs Way. Just beyond the cafe you turn right into Duke's Drive and follow it downhill. You pass Helen Gardens then immediately beyond them turn right along a narrow road signposted Holywell, Promenade (Western Parade); keep along this road downhill, ignoring turnings off, to arrive at the promenade, then turn left and follow the promenade all the way to **Eastbourne**, a walk of about a mile. Look out to your left for Western Lawns and, on the far side of them, the magnificent white-fronted Grand Hotel which dates back to 1875 and whose guests have included Winston Churchill and Charlie Chaplin. You pass a Martello tower known as the Wish Tower, Wish being a corruption of Wash, a stream that used to flow here, then pass the Lifeboat Museum which is well worth a visit. By bearing left up the slipway beyond the museum to the coast road, crossing it and arriving at the start of Lascelles Terrace, a <u>detour D3</u> is possible to access Eastbourne Station and town centre, and/or to view the architectural, cultural and historic highlights of Eastbourne that are away from the seafront, including the Old Town. Eastbourne was just a small village until the mid-19th century, centred round the church of St Mary the Virgin in what is now known as the Old Town. That said, it played an important part in coastal defence against the threat of Napoleonic invasion; to combat this menace, a massive brick building known as the Redoubt was constructed in 1803, and you'll meet this as you head away from the town centre. The village was inherited by William Cavendish, the 7th Duke of Devonshire, in 1834, and together with another local landowner, Carew Davis Gilbert, he set about developing it as a resort, with the main development beginning in 1851. The combination of greenery and fine architecture turned Eastbourne into what was and remains one of the best seaside resorts in Sussex, and it is not surprising that it attracted some notable personalities including Charles Darwin and Claude Debussy. The town remained a prosperous resort well into the 20th century, but it was badly bombed during World War 2. However despite rapid post-war development which rather spoilt its Victorian charm, visitors have continued to be drawn not only to the lovely sands and excellent bathing, but to such features as the stunning Carpet Gardens, established in the town for more than a century; the pier, which suffered a devastating fire a few years back but which has been impressively restored; Devonshire Park with its theatre and tennis courts which play host to an important international tennis tournament in the run-up to Wimbledon in each year; the Towner Gallery with its impressive collection of contemporary art; and a bandstand which was built to accommodate over 3000 spectators. Eastbourne's summer seafront air show, known as Airbourne, is now a major event, drawing huge crowds.

Beyond the Lifeboat Museum, whether you've detoured into the town centre or not, you have a choice of promenades. I suggest that you stick to the lower one, then, just beyond the impressive domed bandstand, a little way short of the pier, climb onto the upper promenade beside the coast road, Grand Parade, enjoying the magnificent architecture along this road as well as the Carpet Gardens. You soon pass (or detour to walk along) the pier, completed by Eugenius Birch in 1872 and, as stated above, recently restored, then beyond the pier you should revert to the lower prom as soon as you are able. It's worth looking back from time to time, in order to enjoy splendid views back to Beachy Head and also to appreciate the variety of buildings around you, ranging from opulent hotels to the flint-fronted Ye Olde Bakery, dated 1790. In just under half a mile from the pier you pass the Redoubt, referred to above. Beyond the Redoubt there's a little kink in the prom to the left and then right, but the going remains quick and easy, your route following a clear and obvious walkway, with sea kale, yellow horned-poppy and sea campion all to be found nearby. Note that the walkway also doubles as a cycleway and you need to watch and listen for cyclists! You've now pulled well away from the centre of Eastbourne, but you should pause to enjoy the view back towards the town and to Beachy Head. You pass the large red-brick water treatment works, then go forward to within clear sight of a Martello tower, where rather abruptly your walkway stops. Don't bear left as signed here, but go straight ahead over an area of shingle, aiming straight for the tower. Immediately ahead of you here is Langney Point and the mouth of Sovereign Harbour, your only natural obstruction on this section but thankfully not requiring as lengthy an inland detour as the Ouse or Cuckmere estuaries have demanded of you! As you reach the Martello tower, turn left and cross rough shingly ground to pick up an excellent harbourside path, now entering the modern and hugely impressive Sovereign Harbour complex. You arrive at two pairs of swing bridges providing entrances and exits for boats entering and leaving the harbour. Simply choose whichever ones happen to be open in order to negotiate the harbour waters, then, before proceeding, pause to enjoy the variety of modern architecture on show, as well as the splendid range of vessels. Having crossed, aim for and pass to the right of the lifeboat station and continue along the waterfront, veering right to arrive back at the beach, now on the east side of the harbour. You then swing left to follow an excellent concrete walkway at the back of the beach, with modern housing alongside you on the landward side.

At the end of the modern housing, it's decision time. For the next 4 miles, past the architecturally uninteresting sprawls of Pevensey Bay and Normans Bay, there is no coastal path or promenade as such. There's a choice between what could be a very tough shingle walk, or the shingle-avoiding route of the Sussex Hospices Trail as shown via its website and the ifootpath app, starting here, proceeding via Pevensey Bay, Normans Bay (with station) and Cooden Beach, and ending at South Cliff, where a slipway takes you down to the promenade on the approach to Bexhill. However, this route is extremely dull and providing you have the stamina I recommend you stick to the beach. Outside high tide you can proceed along the sands, although your progress will be interrupted by the negotiation of breakwaters, of which there are lots. If the tide is too high, it will be a very tough shingle tramp, so do try to choose low tide for this walk! In any case, it's possible to swap from shingle to road (or vice versa) at **Pevensey Bay**, a mile into the shingle walk. Please see the description given in the Sussex Hospices Trail section, which also gives details as to public transport options from there and a possible detour to the historic centre of Pevensey. If nothing else, Pevensey Bay offers the opportunity of refreshment and a break from your labours. Furthermore, as you approach the built-up area incorporating Cooden Beach and Bexhill (signified by Cooden Beach golf course to your left) you can follow the metalled Herbrand Walk parallel with the beach. This road joins you just beyond a level crossing to your left, some 2.5 miles from Pevensey Bay – wooden steps are available for ease of access – and it brings you to Cooden Beach Station and the amenities of **Cooden Beach**, from which you can either return to the beach or follow the Sussex Hospices Trail. Assuming you've stuck to (or returned to) the beach then not long after the Cooden Beach/Bexhill built-up area begins, you reach a very obvious and very splendid mock-Tudor house and garden backing onto the shingle, and shortly beyond that house a metalled promenade commences. Now it's plain sailing all the way to Bexhill and in fact you'll be walking on concrete almost all the way to Hastings. Follow the promenade then at groyne 44 turn left up a slipway leading to South Cliff, a metalled road. Turn right alongside South Cliff, then on reaching a toilet block you can pick up another and wider promenade which takes you on to Bexhill. As you proceed, West Parade is with you to the left; detouring inland up Richmond Road from the west end of West Parade takes you in 300 yards to **Collington** Station, and a detour of just a few yards off the prom at the clock tower, over West Parade and along Park Avenue, roughly 500 yards or so after West Parade joins you, brings you to the excellent Bexhill Museum. This contains a Costume and Social History Gallery and a Motoring Heritage Gallery, in recognition of the fact that in May 1902, as part of a campaign to promote Bexhill as a resort, the town hosted the first international motor racing meeting on British soil, attracting many fine vehicles from the Continent. Shortly beyond Park Road along the prom you pass the unmissable De La Warr Pavilion, the first public building in the United Kingdom designed in Modernist style. It was commissioned in 1935 by Herbrand Sackville, 9th Earl De La Warr, and the designers were German architects Erich Mendlesohn and Serge Chermayeff. While under construction it was nicknamed King Kong's Meccano Museum! It was envisaged as a "palace of culture" featuring white walls, wooden floors and a floating steel staircase, and included a dance floor and restaurant. It was damaged during World War 2 and fell into disrepair, its condition not helped by the effects of the seaside climate, but it was comprehensively restored and reopened in 2005, now once again without doubt the focal point of Bexhill with its galleries, restaurants and roof terrace amongst its many attractions. Continue on past the splendid white Colonnade built to commemorate George V's coronation, with its ornate cupolas and balustrades. Immediately beyond the Colonnade, by the Bexhill Rowing Club, are steps which provide easy access to the De La Warr Pavilion; simply go straight on beyond the steps and round the side of the Pavilion via the car park to reach the entrance. On your way back to the coast path via the steps, look for the distinctive early 20th century domes on the brick-built houses on Marina Court Avenue just ahead. The coast path continues along the prom, turning sharply left and then right just beneath the bottom of Sea Road, but to reach the station and **Bexhill** town centre, cross the coast road and follow Sea Road inland, to reach the station in roughly 350 yards, passing the main shopping area which is to the left via St Leonards Road.

Bexhill is really two towns in one. The old town of Bexhill, where the lovely Manor Gardens are also to be found, was built half a mile inland from the sea and remains the most historic part of today's Bexhill; for a description of this, and how to reach it from the station, please refer to the 1066 Country Walk (Bexhill Link) section. The town was developed as a resort by the Earls De La Warr, who owned the land between old Bexhill and the sea, in the 1880's. It enjoyed many Royal visits; in 1901 it became the first resort in the country to permit mixed bathing; as noted above, the town hosted, in 1902, the first international motor racing on British soil; and 1896 saw the opening in Bexhill of the Kursaal centre, offering traditional pier-type entertainment (the resort was never to acquire a pier!) but this later closed, effectively being superseded by the De La Warr Pavilion. Nowadays Bexhill has become a largely residential and retirement town, and indeed more than half of its population are retired people. The main town centre and its shops do have a delightfully, some might say reassuringly, old-fashioned feel.

East of Sea Road you keep on along the promenade, soon reaching a sculpture depicting the so-called Easter Egg, a racing car driven by Leon Serpollet in motor racing's earliest days, the sculpture a fine commemoration of Bexhill's motoring heritage. When the promenade ends, you can enjoy a bracing clifftop walk using a quiet road going forward to a good concrete walkway, with a fine view to St Leonards and Hastings immediately ahead, and the sea to your right – and you also get a grandstand view of a sprawling retail park across the railway to the left! Following a descent and then another short clifftop walk, it's a straightforward walk on a good firm path along the back of the shingle beach with the railway immediately to the left. You then go on past lines of beach huts to your right and left, and, sticking to the well-signed cycle route 2, continue to the start of the metalled promenade which will take you all the way to Hastings past St Leonards. Note that by turning left up Grosvenor Gardens by the far west end of Sea Road, crossing Grosvenor Crescent into Keats Close, bearing right along West Hill Road and left up St Vincent's Road you reach **West St Leonards** Station, some 400 yards from the ECP. Back on the ECP, the going is now very straightforward, as you follow the prom past St Leonards, looking out for the fine stuccoed Royal Victoria Hotel across the coast road. **St Leonards** was designed as a completely separate development from Hastings by the architect James Burton. The Royal Victoria Hotel, built in 1828, was one of his finest pieces of work, and with its splendid columns it is arguably the best building architecturally in St Leonards. Immediately beyond the Royal Victoria Hotel there's the possibility of a <u>detour D4</u> left up Gardner Way to view some of Burton's other work here and the impressive landscaped St Leonards Gardens, with many examples of fine Regency architecture. Very shortly beyond the Royal Victoria is the huge Marine Court complex, designed in the 1930's to look like an ocean-going liner, and built in 1937-38. This is a real Marmite building, and Pevsner was in the "hate it" category, calling it the "first modernistic affront to the English seaside." Keep to the prom, although by turning inland up the well-signed London Road you can, via King's Road, reach St Leonards Warrior Square Station in about a quarter of a mile. The prom continues past the verdant Warrior Square itself, consisting of a formal garden laid out in 1853 and regarded as the meeting point of St Leonards and Hastings. Just beyond the garden is a splendid memorial to Queen Victoria. Now proceed straight on to reach Hastings Pier, built in 1872, superbly restored and reopened in 2016 following a fire in 2010. It's well worth walking to its end and back. Continue on along the waterfront past the pier and the fine early 20th century White Rock Theatre opposite. Here, by heading inland up the adjacent Schwerte Way, there's the opportunity for a <u>detour D5</u> to the excellent Hastings Museum and Art Gallery (described in the detour description). Beyond the pier you remain on the prom, but in some 375 yards you could cross to the inland side of the coast road in order to visit Hastings True Crime Museum (on the coast road itself) and shortly beyond the museum, a triangle of streets to your left, Robertson Street, Trinity Street and Claremont, making up America Ground, so-called because following a dispute over land ownership a group of residents tried to claim this area as an American state in the early 19th century. This area now houses a splendid variety of quirky individual shops, with Holy Trinity Church making an elegant centrepiece. By following Robertson Street on, away from the coast road, you arrive in the modern centre of Hastings; to reach the station, in some 400 yards from the seafront, turn hard left up Havelock Road. However to continue along the ECP, stay on the prom beyond the True Crime Museum and America Ground, following it till you get level with Albert Road (roughly 825 yards from the pier) across the coast road. At this point the signed cycle route forks right off the promenade. However the ECP crosses the coast road to the inland side and continues along its inland side to the Breeds Place roundabout. By turning hard left here you have another chance to access the modern centre of Hastings.

Founded by the Saxons, **Hastings** was one of the original Cinque Ports and was already an important harbour town at the time of the Norman invasion. During the Middle Ages it regularly contributed ships to the Navy, and although its importance as a naval town declined, it continued to be a bustling fishing port, and beside Rock-A-Nore Road there's still an area of shingle beach, known as The Stade, where the fishing boats were and continue to be kept. The importance of Hastings' thriving fishing industry is reflected in the Fishermen's Museum – once the church of the fishing community – just off Rock-A-Nore Road, near to the tall black-tarred wooden huts or "net shops" where fishermen would store their gear and hang out their nets to dry. The old town grew up in the valley between two sandstone ridges, East Hill and West Hill, and although the old harbour has long since been destroyed by the ravages of nature, there remain a host of historic buildings as evidence of the town's long and colourful history. There are ruins of a Norman castle still to be seen on West Hill; it was built by Robert Count of Eu shortly after the Norman invasion and the keep was built by Henry II in 1172, but most of the castle has now been washed away by the sea. From West Hill, narrow lanes lead steeply down to the old centre. The town boasted seven medieval churches, of which just two remain: the Perpendicular All Saints Church which dates back to the early 15th century and contains a particularly striking wall painting depicting Christ in judgment, and the church of St Clement which was rebuilt in about 1390 having been destroyed by the French during one of their many raids in the course of the Hundred Years War. There are many other buildings of historic interest in the streets of the old town, which is explored in a route variation V7 set out below. Though visitors started to arrive from about 1775 onwards, Hastings was only really developed as a resort in the 1820's, with squares and terraces of seaside houses, many Regency in style, being built to the west of the old town, Wellington Square (seen immediately to the right off Albert Road going inland) being a good example. James Burton and his son Decimus, together with Joseph Kay, were responsible for much of the design. Well known personalities associated with Hastings include John Logie Baird who did much of his research into the formation of television here, and Sophia Jex-Blake, the women's rights campaigner who was born in the town.

From the Breeds Place roundabout stay on the landward side of the coast road soon branching off to follow the Regency Pelham Crescent, passing the church of St Mary In The Castle, built in 1828 and now an arts centre. Follow the crescent round to return to the coast road via the steps, and continue eastwards along the coast road, but shortly turn left along George Street, entering the heart of the Old Town. At the end of George Street you could turn left up the High Street to join a route variation V7 below, which ends at the bottom of All Saints' Street at its junction with Rock-A-Nore Road. However at the end of George Street the main ECP turns right and immediately left along East Street, going forward over the coast road into Rock-A-Nore Road, V7 joining you via All Saints' Street to the left. As you proceed eastwards along Rock-A-Nore Road to continue, note to your right the modern Jerwood Gallery with its displays of 20th century art, including works by Lowry and Augustus John. Shortly, just before the Dolphin, you need to bear left up the Tamarisk Steps, but before doing so you should detour along Rock-A-Nore Road past the fishermen's huts and fish shops, to visit the Fishermen's Museum and just beyond, the Shipwreck & Coastal Heritage Centre, and Blue Reef Aquarium.

Leaving Rock-A-Nore Road to continue your coast walk, climb the Tamarisk Steps and, following signs for East Hill, arrive at the street known as Tackleway. Join this street but almost at once turn right as signed for a stiff climb up a flight of steps onto East Hill, the site of an Iron Age hillfort, and now a pleasant and extensive green incorporating a barbecue area. For reasons which will become clear shortly, you need to know by this stage if Ecclesbourne Glen is open – see below. Very soon after arriving on East Hill you reach an information board and a signpost with an arrow pointing right to Firehills; you will be following signs to Firehills for some miles! Observing this one, bear right to follow the right-hand side of the green, close to the cliff-edge fence, and go forward to a proper path. You are now in Hastings Country Park, an area of magnificent unspoilt countryside including deep wooded glens, heather-clad hills and fine sandstone cliffs consisting of some of the oldest rocks in the south east. Over 540 acres were formed into the country park in 1974 and much of it is designated as a Site of Special Scientific Interest. Of particular assistance to walkers are the park's numbered marker posts, and several of these will be referred to in the text below. And indeed you may meet a good number of walkers hereabouts, as the next four miles or so provide some of the best walking of the whole of the ECP in Sussex. In summary they consist of three spectacular descents to wooded glens followed by steep climbs, but the views throughout are quite majestic; veterans of the South West Coast Path may perhaps for the only time on their Sussex coast pilgrimage be reminded of the narrow precipitous cliff paths of Devon and Cornwall.

NOTE: Ecclesbourne Glen, the first of the glens, has suffered terribly from coastal erosion and resulting cliff slips, and may well be shut. If it is (and you'll need to check this in advance), you'll need route variation V8 below from the top of East Hill. If all is well, keeping the cliff-edge fence to your right you begin your first descent, into Ecclesbourne Glen, a wooded valley that 200 years ago was popular with smugglers and which provides ideal nesting territory for tits and warblers. Steps aid your descent, and after the crossing of the very narrow stream at the narrow valley bottom, you use steps to rise from the glen.

Having risen from Ecclesbourne Glen, continue along the obvious coast path, passing marker posts 8 and 12. You'll be overlapping with the Saxon Shore Way all the way to Cliff End. For a while the going is less strenuous, but then you find yourself descending to Fairlight Glen; make sure that as you descend you fork right as indicated (again observing the Firehills sign). This glen is arguably the loveliest of the trio, with beautiful woodland on your descent, carpeted in spring with bluebells and wood anemones, while at the valley bottom a stream runs between large boulders under the trees. Then up you rise again. Don't be alarmed that on your ascent the path veers left away from the sea; shortly you reach a signed junction, at marker post 17, bearing right and, after a brief level spell, you begin to descend. (A path here provides a detour to the cliff edge with glorious views, but it is a dead end so you'll need to go back.) Now descend past marker post 18 to the final glen, Warren Glen, less thickly wooded than the previous two but still populated with oak, hazel, beech and ash; as well as enjoying these you should listen for the yellowhammer or stonechat. You pass marker post 21 at the very bottom. Your coast path climbs yet again; there's a sharp right turn at marker post 22, and you have another stiff ascent to the hilltop area known as Firehills, enjoying yet more majestic views. There's a superbly sited bench, inscribed to "Sue" where you may wish to sit and rest and thank the benefactors for their thoughtfulness. Beyond the bench you pass marker post 24, arriving at an area of green, just to the right of a mast. Veering slightly left, continue to ascend to reach another expanse of green; make your way to the far right corner, passing between a Doris Noble memorial bench (to your right) and an artistic information board, the work of Julian Hanshaw. Now follow a path away from the green, your line being the Dungeness complex in the far distance, and descend, passing immediately to the right of memorial benches to Beverley Hall and William & Frances Gower, and going forward along a narrower dirt track through the vegetation to reach marker post 25. Go straight on along a wheelchair-friendly gravel track. You shortly pass twin litter bins and then a picnic table, and just by this picnic table you fork right along a reasonably clear path that contours the hillside then drops slowly down to reach marker post 27 at a junction of tracks.

Beyond post 27 you leave the open country behind, but, keeping the sea to your right, you go forward along a narrow path between fences and then a wide stony track, descending gently, and keeping the houses of Fairlight Cove to your left. You arrive at a junction with Shepherd's Way, and at this point you have to leave the cliffs, as a result of subsidence which is a major problem over the next mile, and embark on a rather uninspiring walk through Fairlight Cove. Observing the footpath sign, turn left along Shepherd's Way then shortly right into Bramble Way, crossing over a staggered crossroads junction. At the next junction, turn left down Smugglers Way, veering right with the road which continues as Lower Waites Lane. Follow it all the way along to a T-junction at its end; don't turn right up the road here, but go straight over and immediately right onto what is a signed footpath with fingers pointing right and left. You head briefly with the path towards the sea, but keeping to the path you soon veer sharp left and climb up onto a clifftop, this being your last cliff climb in Sussex, and, you'll be pleased to learn, a gentle one! There now follows a really lovely walk on a clearly defined path in the shade of woodland, with attractive houses to your left and great views ahead to Pett, Winchelsea Beach and, further ahead, towards Camber Sands and the towers of Dungeness. Keeping houses to your left you now descend on a narrow path to a road at the bottom, here arriving at the village of **Cliff End**. Turn right to follow the road, soon passing a toilet block and a telephone kiosk; shortly beyond the toilets the road bends sharp left, and as it does so, bear right onto a signed path. This looks distinctly private, but very soon you're reassured by another path sign pointing left. Follow this signed path, climb the steps to a concrete promenade, then bear left to follow the promenade, which gives way to an embankment path. Hereabouts you bid a temporary farewell to the Saxon Shore Way; this dives away inland to join up shortly with the Royal Military Canal Path which starts at Cliff End, and both routes overlap all the way to the border with Kent. You'll meet the "combined" route, described later in this book, fleetingly at Rye.

Continue along the embankment path which will take you all the way to the straggling seaside community of **Winchelsea Beach**, not to be confused with the old town of Winchelsea which sits well back from the coast. (If you wished to incorporate the old town into your coastal path plans, you could follow the Royal Military Canal Path/Saxon Shore Way from Cliff End to Rye and detour to Winchelsea as described in that section.) The embankment path is excellent and clear, and you can make up time expended on those tough climbs between Hastings and Firehills! At low tide it's possible to see the roots and stumps of the remnants of a forest inhabited by Stone Age people, but whatever the state of the tide you can enjoy views to the left firstly to the Royal Military Canal and then across Pett Level, a wide flat expanse of reclaimed land consisting of marshland stretching to the sea, widening out into the immense Romney Marsh east of Rye, and crisscrossed by drainage ditches and canals, As you continue along the embankment you'll see the disused windmill at Hog Hill which forms an impressive landmark, and there are shortly views inland to the old town of Winchelsea; both the windmill and Winchelsea are visited by the 1066 Country Walk and as stated above you can easily detour to Winchelsea from the Royal Military Canal Path/Saxon Shore Way.

Beyond Winchelsea Beach, there's a brief promenade, then another short section of embankment path. This soon ends and you have a choice between veering left to join a metalled coast road or sticking to the beach. I suggest you follow the coast road initially, then when a wall begins to the right of it, switch to the shingle bank; when the wall ends, return to the road. To your left is Rye Harbour Nature Reserve. The reserve, consisting of 1800 acres of tidal saltmarsh, creeks, river bank and wide expanse of shingle built up by the actions of the sea, has been designated a Site of Special Scientific Interest. It's on a major migration route and is an important wintering place for seabirds, with many species of wildfowl and waders gathering there to feed in winter. The reserve has not only been important for its nature but also strategically: among defensive constructions to be found here are World War 2 pillboxes and, on the west side of the reserve, Camber Castle, more fully described in the Royal Military Canal Path/Saxon Shore Way section. As you proceed, you reach the very isolated Mary Stanford Lifeboat House. This once housed a lifeboat, the Mary Stanford, which with its crew of 17 was called out to rescue the Latvian ship Alice in 80mph winds on 15 November 1928. The lifeboat capsized, and all 17 lifeboatmen lost their lives; the Lifeboat House, now abandoned, remains as a monument to them. I suggest that at the Lifeboat House you return to the beach. By now the breakwaters have relented and you can follow either a reasonably firm course at the bottom of the shingle bank or, when the tide is out, the firm sands, but take care not to be cut off from the shingle bank. You're now hastening towards your final river obstruction and inland detour, the mouth of the East Sussex river Rother; if you've opted for the sands you'll be forced back up onto the shingle bank which veers round the landward side of some sea defence works, and from there you go forward towards the bank of the Rother estuary. Having arrived at the bank, you can turn left to join a metalled track which will take you to Rye Harbour, the coast road coming up to meet you. It's very pleasant walking along the metalled track beside the Rother, with good views across to Camber Sands, and in due course you're able to join an embankment path to the right of the track. As you approach the houses of Rye Harbour, look out on the left for an impressively sited Martello tower; the track and path become separated here, but you should stick to the path which veers round to the right, heading for the Rother. Then, as you get level with a phone box, you descend a short steep slope off the embankment path to join Harbour Road. However if you wished you could, on arriving at the road, bear right and walk the short distance to the William the Conqueror pub and a nicely placed seat with views to the Rother. The village of **Rye Harbour** grew as a result of its important strategic position close to the mouth of the Rother, the retreat of the sea meaning that the old hilltop town of Rye had ceased to function effectively as a port. The harbour benefited substantially as a result of dredging in the mid-19th century, shipyards sprang up, and in March 1854, a railway branch line was built from Rye to Rye Harbour. Following a bad storm in December 1882 the harbour entrance was practically blocked, and by World War 1 Rye Harbour had all but ceased to function as a port. However some industries sprang up in the immediate vicinity, and the railway line came to serve, via sidings, an oil refinery, concrete works and chemical works. Despite the closure of the railway line in the early 1960's, several industrial works have continued to function hereabouts.

Follow Harbour Road north-westwards through Rye Harbour village, passing the Church of the Holy Spirit. Built in Gothic style in 1848-49, it contains fine woodwork in its ceiling, whilst on the wall is a list of those lives saved by the local lifeboat, and in the churchyard there's a memorial to those who lost their lives in the Mary Stanford disaster described above. My father recalls attending an Easter Sunday service here in the early 1950's prior to a day's golf at Rye, and remembers the church standing "in the middle of a shingle quarry against a background of cranes (and) concrete mixing machinery...music was provided by a lady playing a piano and she like doubtless many of her kind was also the sideswoman and general factotum. The salty tang, the cries of the gulls outside and the general surroundings made it seem almost compulsory to sing *Eternal Father, Strong To Save* but of course it was the Easter Hymn that we had and I like to think we did justice to it."

Beyond the church, simply stay beside the same road all the way to its junction with the A259 on the edge of Rye itself. The surroundings are certainly uninspiring at first, with industrial units on each side, but as you progress you can enjoy increasingly fine views to Rye and also the river Brede, a tributary of the Rother, with its many boats. The road swings to the left to follow beside the Brede – you lose the pavement here, so take care – then swings sharp right to cross the Brede and arrive at the A259. Turn right to follow beside the A259 into **Rye**. Rye is a real hub for Sussex name paths, visited not only by the ECP but the Royal Military Canal Path/Saxon Shore Way, Sussex Border Path, High Weald Landscape Trail and 1066 Country Walk! My suggestion is that whatever path you're on or have been on, you find your way to the junction of Cinque Ports Street with Market Road and Station Approach (G). As far as the ECP is concerned this means following beside the A259, veering right to cross the river Tillingham. By detouring 100 yards or so (each way), if you wish, up the signed High Weald Landscape Trail immediately beyond the bridge crossing, you can view the reconstructed 1824 smock mill.) The A259 bends sharp right again beyond the bridge, but you carry straight on up the A268 Wish Street, going forward in the same direction along Cinque Ports Street to the junction (G) above. Now you have a choice. If you're needing public transport, the bus stands and station are just down Station Road to the left. If you're wanting to head straight through Rye without further ado, turn right up Market Road and left up the High Street. For a suggested tour of the highlights of Rye (although there's no magic in it and you may wish to vary it!) please refer to a detour D6 below.

It's hard to believe that during the Middle Ages this town, once a hillfort, was almost ringed by water; it stood on a promontory and was linked to the mainland by an easily defensible neck of land, guarded by the estuaries of the Rother and Tillingham. It served as an important port, exporting a number of products to the Continent, including wool and iron, and also old shoes which the affluent folk were prepared to donate to the poverty-stricken French. In the mid-14th century it became one of the Cinque Ports, but its defensive importance came at a cost, attracting the attention of French raiders who burned the town in 1377 and again in 1448. Its fortunes as a port suffered severe decline from the 16th century as a result of silting which left the town 2 miles inland and, to add to the town's woes, smuggling was rife in the town during the 18th and early 19th centuries. One group of smugglers was known as the Hawkhurst Gang and became notorious among local inhabitants for sitting drinking at the Mermaid inn with pistols cocked on the table in front of them. There was another equally alarming gang known as the Bonfire Boys, who operated in Rye during the 19th century; they would create effigies of public figures they disliked, and then burn them. Despite all this, Rye with its lovely architecture and wealth of history became a magnet for writers, most famously Henry James and E.F. Benson, but other writers associated with the town include Rumer Godden, Marguerite Radclyffe Hall, Conrad

Aiken, Patric Dickinson, Bernard Darwin, and John Ryan who created Captain Pugwash. Though Rye is still a busy workaday little town, tourism has become more and more important to its wellbeing, with thousands of visitors drawn each year to its charms. The streets of the town, many of them cobbled and narrow, are crammed with historic houses, many timber-framed, tile-hung or weatherboarded, and beautifully preserved. The highlights of Rye and brief histories are described more fully in D6 below, but not to be missed are the church of St Mary, the Ypres Tower, the Landgate, cobbled Mermaid Street with its Mermaid inn, and Lamb House where both Henry James and E.F. Benson (whose *Mapp & Lucia* books were set in and around Rye) lived for a time.

To leave Rye, whether or not you've done the detour, walk from (G) up Market Road and turn left along High Street then first right up Lion Street towards the church. Just before the town hall turn left along Market Street and then right along Church Square to the far corner of the square. Now go straight on down, passing just to the right of Rye Castle towards Gun Garden (which you may already have explored in the course of detour D6!). Immediately before the entrance to Gun Garden turn left down the steps to reach the A259. Cross (carefully) straight over this road along Rock Channel. Veer sharp left with this road then turn immediately left to join a metalled path along the right-hand edge of a green. You're here overlapping with the Royal Military Canal Path and Saxon Shore Way. Follow the metalled path to New Road (A259) and turn right along it, aiming for the bridge over the Rother. Cross the bridge using the right-hand pavement, then immediately beyond the crossing bear right to join the embankment path beside the Rother heading seawards. Before pressing ahead, pause to enjoy what is a really lovely view of Rye, dominated by the hilltop church.

The embankment path provides really excellent walking and a very much more enjoyable experience than your journey upstream from Rye Harbour to Rye, with fine views across the river towards Rye Harbour. You pass a lake which is to your left, then beyond the lake your path swings away from the Rother, reaching a junction with a track onto which you turn right. You're now on the course of a former railway, known as the Rye & Camber Tramway, and you may notice a couple of metal strips which have been incorporated into the track, and which provide the only tangible remains of this line. Constructed and run on a shoestring, it opened in 1895, linking Rye with the golf links; it's said that golfing passengers had the habit of pulling out the pin between the first two carriages, leaving the passengers in the second carriage high and dry! An extension to Camber Sands, popular with holidaymakers, opened in 1908. On the outbreak of World War 2, however, sections of the track were concreted over for logistical reasons and, it being decided that the costs of relaying the track after the war were prohibitive, the line was never to reopen. Keep on the track, which skirts Rye golf course, one of the finest links courses in southern England. Go forward on what is signed as a permissive route along the old Rye & Camber Tramway, almost immediately passing to the left side of a large (black upper half, white lower half) house adjoining and just to the left of the Harbour Master building. Just beyond the large house, the fence to your left bends a little further left; here turn right to walk up a green path which takes you up to a clear if stony Rother-side path. Now turn left to follow it. It's a straightforward and enjoyable walk down to the mouth of the Rother, and satisfying to look back across the river to where you left the seashore some miles back. On reaching the mouth of the Rother, strike out onto Camber Sands and veer left to follow them. Camber Sands form one of the best and most popular stretches of beach on your entire walk and indeed on the south coast. The superb expanse of ridged golden sand, stretching out to sea for half a mile or more at low tide, is complemented along the back of the beach by extensive sand dunes among which marram grass has been planted to preserve the special qualities of the sands from the effects of the wind.

Continue to enjoy your walk along the sand, choosing your path carefully. The dry sand further back from the mean high tide point makes for marginally faster walking than the wetter sand which can be rather soft and if you choose to walk on it you'll find your boots sinking rather further than you'd wish! On half-decent summer days especially at weekends you may find yourself in the company of swimmers and sunbathers, as this is an extremely popular section of sand. The unpredictable currents, however, make the seas here potentially lethal for the unwary, with five people being killed on 26 August 2016 after getting into difficulties in the water off the sands. In due course you reach **Camber** village and pass a line of buildings, many of them cafes, on the front. Just before the point where the buildings end, you'll find that when the tide is high you'll have no sand to walk on and shingle takes over. However, beyond the buildings you reach and join a concrete promenade from which there are excellent views forward to Romney Marsh (more fully described in the Royal Military Canal Path/Saxon Shore Way section), the Lydd firing ranges, and Dungeness. Immediately below you to your left is Lydd Road, while the sands to your right (liable to be submerged by the tide) are known as the Broomhill Sands.

Keeping to the prom, you plough onwards, and just over a mile from Camber village you pass the untidy assembly of buildings known as **Jury's Gap** where Lydd Road turns abruptly inland, and you go forward to round a barrier and arrive at a formidable looking gate and fence (H). You're still half a mile shy of the border with Kent, but if red flags are flying here, signifying firing activity on Lydd Ranges, you cannot go further. Bearing in mind that the final half mile offers no essential change to the surroundings – just more tramping along or behind the beach with Lydd Ranges, Romney Marsh and Dungeness in view – you may feel, and I have to say I recommend, point (H) to be a good place to call it a day. If you are a purist, though, and want to say you've walked the whole of the Sussex coastline, you'll have no doubt planned ahead, as I counselled at the start of this section, and will be able to proceed. Alternatively you may just be lucky, finding no firing in place and wanting to satisfy your curiosity! If you are proceeding, I suggest you initially stick to the track beyond the gate; from the track you get a good view of Lydd Ranges and the countryside beyond it, as well as the sea. Before long, however, the shingle bank may become too tall for you to see the sea properly, so you may wish to make your way down to the shore, albeit the going will be rather tougher on the shingle. As indicated above, you will reach the border with Kent roughly half a mile beyond the gate but there will be no sign that you have completed your walk along the coast of Sussex so without the aid of GPS – and incidentally for GPS users the approximate OS grid reference for the border is TR007177 – it will be impossible to ascertain the point at which you've reached it. You could make certain by simply carrying on all the way to Dungeness (6 miles from Jury's Gap, and firmly in Kent), the towers of which will have been in your sight for much of your walk from Firehills! From Dungeness it's a walk of just over a mile along the beach to Lydd-on-Sea for regular buses to St Mary's Bay where you can pick up a bus heading back to Rye and Hastings. The alternative, if you want to say you've walked to the Kent border but can't do so along the coast, is to walk down from the gate/fence at (H) to Lydd Road and follow it north-eastwards for 2 miles to the clearly marked border. It's not the most inspiring of walks!

Unless you've forged on to Lydd-on-Sea you'll need to have a plan for getting back to civilisation. Both the Kent/Sussex border on Lydd Road, and Jury's Gap, are on the Lydd-Rye-Hastings bus route but neither are advertised stops on the official timetable at the time of writing. You can hope that the driver will stop for you anyway but if you're not willing to put that to the test, you will need to have a lift sorted or else will have a really tedious trudge back to Camber (which is 1.5 miles from Jury's Gap), a sad anticlimax after reaching journey's end. At least there is a shop and pub in the village, but you may wish to wait till you get back to Rye, with its rail connections, to properly celebrate your achievement in one of its many cafes, teashops, pubs and restaurants. And celebrate you should: walking the whole Sussex coast is no mean feat and you'll have experienced an unforgettable variety of scenery, history and terrain on your way. Congratulations!

GOOD TO KNOW
Start: Emsworth Station. Finish: Jury's Gap.
Total mileage: 132.
Difficulty: Strenuous.
Stages: Emsworth Marina (R) 1, Prinsted for Southbourne (*RB) 9, Path for Nutbourne (*RAB) 10, A259 for Nutbourne (*RAB) 15, Bosham (*RAB) 15.5, Fishbourne (*RAB) for Chichester (*RAB) 18.5, Dell Quay (R) 20, Itchenor (RA) 25, Snow Hill for West Wittering (RAB) 28, East Wittering (RAB) 31, Selsey (RAB) 37, Crab & Lobster (R) for Sidlesham (RAB) 42, Salt House for Pagham (RAB) 44, Bognor Regis (*RAB) 50, Felpham (RAB) 51, Littlehampton (*RAB) 56, End of Sea Lane for Angmering (*RB) 58.5, End of Sea Lane for Ferring (RAB) 60, End of Sea Lane for Goring-by-Sea (*RAB) 61, Durrington-on-Sea (*RAB) 62, West Worthing (*RAB) 63, Worthing (*RAB) 64, East Worthing (*RAB) 65, Lancing (*RAB) 66.5, Shoreham-by-Sea (*RAB) 70.5, Southwick (*RAB) 72, Hove (*RAB) 76, Brighton (*RAB) 77,

Rottingdean (RAB) 81, Saltdean (RAB) 82, Newhaven (*RAB) 86, Newhaven Harbour Station (*) 86.5, Bishopstone (*RAB) 88.5, Seaford (*RAB) 89.5, Exceat (RB) 92.5, Birling Gap for East Dean (RAB) 96, Beachy Head (R) 99, Eastbourne (*RAB) 102, Pevensey Bay (*RAB) 105.5, Cooden Beach (*RAB) 108.5, Collington (*RAB) 109.5, Bexhill (*RAB) 110.5, West St Leonards (*RAB) 113.5, St Leonards (*RAB) 114.5, Hastings (*RAB) 115.5, Cliff End (RAB) 121.5, Winchelsea Beach (RAB) 123, Rye Harbour (RAB) 125.5, Rye (*RAB) 127.5, Camber (RAB) 130.5, Jury's Gap (B) 132. OS: OL8, OL10, OL11, OL25, 124, 125.

D1 From the pier cross the coast road and head back westwards along the inland side of it, then as it bends slightly right by Clarendon Mansions, turn right along bustling East Street; off to the left is Bartholomews with its majestic Town Hall. Just before the end of East Street, turn left up Market Street (signed The Lanes) to Brighton Place. Turn right here, then immediately left (just right of No.6) into Meeting House Lane, now in the heart of The Lanes, a labyrinth of mainly 19th century streets of medieval origin. Follow Meeting House Lane past the jewellery shops, bearing right at the T-junction by the Meeting House, shortly left at the Lanes Armoury, right again at the Bath Arms, then immediately left along Union Street, turning right into Ship Street then shortly left up Duke Street. At the top of Duke Street turn right, then at the splendid clock tower, built to commemorate Queen Victoria's Golden Jubilee, turn right again down North Street, and left into New Road. You then bear immediately right into gardens, following signs to the unmissable Pavilion described above. Then head for the signed Museum and Art Gallery, with its Art Deco and Art Nouveau furniture, at the top end of the gardens. Turn left here up Church Street to the junction of New Road and Jubilee Street, here bearing left into New Road to view the Dome entertainment centre (to the left) and the red-brick pillared Theatre Royal and impressive Unitarian Church (to the right). Return down New Road and go straight on along Jubilee Street, passing the modern Library; at the end turn left into North Road and second right into Kensington Gardens, now in the cosmopolitan North Laine area. At the end turn right and almost immediately left into Sydney Street, then at the end go right into Trafalgar Street and left into Pelham Street. (To detour to the church of St Peter, built in the 1820's and regarded as one of the finest examples of pre-Victorian Gothic Revival architecture, simply continue on down Trafalgar Street to the end and cross, returning up Trafalgar Street and bearing right into Pelham Street.) Follow Pelham Street, going straight on via St Peter's Street into Ann Street to reach the amazing 19th century brick church of St Bartholomew, again described above. Turn left up Ann Street, continuing up the steps (Fenchurch Walk) then at the very top turn left into Fleet Street. As it veers left, go straight on along Station Street, descending to a T-junction with Trafalgar Street; turn right here, passing the Toy & Model Museum and going under a bridge, emerging to reach a T-junction with Terminus Road immediately adjacent to Brighton Station. Turn right up Terminus Road, passing the left side of the station buildings, continuing to the Seven Dials Roundabout. Take the second (Vernon Terrace) exit, turning immediately left to follow the superb Montpelier Crescent; from there go straight on along Denmark Terrace, bearing second left up Victoria Road past the magnificent church of St Michael, built 1858-61, with particularly fine stained glass and carved misericords. Continue along Victoria Road to its end, going straight over into an alleyway, Vine Place, which emerges onto Dyke Road. Cross over, turning right and almost immediately left to cut down through a small park, aiming for St Nicholas Church, on the far side of Church Street. Turn left into Church Street, shortly reaching the church which is on the right; a flint building with a 14th century tower, it's actually Brighton's parish church. Continue down Church Street to Queen's Road, here turning right and soon passing the Jubilee Tower, then walking down West Street past the exceptional early Victorian church of St Paul, to the coast road. Turn left and follow beside it back to the pier. (Total detour 2.5 miles)

D2 Having left the prom, join Marine Parade and turning left along it, follow it under the railway – Bishopstone Station is immediately to the right before the bridge – all the way to the A259. Cross and walk diagonally right to a signed footpath heading north-eastwards. You descend steps to a stile beyond which you continue north-eastwards along a clear green path, the ground rising immediately to the right. You arrive at a wall that you cross by a ladder stile, then you veer northwards along a clear field path, arriving at a road. Turn right along it to enter the lovely old village of Bishopstone. As the road bends right, turn left along a signed path, shortly bearing left to reach the church of St Andrew, Bishopstone. Return exactly the same way to the prom. (Total detour 2 miles)

D3 If you simply want to reach Eastbourne's town centre and station, walk down Lascelles Terrace to a junction with Compton Street. Cross Compton Street and bear half-right down Chiswick Place. Go forward along Cornfield Terrace to the Memorial Roundabout, going straight on down Cornfield Road to a T-junction with Terminus Road, the town's main shopping area. The station is along Terminus Road to the left. For a longer walk round Eastbourne, don't follow Lascelles Terrace from the inland side of the coast road but take the road just to the left of it, Carlisle Road, with its very Italian feel. At the far end on your right you'll find the Eastbourne Heritage Centre. Turn left at the end along Compton Street past the Winter Garden, almost immediately arriving at Wilmington Square. Bear right along Carlisle Road or the adjacent Wilmington Gardens; to your right is the Congress Theatre and immediately to its left is the Towner Gallery. (NOTE: THIS WHOLE AREA IS BEING REDEVELOPED AT THE TIME OF WRITING, AND ROAD CLOSURES AND DIVERSIONS ARE POSSIBLE.) Having made your way to the Towner Gallery, bear round to the left of it to follow College Road northwards, the Devonshire Park tennis centre to your right. At the top end of College Road kink briefly right into Furness Road and almost immediately reach South Street. To your right is the massive red-brick church of St Saviour, dating back to 1867, but you turn left along South Street through an area known as Little Chelsea with an interesting individual mix of shops and eateries. At the far end you reach Grove Road, crossing over to reach the huge Town Hall, built of brick and Portland stone in the mid-1880's.

Bear left onto Grove Road and immediately right up Saffrons Road, then at its end, cross over Dittons Road and go straight on into Gildredge Park. Follow the path in the same direction, then just beyond a line of trees to the left, strike out across the green to the left-hand corner of the enclosed park ahead. Walk beside the park railings in the same direction, pass through the gate and walk a few steps, then turn left onto a metalled path. Shortly fork right onto a path that goes parallel with a tennis court and veers a little left, keeping a charming flower garden to your right, rising to reach a yellow-painted thatched house known as the Hermitage. Turn right here onto a path *that leads to a T-junction with another path; go straight over and cross the green, keeping the red-brick 18th century Manor House just to your left. At the end of the green descend the steps to arrive at the A259 and the heart of the Old Town. Cross over and bear left, passing the sensational timber-framed Lamb Inn, parts of which date back to the 12th century, cross Ocklynge Road and enter the churchyard. Follow the path aiming for and skirting the north side of the church, to pass the superb 16th century flint Old Parsonage, then carry on along the path to reach Church Lane. Turn left at the end to follow it back to the A259 and left again to the main entrance to the flint and stone church of St Mary the Virgin with several Norman features. Having visited the church, cross over the road and continue eastwards along the right side of the A259 to the end of Borough Lane. It's worth detouring very briefly up the lane to view, on the right, the lovely timber-framed 16th century Pilgrim House where Charles Dickens occasionally stayed, and a fine brick 18th century house immediately adjacent. Now return to the A259 and this time carry on alongside this road (The Goffs) then within sight of the T-junction at the end, bear right onto Southfields Road, following it to its end at a roundabout. Follow the roundabout round anticlockwise, crossing Old Orchard Road and Grove Road. Continue past the station on along Terminus Road, then turn right along Cornfield Road. Go straight over the Memorial Roundabout along Cornfield Terrace, going forward along Chiswick Place to reach Compton Street, noting the fine Devonshire Park Theatre on the right at this junction. Cross Compton Street and walk up Lascelles Terrace to return to the seafront. (Total detour 3.5 miles; to station only, 1 mile)*

D4 Turn left into Gardner Way, then left to pass in front of the splendid Assembly Rooms to reach the top of Burton Way. Turn right here; don't carry on up Quarry Hill but bear half-right into St Leonards Gardens, entering by way of South Lodge with its impressive Doric arch. Now walk straight up through the gardens, pausing to enjoy lovely views back to the sea, with very attractive early 19th century houses and villas around the gardens. Walk uphill, aiming for the north (top) exit at North Lodge, where the author Sir Henry Rider Haggard lived between 1918 and 1923. Exit the gardens by the lodge and continue along Upper Maze Hill to Baston Lodge on the right. A plaque shows that this was the childhood home of Alan Turing, a computer scientist, and whose work was key to breaking the wartime Enigma Code. Now retrace your steps via the gardens to the prom, accessing it via Burton Way. (Total detour 1 mile)

D5 Go over the road here by the White Rock Theatre, following Schwerte Way immediately to the left of the theatre, up to a T-junction. Turn left here up St Margaret's Road and right up Falaise Road, walking all the way to its end at the A21, Bohemia Road. Cross more or less straight over to reach the Hastings Museum and Art Gallery. This includes the Durbar Hall, featuring collections of artefacts from the far East; there are also exhibits relating to John Logie Baird (the inventor of television), the architect James Burton, and author Robert Tressell. To proceed from here, you could simply retrace to the pier via Falaise Road, St Margaret's Road and Schwerte Way. Alternatively you could, having returned to the A21 from the museum, turn left, south-eastwards, alongside the A21, which becomes Cambridge Road. Cross to follow the right-hand side of the road past turnings into Dorset Place and Prospect Place, then bear right down Brassey Steps to reach the America Ground area described in the main body of text. Proceed via Claremont and Robertson Street to reach the coast road; the True Crime Museum is a few yards along the coast road to the right. Go forward from the coast road to the prom to rejoin the ECP. (Total detour or variation is an extra half a mile)

D6 From (G) in the main text walk up Market Road, turning right down the High Street which swings to the left and becomes The Mint. At the junction of The Mint and Mermaid Street turn right and walk straight down past the end of Wish Ward to the main road (A259). As you arrive at this road you'll see to your right the Rye Heritage Centre which includes an amazing depiction, including lighting and commentary, of how Rye was in 1872. Cross over the main road, Strand Quay, and bear right, then shortly left round a barrier to access the quay, turning left to follow the waterfront downstream. At the exit by the left bend of the road, leave the quay and cross the road, going over into and turning left along The Strand, with its restored black-painted wooden warehouses. Follow it to arrive back at the bottom of cobbled Mermaid Street. Now turn right to follow Mermaid Street uphill, passing the timber-framed early 16th century Mermaid inn, and at the top, turn right into West Street, shortly reaching the

18*th* century red-brick Lamb House which is to your right. Follow West Street round to the left, reaching Church Square, then turn immediately right to reach the top end of Watchbell Street. Here turn right again to walk down this beautiful street and enjoy an excellent view from its bottom end by the Hope Anchor inn. Follow Watchbell Street back to Church Square and go straight on to the far (eastern) end, bearing right to reach Rye Castle, also known as Ypres Tower. Built in 1249, it's one of Rye's oldest buildings, being built as the castle of Rye but subsequently becoming a prison. There's a museum within the tower, and beyond it in Gun Garden there's a platform with a display of cannons and cannonballs, and excellent views towards the sea. You could here continue straight on along the ECP continuous route out of Rye, as described in the main body of text, but to complete the tour, walk on round the north-eastern side of the square to a T-junction with Market Street, turning right and walking past the 15*th* century timber-framed Flushing Inn. Veer left down East Street, passing another museum which is to the left; this includes a wide range of attractions, from a 1745 fire engine to a Captain Pugwash treasure hunt. At the end, turn right into the High Street and follow it past Rye Art Gallery, the street becoming Hilders Cliff (or East Cliff, depending on which map you're using!) as you veer left with it, downhill, to reach the 14*th* century Landgate, the last remaining one of Rye's original medieval gates. Walk back up Hilders/East Cliff and along the High Street until you come to Lion Street which is to the left. To your right here is the Old Grammar School dating back to 1636 and boasting distinctive Dutch gables. Turn left by the George Inn up Lion Street, now heading for the church; on the right, just before you reach the church, is Simon the Pieman tearoom and the 15*th* century timber-framed Fletcher's House, the birthplace of the dramatist John Fletcher in 1579, while to the left, pretty much opposite the tearoom, is the fine arcaded 18*th* century Town Hall, from the balcony of which it has been the custom for the newly elected Mayor to throw hot pennies to the children below. The Norman church of St Mary, immediately beyond, is particularly famous for its 16*th* century clock, the oldest working church turret clock in the country. Perhaps the most curious features of the church are the gilded cherubs who strike the bells of the tower clock, although these are modern replicas, the far older originals being kept in the church. Turn right (as you look towards the church entrance) immediately before the church along a pedestrian passage past the lovely pink-painted Old Vicarage and cottages with lovely gardens, arriving back at West Street; follow it back to Lamb House, veering right and walking down to the High Street. Turn right to follow it to the junction with Lion Street, crossing over and now doubling back along the south side of the High Street. Shortly turn right into Market Road to arrive back at point (G) in the main text. To reach the bus stands and the station, cross straight over and walk down Station Approach. (Total detour 1.25 miles)

V1 Having passed the Climping Beach car park, you continue briefly along the back of the beach, keeping a sturdy stone wall to your left, with an area of green behind it. The wall then veers left and you veer left with it, towards a metalled road running behind the beach. At this point there's a public footpath sign including a byway pointing inland. Follow this byway away from the sea, heading just west of north. In just under half a mile you reach a T-junction with Brookpits Lane by Climping Primary School. Turn right along Brookpits Lane then at the end turn left up Crookthorn Lane to a roundabout junction with the A259. Go straight over up Church Lane, and in 500 yards or so you arrive at the church of St Mary, Climping. Having visited the church retrace your steps to the roundabout and turn left alongside the A259 using the footpath/cycleway. Shortly cross using the safe crossing provided, continue briefly beside the A259 then turn right along Ferry Road, following it to its end and being reunited with the coast route just prior to the footbridge crossing of the Arun. (Extra 1 mile)

V2 Leave the promenade at the pier and cross Marine Parade, going straight on up South Street, which becomes Chapel Road, past the church of St Paul, museum and Town Hall. On the right opposite St Paul's Church is Union Place and the Art Deco Connaught Theatre; on the left just before the church is lovely Ambrose Place with its Regency architecture and a plaque to Harold Pinter on the wall of No.14.. Go forward along Chapel Road and over one roundabout then a double roundabout; by turning left at the first of the roundabouts making the double one, along Teville Road, and then turning first right along Oxford Road, you reach Worthing Station. Otherwise continue northwards past the supermarket up the A24 Broadwater Road, across the B2233 Sompting Avenue and on to the church at Broadwater. Just beyond the church turn right along Broadwater Street East, first left along Forest Road, first right along Southfield Road, left at the end up Sompting Road, right at the first crossroads and almost immediately left up Northbrook Road. Then bear right shortly into Clarendon Road and second left off Clarendon Road along Southways Avenue. When the road splits, turn right into Bramber Road which soon peters out; at its far left-hand end join a signed footpath which heads half-left, north-eastwards, across a field. You arrive at Upper Brighton Road (B2222) and turn right along it, passing the Gardeners Arms (2 miles from the start of the variation – there are no further amenities before Shoreham, 5 miles away), then shortly beyond the pub turn left up a signed footpath taking you to the A27. Turn right (eastwards) to reach the crossing point; cross carefully then continue eastwards and shortly turn left up Church Lane, soon reaching Sompting Church which is to your left. Beyond the church, continue along the road past the impressive flint-built Sompting Abbotts. The road, which becomes Titch Hill, soon bends sharply right and then shortly left and there's no pavement, so take care. It rises then drops to the pretty Steepdown Cottage and Titch Hill Farm, opposite which you turn hard right onto a bridleway which heads south-eastwards to arrive at a T-junction with another bridleway. Turn left here and now head uphill for about a mile. Eventually you reach a T-junction of bridleways, turning right and very shortly reaching a crossroads junction with a byway, turning right; having done so, turn almost immediately right again to join a bridleway which climbs steeply to the summit of Steep Down, marked by a trig point. Beyond the trig point continue along the bridleway south-eastwards, dropping down to a T-junction of paths. Turn left here and almost immediately turn right at the next T-junction to follow a clear byway south-eastwards uphill, enjoying magnificent views to the Adur valley. Rise to an area of woodland, part of the Lancing Ring Nature Reserve, notable for its chalk grassland, then keep along the path through the trees. You pass a car park and a fork junction where the byway forks right and a bridleway forks left. Take the left fork, then ignoring a right-hand and left-hand footpath turn, you continue eastwards along the bridleway and descend to Hoe Court Farm. Ignoring a footpath which here goes off to the right, you carry on eastwards, and drop down, keeping Lancing College Chapel to the left. At length you reach the chapel approach road. Turn hard left to follow the road, soon passing a signed footpath going off to the *right (I), going straight on uphill, then veering left to arrive at the chapel entrance. Now retrace your steps to (I), and turn left along the path which proceeds pleasantly through the meadow, south-eastwards. The path is not always well defined but the direction is obvious. You pass over a stile to arrive at the chapel approach road. Turn left then immediately right along a road that takes you past the former Sussex Pad inn to the A27, here bearing left alongside this road then shortly crossing it at the pedestrian crossing. This was the site of the Shoreham Airshow disaster of August 2015 which claimed 11 lives. Having crossed, go straight on along Old Shoreham Road, soon veering left and continuing eastwards, then at the end go straight on over the Old Shoreham Bridge crossing of the river Adur to reach the A283. Immediately across the road is the lovely church of St Nicholas, Old Shoreham. Whether or not you detour to visit it, you now join the Downs Link between the A283 and the river and head coastwards, simply now following the riverside path. Shortly after passing under the railway your walkway veers sharp left; here leave the riverside, walking up Little High Street and forward along the A259 Shoreham High Street past Marlipins to the footbridge, to be reunited with the coast route. (Extra half a mile)*

V3 Having walked up Medina Terrace you reach Kingsway; to the right here is the fine Courtenay House, sometime home of the actress Elizabeth Allan. Go straight across Kingsway along Medina Villas, the heart of the Cliftonville area, and at the top you reach Church Road (J). You could detour left at (J) and follow Church Road westwards; for Hove Station in half a mile, turn almost immediately right up George Street, crossing almost straight over Blatchington Road and going on up Goldstone Villas; and if you carry on westwards past the chiefly 19th century St Andrew's Old Church along Church Road (becoming New Church Road beyond Hove Street) you reach, in roughly a third of a mile, Hove's excellent museum and art gallery on the right. It contains many works by such famous artists as Constable, Hogarth and Gainsborough and superb contemporary crafts and decorative arts collections. Note also the fine Jaipur Gateway in the grounds, built for the Colonial Exhibition of 1886. However the continuous route turns right at (J), eastwards, along Church Road, crossing Grand Avenue, the road now becoming Western Road. You stay on the right (south) side of Western Road past the magnificent 19th century

Palmeira Square, continuing past the top end of Brunswick Square. Shortly beyond Brunswick Square turn right into Brunswick Street East and follow it seawards. Just before the former Conqueror (now Bottom's Rest) pub turn left; don't turn right into Lower Market Street but carry straight on, veering left then right to reach Waterloo Street. On your way you pass firstly the delectable little Old Market Theatre and then the recently restored Waterloo Arch. Turn right to follow Waterloo Street, passing the stunning Victorian church of St Andrew which is to the left. Continue on to the coast road, crossing to rejoin the ECP. (Extra 1 mile; extra 600 yards without museum detour)

V4 Immediately beyond the pier, leave the prom by crossing the lower coast road, walking in front of the Sea Life Centre and walking a little to the right to cross the main coast road, Marine Parade. Now turn left and walk back down Marine Parade, bearing right at its end up Old Steine, shortly turning right up St James's Street. Now follow this road past numerous independent shops/eateries, noting the magnificent red-brick church of St Mary at No.61, and the AIDS memorial in the gardens off New Steine to the right. The road becomes Bristol Road and passes the very fine RC church of St John the Baptist with superb exterior and memorials. Beyond this church the road kinks left and right to become St George's Road; just beyond the kink look up College Road to the left at the splendid red-brick Brighton College. At another fine church, St George's, just under a mile from Old Steine and with the imposing Royal Sussex Hospital visible to your left, turn right down Paston Place, then left alongside the A259 coast road and forward along the parallel Percival Terrace, Clarendon Terrace and Chichester Terrace, noting here a blue plaque for the composer Richard Addinsell. From Chichester Terrace veer left up Lewes Crescent. You're now in the heart of Kemp Town; developed in the early 19th century by Thomas Kemp, this area boasts some of Brighton's grandest architecture. Cross Eastern Road and go all the way round Sussex Square, passing the home of Thomas Kemp himself, then having crossed back over Eastern Road veer left along the eastern arm of Lewes Crescent, keeping lovely (private) gardens to your right. You pass the old Roedean school buildings as well as a plaque dedicated to the dancer Anna Neagle. From Lewes Crescent veer left along Arundel Terrace to reach the A259 coast road; cross using the pedestrian crossing then bear left along the cycle lane parallel with the

A259 high above Brighton Marina, now reunited with the ECP main route. (Extra half a mile)

V5 Cross over the A259 as stated at the crossing immediately level with the Marine Gate complex, bear right and walk briefly on beside the A259; immediately beyond the Marine Gate complex, turn left up a signed footpath, ascending steps then going forward along Cliff Approach to Roedean Road. Cross more or less straight over and turn right, following a slip road parallel with Roedean Road on its far side, leading to the clubhouse for East Brighton Golf Club. Just before the clubhouse veer left through the car park, at the far end of which go forward along a signed bridleway which climbs gently and soon reaches a signed bridleway fork, where you turn right. Your path veers gently right on a clear course, avoiding tracks heading away hard right or hard left. You begin to descend, passing the Ridings turning which is to your left, and go forward along a metalled road, entering Ovingdean and very shortly passing its 11th century church of St Wulfran, noting the lovely flint cottages in the vicinity of the church. You kink left then right, shortly bearing left into Ainsworth Avenue and following it uphill to a T-junction, turning right to join Longhill Road which almost at once veers sharply right. Leave the road here by going straight on, immediately reaching a bridleway fork, here taking the path that strikes out across the ridge top, a delightful walk with great views to the sea and Rottingdean. Ignore forks off the path but follow the central most obvious one, which proceeds through the Beacon Hill Nature Reserve then begins to descend. You soon pass Rottingdean Windmill. Follow the path on to join a road, Sheep Walk, then turn left at the first crossroads, junction with Nevill Road, going on along a path then dropping very steeply to reach Rottingdean High Street. You could turn right here to return to the ECP but I suggest you bear left to join the recommended detour; instructions are given in the main body of text. (Extra two thirds of a mile)

V6 Follow Dane Road, at the top of which you can turn left to immediately reach the station (or right up the A259 Clinton Place, shortly reaching Broad Street on the right – this is Seaford's main shopping area). For the continuous full route variation, however, turn hard right at the top of Dane Road down Church Street past the Norman church of St Leonard, then veer left down South Street past the 18th century Old Town Hall, reaching a crossroads junction with the High Street. I suggest you turn left up the High Street in order to view a number of attractive buildings including the 17th century Old House to your left and the 19th century Regency Restaurant to your right, then return, now crossing South Street, going forward past the imposing Wellington Hotel and continuing over Steyne Road down The Causeway. Cross Esplanade, rejoining the prom and turning left, now back on the ECP . (Extra quarter of a mile)

V7 Having turned left up High Street, shortly turn left again up Swan Terrace, passing or exploring the church of St Clement which is to the right, and go straight on up Cobourg Place, signed for the castle and caves, going forward up quite steep steps. Veer left and pass through a "tunnel" created by the overhanging buildings, and arrive at a crossing of walkways. Here turn right, ascending further steps (and ignoring a path going right) to reach a metalled crossing path (K). Turn left along this metalled path and follow it round to the right, now on West Hill. Soon you're able to detour left to pass the café and cliff railway and ascend onto the highest point of West Hill, enjoying superb views across Hastings and out to sea. Return to the metalled path which you can now follow on to the entrance to Hastings Castle. Built shortly after the Norman invasion, with the keep being built by Henry II in 1172, most of the castle has now been washed away by the sea. Now retrace your steps to (K) but this time walk on to the next set of steps going down to the right, and descend them. By turning left at the bottom (L) you reach Smugglers Adventure (incorporating St Clements Caves), a network of sandstone underground tunnels providing graphic and interactive exhibitions devoted to smuggling. Having visited the caves retrace to (L) but now keep walking to arrive back at the path you followed from Cobourg Place. Simply now retrace your steps back to High Street via Cobourg Place and Swan Terrace, and continue up High Street, passing the tempting Judges Bakery, the lovely Old Town Maritime Garden, created in 2008, the Electric Palace Cinema, and the beautiful flint church of St Mary Star Of The Sea. There are also several fine half-timbered houses in the street. At the top you pass just to the right of the fine mid-18th century Torfield and Old Hastings House. Bear round to the right with the High Street, crossing more or less straight over the A259 (The Bourne) into Harold Road and turning immediately right along All Saints' Street, passing or visiting the church of All Saints. Now walk down All Saints' Street, which boasts some excellent timber-framed buildings including No.58 and No.59, and Shovells, the home of the mother of a 17ᵗʰ century admiral with the splendid name Cloudesley Shovell. Follow All Saints' Street to its end at the beginning of Rock-A-Nore Road. Turn left along this road, now reunited with the coast route. *(Extra 1.75 miles)*

V8 On reaching the top of East Hill beyond the barbecue area, head away from the cliff-edge fence along the grassy plateau, gently rising and following signs for the Fish Trail. As you approach the very top end of the plateau aim for the left corner where you'll see an information board. Pass beyond the board onto a track, going forward along Rocklands Lane. Follow this briefly then as you approach a steep-roofed house to the left of the path, turn right as Saxon Shore Way-signed (though OS maps suggest the Saxon Shore Way takes the more direct Ecclesbourne Glen route) along a permissive path. Keep along it, forking right as Saxon Shore Way-signed at the next signpost, going forward to marker post 5. Turn right here along a narrow path, descending to cross a footbridge. At the path junction immediately beyond the bridge, turn hard right along a track which rises through the trees to a path junction, where you'll find marker post 6. Turn right here and follow the clear track which reunites you with the coast path coming up from Ecclesbourne Glen. It may be possible to detour part-way down to the glen but you'll then need to go back up again the same way. *(Extra half a mile)*

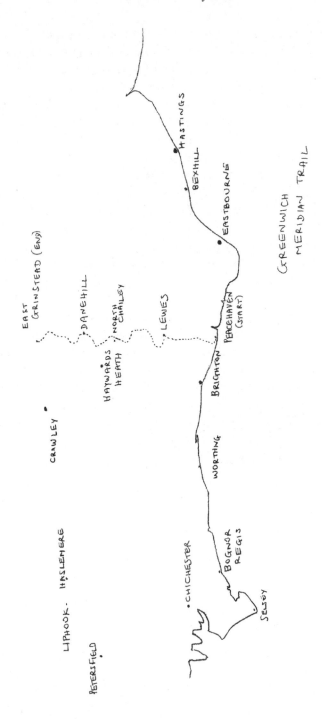

4 GREENWICH MERIDIAN TRAIL

The Greenwich Meridian Trail (GMT) is one of the more recent additions to the family of name paths in Sussex and still awaits the "green diamond" treatment on OS Explorer maps. The trail was the brainchild of Graham and Hilda Heap who wanted to construct a walk that followed the course of the Greenwich Meridian, also known as the Prime Meridian (but referred to hereinafter in this section as simply the Meridian), a geographical line with a longitude of zero degrees. The complete walk, heading northwards, starts at Peacehaven on the East Sussex coast and ends at Sand le Mere in East Yorkshire, a total of 273 miles. Of these, just 32.5 are in Sussex. Just as the Sussex Border Path, about which more later, doesn't follow the Sussex border throughout, the GMT simply cannot, and doesn't pretend to, follow the Meridian all the time. What it does is stick as close as possible to the Meridian, visiting a number of markers or monuments on the line itself. Despite not yet being blessed with those green diamonds, it's relatively easy to follow and well signed, and in Sussex at least, offers a walk of real variety and contrasts, with coastal, downland, forest and Wealden walking.

The GMT starts in the less than lovely coastal town of **Peacehaven**, described more fully in the England Coast Path section. From the A259 in Peacehaven, very well served by buses, walk seawards along **Horsham Avenue** (which leaves the A259 roughly 275 yards east of the roundabout junction with Sutton Avenue) to reach the impressive King George V Memorial on the cliffs. The memorial, situated on the Meridian itself and topped by a distinctive sphere, was erected on 30 May 1936 and not only bears a tribute to the then recently deceased king, but it marks Peacehaven's position on the Greenwich Meridian, and lists distances to all outposts of the Empire. From here the GMT heads westwards along the clifftops towards Brighton. It's a bracing and enjoyable start to the walk, reminiscent of Wainwright's Coast To Coast Walk in beginning with a coastal march before heading inland. And indeed beyond the built-up area, the GMT turns sharply inland, crossing the A259 and now heading north-eastwards across open fields, climbing steadily before joining a track, overlapping now with a section of the Sussex

Hospices Trail and descending on the track to the pretty village of Telscombe. Much of this isolated village, in a hollow at the bottom of a no-through road and therefore not troubled by passing traffic, is owned by the National Trust, with many of the houses surrounded by high flint walls. Properties owned by the Trust include the Manor House with its sheltered gardens and neo-Saxon tower, while the part-Norman church of St Lawrence is built of local flint and Caen stone from Normandy. Beyond Telscombe, still heading north-eastwards, you climb with the road then strike out along a path which drops to a dry valley known as Cricketing Bottom, crossing over the Meridian; you go forward to follow a farm track, soon meeting the South Downs Way (albeit here leaving the Sussex Hospices Trail) and climbing steeply with it northwards to reach the **end of Mill Lane** above **Rodmell**. (By following this road to the end, then crossing straight over, you can continue through Rodmell down to Monk's House, described in the Sussex Ouse Valley Way section. The round trip is 1.5 miles.) Veering north-westwards, the GMT stays with the South Downs Way on the escarpment edge, dropping down and passing a cairn and fingerpost on the line of the Meridian, indicating you are passing from the eastern to the western hemisphere! Soon afterwards at a path crossroads you bear right, away from the South Downs Way, along a track known as White Way, dropping north-eastwards steeply down into the Ouse valley.

On hitting the valley bottom at the buildings of Northease you then veer north-westwards across fields and through Iford, another pleasantly quiet village. Its finest feature is the Norman church of St Nicholas; its tower contains three bells dating from the early 15th century and inscribed for saints Margaret, Botolph and Katherine. Beyond Iford the GMT proceeds across a succession of fields just west of north, with fine views to Mount Caburn and the South Downs east of Lewes. Some 550 yards after leaving Iford village street there's a signed path to the left, the start of what is a route variation V1 which visits a number of places of interest. First there's the very pretty village of Kingston near Lewes, with a fine flint church dedicated to St Pancras. Ashcombe Windmill, sadly not open to the public, lies a little way beyond the village; the mill, boasting six sails, was built in 1828 and destroyed in 1916 but it has recently been restored. Having crossed over the A27 and the railway, the variation leads down the pretty Southover High Street past the magnificent timber-framed Anne of Cleves House, an early 16th century Wealden hall house given by Henry VIII to his fourth wife Anne of Cleves as part of their divorce settlement. It's now an excellent museum. Beyond the house is the Norman church of St John and splendid Priory Crescent, and from here a detour off V1 is possible to view Southover Grange, a magnificent 16th century building of Caen stone and the boyhood home of the diarist John Evelyn, and the adjoining Grange Gardens. (Note that the Grange and gardens are also easily accessible from Lewes High Street, along which the GMT passes later.) The GMT, however, veering north-eastwards from the start of V1, skirts the wetlands of the Lewes Brooks Nature Reserve, walking beside a ditch – crossing back over the Meridian – then passing under the A27 and walking through the grounds of the ruins of the Cluniac 11th century priory of St Pancras, to be reunited with V1. You then veer northwards, away from the priory grounds, passing the Mound from the top of which there's a stunning view of the hills around Lewes, and arriving at Mountfield Road. Turn left along it then immediately right along Station Road, passing the railway station and ascending to reach the junction with Lewes High Street (A), turning left to follow it westwards. While **Lewes** abounds with fine buildings, its main highlights are along or immediately adjacent to this next stretch. (Highlights of Lewes east of (A) as well as the church of St John sub Castro and Pells Pool are described in the section devoted to the Sussex Ouse Valley Way which also passes through Lewes; from Cliffe High Street, reached by descending Lewes High Street eastwards, there's a fine circular walk to Mount Caburn, Glynde and Glyndebourne described in the Sussex Ouse Valley Way section.) You soon pass the Georgian White Hart and, by a detour left into St Andrew's Lane, you reach the fine 16th century Pelham House. Continuing along the High Street, to your left you'll see Bull House, built in 1450 and between 1768 and 1774 the home of Thomas Paine, author of *Rights Of Man*, and then a little further along by the superb timber-framed Fifteenth Century Bookshop is the delightful cobbled Keere Street with many fine brick and flint buildings, leading to Southover Grange and the adjacent Grange Gardens. To the right as you head west on the High Street is the Castle Precinct leading to the ruins of the castle, Norman in origin, although the superb outer gatehouse was added in the 14th century. There's a fine museum in the adjacent Barbican House. By continuing along the road through the castle grounds you'll see several notable houses including Castlegate House beyond which is a green that was first used for bowling in 1640; the road leads past a fine viewpoint and on to the so-called Brack Mound, the original site of the castle. Beyond the Castle Precinct along the High Street is the historic church of St Michael, boasting a twisting needle spire and 13th century tower, with the fine flint-built Church House immediately adjacent, and the very photogenic clock immediately above.

The GMT follows the High Street uphill past the splendid Shelleys and Old Grammar School on your right, and the lovely Norman church of St Anne to your left; look out, on the right-hand side, for a Meridian marker on the pavement and the wall above it. Here you cross back to the western hemisphere again! High Street becomes Western Road and you then fork right up Spital Road, crossing straight over the A275 and continuing along Spital Road followed by a clear track adjacent to the prison and suburban housing, before striking out into open country again. A splendid section follows, as the GMT climbs north-westwards away from Lewes above Landport Bottom along a really excellent track, past the site of the Battle of Lewes of 1264 and a charming dewpond known as Jill's Pond. It's a steady ascent but your patience is rewarded with quite superb views from the crest of the hill, extending to Lewes itself, Cliffe Hill, Mount Caburn, the Ouse valley and the South Downs escarpment. Having reached the crest of the hill, the GMT now veers north-eastwards, descending along a clear and potentially muddy path towards Offham. The views to the Weald, as you descend, are absolutely magnificent; I walked this section in the autumn when the colours added a stunning dimension to the beauty of the scene. You cross back over the A275 at **Offham** and, beyond the 19th century church of St Peter, you now follow a road known as the Drove, going over the Lewes-London railway line by a level crossing and heading north-eastwards. You cross the Meridian again then turn immediately right, south of east, along Ivors Lane; as you walk, you can enjoy views to the impressively large tower of the Norman church of St Peter, Hamsey. As you arrive at Hamsey you meet the Sussex Ouse Valley Way, and you now overlap with it as, skirting Hamsey Place, you turn sharp left with the road. However by detouring straight over the road then veering sharp left and right, you can ascend to the church, a total detour of half a mile, though at the time of writing the church is closed to the public. Back on the GMT, you veer left again with the road, now Whitfield Lane, and pass through the village centre – there's not a lot of it! – then strike out north-eastwards along a path which proceeds initially in the shade of trees then through a long succession of fields past Cowlease Farm. Signage is excellent and the views to Cliffe Hill, east of Lewes, are good too. The GMT leaves the Sussex Ouse Valley Way (but will meet it again later), forking north-westwards across a further field to reach the beautifully situated church of St Mary, Barcombe, much restored by the Victorians but retaining a number of 13th and 14th century features and a notable early 18th century monument to Susannah Medley. A pleasant field walk north-eastwards beyond the church precincts brings you to Church Road and after following this briefly, you then head north-westwards over fields and down into a wooded gully, the course of the old Lewes-East Grinstead line, the northern part of which has been revived as the Bluebell Railway – see the Sussex Ouse Valley Way section. Ascending from the gully and along a field edge you reach the sprawling and frankly uninteresting village of **Barcombe Cross**, passing through the centre of the village.

Beyond Barcombe Cross comes a less interesting interlude of the GMT as you head in a predominantly north-westerly direction, initially along the edge of sports fields then through a large succession of fields, the best views behind you in every sense. You can't even console yourself with the thought that you're on the Meridian, which is some way to the west of you. Carefully observing signage – this isn't a good place to get lost – you pick your way round the edge of a sewage works and arrive at a road by Harelands Farm, turning right (northwards) along it for the best part of a mile. Reaching a T-junction you turn left, westwards, along Markstakes Road briefly, then right, north-westwards, through yet more fields interspersed at one point with a patch of woodland where you cross the Meridian once more. A pleasant walk through rolling farmland and woodland, still chiefly north-westwards, takes you to the pretty houses of Cinder Hill; here you veer north-eastwards along a road then branch left, northwards, off it along firstly a field edge and then driveway, climbing steadily. You pass round the edge of Grove House and close to Vixengrove Farm, and from here, at last, there's reward for your fiddly field tramping and climbing with a wonderful view southwards towards the Downs. For the first time on this walk – not the last – there's then a concerted section of woodland walking, on this occasion along a clear straight track just east of north, veering north-westwards past the backs of houses along the course of the former Lewes-East Grinstead railway line, and arriving at the A272 just east of **North Chailey**. This is an obvious place to break, being exactly halfway up the Sussex section of the GMT and within half a mile of the village amenities including a service station and bus links between Haywards Heath and Uckfield.

Having crossed straight over the A272 (and with it also the course of the Sussex Hospices Trail which you last saw between Telscombe and Rodmell), the GMT leaves it northwards along Coldharbour Lane then heads eastwards past horse paddocks and the buildings of Cox's Farm, over the Meridian and north again along a pleasant wooded bridleway (virtually parallel and very close to the Meridian), turning left onto a road to cross the old railway line. Immediately beyond the crossing you fork right along a path which proceeds north-westwards across Lane End Common. You follow the path beneath power lines, then after 110 yards or so veer right with it, reaching in 70 yards a crossing of tracks. By detouring right for some 45 yards you'll find a stone Meridian marker erected in 1953. It was put up to mark the point "where the Greenwich Meridian crosses the Manor of Balneth," referring to what is the nearby Balneath Manor. The GMT proceeds across the common north-westwards, now on the west side of the Meridian again; you cross the A275 then walk north-westwards across fields, veering northwards, and continuing over fields to reach the fine brick and timbered Wapsbourne Farmhouse, dating from 1606, and described more fully in the Sussex Ouse Valley Way section. There's now another overlap with the Sussex Ouse Valley Way, as you head westwards along field edges; by heading east along the Sussex Ouse Valley Way from Wapsbourne you reach, in half a mile, Sheffield Park and its attractions, described in the Sussex Ouse Valley Way section. Back on the GMT you now head uphill, northwards, into Wapsbourne Wood, now overlapping also with the Sussex Border Path spur route. As you continue through the wood you veer north-westwards, emerging briefly onto an open plateau before descending through Hammer Wood; then, leaving the woods, you follow Sloop Lane briefly northwards past the Sloop inn and across the river Ouse, here leaving the Sussex Ouse Valley Way for the last time.

You now proceed predominantly north-eastwards towards the next village, Danehill, here continuing to overlap with the spur section of the Sussex Border Path. Initially you follow a succession of fields in the Ouse valley, then climb away from the valley floor, passing underneath the old Lewes-East Grinstead railway. You may see trains as this is now part of the Bluebell Railway. Good, open but poorly signed field walking on the plateau brings you to King's Wood; having passed through it, you cross Keche's Lane and continue on a farm track past Northland Farm then on through further woodland before a long section of field-edge walking. The Sussex Border Path strikes away hereabouts north-westwards to Horsted Keynes but the GMT continues north-eastwards to cross the Meridian and reach a road, which you follow just west of north to **Danehill**. You cross back to the west of the Meridian and pass its impressively large late 19th century church of All Saints, then go forward to arrive in the village centre on the A275. The GMT bears left very shortly along Horsted Lane, but at the next (right fork) junction up the A275 is a brick-built monument commemorating both the Meridian, which is met here, and the new millennium!

From Danehill the GMT proceeds briefly along Horsted Lane downhill, then strikes out north-westwards, dropping down steeply; you then rise to enter attractive woodland, before descending to a pleasant mixture of woodland and water with ponds, streams and little waterfalls, your path veering just north of east. Climbing out of the valley, the GMT veers north-westwards again, following the edge of Newnham's Wood. You then follow Birchgrove Road (which links Horsted Keynes and Chelwood Gate) briefly south-westwards, with excellent views northwards towards East Grinstead. Bearing right off this road and heading predominantly north-eastwards, you now enjoy a superb walk along a clear track heading downhill through woodland with a succession of lakes to the left. At the end of the track you turn left to follow Birchgrove Lane briefly and cross a stream, then you begin a really quite strenuous section of the GMT. You turn right to climb north-eastwards out of the hollow on a muddy track; there's then another short road walk following which you fork left, northwards, along a path which heads downhill through woodland. You then begin climbing again. The first part of this climb is on a track, then along a driveway, and, just beyond a redwood planted in 1984 to celebrate the centenary of the Meridian (which in fact is a short way east of this point), you continue along a clear green path, where a detour to the right provides a glorious view of the South Downs escarpment. You cross to the east of the Meridian hereabouts, and will stay virtually parallel and close to it for over a mile. You're now at the north-western edge of Ashdown Forest, and having crossed two roads, **Hindleap Lane** and Priory Road (the former providing easy access to the heart of Ashdown Forest) in close succession, you embark on paths through one of the most thickly wooded parts of the forest. Ashdown Forest is also visited by the Vanguard Way and Wealdway and I refer you to those sections for a little more detail about the history of the forest. It's worth mentioning here, though, that path signage in the forest can be very sparing, so don't rely on it!

Still heading predominantly north/north-eastwards, you drop down beyond the two road crossings through the woods, passing close to a chalybeate spring. Chalybeate means "containing iron" and it's the iron oxide or rust which produces the distinct orange colour of the spring; such springs, with their high mineral content, are believed to have health-giving properties. Immediately beyond the crossing of an adjacent stream the GMT takes a most indistinct, unsigned left turn that could be very easily missed. Keeping the stream close by to your left you descend, then begin to climb again, passing close to another specially planted redwood and in due course emerging from the woods. The signposting now radically improves! You ascend through a succession of fields, passing a lovely pond at one point, and enjoying excellent views to the Weir Wood Reservoir and Standen house beyond; now veering north-eastwards away from the Meridian you go forward to join a track at Mudbrooks House, and follow the track past a number of farm buildings belonging to first Spring Hill Farm and then South Park Farm. Beyond South Park Farm a brief woodland walk brings you to the Weir Wood Reservoir access road. Veering north-westwards you follow this to the reservoir car park and nearby water supply works, then ascend to enjoy a good view of the reservoir of which you'll see rather more on your High Weald Landscape Trail and Sussex Border Path (spur route) walks. Continuing north-westwards beyond the reservoir, you follow a succession of fields, crossing the Sussex Border Path spur once more by a footbridge; beyond this crossing, keeping a sewage works to the right, you follow the edge of a long field then continue through a number of further fields, in each case on a narrow enclosed path between fences, crossing to the west of the Meridian. As you proceed, the outskirts of East Grinstead become more obvious and eventually you arrive at a byway which you then follow into the built-up area, going forward up Hermitage Lane to reach and cross the main street. East Grinstead is also visited by the High Weald Landscape Trail, Worth/Forest Way and Sussex Border Path and there's a little more information about the town in the section devoted to the Worth/Forest Way.

Given that the border with Surrey is just on the outskirts of East Grinstead, you may choose to end your GMT walk at the main street, turning left along it for bus connections towards Crawley and Tunbridge Wells, veering right down London Road and left down Railway Approach for **East Grinstead Station**. Alternatively, you could stay on the GMT, passing the church of St Swithun and heading via the car park (with impressive tower) off Church Lane then via College Lane to the East Court complex. This includes lovely gardens and the impressive red-brick 18th century East Court, on the terrace of which is another Meridian plaque dating from 1977, your last brush with the Meridian on your GMT walk through Sussex; nearby is a Millennium Stone which you are positively invited to touch! However, you don't cross the Meridian here and the GMT remains to the west of it as it proceeds away from East Grinstead. I recommend that you retrace your steps to the centre of East Grinstead (from here proceeding to the station, as directed above, if desired), the mileage below reflecting this. However if you want to follow the GMT to the border with Surrey, continue downhill from East Court, veering away to the west of the Meridian, crossing the main (A264) road and heading northwards up the residential Blackwell Farm Road going forward along Hackenden Lane, crossing the railway and continuing down the path beyond to reach a footpath junction. The border is at the edge of the woodland, Alders Wood, beyond this junction. From the border it's probably easiest just to retrace your steps for the town centre, but for variety you could (having come back up from the border) turn right at the footpath junction to immediately reach Alders View Drive. Turn right along it, then at the end bear left along Charlwoods Road; at the end of that, turn left along Lingfield Road, and then left again onto London Road which brings you to the town centre. For the station, turn shortly right down Station Road. The total walk from East Court to the county border and back to the station is 2 miles.

GOOD TO KNOW
Start: Horsham Avenue, Peacehaven (junction with A259). Finish: East Grinstead Station.
Total mileage: 33.5.
Difficulty: Moderate, very occasionally strenuous.
Stages: End of Mill Lane for Rodmell (RA) 4.5, Lewes (*RAB) 8.5, Offham (RB) 11.25, Barcombe Cross (RB) 14, North Chailey (RB) 18, Danehill (RB) 24, Hindleap Lane 27.75, East Grinstead Station (*RAB) 33.5.
OS: OL11, 135.

V1 Turn left at the path junction and soon arrive at the Lewes-Rodmell-Newhaven road. Cross straight over along a metalled lane into the Swanborough Manor complex. Shortly you reach a signed path fork, here forking right along another metalled lane. Soon you veer sharp right as signed, emerge from the farm complex and continue straight on along an enclosed grassy path which arrives at Wellgreen Lane. Turn left along the lane, soon reaching the centre of Kingston near Lewes where refreshment should be available. Turn left up The Street to reach and pass the flint church of St Pancras. Immediately beyond the church turn right along a signed bridleway, which soon bends sharp left and then sharp right, broadening and becoming Church Lane. Follow Church Lane uphill to its end, then turn right down Kingston Ridge, a public byway. At its end cross straight over the road and continue along Jugg's Road, rising to pass Ashcombe Windmill. Continue just north of east along a clear grassy track, going forward along a lane between buildings and then descending to cross the A27. Beyond the bridge, you veer right with the road and descend along it to arrive at Southover High Street, now in Lewes. Go effectively straight on along the High Street, then just beyond Anne of Cleves House turn right down Cockshut Road (though by walking a little further you reach the church of St John and adjacent Priory Crescent; turn left off the main road on the opposite side of Priory Crescent to detour to Southover Grange and adjacent gardens) and, passing under the bridge, arrive at the signed path to the Priory ruins. Turn left along this path, now back on the GMT. (Extra 2 miles)

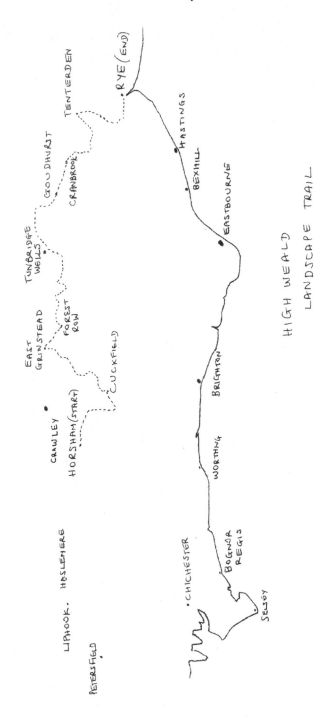

5 HIGH WEALD LANDSCAPE TRAIL

The High Weald Landscape Trail (HWLT) is, as its name suggests, a route which follows the undulating terrain of the High Weald of Sussex and Kent; it begins at Horsham and proceeds all the way to Rye. "Undulating" is perhaps an understatement, as there's a large amount of up-and-down work but with that come rewards in the form of splendid views as well as numerous lovely towns, villages and other places of interest on the route, and while there's a remote feel to much of the walking, you're never actually that far from civilisation and public transport links are excellent. It is a phenomenally good walk which repays your exploration with interest in every sense. While many name paths in this book cross from Sussex into another county, the HWLT is one of just two (the Sussex Border Path being the other) to start and finish in Sussex but visit another county en route. It would in the circumstances be absurd to omit the route detail for that part of the walk, and the full route, including the incursion into Kent, is set out below (although the place descriptions for the Kent part are slightly truncated).

The start of the walk could hardly be more convenient, as it is actually in **Horsham Station**! The centre of Horsham, with its many buildings of interest, is visited by the West Sussex Literary Trail and the Sussex Hospices Trail; please refer to those sections for more details. The HWLT however heads away from the town at once (in fact overlapping with the Sussex Hospices Trail as far as Slaugham), leaving the station by a back exit and continuing with an unexciting eastward walk out of town along Depot Road, crossing Comptons Lane and continuing along Hamper's Lane which emerges into the countryside. At Stew Pond you leave the lane, now heading eastwards along field edges, shortly veering right to descend to cross Sheepwash Gill and enter St Leonard's Forest, so called because legend says that here St Leonard killed the last dragon in England; the forest once supported a flourishing iron-smelting industry, and mounds called pillow mounds were created to provide accommodation for rabbits who were valued for their fur and as food. Proceeding along an excellent track, you ascend Greenbroom Hill then turn southwards to follow a dead-straight track leading to a multi-path junction, where you branch off south-eastwards, descending quite steeply to cross Frenchbridge Gill and then ascending to cross Grouse Road. Now emerging from the woods you descend once more, heading briefly north-eastwards then turning south-eastwards again along the metalled Carterslodge Lane, passing Carterslodge Pond and reaching the **B2110** Lower Beeding-Handcross road. You follow the road very briefly left then bear right, southwards, descending then rising quite steeply through fields. You cross Coos Lane and head south-eastwards along a field edge then through a charming patch of woodland to reach and follow Park Road southwards through the centre of **Slaugham**, overlapping with the Sussex Ouse Valley Way. The village is really very charming and boasts a particularly attractive Norman church which, together with the (very short) detour from the church to the ruins of Slaugham Place, is more fully described in the Sussex Ouse Valley Way section. Beyond Slaugham, having parted company with the Sussex Ouse Valley Way as well as the Sussex Hospices Trail, the HWLT heads southwards, round the edge of a lake, then downhill along a track and across fields before ascending steadily, passing through woodland and reaching the B2115 Cuckfield Lane just east of Warninglid. You head briefly eastwards along the lane before branching off south and then west, picking your way past a number of farm buildings and paddocks. You reach and continue southwards along Colwood Lane, then head eastwards along Jeremy's Lane before striking out southwards along a lovely path taking you through the beautiful woodlands of Wykehurst Park, and down to the straggling village of **Bolney** which is rather marred by traffic noise from the A23. You enter the village at the top end and soon turn eastwards off the village street onto Ryecroft Road but by detouring (roughly 550 yards each way) to the bottom of the village street you'll reach a lovely village inn, the Eight Bells. I visited this inn on a sunny but very frosty January morning, my feet slithering on the ice on my approach, but I was rewarded for my full morning's walk, enjoying a steaming hot coffee in front of a real fire. Bliss!

The HWLT follows Ryecroft Road to its end, passes under the A23 and continues eastwards through the attractive Bolney Wood to reach Buncton Lane; you turn right to follow it briefly south-eastwards before branching left, following a driveway eastwards past the house and farm at Pickwell. Then you swing north-westwards for another road walk through Ragget's Wood before branching off the road for a lovely walk north-eastwards through Long Wood to arrive at Broxmead Lane. After following the lane briefly you have a sharp climb through a field and then an eastward descent along a farm track to Deak's Lane which you follow northwards, then you veer eastwards and descend to pass through Walks Wood and enter Cuckfield Park. This is some of the finest walking on the HWLT so far. Another descent through trees is followed by a very stiff ascent and a terrific high level walk with excellent views to your right to the (private) Elizabethan mansion of Cuckfield Park and South Downs beyond, while ahead you can see the church and houses of Cuckfield. Shortly you reach the B2036, turning left to arrive in **Cuckfield.** The HWLT actually creeps rather diffidently round the west side of Cuckfield, but rather than fork left with the HWLT straightaway via Ockenden Lane you should detour the short way on along the High Street, perhaps visiting the town museum, the highlight of which is its display devoted to the Cuckfield Dinosaurs and the work of a local palaeontologist who reputedly discovered the first fossilised iguanodon teeth. Then on return, bear left down Church Street, noting the sturdy stone Kings Mews on the corner of Church Street and the main street, and the splendid timber-framed Nonsuch House on Church Street itself. There's then a particularly lovely row of brick cottages at the entrance to the church precinct, from which the views southwards are stunning. The 13th century church of the Holy Trinity boasts a very conspicuous 14th century spire and, in the nave, a 15th century roof which was painted in Victorian times with roses and foliage.

As stated, though, the HWLT forks up Ockenden Lane past the very fine 16th century Ockenden Manor, now a posh hotel, then strikes out northwards into the countryside; you drop steeply to a footbridge then rise up a hillside dotted with trees on a clear path albeit with a paucity of HWLT signage. The houses of Whitemans Green, effectively a suburb of Cuckfield, appear to the right and you cross the B2115 (which you last saw near Warninglid many miles back!) in distinctly suburban surroundings. Beyond the B2115 you head predominantly northwards, and shortly a tremendous view unfolds ahead of you, providing definite payback for the somewhat uninspiring tramp from Cuckfield. Your excellent path descends resolutely, keeping a golf course to the left, then switching to an adjacent field (a switch easily missed, so be careful!); at the bottom end you veer eastwards along Spark's Lane to cross the B2036 at the hamlet of Brook Street, passing a chapel that's been converted into an art gallery. You head eastwards beyond the B2036, proceeding messily past Tanyard Farm then rising sharply to follow a field edge, descending to skirt an area of woodland and rising again, with woodland close to you on the right. You then go forward to join a farm lane, following it to the entrance to **Borde Hill Gardens**, one of the finest gardens in the whole of Sussex. The gardens, dating from 1893, boast trees and shrubs collected originally from Europe, Asia, Tasmania and the Andes. You'll find here extensive woodlands including bluebell woods, lakes, 220 acres of parkland, a terraced Italian garden, award-winning collections of azaleas, camellias, rhododendrons and magnolias, and sub-Himalayan species, palms and bamboos. Make sure you leave enough time in your schedule to visit the gardens – and enjoy a cup of tea and slab of cake afterwards.

Beyond the gardens you veer north up Borde Hill Lane and east along the metalled Copyhold Lane, crossing the London-Brighton railway, then, joining the Sussex Hospices Trail and Sussex Ouse Valley Way, following good paths northwards mostly through woodland with one brief field interlude. You then cross over an old railway which once linked Haywards Heath with Horsted Keynes via Ardingly but which closed in 1963, although occasional freight trains still ply the section between Ardingly and Haywards Heath. After a gentle ascent there's then a significant descent and you emerge from the woods into an attractive meadow, here waving goodbye to the Sussex Ouse Valley Way, and also being sure to look to your left towards the splendid Ouse Valley Viaduct, described more fully in the Sussex Ouse Valley Way section. Beyond the meadow there's a sharp ascent to within sight of the popular and attractive Ardingly Reservoir, described in the section devoted to the Sussex Hospices Trail which leaves the HWLT hereabouts to follow the reservoir edge for some distance. The HWLT prefers to follow a series of paths predominantly eastwards some little way short of the reservoir, through a car park at one point, then retreats from the reservoir and joins a driveway that ascends to proceed through the Ardingly College complex. The college dates back to the 19th century and arguably its greatest treasure, as at Lancing College, is its chapel, completed in 1883 in 13th century style. You emerge from the complex to cross College Road and follow a clear easy path eastwards beyond it through Standgrove Wood. Beyond the wood you veer northwards and ascend steadily across fields; do make sure you look back and enjoy lovely views stretching back to the South Downs. At the top of the ridge you reach Lindfield Road (**B2028**). The HWLT turns right, south-eastwards, briefly along this road, but **Ardingly** village is reached by detouring left for 200 yards or so to the road junction. By turning right here up the B2028 continuation you shortly reach the bus stop and village store, but by going straight over into Street Lane, you reach the heart of this attractive village with its pub and delightful Fellows bakery. The church of St Peter, described in the Sussex Hospices Trail section, is half a mile down the lane from the B2028. Ardingly's best-known feature, further north up the B2028, is the South of England Showground which hosts many events including the South of England Show each June.

Having proceeded briefly as stated south-eastwards along Lindfield Road, the HWLT turns northwards along a driveway that descends to the buildings of Withyland, and continues down into woodland. But typically of the switchback nature of the HWLT, your descent is followed by a stiff climb. You pass the buildings of Pickeridge Farm and briefly follow Hook Lane, beyond which there's a steep field descent westwards into a narrow valley. Veering north-westwards you enter a lovely area of woodland where the sight or sound of streams and waterfalls is never far away, and you now head northwards along a really lovely path through East Wood, veering north-eastwards and descending to reach a signed path junction. The HWLT goes effectively straight on but you can and indeed should turn left here to make a detour D1 to Wakehurst Place. The gabled stone house was built by Edward Culpeper in 1590 and the gardens were developed by Gerald Loder over 33 years from 1903; they've been managed by the Royal Botanical Gardens, Kew, since 1965. A mecca for the botanist and garden lover alike, the gardens are noteworthy for their fine collection of hardy plants. One feature of particular interest is its glade, planted with Himalayan species; there are fascinating water gardens too, including a plantation of Japanese irises, as well as two walled gardens and a Millennium

Seedbank that was opened in 2000. The HWLT, having proceeded from the path junction as stated, climbs steadily north-eastwards through the trees to arrive at the buildings of Philpots. Here you emerge from the woods to follow a farm lane, continuing north-eastwards and enjoying extensive views as you keep on climbing, in due course reaching North Lane and following it straight on to **West Hoathly**. Here you're over 175m (about 550ft) above sea level, compared with just 53m (less than 200ft) below Ardingly Reservoir. West Hoathly, with its pretty tile-hung cottages, boasts two gems to your left: the superb 15th century timber-framed Priest House which is open to the public and contains a small museum and attractive gardens, and the early 17th century stone-built Manor House. The Norman church of St Margaret contains a gigantic possibly 12th century chest, and close by the church there's a popular pub, the Cat.

Beyond West Hoathly's centre you descend, heading just east of north, to cross the busy B2028 – visibility to the right as you cross is very restricted, so take care – and then head northwards, following a lane then dropping very steeply through a field and along the edge of woodland, passing a picturesque lake. You then rise, the pain of the ascent mitigated by the excellent views to Gravetye on the left. Gravetye, a stone gabled and mullioned ironmaster's house, was built in 1598, and you can see both the house and lovely grounds from the path. You join a driveway, just by the official entrance to Gravetye in fact, then strike out just east of north to pass the buildings of Home Farm, from which there are great views, and enter woodland. There are numerous tracks but the HWLT is well signed; you reach another driveway onto which you turn right, south-eastwards, and now follow it parallel with the Bluebell Railway, described more fully in the Sussex Ouse Valley Way section. When trains are running you will certainly hear them! You're briefly diverted from the driveway when it becomes private, then return to it and follow it a bit longer before turning sharply north-eastwards, ascending to cross the Bluebell Railway then following meadows and climbing again to join a track heading eastwards past some sandstone outcrops. There are superb views from here to the Weir Wood Reservoir ahead.

You descend to Grinstead Lane, bearing right onto it and shortly left along Admiral's Bridge Lane to descend to and follow beside the reservoir for roughly half a mile, overlapping here with the Sussex Border Path spur route. You then turn left, northwards, away from the Sussex Border Path and climb yet again, through fields interspersed with woodland. As you climb you'll glimpse part of the Standen estate to your right, and there are superb views back to the reservoir. The path levels out and you arrive beside the approach road to **Standen.** a 19th century National Trust-owned property and certainly worth detouring down the approach road to visit. It's a remarkable mix of architectural styles, and is regarded as one of the finest houses of Philip Webb, a close associate of William Morris whose designs decorate the house. Continuing along the HWLT you follow parallel with then along the Standen approach road to meet the road coming up from the reservoir, crossing more or less straight over and heading westwards past a sports field. The HWLT then turns right, north-eastwards, towards East Grinstead but by detouring straight on past the tastefully converted chapel and lovely brick cottage at Milton Mount, then turning left along the road at the end, you soon reach Saint Hill Manor on your right. This late 18th century Sussex sandstone building, in lovely grounds with splendid rhododendrons, is owned by the Church of Scientology; arguably its most interesting feature is its monkey mural by John Spencer Churchill, Sir Winston's nephew. The total detour is just half a mile. The HWLT however proceeds north-eastwards as stated along a reasonably clear path past the right-hand edge of Dunning's Wood. You reach Coombe Hill Road, turning right as signed to reach Dunning's Road onto which you turn left, then very shortly bear left again along Streatfield Place; that said, you may want to detour a few steps further along Dunning's Road to the attractive Old Dunnings Mill Inn, which dates from the 15th century. Beyond the houses of Streatfield Place you continue north-westwards as signed along the clearly defined, occasionally muddy footpath, keeping mainly to right-hand field edges, and, passing a pond with small bird sanctuary, going forward to reach Turners Hill Road. The HWLT turns right alongside it to reach a roundabout. Here a <u>route variation V1</u> is possible here to cut to East Grinstead Station and en route visit the magnificent red-brick Imberhorne Viaduct which carries the Bluebell Railway. However the HWLT goes straight on from the roundabout up West Hill and forward along West Street then East Grinstead High Street. **East Grinstead** is an obvious stopping place on your journey, with its finest buildings concentrated in the High Street; its points of interest are highlighted in the Worth/Forest Way section. For information on reaching the station from the High Street, please refer to the Sussex Border Path section.

The HWLT, now rejoined by V1, continues beyond the High Street along the same road away from the centre, then strikes out south-eastwards for the easiest 2.5 miles on the trail, following the course of the old East Grinstead-Tunbridge Wells railway line and overlapping with the Forest Way. It's lovely easy walking, more fully described (along with a possible detour to Brambletye) in the Worth/Forest Way section, and it's almost a shame to reach and cross the A22 just outside the attractive large village of **Forest Row**, also described in that section. Having followed a lane just beyond the crossing, you cross over the Vanguard Way which skirts the village centre, then very shortly leave the Forest Way and strike out north-eastwards along a track. You soon pass Tablehurst Farm, where at the time of writing there was a useful café/store selling a range of organic products.

After the ease of the last 3.5 miles it's a bit of a shock to be experiencing fiddly walking again. Your track peters out, and you have firstly field-edge then woodland walking north-eastwards on narrow paths, slowly gaining height. At one point there's a key right-hand fork with no HWLT signage at the time of writing, so keep an eye on your map or app. Route finding temporarily becomes easier as you head eastwards along Cansiron Lane, and your direction of travel is predominantly eastwards as you then strike out across fields beyond the lane. This is initially terrific walking, with tremendous high-level views; think of it as a reward for the fiddly slog from Forest Row. In my case the reward aspect was marred when, wearing the wrong kind of footwear, I slipped on a wet patch of grass hereabouts and gave my shoulder a nasty bang. Moral: don't go walking in Converses in monsoon conditions. You descend steadily and continue through Paupersdale Wood, then emerge to walk through fields and reach a lake and campsite by the St Ives farm complex. Here there's another key unsigned turn (well, it was unsigned when I walked it!), as you fork left from the lake across fields. Now heading a little south of east, you descend to pass through another (smaller) patch of woodland which is at its best in spring with a profusion of bluebells. Nondescript field walking brings you to the old railway line carrying the Forest Way which you cross, and a brisk climb away from the old line leads you, still heading south-eastwards, to the very centre of the pretty village of **Hartfield**. This village has strong associations with the Winnie the Pooh creator A.A. Milne who lived nearby. By taking a detour D2 you can visit Poohsticks Bridge, the bridge at the north end of Ashdown Forest said to have been the birthplace of the Poohsticks game, and effectively rebuilt as recently as 1999. In the village itself there's Pooh Corner, a café/shop dedicated to selling Pooh memorabilia, and the village street is dotted with lovely weatherboarded and timber-framed houses.

The HWLT continues up Church Street past the church of St Mary which boasts a superb lychgate effectively incorporating the upper floor of an adjacent timber-framed cottage of 1520. Your route then heads for the next village to the east, Groombridge, but while the Forest Way does the same thing in 3 miles, the HWLT route is nearly twice as long! Initially there's more field walking, south-eastwards from Hartfield past Forstal Farm, then the HWLT turns abruptly just north of east to pass through woodland, emerging to rise through fields to **Withyham**. Overlapping with the Wealdway briefly you now turn left and head northwards to pass Withyham's 17th century church of St Michael, definitely worth a detour and more fully described in the Wealdway section. You descend to the B2110 Hartfield-Tunbridge Wells road and follow it eastwards briefly then, with the Dorset Arms conveniently just adjacent, strike out south-eastwards along a driveway heading for Buckhurst Park. It has a very private feel to it, enhanced by a lot of signage which does make you feel like an intruder; you pass a cricket field and enter woodland, then shortly beyond a lake and a sharp ascent you leave the driveway and follow a woodland track uphill. You emerge to enjoy a fine open walk across fields with glimpses to the early 19th century Buckhurst Park mansion. Veering just west of south, you drop steeply to cross the B2188 and follow a minor road uphill southwards from it, then head eastwards through Legg Wood beyond which there's some tough field walking, culminating in a very stiff ascent to the Groombridge-Crowborough road. Pause as you climb to enjoy lovely views westwards, and also to admire Littlebrook, a delectable timber-framed house, immediately below you.

You bear left to follow the road briefly then turn eastwards along a driveway past the Park Grove complex beyond which you reach a path T-junction. The signage here was very poor at the time of writing but you need to turn left to head north-eastwards, your direction of travel all the way to Groombridge. Initially you follow field edges but then, beyond some further rocky outcrops – you'll see plenty more of same just beyond Groombridge – you enter Jockey's Wood and plunge downhill into an enchanting area with fast-flowing waters, lakes and, in spring, a magnificent patch of daffodils. If you're planning to stop at Groombridge this makes a lovely finale to your day's march. There's a brief walk across a meadow beside a stream, the HWLT now joining hands with the Sussex Border Path, whose advent signifies your closeness to Kent. Beyond the meadow there's a very stiff field climb to a road which you follow past the buildings of Mott's Mill. Having left the road you enjoy a short wooded stretch then, overlapping with the Sussex Border Path still, you follow a good clear path through an area of grass with woodland on either side. Beyond that, there's a brief climb and the landscape opens out to reveal Groombridge ahead and excellent Wealden views to the north and west. It's then an easy and confident descent; having hit the valley floor you pass under the London-Uckfield railway and arrive at Corseley Road which you follow uphill into **Groombridge**. The HWLT rather coyly goes round the edge of the village, heading off south-eastwards by the village school, but by continuing downhill along the road for another 400 yards or so you'll reach its centre and its attractions, described more fully in the Worth/Forest Way section.

Beyond Groombridge the HWLT, now overlapping with the Tunbridge Wells Circular Walk, describes a U shape, firstly crossing the Spa Valley Railway then heading southwards between the railway and Harrison's Rocks, a really impressive line of sandstone outcrops used by trainee mountain climbers and sports enthusiasts. Having been separated from the rocks by an area of grass you come right up close to them in the shade of trees, shortly thereafter arriving at a path junction at Forge Farm. The HWLT goes straight on but by detouring right here along a track over the railway and then turning left along Forge Road for roughly a mile, bearing left at the end, you reach Eridge Station on the main network but also the southern terminus of the Spa Valley Railway. This is a preserved railway linking Eridge with Tunbridge Wells in Kent, the original line having been closed by British Rail in 1985. It's worth riding the railway to the remarkable sandstone rock outcrops at High Rocks, just 2 stations away, while Tunbridge Wells, at the end of the line, is a most attractive town with much fine 18th and 19th century architecture.

Beyond Forge Farm the HWLT swings northwards to meet a road at Park Corner, briefly following the road to the right and then striking out eastwards, initially along a field edge and then, beyond trees, across a very wide field, gradually gaining height. There's then a pleasant woodland walk past the bottom end of Eridge Rocks, another impressive sandstone outcrop. It's now a short walk to cross the busy A26 at **Eridge Green** from which there's an excellent bus service to Brighton, Lewes and Tunbridge Wells. From the A26 crossing the HWLT veers south-eastwards, descending across fields quite steeply and passing through Forge Wood, emerging and rising through open fields on a track through the southern half of Eridge Park. You veer sharply north-eastwards along the fringes of woodland, then turn eastwards through a wooded and watery landscape, keeping lakes to your right as you head along an obvious but often very muddy path through the trees. Veering a little north of east you emerge to walk through the pastures of Old Eridge Park, again on the fringes of woodland, and climb very steeply, re-entering woodland and soon arriving at and crossing another busy road, the A267. You then follow a minor road, The Green, into the village of **Frant**. This is a very pretty village with a wide green, attractive cottages and really splendid views, and there's a shop and pub as well as a bus service linking Tunbridge Wells and Eastbourne. Frant Station is reached as follows: turn right at the road junction at the eastern end of The Green and follow this road for 1.5 miles to a T-junction with the B2169 at Bells Yew Green, turning left here and reaching the station in a further 300 yards.

The HWLT heads north through Frant village and on past the pretty church of St Alban which dates from the early 19th century. North of the church there are quite superb views; make the most of these, as there's nothing better to come for the next five or six miles, during much of which you'll be negotiating the eastern fringes of Tunbridge Wells. Still proceeding northwards you descend steeply, then, veering north-eastwards, you enjoy a straightforward woodland walk, continuing beyond the woods along farm lanes to cross the B2169 Bayham Road and pass the course and clubhouse of The Nevill Golf Club. The HWLT then bears right, eastwards, briefly along a road, crossing the London Charing Cross-Hastings railway and then veering sharply left to descend, parallel with the railway, to Windmill Farm. As you turn north-eastwards again the walking gets a little messy, your route passing along a field edge beside enclosures and then eastwards through woodland which can be very muddy; the path junction at which you turn east is as close as you get to Tunbridge Wells although you wouldn't think so from the surroundings. Emerging from the woodland you swing northwards and climb again, bearing briefly left on a road towards Hawkenbury and then shortly bearing right to head along a path north-eastwards, your direction of travel all the way to the A21. You've now crossed into Kent and you will notice a change in the style of signage: you're still overlapping with the Tunbridge Wells Circular Walk, and Kent County Council have, for this overlap, used a combined path sign logo for both this walk and the HWLT.

You initially follow a good clear path past a sports field with useful bench if you want a sit-down – the suburbs of Tunbridge Wells are very visible from here – then continue on through woodland to arrive at a metalled lane. You turn right along this lane and for the next mile or so it's very nice easy walking, following the lane which continues along a ridge with very good views particularly to the right. You pass the farm complex of Little Bayhall and your lane peters out; the HWLT continues in the same direction on a very thin path, where it would be very easy to get sucked onto wider tracks forking away left and right. Signage could be better! You drop downhill beside patches of trees and at the bottom pass through a thin area of woodland, then having crossed a track leading to the buildings of Great Bayhall you climb steeply, the traffic noise of the A21 getting louder as you climb. You need to follow the course of the path carefully – it's thin in places – but at length you reach the top, crossing the A21 by a bridge and then descending gently to the main street at **Pembury**. The village centre, with its attractive green, is away to the left, and from the village there are excellent bus connections to Tunbridge Wells and Maidstone.

The HWLT bears right, south-eastwards, to follow the main street to its junction with the A21 then strikes away north-eastwards with excellent views ahead. You drop down through fields to reach a road, turning left along it briefly then right along a driveway past houses and forward, just east of north, into Snipe Wood. You need to follow the signage carefully as there are a number of signed tracks. It's not the prettiest woodland walking you'll meet on the HWLT and it can feel somewhat claustrophobic because of the concentration of trees. Towards the end of it the HWLT parts company from the Tunbridge Wells Circular Walk and there's a mileage sign proclaiming Horsham to be 55 miles back (it's actually closer to 57 if you want to be pedantic) and Rye 37 miles ahead. You're well over halfway at any rate! Beyond the sign you veer south-eastwards and ascend to emerge from the wood, passing alongside an orchard, a foretaste of things to come. You turn left to follow Romford Road north-eastwards, then, continuing eastwards, follow a path just south of the road. Your path descends through some lovely woodland, the bluebells and primroses particularly impressive in spring. You cross Bramble Reed Lane and an area of meadow, ascend through further trees and then, still heading eastwards, pass through fields and along farm lanes to arrive at **Matfield**. Matfield is the loveliest village so far on the HWLT, with a big village green and pond, and many attractive Georgian, tile-hung and weatherboarded houses. There are also excellent amenities including bus connections, and by turning north up the B2160 Maidstone Road you reach **Paddock Wood** and its station in 2.5 miles. However the HWLT crosses the B2160 and heads for Brenchley. There's a real "Garden of England" feel now, and this will continue for much of the way to Rolvenden, a good full day's walk ahead. Beyond Matfield you continue eastwards, then on reaching the Brenchley road, you perform another U manoeuvre (remember the one just beyond Groombridge?), heading south-eastwards on well signed paths past a succession of orchards, interspersed with a couple of brief sections of road walking. Having passed Southfield Farm and completed your U, you then head eastwards and just south of east past more orchards to a lane. You turn left alongside it, ascending to arrive at the stunningly attractive **Brenchley** village centre, with fine weatherboarded houses and an excellent 13th century church with a 14th century tower.

The HWLT proceeds eastwards from Brenchley along an excellent path to Palmer's Green, with fine views southwards. It then wends its way south-eastwards down through orchards – it's essential to follow the signage – to pass round the lovely Furnace Pond, an artificial lake created by ironmasters and a reminder of the iron industry that once flourished in this part of Kent. You then follow a clear track southwards to cross **Brenchley Road**, the village of **Horsmonden** a quarter of a mile or so away to the left along this road. However the HWLT continues southwards through the lovely estate of Sprivers with its 15th century house, owned by the National Trust. You swing south-eastwards to cross the B2162 Horsmonden-Lamberhurst road then strike out south-eastwards across hop fields and further orchards, the signage somewhat sparse in places, but there are excellent views northwards to Horsmonden. You emerge from the orchards and veer southwards, dropping down to pass a large lake at Rectory Park then rising to a road. Looking at the map you might initially wonder why the HWLT chooses to go straight on, southwards, rather than left here, effectively doing two sides of a triangle. The reason is to visit Horsmonden Church, which although a very long way from Horsmonden itself, is a really fine church with a prominent tower and a splendid chandelier, the gift of the rector in 1703. The HWLT heads north-eastwards from the church along the road, completing a V shape, then at the crossroads bears right, south-eastwards, along the road towards Goudhurst, crossing over the river Teise just east of the hamlet of Smallbridge. Beyond Smallbridge and the Teise crossing you leave the road to follow a path steeply uphill south-eastwards to arrive in **Goudhurst**, one of the prettiest villages not only on the HWLT but in Kent, with superb brick-built and tile-hung houses, and glorious views across the High Weald. The 13th century church boasts a tower, the top of which is 500ft above sea level; the tower was used as a lookout point during both World Wars. You follow the A262 through the village past the church.

Between Goudhurst and Cranbrook, the next settlement, there's no orchard walking, and your walk is of a very different character. Proceeding south-eastwards from the A262 very shortly beyond the church, you begin with a steep descent along clear tracks then continue through a farmland mix of fields and tracks, the path always extremely well signed and veering in a more easterly direction. There's a real feeling of peace and tranquillity, though looking back you can still enjoy excellent views to Goudhurst. For a while you flirt with a track that's to your left and then join it, veering sharp left then right past the fine 17th century brick buildings of Little Glassenbury, descending then rising to cross the B2085. Beyond the crossing the character of the walk changes again, as, heading just south of east, you follow a lane that takes you into Angley Wood, veering just north of east as it does so. You're then signed off the lane along a narrow woodland path, going forward to meet a fine forest track which proceeds confidently just south of east. Signposting is excellent, and you need to follow it carefully as you strike out from the track along a beautiful path uphill through coniferous woodland reminiscent of the Serpent Trail. You emerge onto another clear track which takes you to the A229; having crossed with care you follow New Road south-eastwards and this leads to Cranbrook's High Street. You turn left to follow High Street just north of east to reach the town centre. **Cranbrook** is a lovely little town with many fine tile-hung and weatherboarded houses; just off The Hill is the restored early 19th century Union windmill, and there's a sensational church, almost cathedral-like in size and grandeur, dating from the 15th and 16th centuries.

The HWLT heads confidently past the church and north-eastwards out of Cranbrook on an excellent path, crossing Waterloo Road, then beyond this crossing turns south-eastwards off the path to skirt woodland and briefly follow Golford Road heading back towards the town centre! Then, however, you do proceed decisively south-eastwards for what is a really fine stretch of the HWLT, comprising good easy field-edge path walking with fine Wealden views and a couple of short woodland interludes. You cross a track then rise to pass the tile-hung Crabtree Farm, one of the unsung highlights of the HWLT both in appearance and situation. Immediately beyond the farmhouse you enjoy a walk through a delectable stretch of woodland, which like all the wooded stretches of the Kent section of the HWLT is best seen in spring with its profusion of bluebells and primroses. A descent through the woods is followed by quite a tough climb, firstly through the trees then up through a field, beyond which you enter the grounds of Benenden School, its buildings visible to the left. The school, built in 1859 and founded as a school in 1923, is one of the best-known girls' public schools in the country, with Princess Anne, charity campaigner Sue Ryder and actress Rachel Weisz among its former students. The HWLT veers from south-eastwards to southwards, leaving the school grounds and arriving at the B2086. The HWLT turns right and immediately left, striking out southwards, descending quite steeply; there's a lake to the left and a most attractive mini-gorge to the right, and really fine views ahead. You reach the bottom of the hill then promptly swing eastwards for a very tough climb, rewarded by great views from the top. You cross New Pond Road and then proceed pleasantly north-eastwards through fields – with lots of spring lambs! – to arrive at the church of St George, **Benenden**. This is another really fine Wealden church right on the route of the HWLT in Kent; rebuilt in the late 17th century following a storm, it has a magnificent tower and a superb east window. Beyond the church you reach Benenden's very impressive village green, and follow down one side to join the B2086, turning right to follow it south-eastwards past the pub and on through the village.

Beyond the centre of Benenden the HWLT heads south-eastwards from the road, rising slightly to provide another magnificent Wealden panorama. You then descend steeply and proceed through another area of gorgeous woodland, picturesquely named Strawberry Wood, with another profusion of bluebells – a further reminder that spring is the best time to walk the HWLT! The going gets a little muddier and steeper as you continue along the edge of Willerd's Hill Wood and drop down to reach a road, turning left to follow it just south of east to the farm complex at Dingle Den. For road walking it's most agreeable, with little if any traffic. As the road peters out by the farm, you head eastwards past a pond – according to the current OS Explorer map, the path goes right through the middle of it, so, purists, bring your swimming trunks! – and then across fields and along the fringes of more attractive woodland, heading predominantly eastwards. Signage remains excellent and it's very easy, enjoyable walking in a totally unspoilt setting. You cross Sandhurst Lane and continue eastwards, the tower of the next on-route Wealden church, Rolvenden, now very conspicuous just ahead, while to your left you can clearly see Rolvenden Windmill, a late 18th century post mill. Easy field walking is followed by a brief woodland interlude – the path into the wood may not be signed, but it's clear enough – and then you emerge from the woods to cross a green and reach the edge of **Rolvenden** village. The HWLT skirts the village centre, crossing the A28 and proceeding south-eastwards past the church, but it's only a short detour left (northwards) to the centre with pretty brick and weatherboarded houses, a shop, pub, motor museum, and – some way beyond the village admittedly – a station on the preserved Kent & East Sussex Railway, about which more in the Sussex Border Path section. The village also has good bus connections. The 14th century church contains a number of interesting features including a "squire's pew" set out like a comfortable room, a tablet to a John Franklin, a vicar who was burnt at the stake during the reign of Queen Mary, and a memorial to a World War 1 soldier by Sir Edwin Lutyens.

From the church the HWLT continues pleasantly south-eastwards across fields before veering southwards through attractive woodland past Great Maytham Hall, then heading just south of east along a clear path to the village of Rolvenden Layne. Here as the crow flies you're barely 7 miles from Rye, your final destination, but the HWLT walk is roughly twice that, choosing to veer here away from Rye, heading north-eastwards towards Tenterden! You now proceed over a succession of fields, climbing to pass the buildings of Lower Woolwich then dropping to follow a watery landscape at the northern edge of the Rother Levels. It's all quite a contrast to the rolling hills and orchards of the previous sections. You then cross the Kent & East Sussex Railway and climb steadily away from it, continuing north-eastwards through fields; you pass West View Hospital and go forward along Plummer Lane to arrive at the A28 which you follow into the very centre of **Tenterden**. This is the biggest settlement on the HWLT between East Grinstead and Rye, very well served by buses, and a lovely place to stop and potter around before continuing. It contains many fine Georgian and timber-framed houses, is the terminus of the Kent & East Sussex Railway down Station Road, and boasts a church (dedicated to St Mildred) with a splendid very prominent pinnacled tower and a 12th century nave.

The HWLT now heads resolutely to Rye. You exit Tenterden south-eastwards along a narrow lane, Six Fields Path; this becomes a good metalled path bringing you to the B2082 Rye road which you'll meet twice more on your walk, and from the road you veer briefly just north of east to pass the buildings and nurseries of Belcot Manor Farm. You then strike out south-eastwards again, initially across fields then down steps and through an area of stunningly beautiful woodland, best seen at bluebell time. The path is very clear and well maintained with some very fine footbridges over the streams that flow through the woods. You emerge from the woods then pass along the right side of a lovely lake, one of the scenic highlights of this section, and continue past the buildings of Dumbourne including a magnificent oasthouse. Beyond Dumbourne you veer south-westwards and it's then a nondescript walk across flat fields, again part of the Rother Levels, as far as the B2082 at Smallhythe. You walk briefly southwards beside this road and as you do so you pass two wonderful old timber-framed buildings, firstly the Priest's House and then secondly Smallhythe Place. Smallhythe Place, a yeoman's house, was built around 1480 for the local harbourmaster and now, owned by the National Trust, houses the Ellen Terry Museum; Ellen Terry was regarded as the leading actress of her time and lived here from 1899 until her death in 1928. Immediately before the museum is a gorgeous cottage garden which in spring is a riot of colour.

Beyond the museum the road veers right but you proceed southwards, continuing across flat fields of the Rother Levels, then climb quite steeply to pass the buildings of Kingsgate Farm and, enjoying good views from the top of the rise, follow an obvious farm lane southwards beyond it. Note that some OS maps show the HWLT as following the fields to the right of the lane but this is clearly now incorrect. The lane takes you back to the B2082 which you cross; you now continue southwards across fields along the top of the ridge, reaching a narrow road, **Swan Street**. The HWLT crosses more or less straight over this road, but by detouring left along it for half a mile you reach the village of **Wittersham**. The HWLT meanwhile veers just south of east past Bates Farm and along the edge of orchards and beside a churchyard; just ahead, a little off route, is the very prominent church of St John the Baptist, Wittersham, which is chiefly 14th century although its most prominent feature, its battlemented tower, was added in the late 15th century. The HWLT now veers south-westwards right through the middle of an orchard, aiming for woodland. Signage is unclear, but once you've reached the woodland edge on the far side the way becomes obvious. You now plunge downhill along the edge of the woods and then along a good clear field path through a rolling landscape, soon arriving at the Wittersham-Peasmarsh road. Still heading south-westwards you turn right along the road, soon crossing the river Rother and returning to East Sussex. You're now briefly overlapping with the Sussex Border Path towards the end of its journey from Emsworth to Rye. The Sussex Border Path route from here to Rye is a good deal more straightforward than that of the HWLT!

Staying with the Sussex Border Path for the time being you follow the road initially beyond the river crossing, then head away south-westwards through farmland, and after the brief orchard/rolling hill interlude it's now more typical Rother Levels fare, the path, fairly clear on the ground, proceeding across a low-lying farmland landscape. You reach the edge of Decoypond Wood and a major path junction, where you part company from the Sussex Border Path and bear left, south-eastwards, round the edge of the pond itself before climbing in the shade of trees to cross Kitchenour Lane. Now heading just south of east, you cross a field; the way on the ground isn't clear but simply watch for the stile at the edge of the wood ahead. You then pass through the wood, the last woodland section on the HWLT and like so much of the woodland walking on this trail it is really enjoyable, especially so in spring. You emerge at the A268 at the buildings of Flackley Ash, a road sign proclaiming Rye to be 4 miles away. The HWLT turns left to follow beside the A268 briefly towards Peasmarsh – thankfully there is a pavement – then uses first a path heading south-eastwards beside a supermarket (the path can get very waterlogged) and subsequently School Lane to enter **Peasmarsh** village south of the A268.

From Peasmarsh the HWLT heads southwards along the eastern side of Peasmarsh Park, and there's a very stiff field climb, the last climb of the walk in fact. Beyond the first intervening strip of woodland you need to take care to follow the left side of the fence, signage initially unclear. Don't be sucked away along the tempting path to the right! Once on the ridgetop you go forward to cross Church Lane, but by detouring right along this lane you reach, in a quarter of a mile, the beautiful Norman church of St Peter & St Paul, Peasmarsh, with fine Norman carvings on the chancel arch while the chancel itself boasts excellent Early

English lancet windows. Beyond Church Lane the HWLT itself heads straight across an orchard to a T-junction with a bridleway. The HWLT turns left here, south-eastwards, your predominant direction of travel all the rest of the way to Rye. Initially the bridleway is a clearly defined farm lane, with excellent views across Brede Level, another broad area of flat fields through which flow the rivers Brede and Tillingham; your ultimate objective of Rye is clearly visible on the hill beyond. As you lose height, however, the path loses its identity and you now need to follow the path/ HWLT signs carefully along the valley floor. If in doubt, aim for the housing estate ahead, keeping the wide river Tillingham to your right. You then veer slightly left (fractionally north of east) to cross a tributary of the Tillingham just below Rolvendene Farm. Now veering right just in front of the farm you stay beside the Tillingham, reaching a T-junction with a clear metalled path. Here you could take a detour D3 to reach the early 13th century church of St Michael, Playden, with its very impressive spire and ancient ladder leading to the tower. However the HWLT turns right along the metalled path, now heading south. You then leave the metalled path to follow a grassy path across a meadow south-westwards beside the river, and having crossed Ferry Road now walk beside the river once more, crossing the Ashford-Hastings railway and passing Rye's reconstructed smock windmill, originally built in 1824. You soon reach the A259 which marks the end of the HWLT. I suggest you turn left alongside the A259 (just here overlapping with the England Coast Path and Royal Military Canal Path) then when it shortly veers right, walk straight on along Wish Street, going forward into Cinque Ports Street, as far as the crossroads junction with Station Approach and Market Road. If you wish to explore Rye, please refer to the England Coast Path section and a suggested described walk which starts and ends at this crossroads junction. By turning left down Station Approach you reach the bus stands and **Rye Station.**

GOOD TO KNOW
Start: Horsham Station. Finish: Rye Station.
Total: 94 miles.
Difficulty: Strenuous.
Stages: B2110 6, Slaugham (RA) 7, Bolney (RAB) 10.5, Cuckfield

(RAB) 14.5, Borde Hill Gardens (R) 17.5, B2028 for Ardingly
(RAB) 21.5, West Hoathly (RAB) 25, Standen 29.5, East Grinstead
(*RAB) 31.5, Forest Row (RAB) 34, Hartfield (RAB) 39.5,
Withyham (RAB) 40.75, Groombridge (RAB) 44.5, Eridge Green
(*RB) 47.5, Frant (*RB) 50, Pembury (RAB) 55.5, Matfield (RAB)
for Paddock Wood (*RAB) 59, Brenchley (RAB) 61, Brenchley
Road for Horsmonden (RAB) 62.5, Goudhurst (RAB) 66,
Cranbrook (RAB) 70, Benenden (RAB) 75.5, Rolvenden (RAB)
77, Tenterden (RAB) 81.5, Swan Street for Wittersham (RAB) 86.5,
Peasmarsh (RAB) 90.5, Rye Station (*RAB) 94.
OS OL34, 135, 136, 125.

D1 Take the path heading left, north-westwards, from the path junction, then turn very shortly left again up a signed steep path. You veer very sharply right and climb to reach Ardingly Road, turning left alongside the road to reach the signed entrance to Wakehurst Place. Return the same way. (Total detour three quarters of a mile)

D2 Having turned right onto Hartfield's village street, rather than turn left with the HWLT towards the church, continue along the street out of the village, passing the left B2026 turn and continuing beside the B2110. However in 350 yards beyond the B2026 turn left along a signed footpath on a right-hand field edge then through trees. Emerging at the end, turn right to walk past the buildings of Gallipot Hill Farm which are to the right, enjoying stunning views southwards to Ashdown Forest. Beyond the farm, turn left as signed to walk downhill through fields to reach a lane; turn left to follow it southwards, ignoring a lane going off to the left, and proceed pleasantly to Poohsticks Bridge. Return the same way. (Total detour 3 miles)

D3 Having turned left along the metalled path, cross over a wide track and climb steps, then continue north-eastwards along an obvious green path, entering Rye Cemetery. Follow the path through the cemetery and pass the chapel that's to your right, going straight on up across the grass then after roughly 75 yards turning right along a metalled pathway that brings you to the cemetery approach road. Turn left along it to reach the A268. Cross and turn left to walk beside it then bear right as signed to reach the church of St Michael, Playden.

Return exactly the same way. (Total detour 1.5 miles)

V1 *Turn left at the roundabout into Brooklands Way and immediately left again up Gardenwood Road, and you'll soon pass under the Imberhorne Viaduct. Turn right immediately beyond the viaduct up a grassy bank leading to a path. Follow this path all the way to a car park beyond which bear right over the railway, then descend the steps to reach East Grinstead Station. To return to the HWLT from the station cross straight over the roundabout by Sainsbury's and walk up Railway Approach then bear right up London Road to reach High Street. (Extra half a mile)*

1 The Pavilion, Hailsham, a short distance from the Cuckoo Trail

2 Cyclists on the Cuckoo Trail between Hailsham and Polegate

3 A lovely section of the Downs Link between Bramber and Henfield

4 The splendidly maintained Baynards Station on the Downs Link

5 *Quay Meadow and church at Bosham on the England Coast Path*

6 *The Look & Sea attraction at Littlehampton on the England Coast Path*

7 The six-sailed Ashcombe Windmill just off the Greenwich Meridian Trail

8 The pretty Jill's Pond on the Greenwich Meridian Trail

9 Splendid Wakehurst Place just off the High Weald Landscape Trail

10 Harrison's Rocks, a dramatic feature on the High Weald Landscape Trail

11 The delightful church at Up Marden close to the Monarch's Way

12 The Devil's Humps above Stoughton on the Monarch's Way

13 Above Woolbeding on the New Lipchis Way

14 Chichester Canal and Cathedral from the New Lipchis Way

15 The ruin of Camber Castle on the Royal Military Canal Path

16 Springtime near Iden Lock on the Royal Military Canal Path

17 On the right track: a Serpent Trail waymark on Chapel Common

18 Pretty in pink at Fittleworth on the Serpent Trail

19 The stunning view to South Harting from the South Downs Way

20 Approaching Chanctonbury Ring, a highlight of the South Downs Way

6 MONARCH'S WAY

The Monarch's Way (MW) in Sussex is just part of a route of 610 miles, at the time of writing the longest inland waymarked name path in Great Britain. It traces as faithfully as possible the route of the future King Charles II following the Battle of Worcester in 1651. It was after this battle that the then 21-year-old Charles was forced to flee for his life, travelling to Shoreham from where he fled to France, returning to reign as the "Merry Monarch" from 1660. The route is a tortuous one, progressing via Stourbridge, Bromsgrove, Chipping Campden, Cirencester, Bristol, Castle Cary, Charmouth and Yeovil. But even though the Sussex section makes up a fraction of the whole route, it is a superb walk in itself, with massively contrasting landscapes and lots of interesting features both on and close to the route.

To join the MW for its journey through Sussex you need to start at the pretty Hampshire village of Rowland's Castle, which boasts a wide village green and attractive shops and houses. Starting at **Rowland's Castle Station**, turn left from the station entrance and walk all the way down the road to the junction, turning left (the green immediately to your right) to pass under the bridge. You walk briefly eastwards on along Finchdean Road, then as this road bends left you strike out just south of east to join an impressive beech avenue, described as one of the best in England. You keep to the left-hand edge of the grass to the very end, overlapping for a while with the Sussex Border Path. Ahead is Stansted House, and having parted from the Sussex Border Path and crossed the Forestside-Westbourne road you follow a driveway which passes the house. The original building was a Royal hunting lodge which in 1686 was replaced by a house designed by William Talman and extended in the late 18th century, the grounds having been laid out in the early 18th century. In 1724 Daniel Defoe commented on his ability to see from the west end of the house right down to the town and harbour of Portsmouth and ships at Spithead. The house was very badly damaged by fire in 1900 and largely rebuilt by Sir Reginald Blomfield although parts of the earlier construction remain; the drawing room retains a distinctly 18th century feel, there are paintings by Joshua Reynolds, the servants' quarters vividly reproduce the

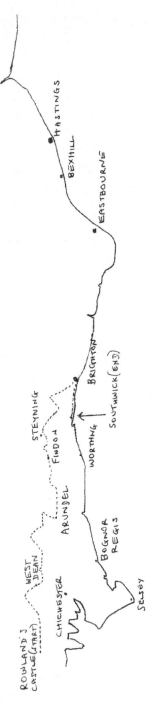

running of a great house in the early part of the last century, and the walled gardens feature restored Victorian glasshouses. There's also a delightful chapel, and a fiendish maze if you've the time (you'll need it)! From Stansted you continue pleasantly along Woodlands Lane, veering south-eastwards and descending to the pretty village of Walderton, crossing the B2146 Harting-Funtington road. You then veer north-eastwards along field paths that climb to provide a quite superb view to the Isle of Wight, the first of many excellent views on this walk, and you reach a signed path T-junction. One feature of interest by the path here is a cairn, a common thing to find in northern England but a very rare phenomenon in Sussex.

The MW turns sharp right at the signed path T-junction here to drop steeply to Stoughton but there's an opportunity here for a route variation V1 to visit the lovely, extraordinary and completely unrestored 13th century church of St Michael, Up Marden, the epitome of a remote country church with its thick walls, brick floor, box pews and wooden benches. Pevsner describes it as boasting "one of the loveliest (church) interiors in England (and) incredibly moving...a visible loving testimony of the faith of successive generations." The MW, however, descends to shortly reach the delightful village of **Stoughton** which boasts a popular pub and, on a hillside just outside the village, the church of St Mary. Described by Pevsner as a complete 11th century church, it boasts a particularly fine chancel arch. You then go forward to a junction with the main street (A), the mapped route bearing left along it past the pub and then forking right at Old Bartons, now joined again by V1. However to complicate matters there's another really fine route variation V2 involving your turning right rather than left at (A) and climbing to the Devil's Humps, four ancient burial mounds that are said to be the tombs of warriors killed in battle against the Danes. The views from the top of the mounds towards Chichester, the Manhood Peninsula and the sea are exceptional, and the chalk grassland hereabouts, part of the Kingley Vale Nature Reserve, is home to nearly 40 species of butterfly as well as numerous orchids, while bird life includes sparrowhawks, tawny owls and woodpeckers. However the mapped MW route from Stoughton heads north-eastwards from Old Bartons, climbing initially quite gently along a farm track past farm buildings then more steeply onto Stoughton Down, towards a thickly wooded area on the northern fringes of Kingley Vale Nature Reserve. Before you enter the woods you should look back for what are superb views towards Portsmouth. On entering the woods you're joined by V2 coming from the right. Woodland walking now takes over for the next two thirds of a mile or so, in a north-easterly direction through the trees, culminating in a descent past the Goosehill Camp earthworks dating back to the late 3rd century BC. You then emerge from the woods and veer sharply south-eastwards, descending to and crossing the B2141 Harting-Chichester road.

Beyond the B2141 there's a brief north-easterly road ascent along Hylter's Lane, the views from the top quite magnificent, and at a crossroads junction of lanes you then turn right to begin your south-eastward progression to West Dean. You initially follow a rough lane, actually the site of a Roman villa, then as the lane veers a little right, you fork left across fields to pass Lodge Hill Farm. Slightly fiddly field walking around the farm is followed by a more straightforward chiefly wooded descent through the Whitedown Plantation; you emerge to cross a road and then follow the western fringes of Warren Hanger, another patch of woodland, beyond which it's a straightforward march to the A286 at **West Dean.** The MW crosses straight over this busy road although by detouring right you'll reach the village pub and bus stops on the Chichester-Midhurst route. There's also a route variation V3 from the A286 crossing, enabling you to visit three features of interest: the church of St Andrew, largely rebuilt in 1934 following a fire but boasting some impressive effigies of 17th century origin; the magnificent West Dean Gardens which in their lovely valley setting contain a rich variety of plants including hydrangea, clematis and climbing roses, as well as an arboretum and lily pond; and the grounds of West Dean College, an impressive and beautifully situated flint building which dates back to 1804. The Weald & Downland Open Air Museum, described more fully in the New Lipchis Way section, is also a possibility! The MW, having crossed the main road, follows a minor road steeply downhill then turns right at a T-junction (where V3 rejoins the MW) to follow Church Lane south-westwards along the edge of the village, passing another road heading right beside which, at the time of writing, is a useful shop. West Dean shouldn't be confused with another predominantly flint-built village of the same name in East Sussex, although its East

Sussex namesake is all one word (Westdean!). Make the most of refreshment opportunities here as, unless you take the East Dean detour or Slindon route variation, there'll be no more till you reach the A29 over 12 miles further on.

You cross the river Lavant and now head south-eastwards, rising steadily through woodland and arriving on the top of a ridge where you meet the West Sussex Literary Trail and New Lipchis Way. Joining hands with them both, you now head eastwards, crossing a signed junction of tracks – where the Sussex Hospices Trail joins you! – and rising to The Trundle, one of the great viewpoints in West Sussex, with views which extend not only to the Isle of Wight but, on a clear day, to the Seven Sisters beyond Brighton. There was a Neolithic settlement here dating from 4000 BC but during the 4th century BC Iron Age people created a ditch, dyke and banks on this site. You'll note the pair of masts on the hilltop but in World War 2 there were eight of them. The West Sussex Literary Trail and New Lipchis Way leave you, going down to (or having come up from) Singleton, while the MW dives eastwards off the summit plateau and drops down to Kennel Hill, the road which links Goodwood's motor racing circuit with Goodwood racecourse. You walk beside it briefly then turn hard left, north-eastwards, onto Selhurstpark Road, which you now have to follow for a mile. To begin with you pass the rear of the Goodwood racecourse grandstand, then can look out onto the racecourse itself. It's not massively enjoyable walking but will certainly be more interesting and inevitably more crowded if it happens to be a race day! There is at least the consolation of a wide grass verge, on which you're still overlapping with the Sussex Hospices Trail. The next part of the MW is fiddly and irritating to walkers anxious to make progress. Evidently to relieve the burden of road walking, it describes 3 parts of a square, heading left – northwards – and descending through woods (leaving the Sussex Hospices Trail) to a valley, veering eastwards to arrive at a road, **Eastdean Hill** (B). By detouring left down this road you reach the very pretty flint village of **East Dean** with its lovely green, pond and the Star & Garter pub, and, by following the village street north-eastwards you reach a grassy path leading to the beautifully-sited 12th century church of All Saints. The total detour is half a mile. However the MW turns right at (B) to follow first along the road then roughly parallel with it, striking out just north of east over Eastdean Hill itself before veering south-eastwards back to Selhurstpark Road. There are good views through the trees but as you reach the road again a look at the map will show how little progress you've made since last on the road, at the cost of a knee-jarring descent and a stiff climb back onto the ridge. Anyway, that interlude over, you cross the road and head resolutely eastwards through the woods of Selhurst Park; when the trees relent the views are magnificent. Slight anticlimax follows as, having emerged from the woods, you veer sharply southwards and then south-eastwards, dropping down to the busy A285 Chichester-Petworth road.

You cross straight over the A285 and take a path bringing you to another road which you follow south-eastwards for 300 yards or so, passing the **Eartham Wood** car park, then bear left off the road as MW-signed to embark on a splendid walk north-eastwards along part of Stane Street, overlapping now with the Sussex Hospices Trail as you'll continue to do until Houghton. However by going straight on here rather than turning left up Stane Street there's an opportunity for a <u>route variation V4</u> in order to visit Slindon Folly and Slindon village, returning to the route at Gumber Corner. Slindon Folly, also known as Nore Folly, is a flint arch built in the 19th century for the Newburgh family who used it as an outdoor dining place. Slindon itself, a lovely village of flint cottages, has two buildings of particular note: Slindon College, a fine flint-built construction which dates from the 16th century and in which there are traces of a former palace for the Archbishops of Canterbury, and the splendid 11th century flint church of St Mary which contains the wooden effigy of a reclining Tudor knight, the only wooden effigy of its period in Sussex. The mapped MW meanwhile strikes out north-eastwards as stated above, along Stane Street. This Roman road, constructed in about 70 AD to connect the port of Chichester with London, was metalled and cambered in most places with a width of up to 25ft. As you might expect, it's dead straight walking, initially along a track through woodland then along footpaths through open country. The views just get better with each step, Halnaker Windmill clearly visible, but on a clear day you should also see out as far as Chichester Harbour and the Isle of Wight. You leave Stane Street as you reach a further area of trees just below the summit of Bignor Hill, and veer east to pass Gumber Corner where route variation V3 meets you.

From Gumber Corner you now enjoy a short but sensationally good hilltop walk just north of east with glorious views to a wide coastal strip including Bognor Regis and Littlehampton. Then you veer south-eastwards and it's a long steady march through the woodland of Houghton Forest, on a good clear track but with very limited views. Signage is good and indeed it's vital not to miss the MW signs as there are so many crossing and forking tracks. In particular don't miss a left fork roughly a mile into the forest. Eventually traffic noise signals the proximity of the **A29** and you need to make a smart left then right turn to cross it at **Whiteways Lodge**. Just south of here on the A29 is a café that's immensely popular with motorcyclists; if you can stand the noise and petrol fumes of the bikes it's a useful amenity for you too! Having crossed the A29 you now plunge eastwards into the Arun valley along a path that runs close to, and more or less parallel with, the B2139. The view across the valley between the trees is stunning. Eventually you have to join the roadside but in doing so you pass another popular watering hole, the George & Dragon at **Houghton**, which dates from the latter part of the 13th century; it's of particular significance to MW travellers in that Charles II stopped to take ale here on 14 October 1651 and there is a plaque here commemorating this event. Just beyond the pub you lose the Sussex Hospices Trail as you turn right off the B2139 along South Lane. Note that **Amberley Station** is another half mile on along the B2139 and **Amberley** village, described more fully in the West Sussex Literary Trail section, a further mile beyond that. Having joined South Lane you very shortly veer south-westwards for a delightful walk beside the river Arun. This is one of the great rivers of Sussex, starting near Horsham and flowing into the sea at Littlehampton; it was once an important river for the transport of cargo, including wine from France and coal from Newcastle, but is now used virtually exclusively by pleasure craft. You veer south-eastwards, keeping to the river bank, but are then signed sharply south-westwards away from the river and now climb steeply yet again, this time into Arundel Park, a former deer park of 1000 acres. You veer southwards and your ascent continues, but you're rewarded with views which from here, the highest ground in the park, are sensational, particularly towards the sea and the Arun valley. You skirt an area of woodland, the Dry Lodge Plantation, then descend southwards, steadily at first then steeply. Ironically there's then a further climb; watch for and take a right turn past the splendid Hiorne Tower, a late 18th century folly which appeared in an episode of *Dr Who* in 1988, then turn left onto a clear track leading out of the park onto London Road in **Arundel**. You turn left along this road to pass the Roman Catholic cathedral, built in Gothic style in the 1870's, and the parish church of St Nicholas. This church is partitioned into separate Anglican and Catholic areas; the Catholic area, viewable only through glass, is known as the Fitzalan Chapel where former Dukes of Norfolk and Earls of Arundel lie buried, and there are some most impressive canopied tombs. Beyond the church is the magnificent flint-built Arundel Priory, which today incorporates a theatre. Now go straight on down the steep hill in the shadow of Arundel Castle, which looks ancient, but was in fact rebuilt in the 18th and 19th centuries after being extensively damaged during the English Civil War; all that remains of its original fortification is the 12th century shell keep and fragments of the 13th century barbican and shell wall. As you continue downhill you find yourself in the centre of Arundel, a lovely place to spend an afternoon or even a full day, with its very attractive shops and cafes. Tarrant Street, a right-hand turn off the main street towards the bottom of the hill, has lots of both. There's also a beautiful riverside area including the historic quay (just to the right before the bridge), and, down Mill Lane to the left, the castle entrance, recently-built town museum, Swanbourne Lake and the Arundel Wetland Centre with its profusion of swans, geese and ducks, including such rare species as blue ducks from New Zealand, in 60 acres of water meadow. Note that the Wetland Centre is a good three quarters of a mile down Mill Lane.

Overlapping again with the Sussex Hospices Trail, you cross the Arun. To reach Arundel Station, half a mile away, continue straight on alongside Queen Street and then the Causeway (part of the A27) using the new cycle route/underpass. The MW meanwhile turns left off Queen Street and enjoys a delightful walk beside the Arun upstream, north-eastwards, as far as **Warningcamp**, where the path veers away from the river to a railway crossing. At this crossing there's the option of a detour D1 to **Burpham** following a further stretch of the Arun. Burpham is a very pretty village of flint, brick and timbered cottages, with an impressive 12th/13th century flint-built church boasting some fine Norman work, the fine flint-built

Burpham House, and the brick/timber/thatched Church Cottage.
The MW crosses the railway (D1 actually rejoining the MW on
the far side of the crossing) and goes up to the Arundel-Burpham
road; you turn left to follow the road briefly, then strike out on a
path eastwards from the road. Indeed eastwards will be your almost
exclusive direction of travel all the way to Findon and beyond. You
enjoy a pleasant woodland walk and follow a charming dry valley,
then ascend steeply to reach a forest track, turning left to leave
the Sussex Hospices Trail and follow the track through the Upper
Wepham Wood and on through the woodlands of Angmering
Park and Michelgrove Park. It's very fast easy going initially, but
in about a mile and a half you need to watch carefully for signage
leading you south-eastwards, still through the woods, then sharply
northwards. You now emerge from the woods, descending steeply
to Michelgrove Lane. There's a short road walk northwards past the
buildings of Michelgrove then you head eastwards again through
more open country, past Myrtle Grove Farm and south-eastwards
to cross **Longfurlong Lane**. Beyond this lane you head for the A280,
contouring a hillside which seems remarkably bare and exposed
after the woodland walking! You now have a stiff climb to cross the
A280, the traffic noise quite a shock after the last few tranquil miles.
There's then a descent south-eastwards along a track past the flint-
built church of St John the Baptist, **Findon**, which contains a 13th
century oak screen and medieval oak pews, and shortly beyond, the
18th century Findon Place. You're now approaching another busy
road crossing, the A24, but just before you get there, you could
turn right onto the signed footpath for a <u>detour D2</u> southwards
to visit the lovely viewpoint of West Hill and also High Salvington
Windmill, a post mill built in 1750.

The tranquillity is again broken by a crossing of the busy A24,
beyond which the MW goes straight on, eastwards, emerging at
the south end of High Street along which you turn right. However
you should detour up this street to the left to arrive, in roughly 400
yards, in Findon's village centre with its 1527 Village House and
Gun inn, cottages of flint and brick, some 16th century, and a good
range of shops and eateries. The MW, though, heads right down
High Street then left, eastwards, along Steep Lane and across the
lovely village green at Nepcote to reach the road linking Findon
with the base of Cissbury Ring. You walk up the road briefly but

soon fork left along a track heading north-eastwards uphill. The ground levels out in just under half a mile and as it does so you find yourself level with the unmistakeable Cissbury Ring hill, reaching a crossroads of tracks where you can detour right to Cissbury Ring, following a <u>detour D3</u>. The 603ft hilltop site at Cissbury Ring was occupied prior to the Iron Age, but the fortifications were built by an Iron Age community around 300 BC. The views from the trig point at the top are astonishing, both eastwards towards Brighton and beyond, and westwards across a massive stretch of coast as far as the Isle of Wight. Pick a clear day!

Beyond the track crossroads, you now continue north-eastwards along a clear track through gloriously lofty and remote countryside, comprising broad rolling open hillsides interspersed with patches of vegetation. You can enjoy really good views left to Chanctonbury Ring and, as you proceed further, towards the coast and the heights of Steep Down; there really is the feeling of being a world away from the busy conurbations of Worthing and Brighton which are only are few miles distant. Appropriately enough, one area of woodland you pass is marked on maps as No Man's Land! A stiff climb brings you up to meet the South Downs Way, which has swept south-eastwards down from Chanctonbury Ring, and for just a few hundred yards, your path overlaps with the South Downs Way, heading southwards, along a track and then briefly beside the Sompting-Steyning road. The views from up here are majestic, encompassing the Adur valley, the masts of Truleigh Hill beyond, and the magnificent 95ft high Lancing College Chapel. And immediately below the road to the left is the remarkable natural phenomenon known as Steyning Bowl, similar in shape to the Devil's Dyke with its deep dry valley guarded by steep hillsides. Very soon after joining the road, the MW, now leaving the South Downs Way, heads off south-eastwards to contour the southern side of Steyning Bowl, soon veering north-eastwards, continuing along Sopers Lane past Upper Maudlin Farm, and going forward between houses to reach a T-junction (C) with **Maudlin Lane**. The MW turns right here and immediately left initially along Maudlin Lane then forks left for a downhill field walk, returning to Maudlin Lane and bearing left to arrive at a roundabout with the busy A283. However by turning left just before the T-junction (C) along the metalled footpath above the road, then beside it, you can walk down to Clays Hill; by turning left here along Clays Hill then Bramber Road you'll arrive, in three quarters of a mile from the MW, in the centre of **Steyning**, more fully described in the Downs Link section. To return to the MW, retrace to Clays Hill and you can choose between returning to (C) or taking a short cut by following Clays Hill down to the A283 roundabout.

From the roundabout the MW heads east along The Street through **Bramber**, once an important seaport on the river Adur. However by crossing The Street at the roundabout and taking the next exit, then turning immediately right onto a track, you very shortly reach the impressive Norman castle, virtually destroyed during the Civil War and now a spectacular ruin; having visited the castle you can then walk back down and veer left along a path leading to The Street past the Norman church of St Nicholas, which itself is well worth a visit. Continuing along The Street, a little further along on the right-hand side you'll reach St Mary's House, a superb timber-framed house dating from around 1470. Among its fine rooms are the Monk's Parlour, notable for its huge "dragon" beam and 17th century inglenook; the Hall, embellished with beautiful 17th century gilded wall-leather; the Octagonal Dining Room displaying over 80 costume dolls; the Painted Room, with its fascinating murals said to have been painted for a visit by Elizabeth I; and the Library, containing a unique private collection of works by the Victorian poet Thomas Hood. You go straight on along High Street through Upper Beeding, crossing the river Adur, one of the major rivers in Sussex and which you'll see (or will have seen) a lot more of on the Downs Link. You continue along High Street to its end then carry straight on beside the A2037 Henfield road, but shortly you bear right (south-eastwards) up a driveway which rises to cross the South Downs Way. The MW then proceeds delightfully along the side of Beeding Hill on a superb green track, just south of east, with great views to the Adur valley and Lancing College Chapel. There's a sharp drop to a narrow valley and a climb onto another ridge where you turn right at a path T-junction and head south-eastwards over Thundersbarrow Hill, named after Thunders Barrow, an earthwork close to the top of the rise. It's superb open walking with wonderful views towards the sea. You drop slightly to enter an area of rough vegetation and pass the trig point on Southwick Hill, now looking ahead to the sprawling Brighton suburbs of Mile Oak and Portslade and passing over the Southwick Tunnel which carries the A27 under Southwick Hill.

The character of the walk now changes and becomes essentially more suburban and less remote. You drop down a hillside towards the houses, then turn sharp left, northwards (the signed route at variance from the OS-mapped route which continues south-eastwards before turning hard left) and follow a track which recrosses the Southwick Tunnel close to its eastern mouth. You're briefly overlapping with the Sussex Border Path spur route here but soon leave it to drop down to the valley by **Mile Oak Farm**. (A road to the right here brings you in half a mile to **Mile Oak**, a suburb of Brighton, with ample amenities.) There's then a messy and poorly signed trudge through the farm complex and then a curious section along a path heading eastwards, keeping the noise and cars of the A27 close by to the right, and rolling unspoilt downland scenery to the left. You climb briefly away from the A27 then, reaching a path T-junction, turn right and head just south of east back towards the main road, looking ahead to the impressive Foredown Tower, built in 1909 as a water tower and latterly containing a camera obscura, one of just two operational camera obscuras in south-east England. It's easy enough to carry on over the road bridge and along the track beyond if you want a closer look. Rather than crossing the A27, however, the MW strikes out north-eastwards, dropping to the farm buildings of New Barn then climbing, dropping to the Benfield Valley and climbing again, going past West Hove Golf Club. You're now back to almost 500ft above sea level – but the good news is that it is (almost literally) all downhill from here! You're as close here as you're ever going to get, on the MW anyway, to Devil's Dyke with its dramatic dry valley and fantastic viewpoint, but none of that's visible here. You instead turn away from the Dyke, sharp right just before the Brighton & Hove Golf Club buildings, onto a metalled path heading just west of south then veering just east of south. This is part of the Dyke Railway Walk along a section of the now disused Aldrington-Devil's Dyke Railway, which opened in 1887 and closed in 1938. For the final time you cross the A27, and enter suburbia; in fact you will have houses, factories or shops close by for the whole of the rest of the walk. Leaving the Dyke Railway Walk you veer south-eastwards along a path from which there are potentially superb views which may extend as far as the Isle of Wight. Make the most of them, as there are no views that are as good for the rest of the walk. You go forward along Downland Drive, then having negotiated the A2038 you arrive at the **West Blatchington Windmill**, a smock mill dating from 1724. While there are more attractively sited mills in Sussex, it's a delightful surprise to discover this fine building in such unpromising surroundings.

From the mill you head south-eastwards, descending via Court Farm Road, Nevill Road and The Droveway past the remarkable Victorian water-pumping station with 100ft brick chimney stack known as the British Engineerium, and down into the picturesque and very popular Hove Park. From the bottom of The Droveway the MW bears right to cross the park diagonally to Old Shoreham Road, but by continuing straight on in the same direction as The Droveway you can join a route variation V5 which takes you to Preston Manor and the Booth Museum. Built in 1738, Preston Manor, once the manor house of a village outside Brighton, is now a museum and evocation of Edwardian life, and is supposedly one of Britain's most haunted houses! The adjoining church of St Peter, with its tall elegant flint tower, dates from the 13th century and boasts some impressive 14th century wall paintings. The Booth Museum of Natural History, purpose-built by the 19th century natural historian and eccentric Edward Thomas Booth, is well known for its collections of stuffed creatures, fossils and ecological displays; its collection of stuffed birds is one of the largest in the country. If you've decided to stick to the MW to Old Shoreham Road, you walk briefly beside it then drop down into **Hove**, turning right down **The Drive**. For Hove Station, just under half a mile away, turn first right along Wilbury Avenue then left down Hove Park Villas and cross the footbridge. The MW proceeds down the Drive, crosses the railway and shortly continues eastwards along Cromwell Road, being joined again by V5 at the junction with Wilbury Villas, and passing just to the north of Sussex County Cricket Ground. You then turn seawards, arriving via Holland Road at Western Road immediately to the east of the splendid Palmeira Square, designed by the well-known architect Decimus Burton. You now follow Western Road eastwards into the very centre of the city of **Brighton**, past numerous shops, cafes and restaurants – you certainly won't go hungry! It's an amazing contrast to the peace and tranquillity you were enjoying only a few miles back. You pass the huge Churchill

Square shopping complex and cross Queen's Road at the imposing clock tower built to commemorate Queen Victoria's Diamond Jubilee, then continue straight on down North Street. This street itself is an uninteresting shopping street, but off New Road to the left is the sensational Royal Pavilion, while on the other side, East Street provides easy access to the narrow streets of shops known as The Lanes. At the bottom of North Street you bear right to reach the seafront by Brighton Palace Pier, the Sea Life Centre immediately to your left. The England Coast Path section provides more detail on the history of Brighton and its highlights, including a suggested circular walk which overlaps in places with the route of the MW.

All the way from Rowland's Castle you've been heading in a predominantly easterly direction, but for the final four and a half miles of your walk you're heading westwards! Your westward walk is along the seafront almost throughout, but again with some amazing contrasts in surroundings. It's all described in rather more detail (in reverse) in the England Coast Path section, including a possible **Hove** detour, leaving the prom at the King's Esplanade via Medina Terrace. Initially it's very cosmopolitan, as, staying on the upper promenade, you pass the large and not hugely elegant Odeon and Brighton Centre and then the opulent Grand Hotel. You soon pass the magnificent new I360 tower, from which you can enjoy sensational and indeed unrivalled views to coastal and inland Sussex. You then pass the fine bandstand and the sad remains of the West Pier out at sea; here you move to the seaward promenade and away from the coast road. To your right, as you proceed towards the King's Esplanade, are the superb Brunswick Square and Adelaide Crescent developments, Adelaide Crescent a creation of Decimus Burton, and Brunswick Square dating from the 1820's. Beyond the King's Esplanade the promenade remains wide and impressive but in roughly two and a half miles after leaving Palace Pier you reach Hove Lagoon and the end of the promenade. Now you need to join the coast road which to begin with is separated from the shore by industrial developments, but thankfully these relent and it becomes a pleasanter walk as far as Shoreham Power Station and beyond. The sea is visible more or less throughout, and there are one or two crude shoreside paths you can follow as an alternative to the road. The mapped OS route keeps you beside the road but there is in fact no MW signage alongside this road at all, so you should feel free to vary things!

Beyond the power station you are able to follow a proper shoreside footpath and arrive at a signed footpath junction (D). You'll eventually need to take the path pointing inland to cross Shoreham Harbour and return to civilisation, but not yet; you've not quite reached the end of the MW. You in fact continue westwards, kinking slightly left and right to follow a permissive route along a seafront wall as far as the breakwater on the eastern side of the Shoreham Harbour mouth. In windy weather and at high tide this is potentially very exciting walking indeed, with waves crashing against the stone wall. It was hereabouts that the future Charles II put out to sea in the "Surprise," landing at Fecamp on the north coast of France and proceeding via Rouen to Paris; he was to remain in exile until after the death of Cromwell, returning to England and being crowned in 1660. The MW officially ends at the breakwater and if you have some energy to spare it's certainly worth walking its full length to enjoy superb views across the harbour, out to sea, and inland towards the South Downs. It's a great climax to a really enjoyable walk. It then just remains for you to retrace to (D) and follow the signed path which goes over the harbour gates – you may be held up when the gates open for passing harbour traffic – and forward to arrive at the A259 Albion Street. By turning right along this street and shortly left up the B2167 you reach the entrance to **Southwick Station** with frequent trains to Worthing and Brighton. The pleasant centre of Southwick is just north of the station.

GOOD TO KNOW

Start: Rowland's Castle Station. Finish: Southwick Station.

Total mileage: 58.5.

Difficulty: Moderate, strenuous in places.

Stages: Stoughton (R) 5, West Dean (RAB) 10, Eastdean Hill for East Dean (RA) 14, Eartham Wood 17, A29 Whiteways Lodge (R) 22.25, Houghton (R) for Amberley Station (*) and Amberley (RA) 23.5, Arundel (*RAB) 27.25, Warningcamp for Burpham (RA) 28.25, Longfurlong Lane 33, Findon (RAB) 34.5, Maudlin Lane for Steyning (RAB) 40.5, Bramber (RAB) 41.5, Mile Oak Farm for Mile Oak (RB) 46.5, West Blatchington Windmill (RB) 50.25, Hove (The Drive) (*RAB) 51, Brighton (*RAB) 52.5, Hove (*RAB)

53.5, Southwick Station (*RAB) 58.5.
OS: OL8, OL10, OL11.

D1 Almost immediately beyond the crossing bear left along a clear path in the shade of trees, emerging and crossing a meadow, veering right to walk parallel with a ditch. You shortly reach a path junction, turning left, northwards, and walking all the way to the river bank, climbing steps to reach the embankment. Turn right along the embankment, reaching a path junction at the edge of trees. Fork right up the steps, continuing northwards along the path, going forward alongside a sports field to reach the road at Burpham, the George pub on the right and the church straight ahead. Return exactly the same way. (Total detour 2.5 miles)

D2 Turn right off the MW onto the signed path and follow it down through the trees. At the end turn left past a lodge, then right onto a metalled farm lane bringing you to Roger's Farm. Shortly before an entrance to the complex marked "Private," turn left opposite the greenhouse along a track then shortly fork right and veer left in front of the white house. Immediately beyond the white house there's a path junction (E). Bear right here up a signed narrow path between fences. You go straight over a path crossroads and, keeping to the path, pass through woods, then emerge and proceed between fields, passing to the right of a mast. Immediately beyond the mast you reach a T-junction of paths on West Hill. Enjoying really impressive views, turn left along the bridleway, going straight on along West Hill to a junction, diagonally to the right of which is High Salvington Windmill. To continue, turn left at the junction along Bost Hill, emerging from the woods to enjoy fine views towards Cissbury Ring. You descend, veering right to reach the Bost Hill car park which is to your left, and immediately beyond the car park bear left along a narrow dirt track keeping the vegetation just to your right. Follow the track north-westwards, going over a signed path crossroads and then soon arriving back at (E) by the white house at Roger's Farm, retracing from here to the MW. (Total detour 2.5 miles)

D3 Having turned right off the MW, follow the track to the car park. Go straight on past the car park, dipping slightly, and continuing through the gate to immediately reach a signed path junction. Take the path signed straight on, aiming for a gate at the foot of the steep hill, passing through the gate and carrying on uphill, going forward to climb steps as the gradient intensifies. You go straight over the outer ring and continue up the steps to reach the inner ring. Go straight over again, onto a green path which takes you unerringly to the trig point at the summit of the Iron Age hillfort of Cissbury Ring. Return the same way. (Total detour 1.25 miles)

V1 Turn left at the signed T-junction (rather than right with the MW) and follow the path downhill through the trees to reach a narrow metalled lane; you turn right up this lane and in just over a mile come to Up Marden village. Just opposite Hill Farm, a little before the post box, turn left up a signed path across a field which brings you to the churchyard and church. Return the same way to the lane. Turn right onto the lane then almost immediately left down a signed path which skirts Hill Farm then descends to woodland. Follow the obvious path through the woods, which are fantastic for bluebells in spring. Near the end of the wood there's a path fork; take the left fork and go forward to exit the wood and continue as signed across a field, heading for a prominent house. You reach a path T-junction, turning left onto a bridleway and descending. At the bottom of the dip, roughly 220 yards from where you joined the bridleway, turn right along a signed footpath, keeping a broad field to your right. Continue on the obvious field path, ignoring a right path fork and going on into the woods. Now simply follow the clear woodland path, ignoring crossing tracks, ascending steadily and enjoying a further profusion of bluebells. You go forward to a clear track and now head downhill, exiting the woods and arriving at a road, turning right to enter Stoughton. To continue straight on along the MW, turn hard left just by Old Bartons to pick up the MW and proceed north-eastwards towards Stoughton Down. Of course you may wish to detour into the village in order to explore it, enjoy a pub drink or meal, and/or embark on route variation V2, described below. (Extra 3.5 miles)

V2 Head briefly south-westwards from the village centre along the road towards Walderton, then between Jeremy's and Tythe Barn House, turn left up a signed bridleway, ascending steeply. You enter woodland and continue uphill through the woods, then at the top, roughly three quarters of a mile from Stoughton, reach a left forking *path. Turn left along this path which takes you past the Devil's Humps. Beyond the Devil's Humps continue along the track, turning right off it as bridleway-signed then at the next bridleway junction turn left and descend to reach a multi-track junction where you turn right to rejoin the main MW route. (Extra 1 mile)*

V3 Don't cross the A286 but turn left alongside it for roughly half a mile, until you reach West Dean Gardens signed to the right. By continuing beside the A286 and bearing first right you reach the Weald & Downland Open Air Museum, described more fully in the New Lipchis Way section, in a further half a mile. Retrace your steps briefly from the gardens but then turn left down the driveway signed for West Dean College. While you may wish to follow the main driveway all the way round to view the front of the college, the continuous route variation takes the first right driveway off the main driveway, passing immediately to the right – the rear – of the college building. Look out to the right for, and walk through, a green door signed for the church and enter the churchyard, walking up the path then left to arrive at the west door. Go forward to the exit gate at the west end of the churchyard and go straight on along Church Lane to be reunited with the MW. The part of the walk through the college grounds isn't a public right of way; if access to the college or through the green door is unavailable you'll need to return to the main road and continue back along it then take the first left road turn beyond the college entrance. This is Church Lane which soon reaches the church (to your left) then veers right to meet the MW. (Extra 1.25 miles)

V4 Instead of turning left off the road onto Stane Street as MW-signed, continue along the road for some 80 yards then bear left onto a signed bridleway. You pass some buildings that are to the left then continue along a good clear track that veers right, just south of east, and ascends steadily through the trees. You reach a signed bridleway junction, turning right (southwards) uphill, reaching, in 275 yards, a T-junction of tracks. Turn left here along the signed footpath which bends right and almost at once reaches a signed path fork. Here fork left to follow a good clear path that soon veers left, eastwards, then curls south-westwards. Suddenly superb views open out ahead and you pass the extraordinary Slindon Folly and trig point beside it. Your track then descends steeply to reach a track T-junction, where you turn left to arrive at a road by Court Hill Farm. Turn right here but in roughly 80 yards join an unsigned path going off to the left, parallel with the road, climbing steeply up through woods to reach a junction with Top Road. Bear left here and walk past the imposing Slindon College to Slindon village itself, 2.75 miles from the start of this variation. Follow Top Road past right turns down Church Hill (on which in 80 yards or so you'll find the church of St Mary, and just beyond it on the other side, an extraordinary thatched railway carriage in the grounds of Church House) and Dyers Lane, then turn left up Mill Lane – though by continuing along Top Road, becoming School Hill, downhill, you reach Slindon's delightful Forge café and shop. As Mill Lane veers sharply right, go straight on up a bridleway, soon getting super views especially to the left. You enter an area of woodland and begin to descend, ignoring a left fork and emerging onto grassland. Go straight over a path crossroads along an excellent path signed as a bridleway to Bignor which proceeds in a straight line. At the signed path junction go straight over and onwards, the path a clear green track through open fields. You climb gently and steadily, crossing a track, veering very slightly right; go straight on along the path through the trees, ignoring paths soon coming in from the left and right and also ignoring two signed paths going off left. The woodland recedes on the right and you arrive at a T-junction at Gumber Corner. Turn right to rejoin the mapped MW. (Extra 3 miles)

V5 Continue across Hove Park in exactly the same direction as The Droveway had been following, and cross Goldstone Crescent, going straight over along a metalled continuation of The Droveway, ascending eastwards to cross Dyke Road straight over and descend along The Drove. Ignore the left fork of Hampstead Road but go straight on very steeply downhill under the railway bridge and on along South Road to reach the A23 Preston Road. Cross over Preston Road and turn left beside it. Just opposite a deli there's a gateway into the Preston Manor complex but if it's shut, go on a little and turn right up Preston Drove then shortly right again into the complex, with separate driveways for the church and manor. Having visited them, make your way via the path just to the left of the front entrance to Preston Manor to follow a path beside the back (southern) end of the manor then at the far end turn left and shortly right into the lovely walled garden. On reaching the centre of the garden turn left, exiting the walled garden and going forward along a path which passes the so-called Preston Twins, a pair of 400-year-old elms, possibly the oldest surviving English elms in the world, though in 2017 one suffered a partial collapse. At the end of the path you reach the A23 Preston Road again. Cross over it and turn right, following beside it to reach South Road although it's worth detouring a few yards further on to see the lovely No.199, home of the Guerrand Hermes Foundation for Peace. Now follow South Road past some excellent flint houses and then uphill under the railway. Immediately beyond the railway bridge turn left up Miller's Road, veering right and going forward into Highcroft Villas, reaching a crossroads junction with Dyke Road. Turn left down this road, in 300 yards or so reaching the Booth Museum of Natural History. Now cross Dyke Road, detouring left if you wish to enjoy the lovely Dyke Road Gardens, then return up Dyke Road on the gardens side and, opposite Highcroft Villas, turn left down The Upper Drive. Cross Old Shoreham Road and take the left fork along Wilbury Villas, crossing the railway and arriving at Cromwell Road. Turn left along Cromwell Road, now reunited with the MW. (Extra 1 mile)

7 NEW LIPCHIS WAY

T he New Lipchis Way (NLW), is a superb walk, combining fine woodland rambling, tremendous downland walking and then a beautiful waterside stroll – truly something for everyone, ranging from very strenuous to very easy. Its name is both rather inelegant and misleading. The reason for the name is clear enough in the sense that it begins at Liphook and proceeds to Chichester – should it not therefore have been called the New Lipchich Way? – but it certainly doesn't have the same ring as, say, the South Downs Way or the Monarch's Way. It's also slightly misleading in the sense that it doesn't end at Chichester but then goes the extra mile – well, eight extra miles – to end at West Wittering near the sea.

Starting from **Liphook Station**, the NLW heads out of Liphook south-eastwards along Midhurst Road, then strikes out eastwards/ south-eastwards into thick woodland, briefly overlapping with the Sussex Border Path and the Serpent Trail (these two routes themselves overlapping here!) and passing from Hampshire into West Sussex. You now proceed predominantly south-eastwards (though for a time veering west of south) across the thickly wooded Stanley Common; this is lovely well-signed woodland walking, through a mixture of birch, pine, oak and sweet chestnut trees between 50 and 120 years old, with an understorey of bracken and bilberry. Using clear woodland tracks, the NLW drops down to the hamlet of **Elmers Marsh** and crosses a road. By turning left along it and first left just beyond Lower Lodge Farm, you reach Shulbrede Priory, described more fully in the Sussex Border Path section, but the round trip from the NLW is 3 miles. By turning right along the road you reach the Hollycombe Steam Collection, this detour involving a round trip of just under 2 miles and better accessed from the Serpent Trail. The NLW, though, goes straight over this road, the rural feel soon interrupted somewhat by an electricity substation just beside the route. However you then find yourself once more in delightful woodland, heading eastwards through Hartley Green Copse, and veering south-eastwards to pass Upper North Park Farm, a Grade II listed building which dates from the 17th century; its exterior consists of a mix of exposed timbers,

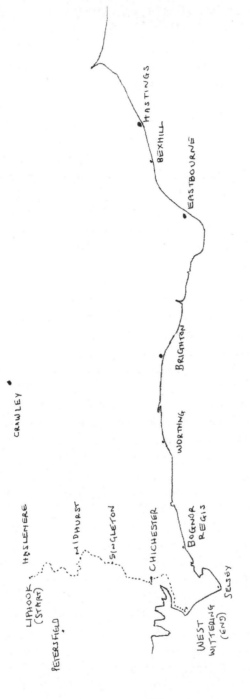

Wealden sandstone rubble and tile-hanging. Sadly it isn't open to the public.

You're now facing some formidably high wooded hills, and after skirting the east edge of woodland, heading south, you're then signed up a steep wooded hillside. You suddenly feel rather insignificant and small, hemmed in as you are by the hills both ahead and behind you, but it is indeed satisfying, as you ascend, to look back at the fine scenery you've already passed through to this point, still so early in the walk. You then have to labour up a possibly very muddy forest track – even in late summer when I tackled it, the mud was atrocious – beyond which a narrow road brings you onto Woolbeding Common. You're here overlapping very briefly with another segment of the Serpent Trail, and now enjoying undoubtedly the finest part of the walk so far and one of the best bits of the whole route. Woolbeding Common is a classic example of a lowland heath landscape created when early man cleared the forests around 5000 years ago. This particular area of heath, standing on a greensand ridge, boasts not only heather – at its brilliant best in August – but gorse, lichen, birch and bilberry. It supports a great variety of wildlife, with birds that include the nightjar, stonechat, yellowhammer and tree pipit, insects including tiger beetles and a profusion of bees in summer, and reptiles including the common lizard and our only venomous snake, the adder, easily recognised with the dark zigzag stripe along its back. As well as enjoying the wildlife and plant life, you can savour sensational views to the west, stretching as far as Butser Hill on the South Downs. Arguably these are the best views on your entire NLW walk. An unremarkable woodland walk along the plateau past Scotland Farmhouse is then followed by a really superb westward march along a path across more open parts of the common, easy to follow and with further breathtaking views, and then a steep descent to cross the Midhurst road.

Beyond this crossing the character of the walk begins to change, as you head south-westwards past Woolhouse Farm and along generally wide woodland tracks. You pass an attractive weir and as you continue just west of south, you cross Stedham Lane and walk across a meadow; you now have water for company, first a stream and then the river Rother, one of the major rivers of West Sussex and the widest and longest river in that county that doesn't flow into the sea. Just to confuse river watchers, there are two river Rothers in Sussex, one in West Sussex and another in East Sussex. The West Sussex one, which you can now enjoy and will see more of as you proceed, actually rises in Hampshire. Your riverside walk brings you shortly to the pretty village of Iping with its 19th century church (declared by Pevsner to be a "heavy, naïve sandstone building: not a lot to be said for it") just beside the route, as well as a five-arch bridge, old cottages and mill. Begging Elmers Marsh's pardon, this is the first settlement of any size since you set out from Liphook. The steeply wooded hillsides and heights of Woolbeding Common now seem a very long way away as you head eastwards along field paths and then beside the Rother again, observing the 17th century six-arch river bridge as you reach **Stedham**. Stedham, accessed in just 150 yards or so by turning right along the road carried by the bridge and going uphill, boasts a long street of brick and sandstone buildings, very typical of this part of Sussex; among the best are Myrtle Cottage on the right and the Old Ale House to the left, while in The Alley, a semi-circular street forking left but returning to the main street, you'll find the fine Old Bakehouse. Stedham's most prominent buildings, off the road to the left between the NLW and the village centre, are adjacent to one another: the church of St James with a Gothic-style 17th century tower, adjacent Saxon or pre-Saxon stone tombs and a hollow yew believed to be 2500 years old, and the impressive 17th century partially-timbered Stedham Hall which lies to the north of the church.

The NLW turns left over the bridge and after passing the fine house Bridgefoot now turns right along a path which follows immediately beside the Rother all the way to Woolbeding Bridge. In fine weather, this provides some of the loveliest riverside walking in Sussex. You soon pass very close to Stedham Hall, a fine sight across the river, and shortly you reach the beautiful waterfall by Stedham Mill, the mill house dating back to the late 18th century. From the mill you continue on a path along the fringes of Woolbeding Wood which lies to your left. It is in fact possible, at a signed path junction a couple of hundred yards or so beyond the mill – the NLW sign pointing straight ahead at this junction – to bear left, using steps to ascend to and follow a more elevated parallel path through the woods. The signed NLW route simply continues along the valley bottom and emerges from the trees to cross a meadow. Current

OS mapping suggests that the elevated route is the correct course of the NLW and I think it's actually preferable: the views through the trees are delightful and the woodland path is easy to follow and not the least claustrophobic. In due course, this path veers downhill to arrive in the meadow and meet the signed NLW route onto which you turn left. Note that the signed NLW route through the meadow doesn't even show on OS maps as a proper path, but fear not: this land is owned by the National Trust and responsible walkers are welcome. The meadow is quite delightful, and in the spring there is a profusion of beautiful wild flowers, with hosts of bluebells, buttercups and cow parsley. The meadow walk ends when you arrive at the medieval triple-arch Woolbeding Bridge bearing the Midhurst road, and the NLW turns right to go over the bridge, crossing to the right bank of the Rother. However it's easy enough to detour here to the lovely buildings of Woolbeding, turning left onto the road and simply following it for roughly half a mile. You'll then arrive at the church of All Hallows, which boasts a Saxon nave and early 18th century tower, and, adjoining the church, the largely 18th century Woolbeding Hall. A little beyond the church along the road are the 26-acre Woolbeding Gardens. These were created over some 40 years by the late Sir Simon Sainsbury and his partner Stewart Grimshaw, the highlights including formal "garden rooms" divided by clipped hedges, a water garden with grotto, Chinese bridge and ruined chapel, and a particularly fine ornamental vegetable garden. Note that to visit the gardens you need to pre-book.

Beyond Woolbeding Bridge the NLW heads for Midhurst but takes a considerably more roundabout route than the direct road walk. Initially, after flirting briefly with the Rother, it veers north again, and for this next section overlaps with the so-called Rother Walk, which is extremely well signed so route finding won't be a problem. Having risen away from the river, you walk across a large sloping field from which there's a quite exquisite view to the buildings of Woolbeding below, but then veer south-eastwards back towards the river again and remain close to it all the way to the A272. You then emerge at the A272 at **Midhurst**, turning right alongside this road and soon passing the bus stand from which a left turn takes you along a path offering a detour D1 to the ruins of Cowdray House and along the fringes of Cowdray Park to Easebourne. Cowdray House dates from the 16th century and was second only to Hampton Court in terms of scale of Tudor mansions, but was devastated by fire in 1793 and never rebuilt. The ruins however have become a major attraction in themselves, being painted by Turner and Constable, and part of the complex, including a tea room, is open to the public. Easebourne (pronounced Ezbourne) contains a former Augustinian priory dating from 1238, the Priory church of St Mary with 11th and 12th century features, and many lovely houses of timber and distinctive local stone. It has one particular curiosity, opposite the church, that is the Private Byepass Bridge adjacent to the main road, which was designed for horse traffic.

The route of the NLW is somewhat debatable from the bus stand. There is signage to suggest that the NLW should bypass Midhurst centre via the Cowdray ruins and accordingly that is set out below as a "Note" to D1. However, the mapped and recommended route continues beyond the stand up the A272, North Street, dominated by its Angel Hotel but including several Georgian facades and a good range of shops and places to eat. H.G. Wells lived for a time in what is now a restaurant on this street, just north of the Angel Hotel. One of the real joys of Midhurst is its variety of independent shops and cafes – there is a delightfully old-fashioned feel about the town, and it all feels a bit like a town centre as it really used to be before the rise of the out-of-town superstores. There is mercifully no sign of those around Midhurst – yet! I suggest you walk straight up North Street (becoming Rumbolds Hill), past the Knockhundred Row turning on your left, to the Wheatsheaf. Pass to the left of it down Wool Lane, where No.3 and Wool Cottage with its overhangs are a particular delight; at the end, bear left briefly along West Street to admire the 1660 timber-framed building on the opposite side. Retrace to, and turn right along, Knockhundred Row, with its tiny museum, veering right and descending gently along South Street to the old town, passing the part-13th century church of St Mary which is to your left. Here you could detour left, going past the main church entrance and forward up St Ann's Hill, through a gateway beyond, then continuing up a path to reach in a few yards, on the hilltop to your right, the remains of a Norman castle. Return the same way and whether you've detoured or not you can enjoy the many fine buildings in the neighbourhood of the church including the timber-framed Spread Eagle which dates back to 1430, the 1550's Market House, and the delightful assembly of old houses, some 18th century, around Edinburgh Square. The mapped NLW then continues via South Street to South Pond, once a breeding ground for fish and later a millpond for fulling cloth, bearing left opposite the pond to leave the town.

The NLW heads eastwards, veering south-eastwards, from Midhurst, initially along the Wharf and then a path, staying above the Rother but enjoying good views towards it. You then cross Selham Road and veer briefly south-westwards along the edge of woodland, before turning south-eastwards, first through trees then open country to arrive at a bridleway T-junction. Here you bear right, south-westwards, onto and across Heyshott Common, an area of quite delightful mainly coniferous woodland, albeit less lofty and steep-sided than the woods around Woolbeding Common. You cross over a bridge which seems somewhat incongruous in this particular setting, but under it is a track, actually the course of the old Pulborough-Midhurst railway line which is covered in more detail in the Serpent Trail section. The course of the track hereabouts is so good it could easily be converted into a cycle track and footpath. Back on the NLW, you continue south-westwards across the common, overlapping briefly again with the Serpent Trail, taking care to follow the signage out of the wood. You emerge from the trees and briefly follow the road linking Heyshott Green and Selham, then proceed southwards across fields to the brick-and-flint village of **Heyshott** with its pretty 13th century flint church of St James immediately adjoining the path. This is a good spot to rest and gird up the loins, for there then follows a huge climb out of the village, your path still heading southwards and aiming unmistakeably for the South Downs escarpment. The gradient is gentle to begin with then gets steeper and steeper, increasing in intensity as you enter the woods. Before disappearing into the trees you should pause to get your breath back and enjoy sensational views back the way you've come; you won't get such good views northwards again on this walk, so make the most of these. It's only when you emerge from the woods that the gradient eases and you reach the escarpment top, crossing (but not joining) the South Downs Way. Sadly the profusion of trees limits the views massively, and it's undeniably disappointing, having gained all the height, to find yourself losing it almost immediately, as you continue southwards through the woods on a broad track.

However, do not despair. After a mile of woodland descent you emerge and veer south-westwards to climb onto Levin Down, passing round rather than over the highest point, but you're unlikely to get into trouble for detouring up to it. I'd suggest that Levin Down is one of the best kept secrets of this part of Sussex, not attracting the popularity or the visitor numbers of its very near neighbour The Trundle which awaits you just the other side of Singleton, the next village. Levin Down is a chalk hillside covered in natural scrubby grassland, its name thought to be derived from "Leave-alone hill," it being too steep for the plough or intense agriculture. It's a Site of Special Scientific Interest, with a wealth of plant life that includes lady's bedstraw, pyramidal orchid, round-headed rampion and marjoram, and birds you might find here include the yellowhammer, buzzard, garden warbler and kestrel. The ascent of Levin Down is admittedly a bit of a slog, the correct path not always easy to discern, but your reward on reaching the highest point is a quite fantastic view which stretches as far as the sea and the Isle of Wight. Then you begin descending again, and in fact drop down steeply to reach a road onto which you turn right to enter **Singleton**. This is one of the loveliest villages in West Sussex, with flint cottages, a small green and pond and church of St John Evangelist with Saxon tower and what Pevsner describes as "extraordinary tall" nave walls that date back to the 11th century. The NLW, rather than veering right with the road, goes straight on at St Francis Cottage and follows the bottom village street westwards then by the Partridge inn turns south to pass the west side of the church and exit the village. However I recommend that, in order you can see more of the lovely houses and village green at Singleton, you veer right at St Francis Cottage to arrive at the green, then turn left just beyond the green to reach the bottom village street at the Partridge. The church and resumption of the NLW are reached by crossing straight over along a lane leading shortly to the north-west corner of the churchyard where a sign reassures you. However by continuing westwards along the bottom village street beyond the Partridge and following it to its end, here turning left to walk beside the A286 and then bearing first left, you almost immediately on your right reach the Weald & Downland Open Air Museum. The detour is roughly a quarter of a mile each way. Founded in 1970, the museum boasts a wonderful collection of reconstructed houses, barns and workshops from centuries ago, with numerous displays of traditional country crafts and industries. There are now over 50 buildings including a Tudor market hall, plumber's workshop, medieval farmstead, brick-drying shed, Victorian village school, Victorian labourers' cottages, wind pump, medieval shop and toll cottage. At the working Tudor kitchen in the 16th century Winkhurst Farm you can taste some of the food from that period, including griddle bread and pottage. Meanwhile, West Dean Gardens, described in the Monarch's Way section, are just over half a mile down the A286 beyond the museum turning.

Beyond Singleton Church the NLW, now on the same course as the West Sussex Literary Trail, continues steeply southwards up a field-edge path, then, after a short road walk up Knight's Hill and a road crossing, climbs to the topmost ring of the site of the massive Iron Age Trundle hill fort. Overlapping briefly here with the Monarch's Way and Sussex Hospices Trail as well as the West Sussex Literary Trail, you follow the ring clockwise, enjoying superb views to Chichester and the Isle of Wight; on a really clear day you may be able to see beyond Brighton and as far as the Seven Sisters. Your route veers towards the hilltop mast, then strikes out westwards, descending to a road/track junction (where the Sussex Hospices Trail leaves you) and continuing on along a lovely hilltop path. Shortly the Monarch's Way forks right and drops to West Dean but, continuing to hold hands with the West Sussex Literary Trail, you keep straight on, enjoying fabulous views towards the wooded heights of the Kingley Vale Nature Reserve, then descend to a path crossroads.

The West Sussex Literary Trail now bears left to follow an ordinary footpath southwards to Lavant, but the NLW goes straight on and joins the course of the old Midhurst-Chichester railway line. The line opened in July 1881 and closed to passengers in 1935, although freight services along the full length of the line continued until 1953. North of this point, the line had to climb towards a gap in the South Downs before descending to Midhurst, and three tunnels were needed, one as long as 744 yards; two of these tunnels were used during World War 2 for the storage of ammunition. After the line closed to passengers, freight trains continued to run along the Lavant-Chichester section until as comparatively recently as 1991. Thankfully the whole of the section from just south of West

Dean to Chichester has reopened as the Centurion Way cycle/ walkway, providing a lovely walk or cycle ride with excellent views to The Trundle and Kingley Vale. The NLW follows the course of the Centurion Way southwards all the way to the Centurion Way's finish at Bishop Luffa School just west of Chichester. With the exception of the built-up area of **Mid Lavant**, where the Centurion Way is forced along roads running parallel with (and close to) the course of the old line, you're actually following the old line exactly as it was. Although by definition it's very level walking, there's plenty of interest in the form of reminders of the old line, such as the old station at Lavant – an impressive affair, as all the station buildings were on this line, with timber-framing and moulded stucco panels – and two or three impressive brick overbridges. The scene is further enlivened by some modern sculpture by David Kemp and, as you near Chichester, the nearby Brandy Hole Copse, a kind of nature reserve in miniature. Despite the proximity of Chichester, the walk has a lovely rural feel throughout, though the heights of Woolbeding Common and Levin Down seem a long way back! At Bishop Luffa School the NLW heads eastwards via Westgate, over the Avenue De Chartres and along a footpath beside a stream, then veers southwards to pass a less than elegant multistorey car park and arrive at Chichester Station. A description of the highlights of **Chichester** is given in the Sussex Hospices Trail section.

Beyond the station the NLW goes southwards to very shortly arrive at the Chichester Canal Basin, a delightful spot with a good pub and café, and a variety of canal craft on the water. You may feel tempted to have a canal ride yourself, and indeed boat trips are available from the basin, but be warned: the narrow boats move slowly, and you may make faster progress on foot! Now heading first just west of south, then veering south-eastwards, you proceed to follow the towpath along the right bank of what is the Chichester Canal, a branch of the Portsmouth & Arundel Canal which in turn linked Ford with Chichester Harbour. The Portsmouth & Arundel Canal opened in 1823 and provided a linkage with other waterways to form a complete Portsmouth-London waterway route; one of the through cargoes was gold bullion that was transported from Portsmouth to the Bank of England, protected by armed guards. The 1.5 mile branch from Hunston to Chichester was designed to accommodate vessels up to 85ft long and 100 tons in weight.

The main canal wasn't a success, much of it seeing no carriage of cargo beyond the 1840's, but the section from Chichester Harbour to Hunston and the branch to Chichester was more successful and continued to be used until 1906. Your canalside stroll is quite delightful walking, and indeed is extremely popular with walkers, so don't expect to be on your own. In fact you may meet more walkers on the 1.5-mile walk between Chichester and Hunston than on the whole of your walk from Liphook to Midhurst. There's a wonderful variety of birds, and besides the mallard, coot and swan, you may also see heron, kingfisher, whitethroat, common sandpiper, spotted flycatcher and greater spotted woodpecker. There's an overlap with the Sussex Hospices Trail, this trail coming down to join you from the nearby St Wilfrid's Hospice at the very start of its long circular journey that extends as far north-eastwards as Etchingham, not far from the border with Kent.

At **Hunston**, where you meet the B2145 Chichester-Selsey road (and lose the Sussex Hospices Trail), you swing sharply south-westwards to join the course of the "through" canal route, following its left bank. The walking remains just as good; look out, a couple of hundred yards beyond the B2145, for the remains of the old drawbridge which once carried the Chichester-Selsey railway (the so-called Selsey Tram, described more fully in the England Coast Path section) over the canal. You may be lucky enough to see a family of foxes, and even a terrapin or two, close to the site of the old bridge. You cross the B2201 at Donnington and continue along the left bank to reach and cross the A286. Here your lovely towpath walk effectively ends as you switch to the right bank and proceed initially along a path then the metalled approach road for the yacht basin. You follow the road all the way to the end, then cross the canal at Salterns Lock close to its meeting with Chichester Harbour.

From here seawards all the way to the broad green of Snow Hill via **Itchenor**, the NLW overlaps with the England Coast Path, and a full description of the walk is given in that section. The NLW leaves the harbour and the coast path (which continues to reach the neck of the superb East Head in just under half a mile) at a 4-way signed footpath junction at the front edge of Snow Hill. It bears left, just south of east, along a metalled lane then a grassy footpath between fences, then another metalled lane; it then bears right at a T-junction, almost immediately reaching a T-junction with Pound

Road. The NLW turns left along Pound Road to shortly arrive at the main street at **West Wittering**, its arrival here marking the end of the route. However by detouring right along Pound Road you'll reach, in 140 yards on your right, the beautiful 12th century church of St Peter. The church boasts a probably Saxon font and a stone carved with a Saxon cross on each side which may have been the original gable cross of around 740 AD from the earliest days of Christianity here. Having made your way, via the church or not, to the main village street, it just remains for you to catch a bus home, with buses back to Chichester departing from both sides of the street. Bear in mind, however, that on summer weekends the road between Chichester and West Wittering is frequently so busy with traffic that buses may be very badly delayed, so you may find your end-of-walk refreshment celebrations lasting longer than you expected!

GOOD TO KNOW
Start: Liphook Station. Finish: West Wittering.
Total mileage: 38.5.
Difficulty: Strenuous in places.
Stages: Elmers Marsh 3, Stedham (R) 8.5, Midhurst (RAB) 12, Heyshott (R) 16, Singleton (RAB) 20, Mid Lavant (RB) 24, Chichester (*RAB) 28.5, Hunston (RB) 30, Itchenor (RA) 35, West Wittering (RAB) 38.5.
OS OL33, OL10, OL8.

D1 From the bus stand follow the obvious, dead-straight path heading just south of east over the marshy grass and across the Rother to a T-junction with a driveway, the ruins directly in front of you and the visitor amenities accessible to the right. To reach Easebourne (1 mile from start of detour) turn left along the driveway, ignoring the left fork at the footpath sign and continuing north-eastwards along an obvious track, passing some gates and rising gently with good views to Cowdray Park opening out to the right. You pass a café and then the Priory which are to your left and arrive at the A272. Cross over, turning left under the Byepass Bridge and then very shortly right, following the village street past the pub. I suggest you walk as far as Ez Cottage which is to the right, passing the lovely timbered houses

Nos. 17-19, which are also to the right. Return to the main road and turn right along it, veering left and descending a little. Shortly, at the timbered Bunch Cottage, cross over and go straight on up the path leading to the church, then return to the main road. Retrace your steps to the Cowdray ruins and turn right, back onto the path towards the bus stand, crossing back over the Rother (A). To rejoin the mapped NLW simply continue your retrace to the bus stand. (Total detour 2.5 miles)

NOTE: To follow the signed (as opposed to the mapped) NLW, having crossed back over the Rother at (A) turn left along a path beside it, veering right and reaching a path junction. Here leave the riverside by forking right, uphill, climbing steps; at the next fork, go right again up further steps, passing (and possibly detouring to) the castle ruin. Continue on to the gate, passing through it and following St Ann's Hill, going forward to the church and South Street to link with the mapped route. (Mileage difference negligible)

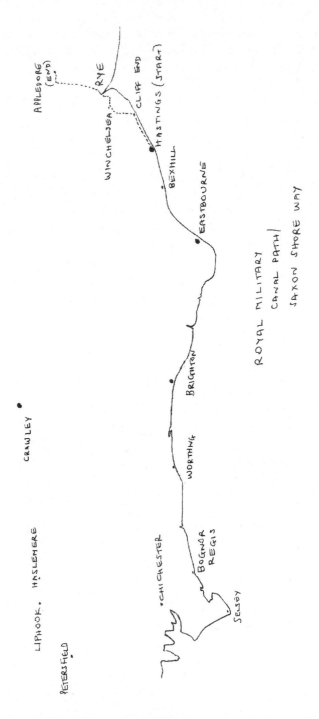

8 ROYAL MILITARY CANAL PATH/
SAXON SHORE WAY

Here we have two paths for the price of one; there is so much overlap between the Saxon Shore Way and the Royal Military Canal Path in Sussex that it makes perfect sense to describe them in a single section. That said, the paths are very different in origin and overall character. The so-called Saxon Shore, not to be confused with the American post-rock band, was a line of fortifications built along the coastline during the period of the Roman Empire, to deter Saxon invaders who came from the southern region of what is now Denmark. The Saxon Shore Way, running from Hastings to Gravesend in Kent for a total distance of 163 miles, attempts to trace the coast of south-east England as it was in those times, visiting the sites of the Saxon Shore fortifications that were constructed before the North Kent marshes and Romney Marsh existed. The Royal Military Canal Path is much shorter, running from Cliff End, just east of Pett, to Seabrook between Hythe and Folkestone in Kent, a distance of 28 miles, following the Royal Military Canal almost throughout and pretty much end to end. The canal, linking Cliff End and Hythe, was built in 1806-7 in response to the military threat posed to England in the Napoleonic Wars, and a road was built behind it, the Royal Military Road, to allow fast transport of troops and equipment. You'll note however from maps that there is in fact an overlap between the canal and stretches of the river Brede south-west of Rye, and the river Rother to the north-east of Rye. The canal was just 30ft wide at most, and William Cobbett, author of *Rural Rides*, was extremely disparaging about its effectiveness to deter potential invaders who would have already negotiated the Rhine and the Danube on their travels!

As stated, there is considerable overlap between the two paths in Sussex. The Saxon Shore Way starts further west, at Hastings; at Cliff End the Saxon Shore Way leaves the coast and joins up with the Royal Military Canal Path in a few yards then stays with the Royal Military Canal Path all the way to the Kent border. It's only on entry to Kent that the two paths diverge and follow very different journeys through that county. It makes sense to continue the route description by following the Royal Military Canal Path to Appledore, where there's a good range of amenities including a station on the Brighton-Ashford line.

I suggest you treat **Hastings Station** as the starting point of the Saxon Shore Way, walking down Havelock Road and at the end turning left (not hard left) along Wellington Place, going via the underpass to the Breeds Place roundabout. From here you simply overlap with the England Coast Path all the way to Cliff End, although you should note that a couple of Saxon Shore Way waymarks suggest a variance with the England Coast Path – see the England Coast Path section for fuller description and in particular route variation V8 for that section. I propose to begin this section's description at **Cliff End** where the Royal Military Canal Path begins and almost immediately joins hands with the Saxon Shore Way.

The mapped Saxon Shore Way does in fact keep its overlap with the England Coast Path just a little way beyond the houses of Cliff End, then turns sharply inland, leaving the promenade to cross the coast road at grid ref TQ894138 and go forward to meet the Royal Military Canal Path. The Royal Military Canal Path, meanwhile, starts by striking north-eastwards from the main road linking Pett and Winchelsea at Cliff End – regular buses serve this spot, grid ref TQ888134. Immediately you find yourself walking beside the old canal and in half a mile or so it's joined by the Saxon Shore Way. For convenience I'll abbreviate these now wholly overlapping paths (as far as the Sussex/Kent border) as RMC. Your route now veers north, keeping the canal immediately to the left, and proceeds almost due north for nearly a mile and a half, then veers north-eastwards with lovely views to the Hog Hill Windmill, Wickham Manor and the wooded hillside around Winchelsea – all of which feature in the 1066 Country Walk. I walked this section on a chilly but clear mid-November day where the colours of the trees decorating the hillside of Wickham Cliff to the north were absolutely stunning.

Sticking to the canal, and in due course enjoying good views to the Strand Gate and other fine buildings of Winchelsea, you arrive at **Sea Road** which links the A259 with Winchelsea Beach. Here is your obvious opportunity to visit the lovely old town of **Winchelsea** (described more fully in the 1066 Country Walk section), reached by turning left along Sea Road, going straight on alongside the A259 for a few yards then bearing left up Strand Hill.

The total detour is three quarters of a mile. Note there is a station at Winchelsea (reached by following the A259 round the village then up Station Road from the hairpin bend) but as it is over a mile from the RMC and trains are infrequent, catching a bus from the centre of Winchelsea may be a better option! The RMC turns right, eastwards, along Sea Road, soon veering north-eastwards; at the very sharp right bend you leave it, going straight on along a lane which then veers left and right to pass Castle Farm. Beyond the farm the RMC then strikes out just east of north along an obvious path through the flat fields of Castle Water Nature Reserve. The path veers just west of north and passes the impressive ruin of Camber Castle, although it's very easy to detour the short way across the grass to reach the castle. Camber Castle was constructed in 1539 on orders from Henry VIII, and at its peak of activity in 1542 it had a garrison of 42 men, but the main fortifications were abandoned and demolished a century later because of the encroachment of the marshland. Returning to the path you now continue towards Rye, veering just east of north again, keeping a fence to the left, and enjoying good views towards Rye and across the valley of the river Brede. You then veer right and follow parallel with a ditch to your right, but in just under three quarters of a mile from Camber Castle you reach a path fork junction (at the time of writing, not signed as such) where the RMC leaves the embankment and ditch and proceeds well to the west of the embankment towards Rye, keeping the river Brede (and canal) just to the left. You go forward to pass through a wooded area and arrive at a bridleway T-junction, bearing left along a wide stony track/bridleway to the Rye Harbour road. Turn left along it, then shortly right along the A259 into **Rye**; just before the river Tillingham bridge crossing you can detour left along a signed path to a railway crossing, immediately before which there's an excellent view of Rye's restored windmill.

According to the OS map, the RMC appears to pass through Rye via The Deals, Traders Passage and Watchbell Street, exiting the old town by descending past Rye Castle and Gun Garden to the A259 and crossing straight over along Rock Channel. However, I'm sure you'll want to explore Rye and may wish to catch a bus or train from here. Accordingly I recommend that where the A259 turns sharply right by the Tillingham bridge (now overlapping with the England Coast Path), you go straight on along Wish Street, then forward along Cinque Ports Street as far as the crossroads junction with Station Approach and Market Road. By turning left down Station Approach you reach the bus stands and railway station. If you wish to explore Rye, please see the England Coast Path section and a suggested described walk which starts and ends at this crossroads junction. To exit Rye and continue towards Appledore, you should head for Rye Castle then follow the England Coast Path directions from Rye Castle as far as the A259 New Road crossing of the Rother. Cross the bridge then while the England Coast Path turns right, you turn immediately left, just east of north, alongside the Rother, now overlapping with the Sussex Border Path at the very end of its journey from Emsworth. There's actually a potential problem just here: the underbridge crossing of the railway, a couple of hundred yards beyond the A259, may be impassable at high tide, so check high tide times before you set out. It may mean you have to spend extra time enjoying the delights of Rye, but that is no hardship!

Beyond the railway it's easy and pleasant rather than spectacular walking, as you follow a clear grassy embankment path beside the Rother, pausing to look back towards Rye and then looking out across the green pastures of Romney Marsh. Romney Marsh was originally a salt marsh but was reclaimed from the sea long ago and is now a mixture of arable land and grazing pasture, and home to the white-faced Romney Marsh sheep. The area is exceedingly rich in bird life, which may include wintering lapwings, golden plovers, migrant fieldfares, wagtails and nightingales. Some 2.75 miles upstream from Rye, you arrive at Iden Lock, one of the best features on the route; it was built in 1808 to link the Royal Military Canal with the Rother and ultimately the sea. Here the Sussex Border Path veers away to the left with the Rother while the RMC continues alongside the Royal Military Canal, sandwiched between the canal and the road, for half a mile north-eastwards. Just before the Kent/Sussex border, the Royal Military Canal Path and Saxon Shore Way part company. If you're planning on continuing along the Saxon Shore Way through Kent (or simply want to see where it meets the border), you need to look out very carefully for the Saxon Shore Way signpost below you to the left, turning hard left off the RMC path to drop to the road. You cross the road, go over a ditch and turn right to proceed parallel with the road for just over 150 yards, passing the border ditch that's clearly visible to the left (and noting the border signpost and boundary stone by the adjacent road), then, if you're so minded, striking out north-westwards towards a stark green hillside known as Stone Cliff and ploughing on to Gravesend many miles distant. The Royal Military Canal Path, however, continues between road (to the left) and canal (to the right), to cross the border – clearly identifiable thanks to the adjacent road signs and boundary stone – and continue on its way to Hythe. Unless you've specifically planned to continue along the Saxon Shore Way I recommend that rather than turning back you stick with the Royal Military Canal Path up to and beyond the border and continue along the clear path between road and canal to Appledore. The views to right and left offer contrasting scenes: to the right is lots more of Romney Marsh while to the left is the green hill which once formed part of what, before the marshes were drained, was the Isle of Oxney. On it is built the (since restored) 15th century church of Stone-in-Oxney, a delightfully photogenic building in a lovely setting, and it's clearly visible from your path. Just under 3 miles into Kent you reach a road on the edge of Appledore. At this point (A) we leave the Royal Military Canal Path although you may feel you want to follow it on towards Hythe and its end at Seabrook. By turning left at the junction (A) you immediately enter the very pretty village of **Appledore** with its brick, tile and timber houses, and fine church with battlemented tower and ornately carved west door. However by turning right at (A) and then veering sharp left, you can follow the road for just over a mile to **Appledore Station** with regular trains to Ashford, Rye and Hastings. Do check the trains are running and on time before leaving the village – the station is not the most congenial place to have to wait for very long!

GOOD TO KNOW
Start: Hastings Station. Finish: Appledore Station.
Total mileage: 18.5.
Difficulty: Strenuous to Cliff End then easy.
Stages: Cliff End (RAB) 6, Sea Road for Winchelsea (*RAB) 10, Rye (*RAB) 12, Appledore (R) 17.5, Appledore Station (*) 18.5.
OS 124, 125.

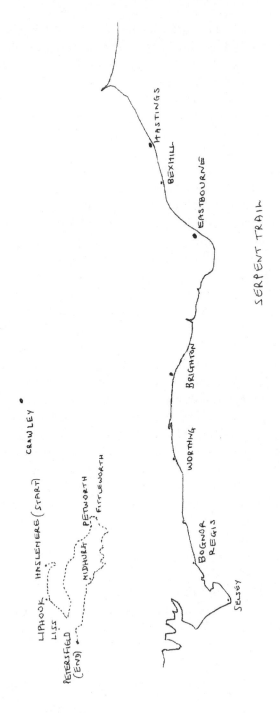

9 SERPENT TRAIL

The Serpent Trail (ST) isn't the longest name path going through Sussex, but is one of the most enjoyable and satisfying. Designed to provide a route across the greensand ridges of West Sussex north of the South Downs, it crosses a succession of commons with lovely mixed (though largely coniferous) woodland, gorse and heather, superb views and firm sandy tracks making for generally excellent walking. Its name is apposite for two reasons. Firstly its course is certainly serpentine, describing two very sizeable loops and creating a crude giant S, and in fact the start and finish of the walk are only a short train journey apart. Secondly the heathland terrain provides an ideal habitat for snakes and you may see a few of them especially in summer. The going is generally easy, with just a handful of stiff climbs, and most walkers will complete it comfortably within a week. The route is exceptionally well signed, far better than some other Sussex trails, and it's not uncommon, if you're overlapping with another name path, to find the ST signed but not the other! That said, it is essential to keep a watchful eye out for the signposts. A good deal of the ST passes through common land within which there are profusions of woodland. In prehistoric times, patches in dense forests were felled by Neolithic settlers to create clearings for hunting. The open heaths were later used by nobles for deer hunting, then commoners for grazing, but, when the land became unproductive for this purpose, bracken and woodland returned and fast-growing pines were planted. Much of this land abounds with paths and tracks, created by the various land users; just one wrong choice of path could send you miles out of your way, and it will be very difficult, especially in the midst of woodland, to establish landmarks necessary to get you back on the right route. That said, while there are a number of quite remote sections, amenities are never too far away with a number of bus routes, railway stations and pubs on or close to the trail itself, and at Petworth, round about the halfway mark, there's ample opportunity to replenish the rucksack with food and drink.

The trail begins at **Haslemere Station** and follows the main road (B2131) eastwards, with a short cut available via an alleyway, to reach Haslemere's charming High Street with its attractive houses and shops. You head south-eastwards out of the town through fields, then ascend through trees to cross the **B2131** again. Beyond that crossing you follow a track south-eastwards past High Barn Farm, veering southwards and gradually gaining height. The countryside is opening out very nicely with excellent views towards the North Downs, and ahead of you is Black Down, one of the major scenic highlights of the whole route. You reach Tennyson's Lane, so named because the poet Alfred, Lord Tennyson had a house, Aldworth House, on the slopes of Black Down; the Sussex Border Path passes its grounds. He lived there for the last 20 years of his life and wrote much of *Idylls Of The King*, based on Arthurian legend, in its back garden. You climb the lane steeply, then turn hard left off the lane and begin what is a lovely walk southwards on the east side of Black Down. Black Down, the highest ground in the whole of Sussex, is described by Nikolaus Pevsner as "a great whale-backed sandstone hill," by Keith Spence as the "nearest approach to a mountain in these parts...shaggily coated in trees like one of the foothills of the Jura," and by Tennyson himself as "exactly like Italy." The views to the left (eastwards) as you proceed are stunning and you should look out for a seat from which you can enjoy them in comfort! After what has been a steady climb the ground levels out and you proceed through the woods along the plateau. You reach a signed path junction by a small pool with a National Trust path going right, and by following this path briefly to the top of the rise and turning right just beyond that point along a further path you will shortly reach a trig point marking the rooftop of Sussex at 280 metres or 919ft. The views are slightly obscured by the surrounding trees but the main point to remember is that you're at the summit of all the Great Walks of Sussex! Returning to the ST the same way, you continue southwards and soon reach a path junction where you go left, dropping down to the so-called Temple of the Winds. There's no temple but there is a stone seat and topograph, as well as a really magnificent view to the South Downs escarpment including the masts of Glatting Beacon and the trees of Chanctonbury Ring. On clear days the views may extend much further.

The ST now swings northwards, immediately returning to the top of the ridge and following the west side of Black Down, its course enabling you to enjoy another, very different view. It's glorious walking along a firm sandy track, the nearby heather providing sensational colour in late summer, and it's a shame when you're signed left, north-westwards, off the top of the ridge and rapidly downhill to enter woodland. You're now sharing your route with the Sussex Border Path and will continue to see a great deal of it as far as Rake and indeed just beyond. You emerge from the woods and follow field paths, now dropping very steeply to just south of Valewood Farm House, the ST preferring a gentler zigzag descent; the Sussex Border Path descent is starker but provides a short cut. Now on the valley floor you skirt the buildings of Valewood Farm House and go forward to Stedlands Farm. You could walk back to Haslemere from here by forking right here up a signed public byway to Scotland Lane, bearing left then immediately right down a path leading to the B2131; turn left here and just keep going straight on to reach the station, 1.5 miles from Stedlands Farm. However the ST continues along well-signed paths and tracks westwards through the woods and past a weir, to reach the **A286** Haslemere-Midhurst road. You've now walked 7 miles but are actually as the crow flies just a mile and a half from where you started! There's here another opportunity to detour up the A286 for those 1.5 miles to access the amenities of **Haslemere**. Buses are available hereabouts to both Haslemere and Midhurst.

It's somewhat ironic that having lost so much height you face, beyond the A286 crossing, a very steep climb past houses. Your climb brings you onto Marley Common, part (along with Black Down) of the so-called Greensand Ridge landscape on the Surrey/West Sussex border, with its sandy soils, woodland and acid grassland, open heath and beautiful mixed woodland including a profusion of silver birch and chestnut. One of the National Trust's earliest countryside acquisitions, back in 1911, Marley Common was used for military training in World War 2 and suffered bad fires in the 1950's and 1960's but has been carefully restored in recent years, helped by the introduction of Galloway cattle. Birds you may see include woodlark, nightjar, Dartford warbler, nuthatch, woodcock, crossbill, meadow pipit, yellowhammer and woodpecker; in the spring there's a wealth of lovely wild flowers, and in the summer you should look out for brimstone butterflies. Once you've ascended onto the common it's a straightforward walk in a westerly direction, though take care not to miss a right fork which takes the ST away from the Sussex Border Path and continues over the common to a road junction. There follows a fast walk along a lane and then another, also important, right turn along a path that heads onto Linchmere Common. This is absolutely lovely walking, the path well signed with great views through the trees.

You go over the Hammer-Linchmere road and continue across Linchmere Common, carefully observing the signage, as your route makes use of tracks that, being situated in access land, aren't marked on OS maps as designated rights of way. You cross another road leading out of Linchmere (whose church and Shulbrede Priory, described in the Sussex Border Path section, are reached down this road to the left – the total round trip is 2.5 miles) and continue in a broadly westerly direction, going quite steeply downhill and now being briefly reunited with the Sussex Border Path as you reach the hill bottom at Lower Brookham. Having passed the buildings you now veer just east of south, climbing again and leaving the marked Sussex Border Path route. You pass through quite thick woodland, albeit enjoying good views through the trees, and again it's vital to observe the signage as you veer south-westwards again, dropping to a narrow valley and then proceeding onto the wooded Stanley Common. Not only are you now back with the Sussex Border Path briefly but also the New Lipchis Way which has just begun its journey from Liphook to West Wittering. However you lose the New Lipchis Way shortly, and again you should take care to observe the signage as the ST leaves the main track (and Sussex Border Path) and heads southwards then westwards across the thickly wooded common. You approach the Liphook-Midhurst road – the fascinating Hollycombe Steam Collection is just over half a mile up this road to the left – but the ST, in keeping with its name, snakes right just before the junction and then twists and turns through the woods roughly parallel with the road north-westwards to reach **Highfield Lane** just by its junction with Midhurst Road. **Liphook** and its station is reached by following Midhurst Road north-westwards for just under half a mile from the ST.

The ST, reunited with the Sussex Border Path, now follows a byway south-westwards from here for a mile and a half, and it is very quick easy walking, if rather dull, although it gets better at the end as you cross Liphook golf course. The course is one of the finest in southern England, very picturesque and beautifully kept, but beware of golf balls! The byway ends and you then follow a road to reach the B2070 by the Black Fox pub; the ST sociably passes immediately beside it, thereby providing you with your first on-route refreshment opportunity since leaving Haslemere. You then strike out westwards from the B2070 onto Chapel Common. Designated as an Area of Outstanding Natural Beauty, Chapel Common is another of the scenic highlights of the ST with its fine mixed woodland, open heaths providing superb views, and plant life which includes a variety of orchids. Expect company in fine weather! The Sussex Border Path, seeking to stay as faithful as possible to the border between Sussex and (at this point) Hampshire, continues northwards towards the railway but the ST heads westwards then southwards across the common; as it approaches the B2070 again it then darts off north-westwards over the common before veering southwards, parallel with and then along a byway taking you back to the B2070. The B2070 used to be the A3 London-Portsmouth road which explains the section of dual carriageway, most unusual for a rural B-road, just to the left as you return to it.

The ST then proceeds the short distance westwards to **Rake** beside the B2070, and you'll note that effectively you've created a crude M shape since crossing this road at the Black Fox. At Rake you're reunited with the Sussex Border Path. You briefly head southwards on the Rogate road away from the B2070 then join a path heading south-westwards initially past houses and then the attractive woodlands of Rake Hanger which is now a Site of Special Scientific Interest with a fine variety of trees including sessile oak, silver birch, whitebeam, rowan and several species of lichen. Note also a number of ponds to the left, which add to the beauty of the scene. There are fine views through the trees, and the path is clearly defined and well signed, making this a very enjoyable walk, but note that towards the end there's a fork junction where it's very important to observe the signage. At the **bottom of Rake Hanger** you emerge at a road, turning right onto it briefly then hard left, leaving the Sussex Border Path. You won't see the Sussex Border Path again until near the end of your journey, roughly 45 miles away, but as the crow flies, this next meeting point is barely 3 miles from here! If you're needing a train, Liss Station is 1.5 miles from here. To get there, stay on the road (rather than turning hard left off it) and shortly bear right onto Rogate Road, ascending to the B2070 at **Hill Brow**, crossing it and following the B3006 downhill to reach **Liss**. The B3006 actually passes the station.

In the course of tracing its S shape, the ST now changes direction and having headed predominantly south-westwards up till now, will be proceeding in a generally easterly direction – south-eastwards or north-eastwards – for virtually all of the next 20 miles or so. Initially you proceed south-eastwards along lovely sandy tracks, obviously well used by bikers, through the woodlands below Combe Hill. After making a stiff climb you follow an attractive path through the woods of Tullecombe then follow a road south-eastwards before striking out north-eastwards along a driveway below Fyning Hill and then south-eastwards again along the edge of Rondle Wood. This is superb walking on a good path with lovely views northwards back towards Chapel Common. You arrive at a road at the hamlet of **Borden** where your direction changes from predominantly south-eastwards to north-eastwards. You enjoy another woodland walk along firm surfaces to reach and follow Borden Lane, emerging and following firstly a farm lane and then field around Kingsham Farm. Now proceeding steadily north-eastwards you pass through Kingsham Wood and then across Iping Marsh, which is as potentially squelchy as the name implies. However the views improve as, having crossed Milland Road and passed an isolated graveyard – there was a church here which has now been demolished – you rise and skirt the northern edge of woodland. Somewhat messy walking follows as you negotiate a cluster of buildings of Titty Hill and follow a rather rough path to reach and cross a road beyond which you enter the woodlands of Stedham Marsh, and again you could be in for some juicy walking during and after wet weather. However after you've crossed Linch Road just south of Redford things improve hugely with a steep ascent, first up a driveway then narrow green paths, onto Woolbeding Common. The climb is the stiffest so far, but the reward is a glorious view across the common, stretching to Butser Hill on the South Downs and beyond. A description of the delights of Woolbeding Common is provided in the New Lipchis Way section.

On reaching the road across the common you head southwards along it briefly, then turn eastwards to climb yet higher, now sharing your path with the New Lipchis Way. You join a track heading south-eastwards then, leaving the New Lipchis Way, bear left, eastwards, to pass Scotland Farm and walk through a wide field forming an extensive plateau. It's lovely fast going and with the prevailing wind on your back you will make rapid progress! You then plunge into woodland and drop down quite steeply to the buildings of Verdley Edge, only then to turn sharp right, south-eastwards, and endure another very steep climb through the trees, unrewarded sadly by any views. Soon the A286 comes into view below you to your left, and you drop down to cross it, descending further to reach the buildings of **Henley** including the 16th century Duke of Cumberland Arms pub, the only on-route amenity between Rake and Petworth! Buses to Midhurst and Haslemere are available nearby. Now heading south-eastwards you make your way steadily along a track through the thickly forested Verdley Wood, the ground rising steeply to the right, and eventually you too rise to arrive at a road at Bexleyhill. You turn left to follow the road briefly eastwards, then strike out south-eastwards along a good firm bridleway, actually a farm track across Bexleyhill Common. Just beyond a path fork you emerge and, still heading south-eastwards, enjoy a lovely steady field descent beside the edge of Snapelands Copse, with tremendous views ahead. You're then signed left to head eastwards across the field towards the hamlet of Leggatt Hill, here enjoying fine views to Black Down which you passed many miles back! You ascend to a road at **Leggatt Hill**; the ST turns left, northwards, along the road here, but by detouring right along the road you arrive, in just under half a mile, in **Lodsworth**. This is one of the loveliest villages in West Sussex, with a superb mix of architectural styles along its main street. You will doubtless have your favourite but arguably among the best are Erickers, a delightful mix of timber-framing and tile-hanging, the timber-framed Old Well House, Woodmancote, sometime home of Pooh illustrator Ernest Shepard, and the impressive early 18th century Old House (formerly Dower House). These last two are by the junction with Church Lane; this lane, itself full of very pretty cottages, leads down to the beautifully situated church of St Peter, beyond which is the Manor House with 13th century features. The village boasts not only a delightful old pub, the Hollist Arms, but the Lodsworth Larder, a combined general store and delicatessen, with a wonderful range of fresh produce. Note that the buses run from the A272 at **Halfway Bridge**, reached by continuing for another three quarters of a mile down the road that runs through the village.

The ST, however, as stated follows the road northwards, then forks off the road to the right, north-eastwards past some cottages, close to which there's a stunning display of daffodils in spring. Your route then veers south-eastwards along the edge of woodland before turning north-eastwards through the woods of Limekiln Rough; although the going can again be very muddy here, the reward is a charming little stream crossing just before you emerge and veer eastwards to Lodge Farm. Here you cross a wider stream, just as picturesque, with lovely wild flowers growing on its banks. There's a brief rest from woodland walking as you head south-eastwards across low-lying fields, and then along a muddy track, but you then enter the thickly wooded Upperton Common and after an innocuous, although possibly muddy, south-eastward walk along the valley bottom you then, still heading south-eastwards, climb very steeply. It's a cruel twist at the end of a long day! At length, however, you emerge at a road just by a prominent monument, one of the landmarks of Petworth Park, through or beside which you will be walking for the rest of your journey to Petworth. You turn right to follow the road pleasantly downhill to the village of Upperton, enjoying fine views, veering sharp left and then sharp right with the road to pass a lock-up garage by Park House.

Now you've a choice. The official, and I have to say vastly inferior, ST route follows roads or roadside paths for much of the way to Petworth, and then passes round the edge of the town. A much better alternative, a route variation V1, leaves the ST route just beyond the garage to proceed to Petworth through Petworth Park, and then through the middle of Petworth, capturing all its highlights. The park consists of 700 acres of beautiful parkland, ponds and woodland including ancient oaks, and accommodates the largest herd of fallow deer in the country. One particular feature of interest in the park is the woodland garden, known as the Pleasure Ground, and believed to be one of the finest achievements of Capability Brown. The park was immortalised by the artist Turner, who was a frequent visitor to Petworth and featured the park in many of his paintings; the 2014 film *Mr Turner* was partially filmed here. Petworth itself is the halfway point on the ST and the only town actually on the course of the ST route between

Haslemere and Petersfield. It was once an important market town and the market square is thought to date from the 13th century. Its chief glory is Petworth House, which dates back more than six centuries, although wholesale rebuilding took place between 1688 and 1696 by the 6th Duke of Somerset, and the Duke's descendant, the 2nd Earl of Egremont, completed the house's construction. Today it contains a magnificent collection of paintings, with works by Turner, Rembrandt, Gainsborough, van Dyck and Holbein, and of particular interest is the Grinling Gibbons Room with many fine examples of Gibbons' work. Just next to the house is the fine church of St Mary with a 13th century chancel and a most unusual red-brick tower. Other highlights in Petworth are the Cottage Museum, providing a fascinating insight into cottage life as it was in the early years of the 20th century, the early 18th century Angel Hotel, the very picturesque Lombard Street, and the late 18th century Leconfield Hall. However there are numerous splendid buildings along its narrow streets and alleys, and plenty of shops and cafes to enable you to recharge your batteries.

If however you prefer to stick to the official marked ST route, carry straight on beyond the above-mentioned lock-up garage along the road and downhill to **Tillington**, branching off the road to follow a path right past the part-Norman church of All Hallows – really the only feature of note on the ST between Upperton and Petworth – with its very distinctive early 19th century tower. The path drops down to the A272 which you then walk beside, eastwards, for just under a mile, keeping Petworth Park to your left. Your A272-side walk ends at a roundabout junction with the A285, the ST going straight across here to enter **Petworth**. You immediately veer left up an alleyway beside the town's central car park, reaching a toilet block; by continuing in the same direction past the block you shortly arrive via the Petworth Bookshop at the west end of the High Street in the centre of the town (and can pick up V1 here if you wish). However the ST bears right just before the block, up another alleyway and forward along Rosemary Lane, briefly left along Grove Street and then right to arrive at the A283 at Angel Street. You follow this very briefly right, south-eastwards, then turn hard left along a path which contours a steep hillside, soon reaching a path junction (A) at which you turn right. At (A) you're rejoined by V1.

The ST strikes out just north of east from Petworth, dropping steeply down into a valley then rising equally steeply the other side, with a superb view back to Petworth once the height is regained! You drop down again then quickly rise, veering south-eastwards, entering an area of woodland known as Brinksole Heath and arriving at a parking area just short of Kingspit Lane. Signage is ambiguous, some signs directing you south-eastwards to join the road a little further down then turn hard left up the road, other signs directing you to cut straight on from the parking area to the road. Either way, you carry on up Kingspit Lane north-eastwards through the trees, soon bearing right, eastwards, along a clear track through the woods of Flexham Park. A good deal of felling has recently taken place so the walking is more open than it once was here. The trail arrives at Wakestone Lane just north of a sharp hairpin bend, and from here the ST has been recently rerouted: it used to follow the lane for some distance but now, having turned right along it, it branches right off it almost at once, heading in a roughly southerly direction along a good woodland track. You turn right at a T-junction of muddy tracks, then shortly bear left at a path crossroads, heading eastwards through Mitfords Copse and emerging to continue eastwards on a field path. This is superb walking with lovely views to the South Downs. You pass through another wooded area then drop down to a valley bottom, entering the woodlands of Lithersgate Common, passing to the right of the house at Warren Barn and then ascending. You go over a path crossroads and reach a path T-junction, the ST turning right here and descending through the woods to reach and turn right along Bedham Lane. However by turning left at the path T-junction it's possible, at the cost of an extra quarter of a mile, to visit Brinkwells, a lovely thatched cottage where the composer Sir Edward Elgar lived between 1917 and 1919. To get to Brinkwells, having turned left as stated, follow the path to the road, turning right then left in 140 yards down the driveway to the house; return to the road, bear left and head downhill, in a quarter of a mile or so being rejoined by the ST. You continue along Bedham Lane for around 270 yards south-westwards towards Fittleworth then branch off left to follow attractive paths downhill through the trees, veering south-westwards and arriving in **Fittleworth**. The ST turns briefly right alongside the A283, shortly left along School Lane then right, north-westwards, to arrive at and cross the B2138 (B). However I suggest and indeed recommend that, in order for you to visit the charming village centre at the cost of negligible extra mileage, you stay beside the A283 rather than going left into School Lane, then as A283 bends left, detour right into Bedham Lane to view the lovely houses along this road, especially a delicious (and apparently nameless) pink timber-framed thatched cottage. Return to the A283 and cross it very carefully then bear right and immediately left to visit the church of St Mary which boasts an Early English tower and chancel and 14th century octagonal font. Then walk down through the churchyard to the B2138 crossing at point (B) above. The ST crosses the B2138 at (B) then heads on to Hesworth Common, proceeding in a somewhat roundabout direction to the trig point at the top. This is a delightfully unspoilt scene with a quite magnificent view to the South Downs escarpment; it's one of the highlights of the whole ST in fact. Hesworth Common supports a fine variety of trees including Scots pine, birch, beech, rowan and oak, and bird/insect watchers should look out for the chiffchaff, willow warbler, chaffinch and brimstone butterfly.

You now head southwards, picking your way carefully down the hillside then veering south-eastwards along a farm lane to reach the B2139 at Lower Fittleworth by the beautiful 14th century Swan inn. Many artists have stayed here and its dining room contains a collection of landscape paintings including a number by George Constable, brother of John. You now follow the B2139 just west of south, crossing the river Rother and the old Pulborough-Petersfield railway beside the former Fittleworth Station. The railway line was opened in 1859 from Pulborough as far as Petworth and was extended to Midhurst in 1866, while the section between Midhurst and Petersfield opened in 1864. It wasn't until 1925 that through services became available – previously a change at Midhurst was necessary – and the line was well used by freight as well as passengers. However passenger usage declined steadily after World War 2 and the line closed to passengers in 1955, while goods services continued between Midhurst and Petworth until 1966. Fittleworth Station was one of a number of delightful intermediate stations and you'll see it's been nicely converted into a private house. You pass the road turning to Coates then shortly turn right, south-westwards. This is a significant right turn as you've reached the south-eastern extreme of the ST and will now be following the bottom piece of the "serpent" all the way to the end of the path at Petersfield. You walk along a driveway past a small industrial estate then forward south-westwards through the woods of Coates Common, crossing a charming stream which you can either bridge or ford! A brief section of road walking is followed by a lovely walk downhill across a small heather-clad common, Lord's Piece, this providing a foretaste of things to come later. You cross a road and, continuing south-westwards, follow a good clear track round the edge of Keyzaston Farm, just north of Sutton; you arrive at another road and turn right to follow it north-westwards, now overlapping with the West Sussex Literary Trail. You then strike out along a lovely woodland path and after another short road walk you join a path along the edge of trees to pass between Burton Mill and Chingford Ponds, a Site of Nature Conservation Importance, and on past the houses of Lodge Green to reach a crossroads path junction. The ST goes straight over, north-westwards, but to visit Burton Park with its fine house and delectable church of St Richard – see the West Sussex Literary Trail section for more information – there's a short route variation V2. However as stated the ST heads north-westwards from the path crossroads and veers westwards to pass the pretty Black Pond and reach a T-junction where V2 rejoins you. Here you turn right, north/north-westwards, along a track past the Burton Farm buildings, heading steadily uphill. You cross a minor road and pass the houses of **Heath End** to reach the busy A285; by looking to the right here you can see the buildings of Petworth which you last saw several miles (and hours) back. Effectively you've almost come full circle! The ST turns left, but by detouring right, and walking beside the A285 for about half a mile, you reach Coultershaw, a heritage site which contains an old waterwheel and 18th century waterpump. Its setting beside the river Rother is quite charming. On your way you pass the Badgers pub and, adjacent to the pub, a road leading to Petworth's former railway station, now beautifully restored as a hotel.

As stated, though, the ST turns left, south-westwards, alongside the A285 very briefly; on the far side there's a useful shop which may do you a welcome hot drink, and you can also pick up a bus from here to Petworth or Chichester but may need to pre-book. These are the last on-route amenities for over 7 miles. Having followed for

130 yards or so alongside the A285 the ST turns right, westwards, away from the A285 and your direction of travel is predominantly westwards for the next 7 or 8 miles. The character of the walk changes here. Up to now you've had a good variety of landscapes including common land, field walking and parkland, but the next 7 miles are monopolised by woodland and common land. It's good straightforward walking to begin with, with a steep drop and then an ascent through the trees of Duncton Common. A little further, the trees relent a little to provide lovely views across the common, with a very pleasant mixture of heather, gorse, pine and silver birch. You pass a car park area (with useful picnic tables) then after a road crossing you go over Lavington Common. Designated as a Site of Special Scientific Interest, the common supports a great variety of bird life including tree pipits, woodlarks, stonechats and nightjars, whilst among the thick heath vegetation you may see insectivorous sundews, adders, common lizards and sand lizards. In areas of wet heath, you may find patches of cotton grass and cross-leaved heather, and indeed there are some sections which could be very badly waterlogged in places. As you cross the common you veer more resolutely north-westwards; there's a short road section over the pretty **Barnett's Bridge**, then you strike out north-westwards across Graffham Common along an excellent and very well-signed track. There's another short road walk southwards within sight of the imposing Millborough House then you continue across the common, initially south-westwards along a smashing path on the left-hand edge of a significant clearing, beyond which, as you veer north-westwards, you follow what is a much narrower path which threads its way through a cluster of rhododendron bushes. Again, however, the signage is excellent and there's no danger of getting lost. Graffham Common, very thick with pine trees, is also an ancient heathland with areas of wet and dry heath, the beautiful heathers supporting many rare wet heathland plants. Among bird and insect life to be found hereabouts is the nightjar, woodlark, tree pipit, spotted flycatcher and the scarce longhorn beetle. You go forward, veering south-westwards, along a wider bridleway onto Hoyle Hanger, then veer sharply north-westwards down a sunken track to reach Ambersham Common.

Some wonderful walking now ensues as you climb very steeply north-westwards – this is the stiffest ascent since Hesworth

Common – enjoying terrific views through a more open landscape along an excellent sandy path. The path levels out and you pass close to the trig point on the plateau, arriving at and crossing New Road, then proceeding straight onto Heyshott Common, veering south-westwards once more. Again this is superb open walking, and there's a real sense of peace and remoteness as you strike out across the heather. The well-signed path is excellent in the main but there is a very soggy interlude where there have been obvious and well-intentioned attempts to create ways round. Once you're clear of that, you enjoy excellent going, which continues as you turn sharply right, north-westwards, at a bridleway crossroads, to follow another super path into thicker woodland. This path brings you to a path junction just short of a splendid red-brick bridge over the course of the Pulborough-Petersfield railway. Here you turn hard left, south-westwards, now overlapping with the New Lipchis Way which is bound for Heyshott and the South Downs on its way to the sea. The sea certainly feels a very long way away just here, as you proceed through further gorgeous, predominantly coniferous, woodland, on another superb path. You part company from the New Lipchis Way (which goes off to the left) and continue through and out of the woods to end this long common-land sequence. There's more common to come but not quite yet! You arrive at Walkers Farm and it's now a straightforward walk along a lane, firstly south-westwards then veering north-westwards to pass Dunford House, a YMCA conference centre, and climbing steadily to arrive at the A286 at **Cocking Causeway**. There's a welcome pub here as well as a really good bus service to Midhurst, just a mile or so to the north, and Chichester, 11 miles to the south. If you'd prefer to access Midhurst under your own steam, you're better advised to wait till you reach the junction of the ST with Bepton Road, just half a mile or so from the centre of Midhurst.

There's a brief break from woodland walking as having followed the A286 very briefly southwards, you turn right, north-westwards, along Pitsham Lane; you go under the old Chichester-Midhurst railway (a brief history of which is contained in the New Lipchis Way section) and pass Pitsham Farm and some industrial works, now veering northwards. You then pass round the edge of the Holmbush estate just to the south-west of Midhurst, and cross **Bepton Road**. By turning right along Bepton Road and going forward along the main road, which becomes Rumbolds Hill and then North Street, you'll reach the centre of **Midhurst**, the delights of which are described in the New Lipchis Way section; having explored, simply find your way back to North Street and then retrace to Bepton Road to rejoin the ST. Your route now strikes out just south of west here onto Midhurst Common. Following excellent and well-signed tracks, you soon veer sharply right, just east of north (crossing back over the course of the Pulborough-Petersfield railway), and climb steeply; it's worth looking back for superb views to the South Downs through the trees. You then turn westwards and enjoy some of the loveliest woodland walking on the ST, crossing Severals Road and entering the woodland of Severals. There's slight anticlimax as you veer sharply northwards and drop down to Woolmer Bridge just short of the noisy and busy A272, but more lovely woodland walking awaits as you head westwards across Stedham Common and, beyond a road crossing, continue onto Iping Common. Stedham and Iping Commons, mostly owned by the Sussex Wildlife Trust, are among the best examples of lowland heath in Sussex, and support an amazing variety of insects and birds. The best time to visit is the summer, when the purple heather is at its most resplendent, and you may see silver-studded blue butterflies, minotaur beetles, swallows, martins, nightjars, siskins and linnets, while spring walkers may be rewarded with the song of the willow warbler, stonechat or tree pipit. You need to watch the signage carefully – there are so many tracks to choose from! – as you head north-westwards and climb steadily through one of the more open and exposed parts of the common, enjoying superb views. Make the most of them as your common-land walking is coming to an end and there's nothing quite as good as this ahead of you. You enjoy an all too brief march along the ridgetop, then drop down steeply through the trees to reach Terwick Lane at **Trotton.** The ST turns left here. However there's a possible route variation V3 here in order to visit Trotton with its fine church of St George dating from around 1300 and boasting two of the finest brasses in Sussex: one is that of Margaret Camoys who died in about 1310 and the other shows later members of the Camoys family, one of whom, Thomas, Lord Camoys, fought at the Battle of Agincourt. The church also has some superb wall paintings depicting the Last Judgment, while visible from the churchyard is the part-16th century

Trotton Place. Also on V3 is the splendidly restored Terwick Mill, a now disused 18th century watermill, which stands beside a weir best seen in winter when the flow of water is particularly impressive.

It has to be said that after so much really splendid walking to get this far, the rest of your journey to Petersfield will seem something of an anticlimax with little or no features of any great interest. You first of all have two miles of road walking, heading westwards along Terwick Lane via Dumpford (where V3 rejoins you) to Nyewood, passing the very prominent Southdowns Manor Hotel, Terwick Lane having become Dumpford Lane. As road walking goes it isn't actually too bad, the road constantly rising and falling, twisting and turning, and offering some excellent views, and there's very little traffic. At length you reach **Nyewood**, turning left down the main street, Nyewood Road, and crossing back over the old Pulborough-Petersfield railway. Beyond the old railway the ST branches off to the right, initially along a lovely path through the trees, then going forward along a narrow field-edge path. This really sets the agenda for the closing miles of the walk, with fields now the predominant terrain. You strike out just north of west along the edge of a long field, the path poorly defined and soggy in places, then veer north-westwards to pass round the buildings of Down Park Farm. Here you join hands briefly with the Sussex Border Path again, and in fact you'd only have to go about three miles northwards along the Sussex Border Path to Rake Hanger which the ST passed around 45 miles back! Overlapping with the Sussex Border Path you head just east of north along the edge of West Heath Common, then at the top edge of the common the Sussex Border Path goes off northwards while the ST bears left, westwards, along a driveway, running roughly parallel with, guess what, the old Pulborough-Petersfield railway. You've never quite shaken it off! You reach a road, turning right to follow it briefly to the buildings of Durleighmarsh, a little shy of the A272, and as at Woolmer Bridge between Severals and Stedham Common the traffic noise from this road can be quite intrusive just here.

Before reaching the A272, however, you bear left to join an excellent field path south-westwards, which goes forward to skirt the buildings of Durford Abbey Farm. Here you cross the border into Hampshire; you can tell you've done so because the footpath signs change! You're directed by the first of the "new" signs over a stile into an area of pasture where the path is invisible, but keeping an attractive pond to your left you veer right along the top edge of the field, then cross a stile. The way over the next field, south-westwards, now becomes clear. Just short of a stile at the far end of the field you turn right, westwards, to follow the field edge then veer left to drop down and cross, by an impressive footbridge, the river Rother which you will last have seen at Fittleworth. It's then nondescript walking across fields to arrive at a road which you follow westwards, crossing Penns Place and continuing along Durford Road to reach and cross the B2199. The final section of the ST involves a pleasant walk south-westwards across a small common to reach Heath Pond. If you're in a hurry you could simply continue along the path you've been following to arrive at a road junction (C), crossing straight over and following the road (Heath Road) going away from the pond. However the official, clearly signed, ST route veers left to follow the east side of the pond and arrive at a car park where the ST officially ends. I suggest that from here you then continue round the edge of the pond to follow its north-west side, along a boardwalk and past a children's play area. Shortly beyond the play area turn left up the slope to the road junction at (C) above, crossing over and following Heath Road away from the pond. At the end of Heath Road cross straight over Dragon Street along Petersfield High Street; to get to the station, bear right into Chapel Street and left up Lavant Street, reaching **Petersfield Station** at the very top end. Petersfield is a delightful market town with many lovely old streets and an unusual feature in its Physic Garden, created in the late 1980's in tribute to John Goodyer, a 17th century botanist. Many features are typical of his time including a topiary walk, knot garden and rose bower. A potter or sit in the garden is an ideal way to relax after your serpentine journey from Haslemere!

GOOD TO KNOW:
Start: Haslemere Station. Finish: Petersfield Station.
Total mileage: 65.
Difficulty: Moderate.
Stages: B2131 (east of Haslemere) 1.25, A286 (B) for Haslemere (*RAB) 7, Highfield Lane for Liphook (*RB) 11, Rake (RA) 15, Bottom of Rake Hanger for Hill Brow and Liss (*RAB) 16.5,

Borden 19.25, Henley (RB) 24.5, Leggatt Hill for Lodsworth and Halfway Bridge (RB) 28, Tillington (RAB) 31, Petworth (RAB) 32, Fittleworth (RAB) 37.5, Heath End (RB) 43.5, Barnett's Bridge 45.5, Cocking Causeway (RB) 51, Bepton Road for Midhurst (RAB) 52, Trotton (R) 57, Nyewood 59, Petersfield Station (*RAB) 65.
OS: OL33, OL10, OL34, OL8.

V1 The much-preferred route from Upperton turns left just beyond the garage by Park House down steps and through a gate into Petworth Park. Beyond the gate follow the obvious path downhill, veering gently right to walk beside the fence, then beyond the fence go straight on to join a clear track running left to right. Turn right to enjoy a super walk through the 700-acre Petworth Park along this track. You pass just to the right of a pond, then immediately beyond the pond veer left off the track, aiming for the far right-hand end of a bank straight ahead, keeping Petworth House across the park to your right. You pass just to the right of the bank and walk down to pass through a park exit gate and then through a tunnel, turning right through the yard to reach North Street. Cross carefully and turn right alongside it, veering sharp right to arrive at the church and, just beyond, the Petworth House entrance. Across the road from the church, turn southwards down Lombard Street to reach the town square, dominated by Leconfield Hall. Keeping the hall to the right, walk on down to the west end of the High Street at Golden Square, in a little courtyard beyond which you'll find the delectable Petworth Bookshop (and a very good deli opposite!) Now head east up the High Street to reach the Cottage Museum which is on the left. Retrace briefly then bear right up Middle Street to Angel Street; it's worth detouring left down Angel Street and back as there are many attractive houses and shops in this street. Then head eastwards along Angel Street away from the town centre past the Angel Inn, veering left just past the RC church down a road then forward along a path to reach the ST at (A) in the main body of text. (No extra mileage)

V2 Turn left at the path junction with the West Sussex Literary Trail and follow it south-westwards, veering right, just north of west, to reach the church and a view to the house beyond. Return to the track from the church and turn left to reach a crossroads of tracks.

Don't take the one going straight ahead towards another church but turn right, pass round the side of the gate and head northwards along the clear track, shortly being reunited with the ST coming in from the right. (Extra quarter of a mile)

V3 Instead of turning left onto Terwick Lane here, turn right and follow the road to the A272. Turn left to walk beside it, crossing a bridge over the Rother, and continue on to the church which is to the right. Having seen the church, return to the A272; cross over and walk a few steps back towards the bridge but then turn right along a signed footpath, actually a driveway past houses. Beyond the driveway go forward along a dirt-track to a T-junction with a lane. Turn left along it and then go forward along an obvious path through a field to cross the Rother again, at the weir. Go past Terwick Mill then bear left as bridleway-signed, soon veering right and ascending gently to the road at Dumpford. Turn right here, now back on the ST. (Extra 300 yards)

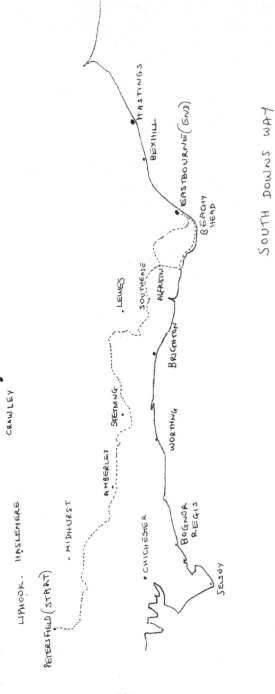

SOUTH DOWNS WAY

10 SOUTH DOWNS WAY

The South Downs Way(SDW) is currently the only name path in Sussex to enjoy National Trail status and the whole route is in the South Downs National Park. With its wide tracks, fine open walking and succession of fabulous hilltop viewpoints, it is arguably the finest continuous walk in Sussex and its completion is a worthy objective for any walker.

The South Downs began as a great chalk mass some 60 million years ago. When the first settlers arrived on this downland 6000 years ago, they preferred to travel using the drier, safer tracks across the chalk rather than follow the soggier Weald below. Thus originated the long unerring tracks over the South Downs, used by generations of settlers including Bronze Age traders and the Romans. More recently, however, the magnificent views from the hilltops and miles of glorious unspoilt countryside have made the South Downs an obvious attraction for walkers and cyclists, and so the SDW was born.

One word of caution is needed before you start. The SDW generally tends to avoid towns and indeed villages, Alfriston being the only place of any size along the 77+ miles of the trail in Sussex. While civilisation is never far away, there are very few on-route or even near-route amenities and there are significant gaps between places served by buses or even spots accessible by car. A number of water points have been helpfully provided, but it is imperative you stay properly nourished and hydrated to avoid getting into difficulties, so stock up your backpack with food and drink before you set out. And don't overdo it: while you do hear of the trail being completed in a single weekend or less, it's too good to be rushed and you'll enjoy it more – and are more likely to stay safe – if you take your time over it.

The SDW actually starts at Winchester in Hampshire and enters West Sussex at Sunwood Farm near Buriton. It's most convenient for us to join the route just west of that point on the Hampshire side, having come up from Petersfield, but note that the walk from Petersfield to Sunwood Farm is 4.25 miles. Exit **Petersfield Station** by the booking hall, walking straight on down Lavant Street to its end, then bear right along Chapel Street and left along the High Street. At the end bear right along Dragon Street; go past the junction with Sussex Road, and also past Tesco, to follow The Causeway uphill, then just short of the roundabout turn left down the road through Broadway Park. Just before it ends, by No. 62, turn right along a footpath, actually the Hangers Way, which you'll follow to Buriton. Follow the path in the same direction through a field, then along a left-hand field edge, then between fields, and along a further left-hand field edge. Observing Hangers Way signage, you're then signed right and immediately left; stay below a steep hillside rising to the right, and follow a muddy path which veers left through woodland. Emerging from the wood you veer right, ignoring paths leading downhill (left) and uphill (right). Reaching a T-junction with a track, turn right along it then almost immediately arrive at a metalled lane; turn left down the lane, and right at the T-junction to reach the very pretty centre of **Buriton**, almost immediately coming to the church. Turn left just beyond the church along a signed path/driveway, the village pond to your right. At the bend bear left along a very good path; at the T-junction at the end turn right along a byway which shortly veers left and rises steeply to a T-junction with a lane. Turn left onto it, now on the SDW. The SDW now follows roads as far as Sunwood Farm, then continues eastwards along Forty Acre Lane, soon crossing the border into West Sussex.

The SDW crosses the Sussex Border Path, and, now veering gently just south of east, continues on a clear track, rising steadily, the folly in the grounds of Uppark visible to the right. You approach the **B2146**, the SDW veering 90 degrees to the right to arrive at the road; at the 90-degree turn a <u>detour D1</u> leads down to the pretty village of **South Harting**, described more fully in the Sussex Border Path section. At the actual junction of the SDW with the B2146, a <u>detour D2</u> takes you shortly to the superb red-brick Uppark House, built in around 1690 and turned into a treasure-house of rare carpets, furniture and paintings from overseas. Damaged by fire in 1989, it's been beautifully restored and many of its previous glories remain including an 18th century doll's house with original contents. H.G. Wells, whose mother was housekeeper at Uppark, spent part of his childhood at the house. Beyond the B2146 you continue uphill, south-eastwards, through the woods, roughly parallel with then over the B2141, now on the 750ft high Harting

Downs; there follows a very straightforward easterly walk along the clearly signed SDW with quite superb views to the left. You then drop down through woods to the foot of Beacon Hill and a signed path junction (A). From here the SDW describes a large V round Beacon Hill but it's possible to (and I recommend you) cut the V, saving three quarters of a mile, by walking over Beacon Hill. To do so, go straight over at (A) and ascend along the obvious path to the top of Beacon Hill, site of an Iron Age fort and providing, from its summit trig point and topograph, fantastic views not only to the north but all the way to the Solent and Isle of Wight to the south. You then continue on the path, soon being reassured by a bridleway sign, and follow the path steeply downhill, turning left at the end back onto the SDW. However the official SDW turns south-eastwards from (A), and, keeping Beacon Hill to the left, rises gently up the hillside before then turning hard left, northwards to descend to the valley separating Beacon Hill and Pen Hill, meeting the path coming down from Beacon Hill.

Now the SDW veers eastwards over Pen Hill, skirting woodland and veering south-eastwards, passing just to the north-east of Buriton Farm, beyond which there's quite an arduous climb into West Dean Woods. The path levels out and continues through the woods, passing a memorial to a wartime pilot, Hauptmann Josef Oestermann. By coincidence I found myself walking this part of the SDW on Armistice Day in 2014 and stopped at 11am to keep the Silence; it really was silent, apart from the very faint rustle of the trees in the fine drizzle that fell from a leaden sky. Veering north-eastwards shortly beyond the memorial, the SDW soon passes the Devil's Jumps, a remarkable line of five Bronze Age burial mounds. Continuing through the woods, veering eastwards, you now pass Monkton House, once lived in by the art collector Edward James. You emerge from the woods and proceed along a straight path between fences for 300 metres or so until a signed bridleway goes away left. It's at this point that a detour D3 takes you to the church at Didling. Known as the Shepherd's Church, it boasts a Saxon font but the rest is deliciously simple early 13th century with unusual bench ends containing candleholders. Beyond this junction as you continue eastwards on the SDW, you can clearly see the 800ft hilltop trig point of Linch Ball, but don't get too excited as there's no right of access to it. Instead the SDW passes just to the right of this hill and goes over a bridleway crossroads, the masts of The Trundle hilltop above Chichester now visible ahead. The walking is level for a time, before a long descent from the top of Cocking Down, heading just south of east, with magnificent views now opening out ahead. The path bottoms out, crossing the **A286** just by a car park and bus stop. The village of **Cocking**, with a good range of amenities, is half a mile down the hill to your left.

From the A286 crossing the SDW continues south-eastwards uphill initially along Hillbarn Lane then along a clear track, climbing onto Manorfarm Down, veering in a more easterly direction and now keeping woodland on your right. Once the woodland to the right is reached and the path has levelled out, you cross the New Lipchis Way and overlap for a while with the West Sussex Literary Trail. It's then straightforward ridgetop walking over Heyshott Down, Graffham Down and Woolavington Down, the views restricted by the trees, but a further climb sees the woods relent to the left and takes you to within less than half a mile of Crown Tegleaze, the highest point on the South Downs at 830ft; even though the SDW only reaches 767ft here the views will be tremendous on a clear day. You swing in a more south-easterly direction to pass over Littleton Down then descend through fields, now enjoying splendid views eastwards towards Chanctonbury Ring, to reach the **A285** Chichester-Petworth road at Littleton Farm. Beyond the A285 the SDW climbs again, proceeding south-eastwards onto Sutton Down. It's a steady climb, shaving the left-hand edge of the woodland of Burton Down, and indeed the shade of the woods will be welcome on a hot day as you ascend. However the path then levels out and there is then a superb walk along a field edge with tremendous views to the Isle of Wight and Chichester Cathedral to the west and beyond Littlehampton to the east. To your left here are twin radio masts on a hill, marked on maps as Glatting Beacon; the masts are very prominent and you'll be able to pick them out numerous times not only from other spots along the SDW but indeed other Great Walks of Sussex. The SDW continues in a generally easterly direction over Bignor Hill, meeting Stane Street, the old Roman road linking London and Chichester, and passing close by the site of a Neolithic camp. A road here drops very steeply down to the village of Bignor and its Roman villa should you wish to detour to visit it. It's a long way back up afterwards, though, and you may prefer to wait till you walk the West Sussex

Literary Trail which goes right past the villa! More details about the villa are contained in the section covering that walk. Beyond Bignor Hill the SDW maintains its height, passing Toby's Stone – a memorial to a local huntsman – from which there are sensational views to the sea, the Weald, the South Downs and the Arun valley, and you should also look southwards to the hilltop Halnaker Windmill, passed by the Sussex Hospices Trail. The SDW swings very sharply north-eastwards, dropping steeply downhill, then veers south-eastwards to climb again, passing immediately below and to the left of Westburton Hill, and skirting the extensive woodlands of Houghton Forest. There's then a descent to cross the **A29**, beyond which the SDW, heading just north of east, descends to the Arun valley, veering sharply south-eastwards and then north-eastwards to drop down to the valley floor and cross the Arun by a footbridge. The descent provides fine views not only ahead to the Arun valley but northwards to the pretty village of Bury, the sometime home of John Galsworthy and also visited by the West Sussex Literary Trail. Beyond the crossing of the Arun the SDW goes forward to arrive at the **B2139** beside which it's a short walk to **Amberley Station** and the fine museum at **Amberley** (both 400 yards along the B2139 to the right, then up the station approach road) and Amberley village itself (just under half a mile away, following the B2139 to the left, then going left again up High Street). The museum and the village are described more fully in the West Sussex Literary Trail section.

The SDW having followed the B2139 briefly southwards then climbs north-eastwards out of the valley via a road, High Titten, before leaving the tarmac and ascending eastwards onto Amberley Mount along a clear track past farm buildings. Watch for cyclists careering down the hill towards you! It's a very steep climb so pause every so often to get your breath back and enjoy the views which improve with each step. At length the ascent becomes gentler and as the path levels out you pass the trig point of Rackham Hill; though this is off the route and on private land, the view as you pass it is still tremendous, particularly westwards to the Arun valley and also northwards, with the fine Parham House and Parham Park clearly visible just to the north-east. Now continue just south of east, passing a wooded area and then, on emerging, dropping down onto **Springhead Hill** but remaining on top of the escarpment. You pass a **car park** where there's a possible route variation V1 along a lovely tree-shaded path to visit the summit and trig point of Kithurst Hill. The main route, meanwhile, continues between areas of pasture and, beyond the point where V1 ends, rises to a car park with signpost known as Chantry Post on Sullington Hill. Now enjoying fine views south-eastwards towards the distinctive hillside beyond Longfurlong and its busy road, you veer left to proceed over Barnsfarm Hill and drop down to the **A24**. To access the picturesque village of **Washington**, including its popular pub, you can simply follow the road beyond downhill, reaching the village in just under half a mile. It should be noted that from Barnsfarm Hill there's an official alternative SDW route, heading north-eastwards downhill to Home Farm Cottages, where you bear eastwards across a bridge over the A24 into Washington then past the church up The Street, through the village centre, and right at the T-junction to ascend to the main route. The alternative, which will add about a mile to the walk, is really intended for horse riders who are anxious about the A24 crossing and I strongly recommend you stick to the official route and detour down to Washington from there. There are buses from Washington to Worthing and Pulborough.

Beyond the A24 the SDW, veering south-eastwards, climbs through a car park and then ascends increasingly steeply through woodland before emerging and bearing left at a T-junction, now heading for the cluster of trees around the famous Chanctonbury Ring hillfort. You pass immediately below and just to the right of the Chanctonbury dew pond, one of a number of such ponds you'll see on the SDW, being man-made shallow hilltop ponds intended for watering livestock and kept supplied with water by dew and condensation. A detour of about 30 yards just beyond the dew pond to the left up the modest hillside takes you to the Chanctonbury Ring trig point from which there are quite stupendous views that on a clear day may extend southwards to Brighton and as far as the Isle of Wight, while to the north you can enjoy a view to a massive expanse of Sussex countryside and as far north as Leith Hill, the highest point in Surrey. Returning to the SDW, you continue on to the cluster of trees that make up Chanctonbury Ring itself, arguably the most famous natural landmark on the South Downs. A large number of the beech trees that made up the cluster were blown down during the Great Storm of 16 October 1987, but an impressive number of trees remain and below them are the rampart and ditch of an Iron Age camp. The SDW now swings sharply south-eastwards, the views hereabouts still really excellent, with another Iron Age hillfort, Cissbury Ring, clearly visible to the south, while just below you to the north are the grounds and church of Wiston House. As you continue across the plateau your views are restricted by trees, but soon things open out again and you can look ahead to the Adur valley, Truleigh Hill and the escarpment leading to the Devil's Dyke beyond. You skirt the summit of Steyning Round Hill then overlap briefly with the Monarch's Way as you come off the plateau and reach the top edge of Steyning Bowl. This is a Devil's Dyke in miniature, a steep semi-circular hillside guarding a dry valley and creating a green bowl-like effect from a distance. The Monarch's Way actually contours the hillside while the SDW prefers to keep its distance, following parallel with the Sompting-Steyning road then heading just north of east roughly parallel with and to the south of the Monarch's Way. There's then a long descent eastwards into the Adur valley over Annington Hill, gentle at first and then steeper, passing a pig farm. You drop steeply and enter an area of trees, then just after the route swings very sharply left, north-westwards in front of a brown shed, a signed bridleway goes off to the right. By turning off the SDW onto this path you can follow a route variation V2 that visits the lovely churches of Coombes and Botolphs. That said, if you want to visit Botolphs only, stick to the SDW as the principal route runs very close to it. Botolphs contains late Saxon features including wall paintings and a splendid Jacobean pulpit, while Coombes is of Norman origin and with further wall paintings, rather more impressive than those at Botolphs, that date back to the 11th century. The SDW continues downhill to the buildings of Annington, bearing right, south-eastwards, along a road that takes you to the valley bottom; a roadside path continues along the valley bottom through **Botolphs** within sight of Botolphs Church. A detour to the church is very easy! However the SDW turns left just a short distance before the church and, overlapping briefly with the Downs Link, goes forward to a bridge crossing of the river Adur. The SDW then leaves the Downs Link, bearing left to arrive at the busy **A283** Steyning-Shoreham road just south of Upper Beeding; buses run from here to both Steyning and Shoreham. Unfortunately the Adur valley hereabouts isn't attractive, and is further disfigured by the nearby Beeding cement works, currently abandoned and, as I said in the Downs Link description, surely one of the biggest eyesores in Sussex.

The A283 is exceedingly busy and there's no bridge crossing, pedestrian crossing or even island, so take huge care when traversing it! From the A283 crossing the SDW heads eastwards then north-eastwards uphill, firstly along a path then along a metalled road followed by a wide stony driveway which passes the Truleigh Hill Youth Hostel at Tottington Barn. The climb is a bit of a slog but it is at least steady and not unbearably steep, and as you climb there are excellent views back to the Adur valley and the stunning and unmistakeable Gothic-style Lancing College Chapel. Beyond the hostel the driveway rises quite sharply to reach the most prominent of a number of masts decorating the hilltop area. From here you drop steeply north-eastwards to the very edge of the escarpment at Edburton Hill, beyond which you veer south-eastwards and rise to proceed in a predominantly easterly direction along the top of the escarpment above Fulking. You descend again before climbing extremely steeply, then after a short drop you embark on a longer steadier ascent towards the viewpoint above Devil's Dyke, joined here by the spur section of the Sussex Border Path. You can tell you're approaching the Dyke, with its very popular hilltop restaurant, by the number of sightseers and kite-fliers. Signage isn't hugely clear and it's important to keep to the right of the grassy bank topped by a trig point, rather than being tempted to keep to the escarpment edge towards the hotel. The SDW continues over the plateau, crossing the metalled approach road; you could detour left for 250 yards along the road to visit the hugely popular viewpoint and pub, a stile to your left en route providing easy access via a muddy path to the trig point. Both the trig point and the viewpoint offer excellent views: from the trig point you have sight of Brighton and the South Downs as far as Firle Beacon, miles to the east, and from the viewpoint you'll see a vast expanse of Weald countryside. Beyond the road crossing the SDW proceeds along the right-hand side of that extraordinary phenomenon, **Devil's Dyke** itself. This is a deep dry valley with Ice Age origins, but legend says that it was cut by the Devil in an unsuccessful bid to flood the churches of the Weald. It is undoubtedly one of the natural highlights of the SDW, the lush green of the valley floor a strange oasis between the uncompromisingly stark steep hills rising on each side, randomly furnished with hardy vegetation. After some 500 yards you reach a signed bridleway crossroads and here you have the option of a route variation V3 which provides a spectacular descent along the Dyke hillside and then visits **Poynings** (which, even if you're sticking to the main route, is worth the detour for the descent and the amenities in the village), Newtimber, Wolstonbury Hill, Danny and Clayton. All are worth visiting. Poynings boasts a pretty flint 13th-14th century church and Royal Oak pub; Newtimber Place is a superb 17th century moated brick house, while the church of St John, Newtimber, is Early English in origin and contains some fine monuments; Wolstonbury Hill is arguably the finest South Downs peak that isn't on or immediately beside the route of the SDW, providing a true 360-degree panorama incorporating views to the Weald and the South Downs escarpment, to the Clayton windmills eastwards, and to Glatting Beacon above Bognor Regis, miles to the west; Danny is a stunning late 16th century brick-built country house with massive mullioned windows; and the church of St John the Baptist at Clayton boasts a pre-Norman chancel arch and superb medieval wall paintings dating from 1140. Do note however that Newtimber Place and Danny are private houses, although Newtimber Place can be visited by appointment.

Back on the SDW, there's now a fine descent north-eastwards high above the Dyke, with views extending to the village and church at Poynings, and indeed as you make progress beside the Dyke, the views to the Weald just get better and better. There's a sharp descent to cross the busy Brighton-Poynings road, immediately beyond which you pass through the picturesque hamlet of **Saddlescombe**, with its small rural life display and farmyard café, food and drink being served from a caravan. A signed path to the right takes you within sight of the 17th century Donkey Wheel, a wheel turned by a donkey to supply water, housed in a mid-19th century wheel house. Continuing north-eastwards, you part company from the Sussex Border Path and climb again, firstly through the trees then steeply through open grassland onto Newtimber Hill. As the ground levels out you reach a gate and here you can enjoy one of the most stunning and yet unsung views on the entire walk, extending back to the South Downs escarpment in the direction of Chanctonbury Ring and forward to Brighton and the South Downs beyond. You can pick out three windmills from here, namely Jack and Jill above Clayton which you'll reach shortly, and Oldland near Ditchling which is visited by the Sussex Border Path spur section. The SDW now drops steeply downhill to a lane which shortly turns 90 degrees to the left to run parallel with the A23; you cross this road by a footbridge then begin a predominantly easterly course, bearing right and ascending to **Pyecombe**. On the right as you enter the village is its church, almost your archetypal Sussex downland country church, built of sturdy flint and boasting a 13th century tower. Very shortly beyond the church there's a crossroads where a right turn brings you into the village centre in 250 yards, but the SDW goes straight on, dropping to reach the A273. After walking briefly northwards beside it, you then strike out eastwards, heading steadily uphill past a golf course. Beyond the course you turn sharply north past New Barn Farm and arrive at a path junction, here being rejoined by V3; you turn hard right to continue along the SDW but by turning left and then shortly right along a signed bridleway you reach, in 150 yards on your left, one (or should I say two) of the best-loved features of the South Downs, the twin windmills **Jack and Jill**. Both date from 1821 and were hauled here in 1850 by oxen. You first pass the tower mill Jack, which has no sails, then soon reach the entrance and parking area giving access to the white-painted post mill Jill, complete with sails. V3 goes past the windmills to arrive back at the main route and indeed by walking V3 in reverse here, following the bridleway beyond the windmills all the way to **Clayton** and turning left at the end along Underhill Lane, you soon reach the A273. Here you can pick up buses to both Brighton and Hassocks, or by turning right briefly beside the A273, crossing the B2112 and turning right onto a signed footpath just before the railway bridge you can walk down to **Hassocks.** On reaching the road at the end of this footpath, cross and turn right, soon forking left up a slipway to reach Hassocks Station, or continuing beside the road for the village centre. Hassocks is nearly 2 miles from the windmills.

Returning to the SDW, you now embark on a straightforward very enjoyable march, initially just south of east, veering just north of east, along the ridgetop, passing a couple more dew ponds and enjoying magnificent views throughout. There's another (and final) brief overlap with the **Sussex Border Path** spur route, before this route sinks down into the Weald via **Ditchling**; see the Sussex Border Path description for accessing the village and its attractions

1.5 miles away. The SDW however stays on the ridgetop and a stiff climb culminates in your arrival at Ditchling Beacon, at 813ft the highest point actually on the SDW and indeed the whole of East Sussex, just under 2 miles beyond Jack and Jill. The Ditchling Beacon trig point is easily found just to the right of the SDW and provides a tremendous panorama not only to the South Downs but also the Weald and the sea around Brighton; in 1588 one of a chain of big fires was lit here to warn of the approach of the Spanish Armada. Returning to the SDW, you proceed past a car park (always busy in good weather!) to shortly arrive at and cross **Ditchling Road,** then continue on a resolute easterly course above Westmeston and Plumpton, passing numerous prehistoric earthworks at Western Brow, Streat Hill and Plumpton Plain, while if you look south-eastwards you'll see the magnificent Amex stadium, the new (well, now not quite so new) home of Brighton & Hove Albion Football Club. Just before the Blackcap woodland and trig point, 2.5 miles east of Ditchling Road, the SDW turns abruptly south-westwards, but I highly recommend a <u>detour D4</u> from here to view Blackcap and, if you've time, Mount Harry. The views from both Blackcap and Mount Harry are superb, stretching from Brighton to Firle Beacon; Mount Harry also boasts a beacon, erected to commemorate the Queen's Golden Jubilee in 2002.

As stated, however, the SDW turns very sharply south-westwards just before Blackcap, following a clear track towards Balmer Down, with particularly good views eastwards to Mount Caburn and Cliffe Hill behind Lewes. You reach a path junction in just under half a mile and here turn off left, south-eastwards. Keeping Balmer Down to your right, you now enjoy some glorious open walking, with a great view ahead to the lush green of the next line of hills, while nearer at hand is the remarkable six-sailed Ashcombe Windmill which you'll meet (or will have met) on the Greenwich Meridian Trail. Despite the nearness of Lewes and the A27, the surroundings are remarkably remote and rural. There's a steady descent and then at a path junction you turn sharply south-westwards, passing through the trees of the Bunkershill Plantation; it's your first woodland walking for many miles, albeit very brief, and there's a stiff climb in the shade of the trees. On emerging from the plantation you look down to the **A27** and there's now a rapid descent to reach this road by **Housedean Farm.** Buses are available to Lewes from the immediately adjacent bus stop alongside the main road. Otherwise bear right up the road past the farm. The SDW shortly forks left to cross the A27 by a bridge, but there's a recommended detour D5 here which gives easy access to **Falmer Station** and possible walks to the old village of Falmer with its lovely pond and massive thatched barn, and/or Stanmer Park, a country estate around a Georgian mansion. Back on the SDW, having crossed the A27 by the bridge, you follow parallel with this road eastwards briefly (buses for Brighton are available just beside the A27 here) then turn south-westwards, passing under the Brighton-Lewes railway. Now, having lost so much height since Blackcap, you start ascending again, climbing south-westwards towards the line of hills you admired as you passed Balmer Down. It's a tough exposed climb into the prevailing wind, and presents a huge contrast to the thickly wooded Heyshott Down and Graffham Down many miles back. Just past the trees of the Newmarket Plantation you veer gently south of east, still climbing; to the west you can now clearly see the village of Falmer and the cars on the busy Falmer-Woodingdean road. Now you veer sharply left to follow, initially, the so-called Jugg's Road north-eastwards, Jugg's Road being an ancient route that was used to carry fish to the market at Lewes. Leaving Jugg's Road you then veer right to proceed south-eastwards over **Swanborough Hill**, high above **Kingston near Lewes** and the town of Lewes itself, described more fully in the Sussex Ouse Valley Way and Greenwich Meridian Trail sections. This is absolutely tremendous ridgetop walking: immediately below you can see both Ashcombe Windmill and the pretty Kingston Church, the village of Kingston half a mile away (and worth detouring to along the signed path off the SDW more or less level with the windmill), while the views further afield to Lewes, Cliffe Hill, Mount Caburn, the Ouse valley, Firle Beacon, the Beddingham masts and Seaford Head are simply unforgettable. You're signed slightly further away from the edge of the escarpment and join a metalled farm lane along which, heading south-eastwards, you now begin a long, long descent past Iford Hill and Front Hill towards the Ouse valley. The descent is harder and more demanding than it looks: the concrete surface is tiring on the feet, and there's no shelter from what could be biting winds. As you continue to lose height you lose the concrete and now begin an overlap with the Greenwich Meridian Trail, actually crossing, during this overlap, from the western to the eastern hemisphere, the moment marked by a fingerpost and an impressive cairn! There's a very short wooded interlude round the buildings of Mill Hill, then you plunge steeply into a dry valley. Leaving the Greenwich Meridian Trail but picking up the Sussex Hospices Trail you turn hard left, north-eastwards, to follow the valley bottom to just short of the **Lewes-Rodmell-Newhaven road**, now joined by the official route of the Sussex Ouse Valley Way and the Sussex Hospices Trail. By going forward to the road and turning left alongside it you reach **Rodmell**; a right turn in the village centre brings you to Monk's House, sometime home of Virginia Woolf – see the Sussex Ouse Valley Way section for more detail. The total round trip is half a mile. However the SDW bears right before this road to walk uphill, parallel with it, then crosses the road and joins a quieter road going downhill, eastwards, through the village of **Southease**. Shortly you reach its delightful flint church with a round Saxon tower, one of only three in the whole of Sussex. The church's original chancel and aisles have gone although some Norman work remains; the present church contains Jacobean box pews, a fine 15th century chancel arch of wood, lath and plaster, and 13th century wall paintings depicting scenes from the life of Christ, while remains of Reformation texts can be made out between the arches. You continue along the road down to the Ouse valley, soon crossing the river Ouse. Shortly beyond the river you cross the Lewes-Seaford railway just by Southease Station, and then go forward to the busy A26 which thankfully is crossed by means of a bridge.

You then start climbing again, and it's a long slog out of the valley as you proceed southwards then north-eastwards onto Itford Hill, climbing all the while. You then veer eastwards, still ascending, and just over a mile from the A26 crossing you pass just to the right of the Itford Hill trig point and the adjacent Red Lion Pond. It's worth detouring from the path to the trig point to enjoy the views which are sensational, particularly to the Ouse valley which you can follow with your eyes all the way from Lewes to the sea. Now having reached the top of the escarpment you can enjoy easy progress north-eastwards then eastwards, passing the Beddingham masts and going forward to a car park at the top end of a road, **Firle Bostal** (a bostal being defined as a small road leading up a hill). By turning left down this road there's the option of a <u>route variation</u>

<u>V4</u> in order to visit **Firle**, Firle Place and Charleston Farmhouse. The 13th century church of St Peter at Firle boasts a stained-glass window by John Piper depicting William Blake's *Tree of Life*; Firle Place, begun by Sir John Gage in 1530, has a lovely drawing room of cream and gold with superb plasterwork and a Great Hall which boasts the second largest van Dyck painting in the country; and Charleston Farmhouse was for over 60 years the retreat of the so-called Bloomsbury Group of artists, writers and intellectuals including Virginia Woolf, Vanessa Bell and David Garnett. The house has recently been restored to re-enact the atmosphere of the house as it was in the 1950's. Note that the Sussex Hospices Trail overlaps exactly with the SDW all the way from Southease to Alfriston, well beyond the end of V4, so you could always undertake V4 when you walk that trail, and stick with the SDW for now – or indeed vice versa!

The SDW continues eastwards beyond the Firle Bostal-end car park along the top of the escarpment, passing the woodland of Firle Plantation, and a gentle climb brings you to the climax of this part of the walk, the 713ft Firle Beacon marked by a large earthwork. This is a quite magnificent viewpoint and one of the highlights of the SDW with glorious views in all directions, including a splendid panorama to the north and north-west as well as a huge coastal strip. The SDW now swings south-eastwards, dropping down to a bridleway junction where V4 ends, and it's a really lovely walk from here to Alfriston. Initially you drop to the car park at Bopeep Bostal, then rise again onto Bostal Hill and now keep a straight and unerring south-easterly course, with fantastic views forward to Windover Hill and left to Alciston, Berwick and the Arlington Reservoir. Soon the village of Alfriston and its magnificent church also comes into view. Taking care to follow SDW signage at path junctions, you swing eastwards to reach a metalled road and now descend to **Alfriston**, one of the loveliest villages in Sussex. You arrive at the High Street by the 16th century Star inn which has ceiling timbers decorated with carved animals, and on the street corner beside it is a large red lion, the figurehead of a 17th century Dutch ship, pilfered from a wreck off the Sussex coast. The SDW turns left along the High Street and right along River Lane, parting from the Sussex Hospices Trail briefly, but it's worth detouring right along the High Street first. By doing so and then soon turning left down an alley by the former Congregational Chapel, you reach a green at the top end of which is the splendid 14th century parish church of St Andrew, known as the Cathedral of the Downs. Across the green from the church is the timber-framed 14th century Clergy House, a Wealden yeoman's house and the first purchase of the National Trust. Alfriston's High Street, worth following for its whole length if you've time, boasts many fine examples of tile-hanging, flint, brick and timber.

The SDW heads eastwards out of the village as stated along River Lane, turning right to follow the delightful Cuckmere river briefly downstream then crossing the river by a footbridge.(Note that the footbridge is adjacent to the green beside which the church and Clergy House are situated, so you could approach it from there.) The SDW now splits in two, and you've a choice between the inland bridleway route and a seaside footpath route. Both are equally enjoyable but the footpath route is undeniably more spectacular. Having done one, you should definitely return another day to do the other!

The **bridleway route** proceeds eastwards beyond the footbridge then just before Lullington Road turns left (B) to head through fields alongside this road. By going straight on at (B) to the road at Plonk Barn a short route variation V5 is possible to visit the tiny 13th century church at Lullington, just 13ft square with room for less than two dozen, making it a contender for the smallest church in the country. However as stated the SDW follows beside Lullington Road just north of east to meet a metalled lane coming in from the left; here you turn right, cross Lullington Road, and, reunited with the Sussex Hospices Trail, you ascend a path to cross the Litlington-Wilmington road, where V5 ends. Beyond the road crossing, the SDW, now heading for Windover Hill, continues to climb, heading just north of east then veering southwards, with superb views southwards to the coast and south-westwards to Alfriston and the 19th century carved Hindover White Horse on a hillside towards the coast. The track bends sharp left (north-eastwards) and levels out; as it does so you should detour shortly to the left across rough grass to the tumulus on the summit of Windover Hill from which you can clearly see the sea, the port of Newhaven, the South Downs escarpment westwards to Firle Beacon, and, to the north, a huge tract of East Sussex farmland. You're right above the chalk figure known as the Long Man of Wilmington, of whom you'll get a proper view on your Wealdway walk. Back on the SDW, you go forward to a gate, now veering south-eastwards, your direction of travel for the rest of the bridleway route to Eastbourne. Beyond the gate, you keep Tenantry Ground, a dramatic dry valley, to your right, and soon you reach a fork junction, veering left here; it's now a magnificent open high-level walk, the views particularly good towards the coast. You veer left into the woods, dropping down steeply, then descend more gently between fields to Jevington, passing its flint-built church which boasts a Saxon west tower and also some Norman and Early English work. You arrive at the road in **Jevington** village centre, roughly opposite the former Hungry Monk restaurant, the birthplace of banoffee pie in 1972! By turning left you could follow the road up to the Eight Bells pub, but the SDW bears right, then second left up a road which soon becomes a track. It's a long uphill slog, overlapping here briefly with the 1066 Country Walk South Downs Link, but at length you pass the trig point marking the summit of Willingdon Hill, another magnificent viewpoint. Now maintaining height and overlapping with the Wealdway as well as the Sussex Hospices Trail (but losing the 1066 route), your SDW path then proceeds decisively seawards. There's quite a contrast between left and right: familiar open downland to the right, and the sprawling suburbs of Eastbourne to your left, separated from you by very steep wooded slopes. The views are tremendous throughout, especially towards Eastbourne and Hastings. Passing Eastbourne Downs Golf Club, you reach and cross over the A259 then proceed to the trig point on Warren Hill. From here, the last great viewpoint on the inland route, the SDW (rerouted from the original) skirts an area of trees separating you from the western fringes of Eastbourne, crosses Beachy Head Road close to its junction with Warren Hill, then ploughs on towards the sea, still high above Eastbourne as though wishing to avoid the town altogether. Then, however, at a path crossroads, it bears left, just north of east, and plunges downhill towards the town. The OS mapping suggests it unites with the footpath route (described below) roughly halfway between this left turn and a café by Duke's Drive, then continues downhill to the café where both alternative routes of the SDW officially end. However, presumably to avoid an awkward stepped descent on the footpath route, the bridleway route is now signed down a narrower and less spectacular path, veering to the left of the mapped route through thicker vegetation, and then, close to the bottom of the hill, swinging right to reach the café. My advice is to stick to the OS-mapped route.

The **footpath route** via Seven Sisters, overlapping with the Vanguard Way as far as Cuckmere Haven, parts company from the bridleway route just beyond the footbridge over the Cuckmere river at Alfriston. You initially walk in a generally southerly direction on a grassy path beside the Cuckmere downstream to Litlington, where you leave the river and walk up to the village street. You turn right along it but could detour left to visit, in 200 yards, the village tea garden and then the pretty Norman church. As stated, though, the SDW turns right (southwards) briefly along the street before striking out first just east of south then just west of south, climbing steeply to enjoy fine views of the Hindover White Horse, then dropping to the north edge of Friston Forest. At the path T-junction here you could turn right to view, below and to the left, the impressive part-13th century flint buildings and medieval dovecote of Charleston Manor (which is not to be confused with Charleston Farmhouse, and is not open to the public). However the SDW turns left at the T-junction and enters the beech woodlands of Friston Forest, heading south. There's a steep stepped ascent then an easy walk on a clear forest track; you veer south-eastwards, beginning to descend, then veer south-westwards to drop to the pretty village of Westdean, the site of a palace of Alfred the Great. Though the SDW bypasses the looping village street it's certainly worth following it round to view the fine Norman church of All Saints, the flint-built Old Parsonage dating from the 13th century, another medieval dovecote, and a number of attractive flint houses. There's then a stiff climb out of the village through the trees, although steps (and hand rail) make the going easier; on emerging from the trees there is a superb view ahead to Cuckmere Haven, the estuary of the Cuckmere. You then have a sharp drop south-westwards to cross the busy A259 just by **Exceat** and its visitor centre, now at the top end of Cuckmere Haven, described more fully in the England Coast Path section. From beyond the A259 crossing the SDW promptly strikes out just east of south, away from the estuary and ascending, then veers sharply right, dropping down to the valley floor and heading seawards. You're now overlapping with the England Coast Path and will continue to do so as you walk all the way up to and over the Seven Sisters, down to **Birling Gap** (where a road leads to the attractions and amenities of **East Dean**), up to the Belle Tout Lighthouse, down to a road and then up onto **Beachy Head**. The England Coast Path section describes this part of the walk, a brilliant climax to your SDW journey, in greater detail. The SDW then continues north-eastwards off Beachy Head to approach Eastbourne; instead of descending with the England Coast Path beyond the clifftop war memorial it maintains height, following a narrow path along the very top of the cliffs and overlapping awhile with the Wealdway. The SDW then veers away from the sea, heading towards the road, until a signpost directs you to the right along a firm wide path going steadily downhill north-eastwards, here overlapping with the shorter Wealdway alternative route. It's fast, easy and confident walking. At a path junction you're joined by the recommended (OS-mapped) bridleway route and now descend very steeply to arrive at the café on Duke's Drive as alluded to in the bridleway route description above.

As stated it's at this café that the SDW officially ends. However, the England Coast Path, which joins Duke's Drive by the café, continues to Eastbourne (and of course beyond) and I suggest SDW walkers continue to Eastbourne along the route outlined in the England Coast Path section, as far as the Lifeboat Museum. Turn left off the prom just beyond the museum and cross the coast road, but (unless you wish to follow the full Eastbourne detour as set out in the England Coast Path section) rather than turn left along Carlisle Road, walk down the adjacent Lascelles Terrace, cross Compton Street and turn half-right down Chiswick Place, crossing straight over the roundabout down Cornfield Road. At the end you reach Eastbourne town centre, turning left along Terminus Road to arrive at **Eastbourne Station**.

GOOD TO KNOW
Start: Petersfield Station. Finish: Eastbourne Station.
Total mileage: 81.5 (via Windover Hill), 84 (via Seven Sisters).
Difficulty: Strenuous.
Stages (NOTE – a number of stages necessarily exceed 6 miles):
Buriton 3, B2146 (B) for South Harting (RAB) 7.5, A286 (B)

for Cocking (RAB) 15, A285 22, A29 27, B2139 for Amberley
(RA) and Amberley Station (*) 28.5, Springhead Hill car park
31, A24 (B) for Washington (RB) 34.5, Botolphs 40.5, A283 (B)
41.5, Devil's Dyke for Poynings (RA) 46.5, Saddlescombe (R)
47.5, Pyecombe (RAB) 49.5, Jack & Jill for Clayton and Hassocks
(*RAB) 51, Sussex Border Path crossing for Ditchling (RAB) 52,
Ditchling Road 53, A27 Housedean Farm (B) for Falmer Station
(*RB) 58.5, Swanborough Hill for Kingston near Lewes (R) 61.25,
Lewes-Rodmell-Newhaven road for Rodmell (RA) 64, Southease
(*R) 64.5, Firle Bostal for Firle (R) 67.75, Alfriston (RAB) 71.5.
Via Windover Hill: Jevington (RA) 76.5, Eastbourne Station
(*RAB) 81.5. Via Seven Sisters: Exceat (RB) 74, Birling Gap for
East Dean (RAB) 77.5, Beachy Head (R) 80.5, Eastbourne Station
(*RAB) 84.
OS OL8, OL10, OL11, OL25.

*D1 At the 90-degree turn, bear left off the SDW along a signed
footpath downhill, ignoring a path forking shortly right and ignoring
other paths signed left and right as you continue. On reaching the
bottom of the hill, continue along the path past a recreation ground
which is to your left, and go forward beyond the recreation ground to
a gate. Go through the gate and follow the road on into South Harting,
the parish church to your left and the pub a little further on. Return
the same way. (Total detour 1.25 miles)*

*D2 Turn right off the SDW alongside the B2146, shortly reaching
a left fork by a lodge, signed Uppark. Fork left here and proceed
along the driveway, but in a couple of hundred yards turn left off the
driveway up a National Trust path, observing the arrow signs; after a
stiff ascent, helped initially by steps, you're signed sharply right, going
forward to pass through the coach park. At the far end bear left into
the upper level car park and follow it on to its end, going forward to
the pay kiosk. Return the same way. (Total detour 1 mile)*

*D3 Turn left off the SDW onto the bridleway and descend steeply.
In 500 yards, turn right along a signed footpath, dropping steeply
through the woods, emerging and descending through two fields to
the start of a lane, arriving at Didling Church. Return the same way.
(Total detour 1.25 miles)*

D4 Instead of turning sharp right with the SDW you continue along the bridleway signed for Lewes, stated to be 3 miles ahead. Your bridleway rises again, keeping to the right of the trees, and levels out just to the right of a trig point and clump of trees known as Blackcap. Leave the track here to enjoy both, as the views from the trig point are stunning. If you wanted to visit Mount Harry as well, return to the bridleway, and head on eastwards, now beginning to descend. Just before a clump of gorse the paths fork; you take the left fork, aiming for a wooden signpost at the bottom of the mini-dip. You descend to pass the signpost, then continue along what is a clear path that climbs again, with trees and bushes dotting the hillside around you. As you reach the top of the rise, you get level with the unmistakeable Mount Harry beacon, turning right off the path to visit it. Return the same way. (Total detour 1.5 miles; Blackcap only, half a mile)

D5 Instead of forking left beyond Housedean Farm to cross over the A27 with the SDW, continue up the road, signed as a cycle track, and go forward on the cycle track beside the A27 and along Middle Street as far as the pedestrian bridge. To reach Falmer old village, cross the bridge to the far end, here bearing right then left to arrive in the village centre. I suggest you walk onto the green then turn left to walk beside the pond, crossing the road to pass or visit the village church. By walking down to the bottom end of the churchyard you get a great view to the huge 13th century thatched barn. Then return to Middle Street. Whether you've visited the old village or not, follow Middle Street on past the Swan, then as the road veers right, take the signed cycle route 90 forking left – IGNORE the fork just before it. Go forward to cross Knights Gate Road then simply go straight on along the cycle route, keeping first a slip road coming off the A27 and then the A27 itself to your left. Your path veers away from the A27 towards the university complex and reaches a signed junction of cycle tracks immediately to the right of a subway. To access Falmer Station walk under the subway and up the steps to arrive at the station at once. For Stanmer, turn right at the cycle track junction and follow the track to a road. Cross and turn left to walk alongside it, but very shortly bear right up the Stanmer Park approach road and follow it, turning left at the road fork junction. Signage is very clear. In 1 mile from the subway you arrive at the country house, in a beautiful park setting across the green from the 19th century church. To reach Stanmer village itself, with its pretty flint cottages and tearoom, continue along the road, soon turning right to pass the church and then left along the street. Stanmer Park is a lovely place to enjoy a lazy day off from your SDW endeavours. Then return the same way to the subway, turning right under it to reach the station, or left to walk back the same way to the SDW. (Straight detour to station 3 miles in total, i.e. 1.5 miles each way; add a quarter of a mile in all for Falmer village detour and 2 miles in all for Stanmer Park detour)

V1 Just beyond the car park, leave the SDW by turning left through a gate and go forward along the car park approach road for a few yards, then turn hard right along a signed bridleway, initially along a track then a much narrower signed path heading east. You ascend gently, initially enjoying great views to the north, and reach the trig point at the top of Kithurst Hill. Go forward a little to a gate, but just before the gate you turn right along a path which initially rises, providing magnificent views ahead as well as north and south, then descends to return to the SDW. Turn left to continue your eastward journey. (Extra 275 yards)

V2 Having turned right off the SDW above Annington, follow the signed path very steeply down through the trees, then turn right as signed along a clear green path following the right-hand field edge. The obvious path passes a white house then descends to arrive at the edge of trees, the ground rising steeply behind. Having entered the wooded area turn right to follow what is a narrow path, then veer left and rise sharply to arrive at a metalled road. Turn right along the road which descends to Coombes. Bear right just before the Church Farm sign up a farm lane, then go forward along a signed bridleway via a gate to the left, up a grassy hillside to reach the church which is to the right. There's a choice of entrances off the path. Having visited the church return via the lane to the road and retrace your steps up the road, but now continue along it downhill to arrive at Botolphs Church. From there, carry on for 100 yards or so to a sharp left bend, immediately beyond which you turn right to be reunited with the SDW. (Extra 1 mile)

V3 NOTE: THIS IS A STRENUOUS VARIATION WITH TWO BIG CLIMBS. Fork left as bridleway-signed off the SDW and follow the path which descends along the right-hand side of the Dyke; it's a spectacular and enjoyable walk. At the bottom of the hill, go straight on as bridleway-signed through the trees. You reach a pond on the left and the bridleway veers left here. Shortly after this bend you fork left off the bridleway along a signed footpath, keeping the pond to your left. At the top end of the pond, kink left and right, walking along a right-hand field edge to reach the main street of Poynings, roughly a mile from the SDW. The Royal Oak is up the street to the left, but you turn right beside the street – a parallel path is provided – soon passing the church. Go straight on, ignoring the road going away left; as your road bends right, go straight on along a signed path eastwards, passing just to the right of farm buildings and then rising to meet the road you just left! Turn left along it, shortly reaching the busy Brighton-Poynings road, now a quarter of a mile from the centre of Poynings. Saddlescombe is half a mile up this road to the right should you wish to return to the SDW there. Otherwise bear left along the road for a quarter of a mile, here turning right along a narrow road. Cross straight over the A281 and continue along the minor road on the other side. As it bends sharply right in three quarters of a mile, bear left as footpath-signed to Newtimber Place. Unless you've booked a visit, you must stick to the footpath round the side of the house, then backtrack. Now walk back up the road towards the A281 but in a quarter of a mile turn left as path-signed at the church of St John, Newtimber. Walk round the right-hand side of the church, going forward through a gate into a broad field, and turn left, north-eastwards, heading for the busy A23. At the end you reach a road; turn right along it then immediately left, under the A23. In a few yards turn right as path-signed, then very shortly left, again as path-signed, up a footpath which at times is extremely steep. At the end you reach a path T-junction, turning left, then in a few yards you reach 2 signed paths going off to the right. Take the nearer of these, a bridleway-signed path which climbs steadily up the side of Wolstonbury Hill and in roughly 700 yards reaches a path junction. Here turn left along a green track, then by a metalled post fork left to join a path which leads you to the trig point at the summit. From the trig point, bear right and take an obvious green path heading steeply downhill eastwards (using as your line a clear straight road running eastwards just below the escarpment you can see ahead) as far as the edge of trees, reaching a path junction with a bridleway sign pointing right and the way you've come. Turn left here, soon being reassured by a footpath sign, and continue straight on downhill along an obvious wide path through the trees. Ignore a left fork and emerge from the trees, passing round a gate beside buildings and going forward downhill to a road. If you wish to miss out Danny you can turn right here, heading for the A273, but for Danny, turn left along the road, which soon bends sharp right and in 300 yards or so again veers significantly right. At this bend, turn left along a signed footpath which takes you, in 500 yards or so, to the driveway for Danny. The view to the house is magnificent. Sadly the house is private so you must stick to the signed footpath round the side, then backtrack to the road. Retrace your steps along the road and this time (in common with those who've missed Danny) keep straight on along it, arriving at the A273. Here turn right, crossing the railway; as you do so, look to the right to see the superbly crafted 1840 brick baronial entrance to Clayton Railway Tunnel. Now cross the A273. Just by the bridge on the far side a footpath signed left takes you down to Hassocks Station – see main body of SDW text. However V3 turns right to walk beside the A273, crossing over the B2112 and shortly turning left along Underhill Lane in Clayton village, soon reaching the church. Continue down Underhill Lane, shortly turning right up a South Downs-signed bridleway; keeping to the blue-arrowed bridleway, you rapidly ascend, looking back to enjoy magnificent views. You now approach the two windmills, Jack and Jill, to your right, and aim for the clear path skirting the left (near) side of the mills. Beyond the mills, keep along the path uphill to a T-junction, turning left and arriving at a fork where you rejoin the SDW. (Extra 3 miles, but only 2 miles if Danny omitted)

V4 Turn left to walk down Firle Bostal off the ridge, and at the very bottom of the hill in roughly three quarters of a mile, you reach a crossroads with tracks going left (to a big barn) and right. Turn right along the track here, unsigned at the time of writing but a public byway, and follow it to its end at another crossroads by farm buildings. Turn left here along a track which matures into a metalled road, past the church of St Peter, Firle, roughly a mile from the SDW. Shortly you reach the village store/café – the pub is a little further along the road – and immediately to the right of the store, fork right onto a signed path along a gravelly track which takes you to a gate. Go through the gate to enter the Firle Place estate. Now you need to take care with navigation. DON'T follow the obvious track just beyond the gate; the right of way proceeds just parallel with and to the right of it, soon reaching the main approach road to Firle Place which is to your right. Unless you're detouring here to visit Firle Place, cross straight over the approach road. Now you need to veer very gently right from your previous course and look out for a large patch of trees ahead of you, with a red-brick farmhouse and farm buildings at the left corner of the trees; you need to aim for the large flint and brick house below the trees and a little to the right of the farm. Simply now walk across the park towards the flint house, soon being reassured by signage. Immediately in front of the house is a lane which you cross. Now follow a very narrow path just past the left side of the house. Continue along it, soon going forward along a left-hand field edge and then veering sharp right along an obvious path through the field uphill. Follow the left-hand top edge of the field briefly, then bear left with the path through the trees to cross over a track. Just up to your left here is an estate folly, Firle Tower. Now follow a clear path through two crop fields, heading just south of east and descending to a meadow. Walk on across the meadow in the same direction, going forward along a left-hand field edge, then kinking left and right as signed to join a very clear wide (if muddy) track and go forward to Charleston Farmhouse where refreshment is available. Beyond the farmhouse follow the farm lane to a T-junction of tracks, here turning right and following a clear track to Tilton Farm. At the farm you veer right again and head towards the steep South Downs escarpment at Firle Beacon. At length, after rising steadily, you reach a path crossroads junction. Cross straight over the (red arrow-signed) public byway and follow the path going uphill, the gradient intensifying as you continue. At length you reach the top of the escarpment and rejoin the SDW, turning left to continue towards Alfriston. (Extra 2.5 miles)

V5 Having reached Lullington Road cross it, turn right then bear immediately left up a signed path which soon reaches a field and proceeds uphill on the left-hand field edge; there's a super view across the Cuckmere meadows south of Alfriston from the top corner. Continue into the trees, your firm path soon passing the signed access to Lullington Church. Keep on along the firm path; at its end, turn left up the road, soon reaching the SDW coming up from the left. Turn right here to rejoin the SDW. (No extra mileage)

11 SUSSEX BORDER PATH

The Sussex Border Path (SBP), dating from 1989, essentially does what it says on the tin: the main route follows the borders of Sussex and its neighbours Hampshire, Surrey and Kent all the way from Emsworth, at one end of Sussex, to Rye at the other, while a spur route, linking with the main route at East Grinstead, follows initially the border of West Sussex with Brighton & Hove, and then the border between West and East Sussex. For obvious practical reasons, often because the border is marked by a river or ditch, it's not always possible to follow these borders exactly. Where it isn't possible, the nearest available rights of way are used, some of these making incursions into neighbouring counties. These incursions are fully described in the text. Essentially, however, the SBP is a Sussex walk, and necessarily a long one. I will be honest and say it isn't my favourite name path in Sussex: while there are some fine stretches and interesting features, there are several dull and fiddly stretches with no memorable aspects or scenery, and there's a great deal of mundane field walking. The journey from Charlwood to Burstow, negotiating Gatwick and the M23, has to be the grimmest piece of walking described in this book, with a combination of underwhelming scenery and appalling traffic and aircraft noise. It is perhaps no coincidence that the best bits of SBP walking come where there is overlap with other routes described in this book. Signage has improved greatly in recent years, but there are still some confusing sections where you will certainly need the map or technology to keep you on the right track. All that said, there's plenty to see and enjoy on the SBP and if you finish it all you will have the satisfaction of having walked Sussex from end to end and from top to bottom, and therefore, arguably, of having undertaken the two longest possible continuous Sussex walks!

Main Route

To access the start of the SBP main route from **Emsworth Station,** follow the directions given for the very start of the England Coast Path section, bearing right just beyond the Lord Raglan on Queen Street (where the SBP begins), following the causeway towards the harbour, then veering left to reach Slipper Road. You

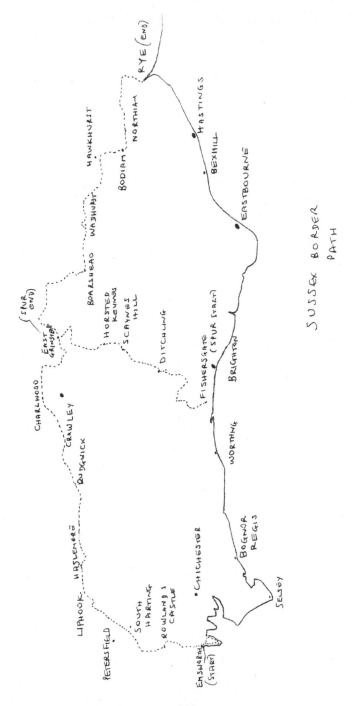

then head southwards down Slipper Road, going forward into the Emsworth Marina and Yacht Harbour area, kinking left and right to pass the red-brick Yacht Harbour complex and continuing beside the marina basin along a wide gravel drive, keeping a line of "houses on stilts" to your left. You then leave the England Coast Path, turning left at the end of the drive then shortly right along a path between trees and more houses on stilts. In 150 yards or so you bear left, eastwards, soon crossing Thorney Road and continuing past Thornham Farm to reach the edge of Chichester Harbour just south of **Prinsted**; see the England Coast Path for directions to the village and **Southbourne** beyond. The SBP climbs up onto the embankment and bears right to begin a waterside clockwise walk round the edge of Thorney Island. You're now overlapping with the England Coast Path in reverse, and this part of the SBP, as you walk beside Chichester Harbour, is described more fully (albeit in reverse) in the England Coast Path section. The going is very easy indeed, as you proceed in a predominantly southerly direction on an extremely good coastal path. You soon pass Thornham Marina and shortly beyond that, Prinsted Point and Thornham Point; you arrive at a gate where to proceed you will need to press a button (or phone 01243 388269) and seek entry. Once the gate has clicked open for you, you can enjoy easy walking past Stanbury Point. You find yourself on the shore (although at high tide you may need to veer briefly inland here) as you pass the island church of St Nicholas, beyond which it's straightforward walking, southwards, to Longmere Point. You veer westwards here, bypassing Pilsey Island but enjoying superb views to East Head near West Wittering to the east, and Hayling Island to the west. Now you head north-westwards along a really good clear path, and it's fast easy walking all the way to Marker Point, the most westerly point of the island; you then veer sharply again to the right and now make your way northwards again towards Emsworth, enjoying great views ahead to the South Downs and Kingley Vale Nature Reserve. After negotiating a couple of mini-inlets it's a virtually straight run until you arrive at Emsworth Yacht Harbour. The SBP heads eastwards away from the water, then after 200 yards or so forks left to return to the wide gravelled driveway you followed on your outward journey. You now retrace past the Yacht Harbour complex and back up Slipper Road, this time following it all the way to the **A259**. I don't wish to demoralise you too much, but you have effectively just completed a giant circle and progressed only about 80 yards from the Lord Raglan where the SBP started! The plus side is that by turning left and then shortly left again up Queen Street you will be able to enjoy the delights and amenities of **Emsworth** a second time.

The SBP, bordering Hampshire (as it will do to just beyond Liphook), crosses pretty much straight over the A259 along Lumley Road, passing under the railway bridge, turning hard left onto a path heading just south of west and hard right along another path which passes under the A27 and just east of north through fields, keeping the buildings of New Brighton to the left. You are here actually right on the border between West Sussex (to the right) and Hampshire (to the left). You arrive at the B2147 Emsworth-Westbourne road and by turning right along it you will immediately arrive in the very pretty village of **Westbourne** with its fine 14th century church of St John the Baptist to the left, and a number of very attractive houses in and around Church Road just beyond. However the SBP turns left to follow the B2147 to a roundabout, and at the roundabout bears right onto Redlands Lane, northwards, continuing along a path which widens and rises to a T-junction with Long Copse Lane. You follow this westwards, along what is the very northern edge of the Emsworth/Westbourne/New Brighton sprawl, then bear right, just west of north, and at last you're back out in the countryside again. You now follow a lovely path through Hollybank Woods where there's a splendid variety of bird life to be found including tits, bats, warblers and woodpeckers, and plants include early purple orchids. You rise to Emsworth Common Road, and turn right (just north of east) to follow it, soon turning left onto a path through woods, dropping gently then rising to cross Woodberry Lane. The SBP continues north-eastwards along a track for just under half a mile, passing through the hamlet of Stubbermere, then bears left (westwards) through the Holme Farm complex and across fields, soon passing just to the left of woodland. You then veer northwards to reach one of the scenic highlights of the early miles of the SBP, the broad avenue linking Stansted House and Rowland's Castle, and by looking to the right here you can clearly see Stansted House. This is more fully described in the Monarch's Way section, but it's worth repeating here that in 1724 Daniel Defoe commented on his ability to see from the west end of the house right down to the town and harbour of Portsmouth and ships at Spithead. While you may not get that clarity, it's worth pausing to enjoy the view which on a half-decent day is still magnificent. You reach a path junction in the middle of the grassy carpet between the lines of trees; the Monarch's Way, with which you now overlap briefly, proceeds eastwards to Stansted House, but the SBP turns left to follow a clear path along the avenue westwards, going forward into and through woodland and descending to arrive at Finchdean Road just outside **Rowland's Castle**. The SBP turns right up Finchdean Road, parting from the Monarch's Way, but by going straight on rather than turning right here you reach, in just over 100 yards, Rowland's Castle with its excellent range of amenities including a railway station, just up the road to the right beyond the bridge.

The SBP, now overlapping for some time with the Staunton Way, proceeds up Finchdean Road on the Hampshire side of the border then passes over the London-Portsmouth railway and strikes out north-westwards along a clear green path. You then veer just east of north to follow the narrow Wellsworth Lane, continuing on a lovely path across open fields. You descend through the trees to reach a road, turning right and dropping down to **Finchdean,** a delightful village, with the bonus of the pretty George inn to help quench thirsts. Now well over into Hampshire, you follow the Chalton road north-westwards out of Finchdean then bear right, northwards, to walk uphill along a lovely path with views to Idsworth Church. You pass through an area of trees, veering north-westwards then north-eastwards, and it's now straightforward going as you follow the clear path through fields over Chalton Down, enjoying the best views so far. Your dead-straight path then begins to dip, and the SBP turns left onto a path leading down to enter the churchyard of Chalton's 13th century church which boasts a particularly fine east window.

The SBP follows a road eastwards out of Chalton but soon branches off, again eastwards, on a field path, descending steeply to cross a minor road and the railway again. You then go forward north-eastwards along Harris Lane, soon entering woodland. You now have a good two miles of walking through woodlands on the slopes of West Harting Down, re-entering Sussex hereabouts, and although your north-easterly course looks clear enough on the map, you need to follow signage, map and/or technology very carefully as there are so many forks and crossing tracks. At last, at Foxcombe Farm, you emerge from the trees and follow a lane past Foxcombe Cottages, crossing over the South Downs Way, beyond which a pleasant descent through the trees takes you to the **B2146** South Harting-Petersfield road. The SBP goes straight over, but by turning right and following the B2146 for less than half a mile you'll reach **South Harting**. Not only are there buses available here to link with the rail network at Petersfield, but it is a large and attractive village, with thatched and timber-framed cottages and the splendid church of St Mary & St Gabriel, containing nave walls which could be pre-Norman, an impressive Victorian tower linked to the church by a splendid wooden staircase, and part of a 13th century effigy in the chancel.

Beyond the B2146 the SBP continues northwards, rising and then proceeding parallel with the West Harting road through woods immediately below Torberry Hill. You're then forced down to the road which you follow to the hamlet of Quebec, then veer north-eastwards and north again with the road. Shortly you fork right and now proceed in a predominantly north-easterly direction, initially beside the road, along the south fringe of woodland and then across fields past Down Park Farm and past Downpark Common onto West Heath Common. Here you briefly overlap with the Serpent Trail which you'll see a fair bit more of in the miles ahead. The Serpent Trail goes off to the left while the SBP continues just east of north past Wenham Common, crossing an old bridge which once carried the now disused Pulborough-Petersfield railway, more fully described in the Serpent Trail section. You then carry on through meadows, crossing the West Sussex river Rother and then veering just west of north past Wenham Manor Farm to reach the A272. The SBP bears left to walk beside this busy road, but thankfully soon bears right along the approach road to Durleighmarsh Farm. You continue just east of north through open country on a byway before entering and passing through Durford Wood; the SBP's course is very obvious and well signed, and this is a really enjoyable woodland walk. Veering north-eastwards, then north-westwards, then north-eastwards again, you go forward to arrive at the Hill Brow-Rogate road. The SBP turns left to follow this road briefly but shortly bears right at the next road junction, now at the **bottom of Rake Hanger**. However, by continuing straight on along what is Rogate Road to the B2070, crossing straight over it at **Hill Brow** and continuing downhill along the B3006, you reach **Liss** and its station, 1.5 miles from the SBP. As stated, though, the SBP bears right at the aforementioned road junction and proceeds quite steeply downhill. Very shortly the road bends left; soon after the left bend you rejoin the Serpent Trail which has come in from the right, and shortly the SBP and Serpent Trail together bear left to proceed north-eastwards along a good clear path through Rake Hanger described (in reverse) in the Serpent Trail section. You go forward along Sandy Lane and rise gently to arrive at Bull Hill, turning left and ascending to reach and cross the B2070 at **Rake**. This was once the main A3 London-Portsmouth road; despite its demotion, it is a busy road, so cross with care.

Having crossed, the SBP turns right and almost immediately goes left along Brewells Lane, entering Hampshire and leaving the Serpent Trail but now overlapping with the Shipwrights Way. You follow the lane roughly northwards, then bear right at a crossroads by Brewells Farm, and left at the T-junction to cross the London-Portsmouth railway at Langley. You've returned to Sussex again! Now you leave the tarmac and strike out north-eastwards on a lovely path which passes the houses of Langley then skirts the edge of woodland and descends to arrive at a multi-path junction. Here you bear right, eastwards, again along a woodland edge, passing close to Folly Pond which is to the left. You then swing south-eastwards, keeping woodland to the left and crossing the railway again, then proceed between fields and enter the woodland of Chapel Common (described a little more fully in the Serpent Trail section). Here, reunited with the Serpent Trail which traverses the common, you bear left, eastwards, to shortly reach the B2070 again and turn left to follow it briefly, past the welcome Black Fox pub. You very soon turn right at the next road junction, signed Milland and Iping, almost immediately reaching a road T-junction, and go straight over onto a footpath/byway which now heads north-eastwards in a straight line, initially across Liphook golf course, so do be careful and give way to golfers. It's then dull but easy and quick walking of about a mile and a half, all the way to the Midhurst-Liphook road at its junction with **Highfield Lane**, hugging the Hampshire/Sussex border but just staying within Sussex throughout. The village of **Liphook** with its railway station is less than half a mile to the left down Midhurst Road. By detouring right along Midhurst Road you would reach the impressive Hollycombe Steam Collection in just under a mile.

The Sussex Border Path now heads eastwards across the thick woodland of Stanley Common, overlapping briefly with the New Lipchis Way and the Serpent Trail. It drops steeply downhill into a valley and veers north, descending to a beautifully sited house, Lower Brookham. Beyond the house you rise steadily, veering eastwards, your predominant direction of travel virtually all the way to Valewood Farm House below Haslemere. This section of your route, where again you and the Serpent Trail part company for a time, takes you across Linchmere and Marley Commons, part of the so-called Greensand Hills landscape on the Surrey/West Sussex border; both are described in the Serpent Trail section. Your going is mostly along woodland paths, with just a short stretch of road walking near Linchmere village taking you to Linchmere village green where the SBP turns left along a road. However, there is the possibility of a <u>route variation V1</u> by the green to visit the church of St Peter, Linchmere, and Shulbrede Priory. The church is of 11th century origin and among its interesting features are a double north aisle, carved wooden cherubs adjacent to the old organ, a bas-relief of the Seven Deadly Sins thought to date from about 1300, and a glass south door giving fantastic views to the nearby hills and woodlands. Shulbrede Priory is an Augustinian priory, founded about 1190 and converted into a farmhouse at the Dissolution; it is now a private dwelling but with its fine exterior and delightful setting it is well worth seeing. The SBP main route continues in its resolute easterly direction, ascending and being joined by V1. Signposting is good, tracks are firm and it's straightforward if not desperately exciting ridge walking; your county neighbour is no longer Hampshire but Surrey, although you remain in Sussex. As you approach the eastern end of Marley Common, reunited with the Serpent Trail again, you walk very steeply downhill through the woods, to cross the A286 just north of Kingsley Green with bus connections to Haslemere and Chichester. I recommend that to access Haslemere on foot, you plough on along the SBP, initially along Fernden Lane then along tracks through the trees and past ponds and a weir, to **Stedlands Farm**, where the SBP forks right towards Valewood Farm House. To reach **Haslemere**, 1.5 miles away, fork left here up a signed public byway to Scotland Lane, bearing left then immediately right down a path leading to the B2131. Turn left here and just keep going straight on to reach the station.

Beyond Stedlands Farm the SBP passes Valewood Farm House, veers sharply south-eastwards and climbs very steeply up a grassy hillside. The Serpent Trail, with which you otherwise continue to overlap up on to the Black Down plateau, prefers a more gentle zigzag. The SBP continues first across a field and then into woodland to begin the climb onto Black Down, which together with its connection with the poet Alfred, Lord Tennyson is described more fully in the Serpent Trail section. Still overlapping with the Serpent Trail, the SBP goes all the way up to the plateau, but once there bears left, parting company from the Serpent Trail. However by bearing right here along the course of the Serpent Trail, following the track and forking right as it bends sharp left, you reach the superb Temple of the Winds viewpoint, with views stretching all the way to the South Downs. The total detour is 1.25 miles. As stated, though, the SBP bears left, veering north-eastwards, swinging to the east side of the plateau to provide a great eastward view just off the route to the right. Then, flirting briefly with the Serpent Trail again before bidding it a final farewell, your route dips down to just short of Tennyson's Lane. You skirt the grounds of Aldworth House, sometime home of Lord Tennyson (but not open to the public), and head steeply downhill south-eastwards through woods above Upper Roundhurst Farm. You then bear sharp left for about a mile of road walking, northwards then just north of east along Jay's Lane as far as Gospel Green, and from there you continue north-eastwards along a bridleway through a strip of woodland with fields to the right and left. The path begins to gain height and soon reaches and crosses the **A283** Milford-Shoreham road.

Beyond the A283 crossing, the SBP heads north-eastwards through the trees of Big Copse then veers just south of east, skirting the grounds of Shillinglee Park and crossing horse gallops. Look out for fast-moving horses! You pass through the northern fringes of Manorhill Copse, then proceed along the southern fringes of a much larger area of woodland, veering north-eastwards again and crossing the Plaistow-Dunsfold road at **Dungate Farm**. Although the walk from the A283 to Dungate Farm is unremarkable, the footpaths do actually follow the Sussex/Surrey border throughout! Beyond Dungate Farm you tend, for the time being, to stay well within the Sussex side of the border. Now, having skirted so much woodland, you pass through the middle of a large patch of it, firstly Upper Ifold Wood and then Hog Wood; once again, you're heading south-eastwards then on emerging from the woods you veer north-eastwards, passing Oxencroft Copse and crossing Barberry Bridge which takes the SBP over the Wey & Arun Junction Canal. The canal has spawned its very own name path, the Wey South Path which you also cross here, and the Wey South Path section of this book provides a more detailed guide to this waterway, now being gradually and impressively restored. You continue north-eastwards beyond the canal through fields to cross the **B2133** Loxwood Road at Alfold Bars. **Loxwood** village is just under a mile southwards along this road – see the Wey South Path section for more detail. Beyond the crossing you head eastwards along a lane through farmland, entering another area of woodland. Veering north-eastwards, you pass the buildings of Rikkyo School, possibly the oldest Japanese boarding school in Europe, and cross the very busy A281 Guildford-Horsham road. Continuing north-eastwards you follow Hillhouse Lane, cross the Cranleigh-Rudgwick road and follow a path that rises, skirting woodland and passing a trig point; you reach and briefly overlap with the Downs Link which at this point in its journey is actually passing over the Baynards railway tunnel. Beyond the Downs Link overlap, you proceed eastwards through fields to reach the main street at **Rudgwick**. You turn right to follow the street southwards, soon reaching the chiefly 14th century church of the Holy Trinity with 13th century tower and 12th century font made of Sussex marble. The SBP strikes out eastwards just beyond the church but by detouring on for half a mile down the village street you'll reach the village centre. The village, with its attractive tile-hung cottages, has a shop and bus links to Guildford, Cranleigh and Horsham.

The SBP heads north-eastwards from Rudgwick, wending its way along farm lanes and tracks all the way to the Rowhook-Ewhurst road, and once again you are actually following the Sussex-Surrey border. Beyond the road crossing you continue north-eastwards through woodland, then just before Honeywood Lane you turn sharp right, south-eastwards, down Monks Lane to arrive at Stane Street, the course of the old London-Chichester Roman road. You bear left to follow it north-eastwards briefly, then head eastwards along a most attractive bridleway, going forward through woodland to cross the **A29**. Beyond the crossing, the SBP continues to Denne Farm then (passing into Surrey) heads northwards via Rowland Wood to Weare Street, proceeding eastwards along this road and south-eastwards along Smugglers' Lane. You follow the lane past Oakdale Farm then, veering north-eastwards, ascend to Wattlehurst Farm and proceed along field paths and through Grove Copse to reach Bonnetts. From here you head eastwards to cross the very busy A24 London-Worthing road, here just single carriageway. Beyond the crossing, continuing eastwards, you soon go over the Dorking-Horsham railway, then after following Rusper Road briefly, you veer southwards past a scramble track, heading downhill and returning to Sussex. Then the SBP resumes its easterly course, in fact just north of east, crossing Friday Street and proceeding through farmland before entering and passing through Horsegills Wood. It's a lovely stretch of woodland which will seem especially refreshing in summer. You descend to cross a stream, then rise up again, and emerge from the wood along a clear path to Rusper's main street. **Rusper** contains a lovely mixture of half-timbered and tile-hung cottages, while the church of St Mary Magdalene boasts a magnificent tower, chiefly 16th century, and a fine 14th century brass of John de Kyggesfold. The village once boasted a Benedictine nunnery.

You continue north-eastwards from Rusper, veering north-westwards to pass through Furzefield Wood, taking care not to get sucked away to the right, which you could very easily be. Then, on emerging from the wood, the diet of north-eastward field/farmland walking resumes, with just one short section of road at the hamlet of Orltons; again your path hereabouts is very faithful to the Sussex/Surrey border. The noise of planes is now all too obvious, signifying your approach to Gatwick Airport. You arrive at another road, Russ Hill, by the Russ Hill Hotel, here crossing into Surrey, and walking parallel with it; by detouring along it rather than leaving it as per the SBP you'll reach the restored Lowfield Heath post mill in about 250 yards. The SBP then continues across further fields north-eastwards. Your field walking brings you to **Charlwood**, and past the church of St Nicholas which is a little to the west of the village centre. The church dates back to around 1080, the north aisle and tower base considered to be its oldest parts, and there are very fine wall paintings on the south wall which are believed to date from 1300. The village, which apparently boasts more timber-framed houses using the so-called "crown post" construction method than any other village in Britain, was the sometime home of David Sheppard, a former England cricket captain and Bishop of Liverpool, and the motorcyclist Barry Sheene. Sadly these days it does suffer very much from the proximity of Gatwick Airport. The SBP strikes out north-eastwards from the village then veers eastwards across fields to reach the Charlwood-Hookwood road. The next section can only be described as surreal and unlike any other you'll have experienced on a name path walk in Sussex! Beyond the road you shortly reach the river Mole and the SBP now proceeds beside it, heading essentially north-eastwards but doing a lot of meandering – path and river alike. The Mole enjoys just a modest flow here, having risen just east of Horsham and only becoming a river of any significance once it reaches Surrey. Behind the Mole there's a huge embankment with the North Terminal building of **Gatwick Airport** immediately beyond it. Now back in Sussex again, the SBP comes up to just short of the A23 London-Brighton road then slips south-eastwards, keeping the A23 close by to the left; you cross a road leading to the North Terminal, proceed under the monorail linking the North and South Terminals and continue along Perimeter Road North, soon turning hard left. Gatwick Airport Station is in the South Terminal a short way south along the perimeter road. Having turned hard left, the SBP follows the pedestrian route under the A23 and monorail then bears left, northwards, as clearly signed. You pass under the A23/M23 link, now walking parallel with the railway which is to the right, then turn eastwards, crossing the railway and going along a path taking you eastwards to the **B2036** Balcombe Road. The SBP turns right, south-eastwards, here along the road; **Horley**, and its useful station on the London-Brighton line, is just over half a mile to the left, up the road to the roundabout then left again. The peaceful slopes of Black Down seem a very long way back indeed!

Having turned south-eastwards onto Balcombe Road, the SBP then veers left, eastwards, to run, again on the actual border between Sussex and Surrey, parallel with the A23/M23 link. Then, just on the Sussex side of the border, you turn south along Peeks Brook Lane (which sounds a lot prettier and more intriguing than it is) under the A23/M23 link, through Fernhill. You stay parallel with the M23 itself before turning east to follow Church Lane over the M23 and pass back into Surrey. This is probably the worst bit of the whole SBP and indeed any of the Great Walks: not only are there no views to speak of, but it's extremely noisy as well, both from motorway traffic and aircraft. You then veer north-eastwards still on Church Lane which is now a path, passing to the left of a lake and arriving at Church Road, turning right, south-eastwards, to walk along it through Burstow. If it were anywhere else on the SBP it would probably feel unremarkable, but the fact that it is on such an uninspiring part of the route makes it seem a good deal more quaint and picturesque than it is. That said it is certainly worth exploring the village church with features which date back to the 11th century. John Flamsteed, the first Astronomer Royal in 1675, was rector of Burstow from 1684 until his death in 1719; he is buried below the chancel, and he is commemorated by, appropriately enough, a star set in the large window above the altar. You now continue south-eastwards, then at a sharp left bend use a field to cut a road corner, rejoining Church Road and following it to the B2037 Antlands Lane. Crossing straight over, you then continue south-eastwards on a path across fields, reaching another road, Copthorne Bank. You turn right to follow the road past the **Cherry Tree inn** – if you continue along this road you reach the centre of **Copthorne** in just over a quarter of a mile – then bear left, just south of east, along Clay Hall Lane, before heading just east of south across fields, re-entering Sussex and arriving at the very edge of Copthorne. Copthorne is a large sprawling village, a dormitory for nearby Crawley and a popular overnight stopping place for would-be Gatwick passengers – as if you needed another reminder that you are still very much in the shadow of the airport! You head sharply eastwards then south around the far eastern side of Copthorne, emerging at the A264. More traffic noise! Having crossed over this very busy road, linking Horsham, Crawley, East Grinstead and Tunbridge Wells, you head southwards through predominantly woodland scenery – most refreshing after the soulless road and field walking that's dominated since Charlwood – to arrive at Rowfant House. This is a splendid building which was originally constructed in the late 16th century, probably for an ironmaster; although it was extensively restored in the 19th century it retains a number of late Elizabethan features.

Having passed through the grounds you arrive at Wallage Lane, turning left to follow it eastwards then right to reach the course of the defunct Three Bridges-East Grinstead railway, described more fully in the Worth/Forest Way section. And indeed, overlapping with the Worth Way, you now enjoy a straightforward walk just north of east along the old line for roughly a mile, passing over Wallage Lane and then under the Turners Hill Road bridge (the only overbridge in this mile). Beyond the overbridge you switch to Grange Road which you follow downhill to **Crawley Down**. Like Copthorne this is a rather sprawling village, but there is a useful row of shops to the left, and there's a good bus service to Crawley and East Grinstead if you're flagging. On reaching the village centre, the Worth Way finds the shortest way back to the course of the old railway, but the SBP chooses to embark on a more adventurous course, striking out south-eastwards from the village along Sandhill Lane and eastwards along Burleigh Lane, then beyond Burleigh House Farm continuing eastwards along good paths. The views are really lovely, and the noise of Gatwick seems like a distant memory. You dip down to cross a stream, then gently rise, and just north of Tilkhurst Farm veer just west of north to follow a clear green path, passing the left edge of a pond and going forward to arrive back at the Worth Way and the course of the old railway. You turn right to follow it to **East Grinstead**, reaching the station car park and crossing the existing line, dropping down to the railway station and Sainsbury's. The SBP continues eastwards from the station via Railway Approach to London Road, soon turning left off this road and keeping to the north of the town centre, but by continuing along London Road you reach the centre of the town, described more extensively in the High Weald Landscape Trail, Greenwich Meridian Trail and Worth/Forest Way sections.

Having cut round the northern edge of the centre of the town eastwards via King Street, Institute Walk and De La Warr Road, the SBP soon reaches the B2110 College Lane. You turn left to follow it northwards and cross over the A22 by a bridge, then just past the Estcots Drive turning you strike out north-eastwards. Initially you follow a driveway, then, beyond the splendid timber-framed

Estcots Farmhouse, go forward along a path running parallel with Estcots Drive, descending to pass close to a stream to your left. You then continue along a sometimes narrow but obvious and well-signed path through Ashplats Wood, keeping the suburban housing immediately to your right. You rise to meet – again! – the A264 (here Holtye Road), crossing more or less straight over, then, enjoying fine views, striking out north-eastwards, descending steeply through pasture to the edge of Blackhatch Wood. Here you say a final farewell to West Sussex, as you cross the border into Surrey; the West Sussex-East Sussex border is just south of here. There follows a splendid march north-eastwards through two broad fields and then on through Blockfield Wood, bringing you to the superb timber-framed buildings of Old Surrey Hall. It is believed that the buildings date back to the 15th century; during World War 2 the then owners turned it into a maternity home rather than let it be requisitioned by the Army. From here you ascend again, north-eastwards between fields, enjoying excellent views to your right including, near at hand, the timber-framed Lullenden. You arrive at **Hollow Lane**, following it north-westwards, then just beyond Two Houses (sic) branch off downhill, north-eastwards and eastwards to Upper Stonehurst Farm. Here you veer sharply north-westwards, climbing to Old Lodge Farm, and reaching a clear metalled track. You bear right, just north of east, along this track, enjoying super views, and arriving at the extensive buildings of Dry Hill Farm where you meet, very fleetingly, the Vanguard Way. However while the Vanguard Way heads southwards towards Ashdown Forest, and northwards on through the heart of Surrey, the SBP continues eastwards along the fringes of Reynolds Wood before veering south-eastwards, your predominant direction of travel all the way to Cowden. It's as you veer south-eastwards, now in Jules Wood, that you cross from Surrey into Kent, and for the rest of the walk you'll be either in Kent or East Sussex.

You follow a lovely path through Jules Wood, with the embankment of Dry Hill Reservoir just away to your right, then emerge from the woods to enjoy quite fantastic views across to the North Downs. There's a surprisingly remote feel to this part of the walk, and East Grinstead seems a very long way away. The SBP briefly enters the woods of Willow Bed then proceeds through fields, just skirting another couple of areas of woodland. There are further superb views hereabouts; make the most of them because you're now coming off the hills and won't get back up this high for several more miles. You enter and pass through Clay's Wood then enjoy a very easy walk downhill through the field ahead – you can really get up some speed here – with the splendid buildings of Waystrode Manor, a Tudor manor house, ahead of you. There's a further steep descent and, ironically, a stiff climb, to pass the manor buildings beyond which you continue eastwards to reach a road, your first for what seems like many miles! You follow the road straight on to reach the centre of the village of **Cowden**. The village, which had its own blast furnace from 1573 until sometime in the 18th century, boasts a 13th century parish church built of sandstone with a restored shingle-covered spire which was bomb damaged during World War 2. By turning left at the T-junction in the village centre and following the road, crossing straight over the B2026, you reach Cowden Station in just over a mile.

You head southwards out of the village, dropping down to a stream known as Kent Water and now veering left to head in a predominantly easterly direction beside the stream, first on its right bank, then its left. The character of the walk has completely changed: you've left the wooded hills behind and are now strolling through low-lying meadows, which have their own serene scenic charm – as long as they're not too muddy! The stream marks the Kent-East Sussex border, so again this is border walking in the purest sense. You make easy progress to the B2026 Edenbridge-Hartfield road where you see signs marking entry to Kent on the left, and East Sussex on the right! Fast, easy eastward walking beside or roughly parallel with Kent Water continues beyond the B2026, with sections of right bank and left bank walking. You pass underneath the London-Uckfield railway line, then cross a minor road just north-east of Blackham, now veering south-eastwards past a golf course. The SBP then abruptly leaves Kent Water (and the border – you're now firmly in East Sussex) and veers south-westwards, climbing to Willett's Farm then descending southwards through fields, enjoying a good view ahead which includes the infant river Medway. You drop down to the water meadows and enjoy a brief walk beside this river; it's hard to believe this is going to become Kent's widest river, after the Thames, emptying into the Thames Estuary beyond Chatham and Rochester. You pass underneath the railway again and continue across the meadow to arrive at the A264. As the crow flies this is just over 5 miles from where you last saw it, but you've covered getting on for twice that! The SBP turns left to walk beside the A264 over the Medway into Kent, goes under the railway bridge then turns right shortly along the road past **Ashurst Station** on the London-Uckfield railway.

Beyond the station the SBP remains briefly on the east side of the railway as it proceeds south-eastwards towards Groombridge; it rises and contours a steep hillside, then joining with the Wealdway descends, passes to the west side of the railway and crosses meadows close to the Medway, returning to East Sussex. In fact the SBP will remain well in Sussex for many miles, and will be nowhere near the border with Kent! The Wealdway then heads westwards while the SBP turns south-eastwards, passing Ham Farm and crossing the B2110 to join and briefly follow the Forest Way, another section of disused railway which once linked East Grinstead with Tunbridge Wells and has now become an excellent footpath fully described in the Worth/Forest Way section. However barely have you got into your stride than you leave the Forest Way, striking out south-eastwards across meadows, crossing the B2188 at Hendal Bridge, crossing the London-Uckfield railway again and reaching **Corseley Road**. By turning left here you could walk the half mile on into **Groombridge**, again described more fully in the Worth/Forest Way section. However the SBP turns right and, now overlapping with the High Weald Landscape Trail, almost immediately leaves the road, heading south-westwards. You go back over the London-Uckfield railway and walk between two strips of woodland to the hamlet of Mott's Mill, beyond which there's a brief road walk south-westwards. You then leave the road by turning left along a path heading south-eastwards; from here the High Weald Landscape Trail now strikes out south-westwards through Jockey's Wood while the SBP continues south-eastwards, your predominant direction of travel all the way to the A26 crossing at Boarshead. Initially you skirt the southern end of Rocks Wood, then head through a succession of fields, passing just to the right of the buildings of Bullfinches and enjoying some really splendid views. There's then a lovely long descent through a field to a path crossroads and footbridge. Pleasant up-and-down walking then takes you through fields and along the edge of woodland, past Renby Grange to cross the **A26** Tunbridge Wells-Newhaven road. Just over a quarter of a mile along the road to the right – you've a choice of the main road or a parallel minor road! – is the hamlet of **Boarshead** where there's a pub and excellent bus services to Tunbridge Wells and Brighton. **Eridge Station** is roughly a mile up the A26 to the north-east.

Having crossed the A26 you continue initially south-eastwards; to your left you can see the Bowles Rocks outdoor activity centre and may derive some free entertainment from watching some of the participants attempting the activities on offer. You then however veer just north of east, soon crossing Sandhill Lane, skirting Roughets Wood and passing under the London-Uckfield railway. This is the last time you'll see it! It's then a steady climb through open country past Stitches Farm to meet the Eridge-Rotherfield road, turning right (south-eastwards) to follow it briefly then bearing left along a minor road towards Great Danegate. In a fraction under 500 metres along this road you're signed left (A), north-eastwards, but at this point there's the opportunity of a very substantial and most enjoyable <u>detour D1</u> to Rotherfield, Argos Hill Windmill and Mayfield, a maximum of 11.5 miles in all and effectively adding an extra day to your itinerary (or two, if you choose to break your journey or stay over in Mayfield). Given the lack of places of real interest or amenities on this section of the SBP, you may find this appealing, especially as both Rotherfield and Mayfield have ample amenities including good public transport links. Rotherfield has many fine buildings and a lovely old-fashioned feel, but its undoubted highlight is its quite magnificent early 13th century church of St Denys, one of the finest churches in Sussex, with a superb pulpit, wall paintings, box pews – note the sloping ones at the back, creating a grandstand effect – and chapel screen. At Argos Hill there's a post mill, dating from about 1835, recently restored and looking magnificent with its four sails; across the road here you can enjoy an excellent view south-eastwards to Mayfield. Mayfield boasts many beautiful buildings on its main street, including the timber-framed Middle House Hotel of 1576 and church of St Dunstan with its Jacobean pulpit and 17th century octagonal font. The car park off the right-hand (south) side of the main street offers an excellent view to the countryside south of the village. At the top end of the High Street, you reach the entrance to St Leonards Convent; this incorporates the remains of the medieval

Archbishops' Palace, whose 14th century great hall survives and is now used as a chapel. A number of Archbishops of Canterbury lived here, St Dunstan being the first. There's apparently nothing to stop you entering the grounds, but check at reception before wandering! One other feature you will see on three separate occasions on this detour is the course of the now disused railway branch linking the extant London-Uckfield line with Polegate; a number of pieces of railway paraphernalia survive to this day. The history of this line, known as the Cuckoo Line, is explored more fully in the Cuckoo Trail section.

As stated, however, the SBP turns left, north-eastwards, at (A) on a clear wide path, dropping steeply and veering eastwards then north-eastwards; you continue on a clear path through the woods, crossing a stream which flows from a chalybeate spring just to the north of here. Greenwich Meridian Trail veterans may recall the chalybeate spring in Ashdown Forest! As I mentioned in that section, such springs are known for their high mineral content and health-giving properties. You emerge from the woods and, heading just south of east and regaining height, you walk through the old Eridge deer park. This was reputedly the oldest enclosed deer park in England, mentioned in the Domesday Book; in the late 19th century the then Prince of Wales was a frequent visitor at shooting parties held in the park. Follow signage carefully – the paths aren't well defined – and pause from time to time to enjoy superb views across the park and beyond. At length you reach and cross the **A267** Tunbridge Wells-Hailsham road. The amenities at **Frant** are just over a mile up the A267 northwards, and the High Weald Landscape Trail description states how to access Frant Station from the village. Beyond the A267 you proceed in a predominantly south-easterly direction across farmland, gradually losing height. It's fiddly walking for a while but improves, and the views, especially round Lightlands about a mile from the A267, are tremendous. It really is Wealden countryside at its best! At Lightlands you veer in a more pronounced south-easterly direction, dropping then rising through woodlands to pass Earlye Farm, then dropping again to enter woodland and go forward to Partridges Lane. You turn right along it briefly then, veering in a more easterly direction, you veer left and climb again, initially through woods and then fields past Buckhurst Place, reaching Buckhurst Lane. You follow it briefly left, then bear right and descend, skirting woodland, to the buildings of Ravensdale Farm, and then follow a farm lane, crossing Faircrouch Lane and heading eastwards along Tapsell's Lane. Shortly, however, the SBP turns left, north-eastwards, going through more woodland and crossing the London-Hastings railway, beyond which you ascend to and cross straight over the B2099. **Wadhurst Station** is just 100 yards down the road to the left. Whether you're stopping off here or not, you may want to detour up the road to the right to visit the lovely village of **Wadhurst**, but be warned that it's 1.5 miles away, mostly uphill! It boasts a number of very attractive houses along its main street, the finest being arguably the early 18th century red-brick Vicarage, as well as many tile-hung and weatherboarded cottages. By leaving Church Street at the tile-hung Churchgate House you'll reach the church with its Norman tower and 130ft spire. It's worth proceeding to the churchyard's top end for a tremendous view to Bewl Water, which you'll be seeing a lot more of on the next part of your SBP journey.

In some ways it would be a lot more logical for the SBP simply to (and you may indeed prefer to) follow the road to Wadhurst, turn left in the village centre down Blacksmith's Lane and, at the sharp left bend, continue straight on along a path past Little Pell Farm and on down to Bewl Water, turning left along the reservoir-side path, almost immediately reaching the actual SBP route. However, presumably to avoid an uphill road trudge to Wadhurst, the SBP opts for a two-sides-of-a-triangle walk to reach Bewl Water, requiring over a mile extra walking, eschewing Wadhurst altogether and still not pretending to follow the border with Kent! Beyond the B2099 crossing the SBP heads north-westwards parallel with the road, rather messily through trees – follow the signage carefully! – then turns right briefly along a minor road before bearing left, just east of north on an excellent woodland bridleway. You reach Whitegates Lane and turn left along it, veering gently left to the edge of woodland then striking out north-eastwards along a track as far as Great Shoesmiths Farm. The SBP turns right here, heading south-eastwards to Wood's Green, but there is a route variation V2 possible here to enable you to visit the Bayham Abbey complex. The complex consists of a Tudor-style (actually 19th century) mansion, and the ruins of the 13th century Premonstratensian abbey. There's lots still standing, including sections of the nave, cloister, chancel and transepts in a quite glorious setting, and there are beautiful views across the meadows. As stated, however, the SBP turns south-eastwards at Great Shoesmiths Farm, following field paths to Wood's Green and arriving at a road. You turn left and almost immediately right at a T-junction with Osmers Hill, then, leaving the road, strike away just south of east, rising and following field paths to reach the B2100 at Pell Green. You then turn left, north-eastwards, alongside the B2100 to shortly reach **Cousley Wood**, turning right just by the Old Vine inn, reunited here with V2.

The SBP heads just west of south away from the inn along Butts Lane, then as the lane veers left, you continue on a path heading just west of south, veering south-eastwards and descending to reach Bewl Water Reservoir, going forward to join the path heading round the northern fringe of the reservoir. The reservoir, completed in 1975, was part of a project to increase water supplies in the area; it is now the largest body of inland water in south-east England and is very popular as a sailing centre and for trout fishing. You'll get to know it quite well as you'll be walking beside it for most of the next 5 miles, initially in a predominantly north-easterly then south-easterly direction. Generally the waterside path is well defined. However even though the going appears to be straightforward, it's not hugely quick, with numerous inlets to negotiate and you need to watch for signage to steer you round any necessary deviations from the water's edge, particularly at Hook Farm, just a couple of miles in. Here, at OS ref TQ669334 (B), the SBP leaves the water and heads north-eastwards, then veers just west of north, following a road to a T-junction. Here you turn right and follow this road for around half a mile, bearing right at a kiosk to follow what is the vehicle approach road for the reservoir. You veer right with it and, beyond the wooden-clad buildings on the left but just before the parking area, turn hard left down to the reservoir at the north-west end of a dam, bearing left to follow the top of the dam wall. (The visitor centre and café can be reached by turning right on reaching the dam, climbing the steps and bearing briefly left at the top.) However a slightly shorter and pleasanter alternative route is available from point (B) to the dam, requiring less tarmac crunching, and passing right beside the café and visitor centre; this is described in a <u>route variation V3</u>. Whichever route you've followed, it's then a straightforward walk south-eastwards beside the dam, the SBP veering briefly south-westwards before continuing more resolutely south-eastwards, and the going is in fact exceedingly enjoyable on really good paths, mostly in the shade of trees and actually following the Kent border again. Eventually you reach a road, turning right, southwards, to cross what is the most easterly incursion of the reservoir. There's a particularly photogenic oasthouse in view to the right as you cross. Having crossed, turn left, eastwards, along a path which soon veers south-eastwards, climbing through lovely woodland to reach and cross the **B2087** Flimwell-Ticehurst road at Union Street, the SBP now firmly back in East Sussex! **Flimwell**, which boasts modest amenities, is roughly a quarter of a mile along the B2087 to the left.

The SBP now heads southwards and, with excellent views ahead, proceeds past the buildings of Quedley and across the Dale Hill golf course – be very careful of golfers and low-flying balls! – then enters woodland. There's quite a steep ascent on a rough path to a stile at which you exit the wood (C). Here the SBP veers gently left across the field ahead but by turning right at this point there's a possible detour **D2** to Pashley Manor Gardens and/or **Ticehurst**. Pashley Manor Gardens are among the finest in Sussex and well worth a visit with their blend of fine old trees, fountains, springs and large ponds with tremendous views across the surrounding countryside. In spring there's an abundance of tulips while later months bring lavender, sweet peas, lilies and late-flowering herbaceous perennials. The manor house, not open to the public, dates back to the mid-16th century. Ticehurst is a lovely village with many old weatherboarded and tile-hung cottages, a couple of pubs and several traditional shops; look out for the Coopers sign, indicating a former retail business, the site now occupied by a café. The church of St Mary dates back to the 13th and 14th centuries and contains wooden choir stalls carved by Robert Thompson whose trademark was the addition of a lifelike mouse to each of his carvings. As stated, however, at (C) the SBP veers gently left, south-eastwards, across the field ahead, descending to a footbridge; it then veers in a generally easterly direction and ascends, passing the Roughfield complex on woodland paths, going forward to arrive at the A21 by the buildings of Mumpumps.

You carefully cross the A21 and now head eastwards towards Delmonden Manor. This isn't necessarily the most memorable section of the SBP; that said, you may find it memorable for the wrong reasons, as it's fiddly field/woodland-edge walking and you could easily lose the route. Trusting to your map-reading skills and/ or technology you make your way along a mixture of field paths and tracks via Brookgate Farm to Delmonden Manor, crossing the border into Kent. Beyond Delmonden Manor, further field walking brings you to a Delmonden Road; having crossed it, you now head south-eastwards through an orchard. Welcome to the Garden of England! Beyond the orchard, bitty field walking takes you past Rowland Farm, and there's then a descent and ascent on a track going forward along Heansill Lane. This brings you across Talbot Road to the A229 at the pretty village of **The Moor**, with the church of St Laurence directly opposite. Much of the church dates from around 1450 but the great east window, built around 1350, is regarded as one of the finest pieces of architecture of its kind in the country. By following the A229 north-eastwards for just over half a mile, you'll reach the centre of **Hawkhurst** with its excellent range of amenities including bus links with Maidstone and Tunbridge Wells.

From The Moor you head east/south-eastwards along Stream Lane then strike out, in a south-easterly direction along a clear path past the buildings of East Heath, descending to cross Conghurst Lane and pass Conghurst Farm. Beyond the farm you head initially eastwards then turn sharp right, southwards, on a good path with splendid views. Again you veer south-eastwards, re-entering East Sussex, ascending to the buildings of Northlands; the footpath junction with SBP sign just beyond has to be one of the most picturesquely sited SBP signs on the whole walk, with delightful unspoilt rolling scenery all around you. Continuing south-eastwards you proceed through woodland then rise, still on a good path, to reach the buildings of Lower Northlands Farm and follow a farm lane to cross Bodiam Road at Peter's Green. (Bodiam Church is 275 yards down this road to the right but isn't particularly interesting.) There's then a stiff climb, still heading south-eastwards, to the buildings of Court Lodge from which there's a terrific view to Bodiam Castle just below you. Veering just west of south, you now descend to enter the castle area, veering south-westwards to cross the grounds and reach the castle shop and café. Arguably the finest and most photogenic castle in Sussex (though fans of

Herstmonceux might have something to say about that!), it was built in 1385 as a response to fears that the French might attempt an invasion via the nearby river Rother. It suffered severe damage in the English Civil War and fell into decay, but was restored at the end of the 19th century and a number of impressive features remain including rounded corner turrets, battlements, moat and gatehouse with original portcullis, claimed to the oldest in the country, as well as the great hall, servants' hall, chapel and kitchen.

Beyond the shop/café you proceed to the road, turning left to cross the East Sussex river Rother by means of Bodiam Bridge. The East Sussex Rother is one of the great rivers of Sussex, beginning somewhat indistinctly just south-east of Mayfield and emptying impressively into the English Channel at Rye Harbour. You'll see a lot more of this river later in the walk. At the same time you may need to rack your brains to recall the *West* Sussex river Rother which you crossed just north of Harting all those miles back! The SBP then turns left to follow the embankment eastwards by the Rother, but by continuing along the road through **Bodiam** you will soon reach the station at the western end of the preserved Kent & East Sussex Railway. The original railway ran from Robertsbridge to Headcorn via Tenterden, opening in the first decade of the 20th century; it closed to passengers in 1954 but twenty years later the section between Tenterden and Rolvenden was reopened as a preserved steam railway and the extension to Bodiam was effected in 2000. You may decide to indulge in a ride before continuing with the SBP! Back on the walking route, the SBP follows the right bank of the Rother eastwards of Bodiam Bridge then turns sharp right to cross the meadow before heading westwards to cross over the railway. Now you strike out south-eastwards from the railway on a field path, soon forking left onto a path which continues south-eastwards uphill, skirting woodland and reaching a road at Ewhurst Green. Look back here for a stunning view of the Rother valley and Bodiam Castle. You turn left, north-eastwards along the lovely main street at Ewhurst Green, going past the fine tile-hung Preacher's House and 12th century church of St James to your right.

Just beyond the church you bear right, south-eastwards, downhill, soon veering north-eastwards to pass along the bottom edge of further orchards, and reaching a road; the SBP follows this briefly south-eastwards then bears left to proceed north-eastwards beside a stream. You bear right to cross the stream and enter another field, walking straight across it as signed and approaching another footbridge crossing. The SBP turns right (D) just before this crossing, but by going straight on there's the chance of a <u>route variation V4</u> to Northiam via Great Dixter. I really recommend this; it'll be one of the highlights of the whole walk. Great Dixter is a 15th century half-timbered house which was home to the gardener and writer Christopher Lloyd until his death in 2005. Lloyd's parents bought the house in 1912 and with the assistance of Edwin Lutyens redesigned and extended it; Lutyens also helped design the quite magnificent gardens, planting hedges and topiary. Striking features are its series of intimate garden rooms including the meadow garden, the colonies of bulbs, the orchard with its early purple orchids, the famous Long Border with its spectacular mixture of shrubs, climbers, perennials and annuals, and a sheltered Exotic Garden which is a riot of tropical colours. However as stated the SBP turns right at (D) and heads just south of east through fields with woodland close by, the ground rising to your left while you remain on the valley bottom, roughly parallel with a stream. You cross a road at the picturesquely-named Strawberry Hole Cottage, then head uphill just north of east, initially across fields then along a lane to the main street (actually the A28) at **Northiam**, reaching this road in the old part of the village by the green. There are delightful tile-hung, timber-framed and weatherboarded old houses round the edge of the green, while at the green's top end is the ancient battered oak under which, in 1573, Elizabeth I sat and changed her shoes, leaving her old ones behind! The 12th century church of St Mary is a little way along the lane just beyond the oak. Northiam offers a good range of amenities including shops and bus links not only in the old part of the village but in the newer part just to the north (left) of where the SBP reaches the A28; it's the last settlement of any significance before the end of the walk at Rye.

The SBP turns right to walk briefly south-eastwards beside the A28 then strikes out south-eastwards from the village, descending quite steeply and skirting Hilly Wood, veering just north of east to pass through the pretty Gilly Wood with its profusion of wild garlic in spring, and ascending eastwards past Woodgate House to reach Church Lane. You turn left onto it then immediately right along Rectory Lane, soon forking left and continuing just north of east across fields, veering eastwards and then south-eastwards along the edge of trees to reach the B2088 at Beckley. You follow the road briefly eastwards initially then turn left, northwards, for a walk which begins pleasantly enough but continues uninspiringly past a sewage works and what at the time of writing was an area of general farm/works debris, veering north-eastwards to cross the A268 Hawkhurst-Rye road. From here things improve as you continue north-eastwards uphill through fields, soon passing a narrow strip of woodland, then walk eastwards along the north fringe of Dean Wood. There's a stunning view from here along what is an excellent path, and there are seats provided for you to sit and enjoy the view. You drop down slightly to reach Hobbs Lane, turning right (southwards) along it then turn left to follow a footpath eastwards, shortly passing through the very pretty Barber's Wood. Emerging from the wood and heading just south of east, you aim to the right of a pond at the edge of the trees of Decoypond Wood, reaching a path fork. You've now reached the Rother Levels, a large and extensively farmed area of lowland marshes, full of ditches and channels around the Rother. At the fork you once more meet the High Weald Landscape Trail which you previously saw near Groombridge many miles back and which you now overlap with for the next mile or so. Forking north-eastwards, you now follow what is a sometimes indistinct path across a section of the Rother Levels. On a dry sunny day this will seem pleasant and relaxing, but on a grey, wet windy day it will feel quite inhospitable. You'll doubtless be relieved to learn that the walking is about to get much easier! Your path arrives at the Wittersham-Flackley Ash road and you turn left along it, shortly reaching the **Blackwall Bridge** crossing of the Rother and passing temporarily back into Kent.

Now the going gets very easy indeed and will remain so for the rest of the walk. Having crossed the bridge, now on the Kent side of the border, the SBP turns immediately right, south-eastwards, to join a clear path along the left bank of the Rother. You simply follow this for 2 miles or so, initially just south of east then – returning to East Sussex where you'll remain for the rest of the walk – just north of east, until you reach the B2082 Wittersham Road. As you walk between Blackwall Bridge and the B2082 there are fine views to Wittersham Church, visited by the High Weald Landscape Trail, to the left. The SBP crosses straight over the B2082 and continues eastwards then south-eastwards along the left bank of the Rother for just under 2 more miles. To your right across the river is the particularly fine set of hilltop buildings of Thornsdale Farm, with a splendid oasthouse, while ahead of you to the left is Stone Cliff, a prominent hillside just to the south of the historic village of Stone-in-Oxney. In due course you reach the Military Road which you cross straight over; to your left is the Royal Military Canal, built in 1807 and described more fully in the section devoted to the Royal Military Canal Path and Saxon Shore Way. South of here the canal actually overlaps with the Rother. Having crossed straight over the Military Road, you turn right and then bear immediately left to cross the Rother/Royal Military Canal, now turning south-westwards at **Iden Lock** to follow its left bank all the way to Rye, just under 3 miles distant. The waterside walk, overlapping with the Royal Military Canal Path and Saxon Shore Way, is enjoyable and largely straightforward, with extensive views across Romney Marsh (again, described more fully in the Royal Military Canal Path/Saxon Shore Way section) to the left. There is one point where you are signed round the left-hand side of a riverside house, but as you reach a point where you have to pass under the Rye-Ashford railway a more potentially awkward logistical problem presents itself: the path under the railway may flood at high tide and thus be impassable with no other way round. You may just have to wait for the tide to recede. At length, not long after passing under the railway, you reach the A259 coast road, which you last saw in Emsworth right at the start of the walk! Now turn right alongside the A259 over the Rother to enter **Rye**. On reaching the roundabout turn left as far as the pedestrian crossing, crossing here and walking up the slipway to reach a street, East Cliff, also known as Hilders Cliff. Turn right along it, passing under the Landgate – one of three gates into the town built under Edward III – and turning hard left down Tower Street, going forward along Cinque Ports Street as far as a crossroads junction, with Market Road to the left and Station Approach to the right. For a suggested walking tour of Rye which starts at the crossroads junction, please refer to the England Coast Path section. To reach the bus stands and **Rye Station**, turn right into Station Approach.

That then completes the main SBP route but if you want to say you've walked the entire SBP you need to complete the spur route as well.

Spur Route

According to OS maps the spur route begins at Mile Oak Road just west of its junction with Portslade High Street. However I suggest you begin from **Fishersgate Station**, taking the footpath heading north-westwards from the east end of the north platform, then following it through the sprawling outskirts of Brighton along paths marking the exact border between West Sussex and the unitary authority area of Brighton & Hove. You soon cross the A2070 Old Shoreham Road and shortly you reach Mile Oak Road. Continuing north-westwards beyond Mile Oak Road, you begin to emerge from the housing, gaining height all the while and climbing onto Southwick Hill, overlapping briefly with the Monarch's Way, then descend, passing over the Southwick Tunnel which carries the A27, and skirting the buildings of Mile Oak Farm. At last you've emerged from suburbia! Having dropped down to the valley you leave the Monarch's Way, swinging north-eastwards and properly entering Brighton & Hove. Climbing again, you skirt the summit of Cockroost Hill, which is to your right, and veer quite sharply right, just north of east, to reach a path T-junction; here you turn left and head resolutely uphill just west of north, then veer north-eastwards, still climbing. At length, crossing into West Sussex, you reach the top of the ridge on Fulking Hill, now turning right to join the South Downs Way. Pause for a moment to admire the superb views, then continue eastwards to arrive at a road along which, to the left, is the **Devil's Dyke** pub/restaurant and spectacular viewpoint, 250 yards away; you may feel you've earned a rest and a drink here, but be warned that it is exceedingly popular in summer. The South Downs Way section describes how to gain access to the magnificent nearby viewpoints.

The SBP goes straight over the road and now follows the South Downs Way along a clear path going gently downhill north-eastwards, keeping Devil's Dyke, more fully described (as is a possible detour to **Poynings**) in the South Downs Way section, to your left. You keep going along the South Downs Way, at length getting within sight of a car parking area and a road coming in from your right. Here you veer left with the South Downs Way, downhill, to cross a road at the hamlet of **Saddlescombe** and pass round the edge of the farm buildings. Beyond the buildings the SDW heads north-eastwards towards Newtimber Hill and Pyecombe but the

SBP now branches off south-eastwards, back towards Brighton again! Crossing back into Brighton & Hove, you drop down, passing Sweet Hill and its trig point with good southward views to Waterhall Windmill, a 19th century tower mill, to the south; you then cross the A23 and skirt the A27 just beyond its junction with the A23. Now you turn northwards again, pulling away from Brighton for what will be the second and last time. You join a path heading uphill; ahead of you, to your half-right on the hillside, is a clump of trees and you can see the white Chattri Indian War Memorial. Unveiled in February 1921 by Edward, Prince of Wales, it is dedicated to Indian soldiers who fought on the Western Front during World War 1 and stands on the site where a number of them were cremated. Your clear path continues northwards then veers elegantly north-eastwards, passing above trees and just to the left of the war memorial; the going remains very well defined and easy. You exit Brighton & Hove and re-enter West Sussex, going forward past the right of another area of trees and above the buildings of Lower Standean that are to your right, rising steadily, to arrive eventually at the South Downs Way again, crossing just here into East Sussex. The SBP spur turns right here to follow the South Downs Way for roughly 150 yards eastwards, but all too soon you then leave the escarpment and the South Downs Way, turning left (north-eastwards) to walk very steeply down the hillside of Burnhouse Bostall, veering to the right and then left, steeply descending all the time; do pause to enjoy the magnificent views across the Weald as you proceed downhill, as there is nothing quite as good as this to come. The gradient eases and it's then a straightforward descent to Underhill Lane. The SBP turns right onto Underhill Lane and shortly left onto a signed path which heads in a north/north-easterly direction between fences and forward along the B2112 South Street into the delightful centre of **Ditchling**, crossing over West Street; by turning left in the village centre along the B2116 West Street you reach **Hassocks Station** in 1.25 miles. However the SBP proceeds northwards beyond West Street through the village up High Street, past the end of Church Lane. You can and should detour left via Church Lane to reach two features of particular interest, namely the church of St Margaret, with both Norman and Early English features, and the new and excellent Museum of Art & Craft. From in front of the museum there's a fine view southwards to the magnificent timber-framed

Wings Place on West Street. Meanwhile, to the right up High Street is the lovely Conds Cottage, sometime home of the writer Esther Meynell, and next door is the house where the sculptor Eric Gill made his home for a time. The SBP then bears right off the village street along East Gardens. However by turning left rather than right, along Boddingtons Lane, there's the option of a <u>detour D3</u> to Oldland Windmill, a delightful post mill which dates back to around 1700.

Beyond East Gardens the SBP proceeds in a generally north-easterly direction through fields with just one lovely woodland interlude. You cross the Burgess Hill-Lewes railway line, then continue in an essentially north-easterly direction, again through fields, veering sharp right to cross Folders Lane, following another road very briefly eastwards then striking out just east of north on a path that skirts an industrial estate. You now go forward along a clearly signed bridleway heading northwards through the edge of woods, with fields visible to the left. This is certainly the most enjoyable walking since Ditchling and particularly pleasant and refreshing in hot sunshine. You emerge from the wood and shortly reach **Wivelsfield**, turning right along Eastern Road to a crossroads junction with Green Road. (Wivelsfield Station, reached by turning left along Green Road, left at the end down the B2112, then first right up Janes Lane, is 2.5 miles away! Beyond the crossroads you continue just east of north along Slugwash Lane, walking uphill past Townings Place, then head north-eastwards through Ham Wood along Ham Lane. From here you continue north-eastwards over Ham Bridge (returning to West Sussex), the walking now becoming quite fiddly as you follow a succession of paths, incorporating a steep climb, north-eastwards. Things get easier as you join a metalled lane and, continuing north-eastwards, now follow it past Ham Lane Farm and into **Scaynes Hill**, reaching the A272.

Beyond the A272 the SBP heads eastwards along Clearwater Lane, overlapping here with the Sussex Hospices Trail as far as the Hammond's Farm buildings, then the SBP continues along a path through farmland, descending then veering just east of north and rising to arrive at the picturesquely-named Butterbox Lane.

You turn right, south-eastwards, along the road, passing the entrance to the buildings of Massetts, beyond which you proceed first north-eastwards along the edge of Lye Wood then north-westwards through Hammer Wood. For just a little while now you overlap with two other name paths, the Sussex Ouse Valley Way and the Greenwich Meridian Trail. Beyond Hammer Wood you reach Sloop Lane, turning right along it past the Sloop pub, a welcome watering hole for three sets of name path walkers! The Sussex Ouse Valley Way leaves you here, but the Greenwich Meridian Trail stays with you as you cross the Ouse then head eastwards (entering East Sussex), past the left-hand side of the buildings of Freshfield Mill Farm and on through the water meadows close to the Ouse. Veering north-eastwards, you pass under the Bluebell Railway, skirting the right-hand edge of woodland. You ascend through grassland and pass through King's Wood to cross Ketche's Lane, then continue north-eastwards on a farm lane and then, beyond Northland Farm, pass through Northland Wood to reach a path junction. Here you at last leave the Greenwich Meridian Trail, heading initially south-westwards, veering north-westwards to skirt Cowstocks Wood and cross Freshfield Lane. Pleasant woodland walking past Latchetts and Hole House (where you return to West Sussex) brings you to another lane at Wyatts, from which you continue northwards to **Horsted Keynes**. Horsted Keynes' most iconic feature is its splendidly wide village green lying between the Crown inn and an old forge, while the village sign on the green shows a knight and squire from the Bayeux Tapestry. The village has many attractive cottages including some timber-framed houses, while about a mile to the north-west is Horsted Keynes' railway station on the Bluebell Railway, more extensively described in the Sussex Ouse Valley Way section and easily accessed at the end of the SBP spur route in East Grinstead.

The SBP continues northwards from the village centre, descending then climbing to pass the church of St Giles; it's mainly Norman in origin with a tall shingled spire, and two other features of interest are a pigmy Crusader's effigy, which may have been scaled down to fit a niche in the chancel, and a headless brass of a lady with hands clasped in prayer. Beyond the church you follow a really lovely path just east of north which passes between large ponds. Seats are provided, and you may well be tempted to sit and relax and enjoy the tranquillity. You pass just to the left of the fine Broadhurst Manor, mostly built in 1934 but containing some 16th century features, then turn left onto Broadhurst Manor Road and right at the T-junction.

Shortly you head north-westwards, descending then ascending steeply, descending once more and veering briefly south-westwards to join Horsted Lane and follow it briefly northwards. You then resume your north-westward progression through rolling fields, roughly parallel with the Bluebell Railway which is to your left, to reach the village of **Sharpthorne**. You cross the main street and walk north-westwards along Station Road to cross the railway then continue northwards; you're now immediately beside the railway, keeping it to your right, and if trains are running you can enjoy the sight and sound of the magnificent old steam engines. You cross back over the railway then strike out enjoyably north-eastwards on a lovely path that goes past New Combe Wood and then through Blackland Wood, reaching **Grinstead Lane**. You turn left to follow this lane northwards, cross the end of Weir Wood Reservoir, and carry on north-eastwards uphill along the lane, here flirting with the East/West Sussex border. Shortly you bear just east of north along a road then, overlapping with the High Weald Landscape Trail, go forward along a path which snakes along the reservoir edge, keeping it to the right albeit sometimes separated from it by vegetation. Ignore two signed paths going off to the left (unless you wish to detour up the High Weald Landscape Trail which brings you in half a mile to Standen, more fully described in the High Weald Landscape Trail section) and pass through some lovely woodland; with all the twists and turns, this waterside walk may take quite a lot longer than one perhaps thinks it should. The reservoir was completed in 1953 and is now designated as a Site of Special Scientific Interest. The SBP is one of three name paths (High Weald Landscape Trail and Greenwich Meridian Trail being the others) to visit the reservoir which boasts a breeding colony of crested grebes and migrating ospreys. Throughout your reservoir-side walk on the SBP you're on the border of East and West Sussex. Not far short of the east end of the reservoir you pass a picnic area and a little way beyond that, you veer northwards away from the reservoir (now in West Sussex again) to Busses Farm. Here you veer north-eastwards and then eastwards, skirting woodland and descending to pass a sewage works which is to your left and Horseshoe Farm to the right. You then veer north-eastwards along a lane, marking the East/West Sussex border, to arrive at the Forest Way (which you crossed on the main SBP route), accessing it via a slipway. Now back in West

Sussex, you follow the Forest Way north-westwards to reach the main street at East Grinstead. To get to **East Grinstead Station**, turn right off the main street down London Road and left down Railway Approach, crossing the roundabout at the end and passing Sainsbury's to arrive at the station. By turning left just before the mainline station and walking alongside Sainsbury's and its car park, you reach the northern terminus of the Bluebell Railway.

GOOD TO KNOW

Main route start: Emsworth Station. Main route finish: Rye Station.

Spur route start: Fishersgate Station. Spur route finish: East Grinstead Station.

Main route mileage: 140. Spur route mileage: 34.5.

Difficulty: Moderate.

Main route stages: Prinsted for Southbourne (*RB) 2, A259 for Emsworth (*RAB) 10, Westbourne (RAB) 11, Rowland's Castle (*RAB) 15, Finchdean (R) 16.25, B2146 for South Harting (RAB) 22, Bottom of Rake Hanger for Hill Brow and Liss (*RAB) 26.5, Rake (RA), 28, Highfield Lane for Liphook (*RB) 32, Stedlands Farm for Haslemere (*RAB) 37.5, A283 41.5, Dungate Farm 46, B2133 for Loxwood (R) 48.5, Rudgwick (RAB) 51, A29 57, Rusper (RA) 61, Charlwood (RB) 66.5, Gatwick Airport (*RAB) 69, B2036 for Horley (*RAB) 70, Cherry Tree inn (R) for Copthorne (RAB) 74, Crawley Down (RB) 78, East Grinstead (*RAB) 82, Hollow Lane 84.5, Cowden (*RA) 89.5, Ashurst Station (*) 92, Corseley Road for Groombridge (RAB) 95, A26 for Boarshead (RB) and Eridge Station (*) 99, A267 for Frant (*RB) 103, Wadhurst Station for Wadhurst (*RAB) 106, Cousley Wood (R) 108.5, B2087 for Flimwell (RAB) 114, D2 start point for Ticehurst (RAB) 115, The Moor (R) for Hawkhurst (RAB) 119, Bodiam (R) 123, Northiam (RAB) 128.5, Blackwall Bridge 133, Iden Lock 137.25, Rye Station (*RAB) 140.

Spur route stages: Devil's Dyke (R) for Poynings (R) 5, Saddlescombe (R) 6, Ditchling for Hassocks Station (*RAB) 12, Wivelsfield (*RB) 15.75, Scaynes Hill (RAB) 18.5, Horsted Keynes (RAB) 23.5, Sharpthorne (RAB) 27, Grinstead Lane 28.5, East Grinstead Station (*RAB) 34.5.

OS: OL8, OL33, OL34, 135, 136, 125, OL11.

D1 NOTE: THIS IS A LENGTHY DETOUR, 11.5 MILES IN TOTAL. From (A) go straight on past Little Danegate then in 130 yards fork right along a signed byway, passing charming ponds on both sides and then the lovely buildings of Colshorn Oast and Hoth Farm House. You descend steeply into woods, at the very bottom of the descent using a parallel path with bridge to avoid fording a crossing stream. You rise for a few yards beyond the stream then turn right as footpath-signed and almost immediately left, steeply up a narrow path through the trees, veering left and then hard right to rejoin the byway. At the end turn right along the road then in 30 yards turn left as footpath-signed into Big Millhole Wood. Follow the clearly signed footpath downhill to cross under the old railway, then veer left to cross a stream and head uphill as signed on the obvious path – don't be tempted onto the old railway line that's away to your left. At the path T-junction at the top turn right along a wider path, then in roughly 80 yards turn right again along a signed path taking you to Eridge Lane. Turn left (south) along the lane which takes you past a small cemetery and the impressive St Denys Lodge into Rotherfield (2.5 miles from start of detour). Turn right into Church Road, the B2100, to visit the church of St Denys which is immediately to your left. (By continuing along the B2100 westwards you reach Crowborough Station in 1.25 miles.) Return to the High Street and turn right along it, then, just past the Station Road turning, cross the road to reach the adjacent Kings Arms, and take a signed path immediately to the right of the pub. The path soon veers right, going forward across New Road and along Horsegrove Lane. At its end you reach a path fork, bearing right downhill along a right-hand field edge; at the stile, veer left as signed across the field down the hillside, aiming for a stile which you cross, then continue along the path beyond, through an area of woodland. You cross a stream then continue through the trees, emerging and rising to follow an obvious path through a meadow then dropping to another stream crossing followed by a sharp ascent. You then follow a left-hand field edge to a gate, veering left beyond the gate to reach a farm lane, and turning right along this lane to shortly arrive at Sheriff's Lane. Turn right along it to a T-junction, turning left here along the B2101 for just over a quarter of a mile, then as the road bends gently left, bear right up Argos Hill Lane. Go straight over at the crossroads (detouring left here if you wish to shortly enjoy a fantastic view to the north) and continue past Argos Hill Windmill. Proceed on along the road which begins to drop steeply, but shortly before reaching the A267 turn right along a plinth-signed bridleway, also signed for Spring Place. Just before the house go left as signed along a delightful path in the trees, descending to Pages Farm, beyond which continue in the same direction along the farm lane, veering sharp right and then left to reach Fir Toll Road. Turn left along it to the A267, crossing straight over onto signed cycle route 21, climbing up a metalled slipway, then going on along Fir Toll Close to a crossroads junction with Love Lane and Stone Cross. Go straight over along Station Road (becoming High Street) to reach Mayfield's centre, boasting many shops and eateries, 6.5 miles from the start of the detour. Note that there are regular buses linking Rotherfield and Mayfield.

Now return all the way to the B2101 as follows. Go back down the High Street, on along Station Road, across Love Lane/Stone Cross, down Fir Toll Close (NOT the adjacent Mayfield Close), down the slipway, over the A267 and along Fir Toll Road. Fork right up the lane signed Burnt House and Downford, past Pages Farm and on up the woodland path to Spring Place, following the driveway then turning left at the end; ascend and pass the windmill, going straight over the crossroads (keeping Postmill Cottage to the left), descending to the B2101 and turning left alongside it. After roughly a quarter of a mile turn back down Sheriff's Lane, this time following it to its end, passing under a bridge which carried the now disused railway linking Tunbridge Wells and Eastbourne, the so-called Cuckoo Line. At the T-junction at the end turn left down Yewtree Lane, passing the Cuckoo Line Stores (the only refreshment option between Mayfield and the end of the detour) and reaching a T-junction with the B2100 at Town Row. To avoid what is an awkward crossing of the B2100, turn left just before the T-junction along a path which veers right, across the course of the old line, to the B2100. Cross here and turn right under the splendid old bridge, then bear immediately left up Spouthill, noting the superbly kept old Rotherfield & Mark Cross station to the left. Now follow this road for roughly a mile in total. You pass (but don't take) a road forking right, and just over 275 yards beyond the fork you reach the southern end of the byway you followed at the start of the detour. Turn right along it and simply retrace your steps to the SBP, as follows. Turn shortly hard left along a signed footpath which hairpins back and then turns sharp right, downhill to a path T-junction; you turn right here to return to the byway. Turn *left onto the byway, soon switching to the parallel signed path to avoid having to ford the stream, then, returning to the byway and sticking with it, climb past Hoth Farm House and Colshorn Oast to arrive at the road. Turn left and shortly beyond Little Danegate you reach point (A) in the main body of text, turning right to resume your SBP walk. (Total detour 11.5 miles)*

D2 At (C) turn right and proceed uphill on the right-hand field edge. You pass a hedge at right-angles to your path and keep rising to shortly reach a second hedge, also at right-angles. Turn left to follow parallel with the hedge, keeping it to your right, then at the end veer right as path-signed, and walk straight across the field ahead, rising gently and heading westwards. At the trees on the other side go forward in the same direction on a narrow fenced path, at the end of which turn left along a driveway bringing you to a junction (E) with the B2099. To visit Ticehurst (1.25 miles from the start of the detour) with its ample amenities including buses, turn right and simply follow the road to reach the village centre, walking back the same way to (E). To visit Pashley Manor Gardens, then, coming from the driveway, turn left at (E) – or, if you've detoured to Ticehurst, carry straight on – and follow the B2099 for half a mile, the gardens clearly signed on your right. Then return to (E) and retrace your steps via the driveway, fenced path, gentle field descent, left as signed along the right-hand side of the hedge, and right, downhill, along the left-hand field edge past the lower hedge to arrive back at point (C). Turn right as signed to resume your SBP walk. (Total detour 3.5 miles)

D3 Having turned left along Boddingtons Lane, continue in the same westerly direction, passing through the gate – don't be tempted to veer right – to arrive at Lodge Hill Lane. Turn right up the lane, ignoring the first footpath signed left. In about 300 yards beyond that first footpath turning, fork left onto a footpath running parallel with the lane, very shortly having the choice of an enclosed narrow path between fence and vegetation, or (via a gate) an open grassy permissive path alongside but just below the fence. In due course the latter path ends and unites with the enclosed one, continuing to shortly reach Oldland Windmill. Return the same way via Lodge Hill Lane and Boddingtons Lane to rejoin the SBP spur route. (Total detour 1.25 miles)

V1 Instead of turning left by the green at Linchmere, continue along the road heading south-eastwards, soon reaching and perhaps visiting the church which is to your right. Beyond the church follow the road as it descends, veering just west of south then south-eastwards and negotiating a sharp left bend. Now continuing south-eastwards you emerge from the trees, crossing a stream and descending gently to reach the well-signed Shulbrede priory. The best views of the Priory are from the roadside just beyond the driveway to the house. Retrace your steps briefly but just after crossing the stream referred to above, as you enter the woods roughly 500 yards from the priory, bear right up a signed footpath. Ignore a left path turn and cross a private driveway then, heading north-westwards, ascend to a T-junction with a path coming hard in from the right. Turn right along this path which soon reaches a left bend from which there are fine southward views. On this bend, turn left along a signed path which heads uphill through the trees, heading north-eastwards. Signage is excellent. You emerge from the woods at the top of the ridge and go through a metalled kissing gate then forward, north-eastwards, across an area of grass. You dip down slightly and pass through another gate, turning right at the path junction here to rejoin the SBP. (Extra 1.25 miles)

V2 Instead of turning right at Great Shoesmiths Farm, walk straight on through the complex, ignoring paths signed right and left, then follow the signed bridleway on along a left-hand field edge with woodland to your left. Beyond the woods you veer very gently left, keeping to the field's left side, crossing a footbridge then veering gently right, past a pond and the lovely Bartley Mill to reach Bartley Mill Road. Turn left to follow it briefly, in 275 yards forking right up what is a continuation of Bartley Mill Road to reach Bayham Road (B2169). Turn right to follow it eastwards for just under a mile, reaching the well-signed Bayham Abbey driveway to your left. Having visited the abbey continue eastwards along the B2169 which in some 275 yards bends left; immediately beyond this bend you fork right onto a rather inconspicuous plinth-signed path which immediately veers left to follow the right-hand edge of trees to a footbridge. Turn right to cross the bridge and proceed along a left-hand field edge, shortly reaching a metal gate on the left. Turn left through the gate and over the stile immediately beyond, joining a driveway briefly; 100 yards or so along on the right, turn right along a signed but easily missed woodland path. You soon cross a boardwalk, beyond which continue past a path going off to the right, then, very soon beyond a path coming in from hard left, you reach a fork. Signage hereabouts is conspicuously non-existent! Fork right, soon reaching another fork; fork left here, going forward to a path T-junction where you turn right. Continue to another path T-junction, turning left and arriving at a footbridge which you cross, immediately then turning right up Free Heath Road. You reach a crossroads in the woods, going straight over (although a short detour up the road to the left provides a superb view northwards across miles of Kent countryside) and following the road to a T-junction. Turn left here along Sleepers Stile Road for 300 yards past an area of woodland that's to your right, then, close to the end of the woods, turn hard right along a signed path. Ignore left forks but veer left with the path, emerging to cross a field to Newbury Lane. Turn left along it then in 75 yards bear right onto a footpath which from its elevated spot enjoys superb views, especially to Bewl Water ahead. Follow the path down to Windmill Lane, bearing right along it then left at the end, and follow the road (ignoring the left fork) to reach the B2100 at Cousley Wood. Cross straight over to the Old Vine to be reunited with the SBP. (Extra 1.75 miles)

V3 Having turned away from the reservoir at point (B), take the second drive on the right, signed as footpath only. You reach a parking area; at the end of it, don't continue down the access road to the bistro but turn left and almost immediately right along a path signed to Public Car Park. Cross an access road and follow the path ahead past a sign pointing to an Adventure Playground. You go forward along an area of green, passing to the right of (and perhaps visiting) Bewl Water Visitor Centre whose restaurant provides an opportunity for refreshments. Having passed the visitor centre and restaurant, continue to the left of a small children's play area then shortly turn right down the steps. You here reach the dam and go forward beside it, soon being rejoined by the SBP route. (Just under 400 yards saved)

V4 Go forward over the footbridge, then (going straight on) follow an excellent path uphill, aiming for the left edge of the trees. Now simply continue as signed, veering right across the field and aiming for the field boundary at the top. On reaching the boundary by a pond, veer left along the right-hand field edge, then go through a metalled *gate and forward along a driveway to reach Great Dixter. Having visited it, follow the path parallel with the driveway from the house to a road fork of High Park and Dixter Road. Fork right down Dixter Road which takes you all the way to the A28 Main Street. Turn right to follow it to the old part of Northiam, being reunited with the SBP which comes in from the right almost opposite the green. (Extra half a mile)*

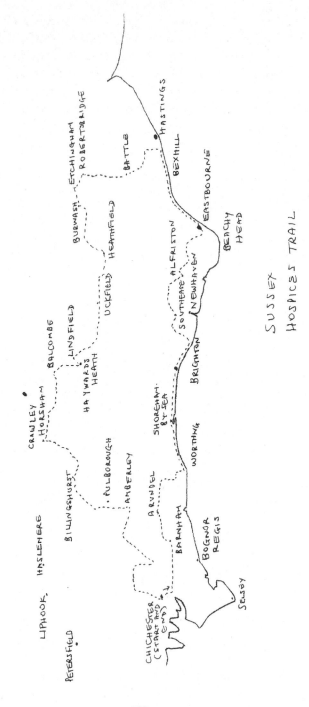

SUSSEX
HOSPICES TRAIL

21 The Vicarage, Wadhurst just off the Sussex Border Path

22 The church and Wings Place at Ditchling on the Sussex Border Path

23 Kipling's beloved Bateman's on the Sussex Hospices Trail

24 Boxgrove Priory near the end of the Sussex Hospices Trail

25 The Ouse Valley Viaduct, the finest feature of the Sussex Ouse Valley Way

26 The Ouse at its best: approaching Lewes on the Sussex Ouse Valley Way

27 Herstmonceux Castle, one of the highlights of the 1066 Country Walk

28 The beautiful church at Penhurst just off the 1066 Country Walk

29 The remarkable interior of Berwick Church on the Vanguard Way

30 A broad track on the top of Ashdown Forest on the Vanguard Way

31 The magnificently-sited trig point by Camp Hill Clump on the Wealdway

32 Horselunges Manor, one of the best features on the Wealdway

33 The isolated and beautiful Blue Idol on the West Sussex Literary Trail

34 Ebbsworth at Nutbourne close to the West Sussex Literary Trail

35 Loves Bridge near Newpound on the Wey South Path

36 The Wey & Arun Canal at Loxwood on the Wey South Path

37 The church of St Nicholas, Worth on the Worth Way

38 A picturesque section of the Forest Way just east of Hartfield

39 Lamb House in Rye where many Great Walks of Sussex meet

40 St Richard's statue in Chichester where two Great Walks of Sussex end

12 SUSSEX HOSPICES TRAIL

The Sussex Hospices Trail (SHT), starting and ending in Chichester, is the newest in the family of name paths of Sussex, being established in 2016 – and officially launched in September 2017 – to celebrate the 21st anniversary of the Friends of Sussex Hospices (FSH).   For the Sussex walker it presents a terrific new challenge, it being the longest waymarked path passing exclusively through Sussex. It's a very satisfying walk indeed, starting and finishing at Chichester, at the south-west corner of Sussex, and going right up to the very north-east corner at Etchingham. It is the culmination of a huge amount of work by Sue Korman and her colleagues at FSH, who hope that the trail will be used as a vehicle for sponsored walk challenges, particularly to raise money for their fantastic organisation. It's worth reiterating that by buying this book you are contributing to its work. (So thank you!)

Two things should be borne in mind before you set out. Firstly, although the trail goes quite close to some of the places helped by FSH, it only visits a handful of them. That said, the aim was always to link the areas served by the 12 Sussex hospice care providers rather than buildings. Secondly, there is – perhaps inevitably – significant overlap between the SHT and sections of other name paths in this book. In the interests of space, where such overlap occurs, there will be little or no description of the route in this section. But even if you do find yourself repeating bits of other routes you've already done, this walk is still well worth doing. It is a very long walk but easily broken down into bite-size chunks, with amenities far more easily available than on the South Downs Way.

I suggest this circular (2.5 mile) tour of Chichester before you start. Turn left out of Chichester Station approach road and walk up past the Globe, crossing the Avenue de Chartres and continuing up South Street. On the left is the fine Canon Gate and then the brick and flint-built Vicar's Hall which stands immediately above the late 12th century Crypt. Continue on to the Cross, built in 1501 as a covered market, and turn right here into East Street. Take the first left turn into St Martin's Street; soon bear left into Lion Street but do detour to St Martin's Square which is immediately beyond, and which contains the entrance to St Mary's Hospital, once occupied by Franciscan monks, with almshouses adjoining it. Now follow Lion Street to its junction with North Street onto which you turn left, immediately passing the red-brick and pillared 1731 Council House. Continue past the 13th/14th century church of St Olave, now a bookshop, and further down on the left is the beautifully restored Buttermarket, built by Nash in 1807. Continue to the Cross and turn right along West Street. Immediately beyond the 15th century cathedral bell tower turn left past St Richard's statue and the west door of the 11th century cathedral with its Norman sculptures, 14th century choirstalls, imposing 15th century Arundel screen, shrine of St Richard, John Piper's altar tapestry, and Marc Chagall's stained glass window.

Continue beyond the west door along the pavement, turning right into the cloister and shortly left, then just before the cathedral shop/restaurant, turn right down pretty St Richard's Walk to Canon Lane, the 18th century Deanery facing you as you reach the junction. Turn left for the 13th century Chantry and another alleyway, the Vicars Close, consisting of 15th century houses, then return along Canon Lane, following it to its end; go under the archway and veer left as signed towards Bishop's Palace Gardens. Pause to admire the 13th century flint-and-brick palace itself, to your right, then pass under an archway to enter the gardens, following a metalled path through a lovely flower garden. At the far end bear left and then right under the archway. Go straight along to the water feature, veering right here to reach a T-junction of paths, turning left; bear left at the next T-junction and follow it to exit the garden, arriving at the Avenue de Chartres. Turn right to reach a roundabout at which you bear right along West Street, passing the 17th century Edes House that's on your left. A little further up on the left is the former mid-19th century church of St Peter the Great, latterly a bar. Turn left into Tower Street, passing the Novium (the city museum/information centre), and opposite the library turn right into The Woolstaplers, bearing left at the T-junction along Chapel Street past the 1809 Providence Chapel to the left. Cross North Walls and climb the steps leading onto the walls which date from 100 AD; turn right to walk along the city wall path, enjoying good views down to the backs of the neat terraced cottages of Orchard Street. Cross straight over North Street along Priory Road then, as it bends sharp right, turn left to resume your walls walk, with Priory Park immediately to your right. At the end drop down to Priory Road. Turn right along this road, going forward along Guildhall Street, noting the impressive former Ship Hotel to your right. Before the left turn into Guildhall Street it's worth detouring right into the park to view the fine Guildhall itself, a former Franciscan friary chapel. At the end of Guildhall Street turn left down North Street and continue past the Cross down South Street, turning left along West Pallant past the 13th century All Saints In The Pallant. At the crossroads carry straight on along East Pallant, going forward along New Town, up to the T-junction with St John's Street.

Turn left along it, passing the chapel of St John that's to your right; built in 1812-13, its features include gallery and 3-decker pulpit. At the end, go straight over East Street along East Walls, using the wall if you prefer. Turn left along Priory Road then shortly bear left down Little London with many fine red-brick 18th century houses, and, at the end, right along East Street. You pass the six-column Greek Doric portico of the former Corn Exchange, built in 1832, then turn shortly turn right up a signed alleyway leading to the former (13th century) church of St Andrew Oxmarket, now an excellent arts centre. To the right of the wall of the car park in front of you there's a good view to St Mary's Hospital and chapel. Return down the alleyway to East Street, bearing right then shortly left along North Pallant, past the 18th century Pallant House and adjacent gallery containing a splendid collection of 20th century British art. Go straight on down South Pallant then veer right along Old Market Avenue; turn left down South Street, crossing the Avenue de Chartres, and continue in the same direction to Chichester Station. That was the easy bit – now it gets serious!

The SHT leaves the centre of Chichester via Stockbridge Road – for those coming from **Chichester Station**, turn right out of the station car park and simply head south-westwards alongside the A286 – and then uses the footbridge to cross the A27. (At the time of writing the bridge was shut and pedestrians were having to cross the A27 using a special light-controlled crossing.) You continue alongside the A286 signed for the Witterings, but then shortly turn left along Grosvenor Road, passing St Wilfrid's Hospice, a much-loved and crucial facility supported by the Friends of Sussex Hospices. At the time of writing there are plans to relocate it in Bosham, to the west, meaning the route may need to be extended or revised accordingly! You bear left into Waterside Drive and then right down a path bringing you to the canal bank, here turning right to follow beside the Chichester Canal, more fully described in the New Lipchis Way section. You're overlapping now with the New Lipchis Way which you continue to do as you walk along the canal towpath south-eastwards. It's lovely relaxing walking and a nice way of getting into your stride with more rigorous challenges ahead. As you approach Hunston you cross over the canal and go forward to the B2145, crossing over and turning right to walk beside it into the centre of **Hunston**, leaving the New Lipchis Way. Just beyond Meadow Close you turn left and strike out eastwards along a pleasant footpath, veering left (northwards) to follow the edge of woodland then veering east again through pasture and arriving at Church Road in North Mundham. You turn left to immediately pass the 13th century church of St Stephen, which boasts a proud flint tower, before bearing right along Post Office Lane and then left, south-eastwards, along an attractive path that veers north-eastwards to reach North Mundham's sister village of **Runcton**. Having paused to admire the mill to your left as you reach the road, you head briefly eastwards along Saltham Lane then north-eastwards along Brookside, crossing the B2166 Lagness Road and heading north-eastwards along the metalled Marsh Lane to Merston. Shortly before reaching Merston you pass the 13th century church of St Giles, its most remarkable characteristic being a north aisle roof that sweeps down to within a few feet of the ground.

As you reach the pretty buildings in the centre of Merston you turn right, and shortly right again, southwards, along a track, then on reaching a path junction you bear left, just north of east, veering in a more north-easterly direction through flat fields past lines of polytunnels. You cross the busy A259 with care then cross further fields to a road at the hamlet of Colworth; beyond there, field walking dominates as you proceed, in a predominantly easterly direction, to a crossing of the A29 at Lidsey, your field walk giving way to a pleasant green path above a ditch as you approach the A29. This section, a total of some 3 miles from Merston to the A29, is something of a Marmite section. On a clear sunny day with the prevailing wind on your back you'll doubtless love the serenity and excellent views to the South Downs escarpment as far as Bignor Hill and beyond. But, particularly if the weather is unkind, you may find this tedious and frustrating, with no hills to relieve the monotony, a lot of industrial work within sight of the path, and a sense that you've not really achieved much and it's all taking longer than it should be. On many a winter's day, what you'll notice more than anything is the wind: this part of the walk is super-exposed with nowhere to hide and not much incentive to linger. Beyond the A29 – you have to turn right briefly alongside it before striking out eastwards from it – there's the reassurance of what is a clear more sheltered metalled road and then track, just north of east, taking you to a crossing of the Barnham-Bognor Regis railway line. A tramp through rougher grass just south of east takes you round the southern end of the buildings of Church Farm and brings you to a wide track which is part of an excellent cycle route linking Barnham and Flansham. It feels as though it should be part of a disused railway but it isn't! Despite the new relief road within sight to the south, there's a lovely rural feel just here and yes, it is a place you might want to linger. You turn left up the cycle track to reach a road at the Norman church of St Mary, Barnham. The setting of the church is idyllic, quite Betjemanesque in fact, and its beautifully kept interior does not disappoint. The SHT then follows the lane – Church Lane – north-eastwards into **Barnham**, turning left along Yapton Road under the railway. The village, straight ahead, offers ample amenities including a busy railway station 150 yards up on the left. There's also the chance here of a <u>detour D1</u> via the pretty village of Eastergate, with its Norman church of St George and its fine early 17th century Manor Farmhouse, to Denmans Gardens and its four acres comprising gravel beds, walled garden and pond with moorhens. The gardens have recently reopened to the public after a period of renovation.

From Yapton Road you turn right, north-eastwards, up Lake Lane, taking care to fork right at the first fork junction, then as the lane veers eastwards you strike out northwards along Park Road past nurseries. Then you continue just north of east across fields past Walberton Park, arriving at a path junction some 600 yards beyond the nurseries. Here you can detour briefly right to visit the church of St Mary, Walberton, which is much restored but which still boasts a 13th century chancel. Beyond the path junction you veer just west of north to enter Walberton, bearing right to proceed eastwards through this pretty flint-and-brick village. Soon after joining the main street you pass William Booker Yard where you'll find the headquarters of the Sussex Snowdrop Trust. The Trust helps families whose children have life-limiting illness and works closely with local hospices; again there's a strong link with FSH and the headquarters themselves have a lovely friendly and welcoming feel. Further down the main street there's a parade of useful shops, and there are buses to Arundel, Chichester and Bognor Regis. Beyond the village you cross the busy B2132 then eastward field walking takes over again, culminating in a sharp descent and climb (your very first on this walk!) just north of east to Binsted with the pretty church of St Mary on the right, immediately adjoining the path; the church, in a lovely rural setting, boasts some Norman windows and 12th century wall painting. You now enjoy attractive field walking with woodland views, albeit with the noise of the A27 not far away, eastwards through the southern edge of Binsted Wood to Binsted Lane. Then continuing eastwards, veering just north of east, you pass through the woods of Tortington Common – your first proper woodland walking of your journey. Be warned, however, that this area of countryside may become part of the route of the new A27 bypass west of Arundel, a matter of huge controversy at the time of writing, so watch out (and listen out!) for route changes in future. You cross over two minor roads in close succession then go forward into first Dalloway Road and then Torton Hill Road, turning right down Kirdford Road to reach Ford Road. You turn left up Ford Road to just short of the A27 roundabout, now in the suburbs of Arundel, then follow the pavement round to the right, going forward to a slipway taking you under the A27 and briefly beside the river Arun. Beyond the underpass you turn shortly left between modern houses to reach the end of Tarrant Street, here bearing right to follow it into the centre of **Arundel**. Arundel's delights, including the cathedral and castle, are fully described in the Monarch's Way section and you will undoubtedly wish to enjoy them before pressing on. At the end of Tarrant Street the SHT turns right, veering left to pass the quay and reach the bridge over the river Arun which the SHT crosses to continue along Queen Street. Shortly, though, you turn left to join the waterside and, overlapping with the Monarch's Way, follow the right bank of the Arun upstream. To reach the station, half a mile from the town, keep on along Queen Street and then straight on alongside the A27, using the new underpass to access the station on the right-hand side of the main road.

Beyond the centre of Arundel the SHT stays with the Monarch's Way – see that section for a fuller description including a Burpham detour – via **Warningcamp**, all the way up into the heights of the Angmering Park estate. However on reaching the estate, rather than turning left with the Monarch's Way along the obvious track through Upper Wepham Wood, the SHT dives south-eastwards through Lower Wepham Wood, bearing right onto a bridleway to reach a parking area at The Dover. By detouring here down a metalled road southwards you'll reach, in just over a quarter of a mile, the Chestnut Tree House Children's Hospice, one of the many projects helped by FSH. The hospice building is unremarkable but there's a very poignant sculpture in the grounds on the approach to the building, and you should look out also for the box tree shaped like a teddy! Back on the SHT, you now head resolutely along a bridleway just north of east from The Dover, passing along the northern fringes of Hammerpot Copse, Kitsease Copse and Olivers Copse, then proceed through the heart of a further area of woodland, Selden Fields and Surgeon's Fields. Just under 2 miles from The Dover you emerge from the woodland and contour the more open slopes of Patching Hill, then turn sharply right, just east of south, to reach the buildings of **Patching** including a farm and the 13th century church of St John which boasts a particularly fine spire. Beyond the village, the walking is fiddly for a while, following lanes first southwards then eastwards out of the village followed by a footpath south-eastwards across fields. You reach a crossroads where you veer sharply south-westwards past Patching Pond and over Arundel Road by the World's End pub, using a bridleway to pass under the A27, veering just south of east along a track that's sandwiched between the A27 and A280. It's noisy and uninspiring! You then cross the A280 and after hugging it briefly head southwards away from the traffic along a clear farm track, entering the woods of Highdown Copse and ascending onto Highdown Hill. You need to veer to the right to reach the summit. This hilltop, site of an Iron Age hillfort which was refortified in the 3rd century AD, is perhaps the best natural feature on a Great Walk of Sussex that's unique to the SHT, with magnificent views extending as far as Selsey Bill, perhaps beyond, and Beachy Head. There's a bewildering choice of paths up on the hilltop, and you may well not be assisted by waymarking, but having found your way to the highest ground, head eastwards off the hilltop, passing through a thicket containing the so-called Miller's Tomb, the tomb of the 18th century eccentric John Olliver. Beyond the thicket, aim just to the left of the parking area. The descent past the car park is pleasant enough, good views maintained throughout, and you arrive at Titnore Lane without difficulty.

Now, unfortunately, there is a profound deterioration as, east of Titnore Lane, you pick your way south-eastwards through a succession of residential streets in the West Durrington area of Worthing; you head eastwards to reach Romany Road then follow south-eastwards beside it, the St Barnabas Hospice just to your right here, but not accessible from the SHT. You arrive at Yeoman Road and follow it south-eastwards to the A2032 Littlehampton Road, heading southwards from here via Limbrick Lane and Mulberry Close (with a railway crossing in between), veering south-westwards via Jupps Lane to reach the A259. Here you could turn left to reach, in roughly a quarter of a mile, the shops of **Goring-by-Sea**. However the SHT turns right, westwards, from Jupps Lane along the A259. There is here at least the consolation of a most interesting church, just over the A259, namely the English Martyrs Catholic Church, which contains a reproduction of the Sistine Chapel ceiling, two thirds of the size of the original. If you're anxious to include it in your itinerary, do be sure to check opening times, as it tends to close to visitors in winter. Beyond the church you go forward to a roundabout junction where to your left is a useful parade of shops and refreshment opportunities. The SHT goes straight over at the roundabout, soon reaching Goring Street going left and right. By turning right you reach Goring-by-Sea Station in 200 yards but the SHT turns left, proceeding down Goring Street to Fernhurst Drive along which you briefly turn right. You then head left down Bodiam Avenue and right again along Ilex Way, an avenue created in the 1840's by the Lyon family to provide carriage access to their home at Goring Hall; it's now a wildlife haven where you may find bats, beetles, shrews, foxes, squirrels and hedgehogs, and plants including the red campion and hairy violet. The SHT turns very shortly left, southwards, off Ilex Way across a large partially wooded recreation area, a huge favourite for dog walkers. Make sure you watch where you're treading! You head south-eastwards across this area, keeping Goring Hall Hospital to your left, to pick up a pleasant path through the trees, crossing Amberley Drive and continuing southwards to reach the England Coastal Path just east of Goring Gap.

The SHT now overlaps with the England Coast Path route via **Durrington-on-Sea, West Worthing, Worthing, East Worthing** and **Lancing,** staying with it all the way past the Widewater Lagoon just east of Lancing; please refer to the England Coast Path section which also contains a described and very fine inland alternative route between Worthing and Shoreham. Just beyond the lagoon and the church of the Good Shepherd, however, the SHT leaves the coast and heads directly to Shoreham. (The England Coast Path, by contrast, takes a very much longer route all the way to the harbour mouth and back!) You strike out briefly north-eastwards across the road Beach Green, going over a recreation ground and rising to a path following the south side of the Adur estuary. On reaching this path, you could turn left to undertake a detour D2 to view the impressive Art Deco Shoreham Airport. However the SHT turns right along the path past a line of boats (though at the time of writing this path was shut and pedestrians had to use the parallel road), entering **Shoreham-by-Sea** via the new footbridge and crossing the A259 coast road. The SHT passes round the right-hand edge of the church of St Mary de Haura, bearing right then left up to Shoreham-by-Sea Station. The town is more fully described in the England Coast Path section. You cross the railway then after heading north up Buckingham Road bear right along Rosslyn Road, left up Rosslyn Avenue then right, just south of east, along Nicholson Drive, going forward along Middle Road for the best part of a mile. It's desperately unexciting suburban walking. You then head south-eastwards along St Julian's Lane beyond Middle Road, passing the attractive flint-built church of St Julian, then walk briefly up Kingston Lane and make your way on to Southwick just south of east via Park Lane. You briefly follow The Green – the centre of **Southwick** is reached almost at once by following The Green to the left – then turn right down Grange Road under the railway; to access Southwick Station, turn left along Butts Road for 100 yards or so just beyond the railway bridge. Otherwise continue to the A259, reaching it at the entrance to Shoreham Port. One is tempted to ask if it would have been better simply to follow the A259 from the centre of Shoreham-by-Sea with the England Coast Path route! There's no immediate improvement either. For a mile or so beyond the entrance to Shoreham Port, the trail alternates between quiet roads or paths immediately beside the eastern arm of Shoreham Harbour, and a pavement beside the A259, then follows the A259 as far as Hove Lagoon where it returns to the coast. The views across the very busy industrial works around the harbour are impressive but the noise of the traffic and the profusion of nearby suburban houses and shops is all less appealing, and again you wonder if the coastal route would have been a better option for the SHT. At the lagoon, however, the SHT does finally come down to join the promenade and overlaps with the England Coast Path all the way on via **Hove** to **Brighton** along the prom. This part of the walk, and possible offshoots, is more fully described in the England Coast Path section.

From Brighton Palace Pier the trail sticks to the lower promenade immediately adjoining the electric railway, switching to the beach side of the track and following a path parallel with the railway line all the way to the Brighton Marina complex, passing under the marina approach road and going forward to an undercliff path to the left of the Asda store. You then follow the undercliff path all the way to Saltdean, initially keeping the impressive marina, then the open sea, to your right. Note that in stormy conditions while the walking will be particularly dramatic the undercliff may be unsafe in which case it would be more prudent to use the cliff path described in the England Coast Path section. No extra mileage is involved. You pass below **Rottingdean**, which is well signed, and continue on the undercliff path, now overlapping with the recommended England Coast Path route. (Note: I have in the England Coast Path section also suggested a clifftop alternative.) In just under a mile from Rottingdean you reach a flight of steps leading to a café at **Saltdean**; the SHT in fact uses a subway just below the café to leave the England Coast Path and pass under the coast road to begin heading inland, north-eastwards. You pass Saltdean Lido (see the England Coast Path section) then go diagonally uphill aross a green, Saltdean Park, and ascend along Linchmere Avenue through an area of suburban housing. It's worth detouring right off this road up Wicklands Avenue (about 250 yards beyond the park) to view the remarkable Grand Ocean building, constructed in Art Deco style and once a hotel, but now converted into flats. Beyond Linchmere Avenue you turn left into Longridge Avenue then strike out along a track across open grassland with fine views back to the coast. Your clear track veers eastwards across the plateau, providing some of the best walking on the trail so far, passing the south end of Homebush Avenue and arriving at the top end of a lane leading down to Telscombe. Now overlapping with the Greenwich Meridian Trail you descend along the lane through Telscombe, more fully described in the Greenwich Meridian Trail section. You then ascend sharply and, staying with the Greenwich Meridian Trail, join a path that descends into a dry valley then rises to reach a farm lane. You now follow this lane north-eastwards. The Greenwich Meridian Trail leaves you by taking a path steeply northwards up the hillside, but this path also carries the South Downs Way which now comes to meet you, and as you continue along the track north-eastwards you're overlapping with the South Downs Way with which you will continue to overlap virtually all the way to Eastbourne! There are lovely views northwards to Mount Caburn just east of Lewes. Just short of the busy **Lewes-Rodmell-Newhaven road** (please see the South Downs Way description for a **Rodmell** detour here) the SHT turns sharp right and climbs parallel with the road, then crosses it at a junction with the road from Telscombe. Overlapping here with not only the South Downs Way but also the Sussex Ouse Valley Way you now have an easy road descent to **Southease**, passing the church (briefly described in the South Downs Way section) and dropping down to cross the river Ouse. Here you leave the Sussex Ouse Valley Way but, staying with the South Downs Way, you go forward to cross the railway just beside tiny Southease Station, one of the most rural in Sussex.

From here to Eastbourne, save for one tiny stretch at Alfriston, the trail follows the South Downs Way exactly, and you should refer to the South Downs Way description elsewhere in this book. Your route can be summarised thus. After crossing the busy A26 you have a steep ascent to Itford Hill and then a superb ridge walk past the prominent Beddingham masts and on to a car park at the top of the **Firle Bostal** road. Here you have a choice of continuing along the South Downs Way over Firle Beacon, followed by a sweeping descent towards Bopeep Bostal, or taking an alternative route via the lovely village of Firle, Firle Place and Charleston Farmhouse. This route variation is fully described in the South Downs Way section; if you walked the official South Downs Way route when following that path, you may prefer to try the alternative route when walking the SHT! Both routes join up just above Bopeep Bostal and you now descend to **Alfriston.** Immediately beyond Alfriston there's a slight divergence from the SDW, the SHT route preferring to exit the village via North Street and cross the river via Long Bridge, rejoining the South Downs Way bridleway section just beyond the bridge. There's then a climb above the Long Man onto Windover Hill, beyond which the route passes Tenantry Ground and descends to **Jevington**. There's another ascent onto Willingdon Hill and then an overlap with not only the South Downs Way but also the Wealdway along a ridge above Eastbourne to the A259. Shortly beyond the A259 you reach the trig point at Warren Hill, then drop to cross the B2103 before rising again, heading towards Beachy Head. While the Wealdway continues towards Beachy Head, the South Downs Way and SHT turn sharply left, north-eastwards, dropping down steeply to a café on Duke's Drive. Here the South Downs Way ends. The SHT now however overlaps with the England Coast Path all the way into Eastbourne via the promenade, passing the Wish Tower and Lifeboat Museum where a detour via Lascelles Terrace, this detour fully described in the England Coast Path section, provides quick access to **Eastbourne** town centre and station.

The SHT now continues to overlap with the England Coast Path, following the promenade past the pier and the Redoubt, and you now then stick to the seafront walkway/cycle track towards Sovereign Harbour. Just short of the harbour, as with the coast route, you cross the shingle to pass the Martello tower, negotiate the pavements and locks round the edge of the complex, and then keep on along the pavement till its very end (A), where shingle takes over. According to the SHT website, there's now a choice. You could join the shingle and follow it for a mile to the car park at **Pevensey Bay** (just short of the Aqua Bar, by the red board bearing the code WN16), cutting through the car park and walking up Sea Road to the A259 and its junction with Coast Road on the right. If you don't fancy the shingle, and it can be tough going and feel a lot longer than it really is, an alternative route is offered from (A). This follows a road inland past a caravan park and golf course to the A259, then bears right to proceed for over a mile beside the A259 through Pevensey Bay village, turning sharp left with the A259 to reach the junction with Coast Road. The village is well served by buses to Eastbourne and Hastings, while Pevensey Bay Station is roughly 600 yards up the A259 Wallsend Road, heading north-westwards from the village. However, trains are very infrequent from this station. By continuing up the A259 beyond the station and then turning left along the B2191 Pevensey High Street, you reach Pevensey & Westham Station with more frequent trains. That said, although this gives you the opportunity to explore Pevensey's attractions, more fully described in the 1066 Country Walk section, this station is nearly a mile and a half from Pevensey Bay. The bus may be a better option.

The next section of the SHT, as far as the slipway leading off South Cliff to the promenade approach to Bexhill, is undoubtedly one of the most tedious sections of walking in this book. You may prefer to leave it out and stick to (or here join) the beach, particularly if the tide is out, and instructions on how to do this are contained within the England Coast Path description. However, the official SHT now follows Coast Road for roughly 2 miles to **Normans Bay**. At the station here the SHT crosses the railway and there's more tarmac crunching, north-eastwards, past the ancient Star inn, the only redeeming feature on this section; the inn, once a smugglers' haunt, is thought to date from the 15th century. Unless you simply stay with the road all the way to Cooden Sea Road at Cooden Beach – this is a perfectly feasible and not unpleasant option – there then follows a fiddly field walk and a potentially confusing (and scenically unrewarding) tramp first north-eastwards then eastwards across Cooden Beach golf course. Thankfully the website directions are excellent so make sure you have them. At length tarmac takes over as you hit Clavering Walk and proceed along it south-eastwards to Cooden Sea Road at **Cooden Beach**, then turn right along this road. Continue seawards along Cooden Sea Road, passing the entrance to Cooden Beach Station and then going under the railway, beyond which Herbrand Walk (the road from Normans Bay) comes in from the right. It is possible to go forward to the beach here and turn left to follow it, effectively joining the England Coast Path. However the SHT turns sharply left, just north of east along Cooden Drive, leaving it to walk along the parallel Beaulieu Road and Hartfield

Road, then returning to it before shortly striking out along South Cliff. It's not great, frankly, and will seem even less great at the end of a long day. At last, however, shortly after joining South Cliff, you leave it by turning right opposite No. 58 down a slipway which takes you to the promenade, and you turn left to follow it. You then overlap with the England Coast Path all the way past **Collington** and **Bexhill** as far as the start of the promenade at St Leonards, and a full description of this walk is to be found in the England Coast Path section.

Having reached the promenade at St Leonards, the SHT turns away from the sea, heading northwards via Grosvenor Gardens and over the A259, eastwards via Keats Close and West Hill Road, and north-westwards via St Vincents Road past the station at **West St Leonards**. Having crossed Filsham Road you then follow paths running beside the Hastings-Tunbridge Wells railway, which you will see a lot of between here and Etchingham. You cross the B2092 Harley Shute Road then continue heading north-westwards, parallel with the railway. You soon reach a path (B) heading westwards away from the railway which the SHT follows. (If it's flooded, you'll need to continue along the railway-side path, rising to a path junction, here turning left and in 130 yards bearing left again on an unsigned but clear path, descending to the main path (B) and turning right to rejoin the main route.) You now head south-westwards across the Filsham Reedbed Local Nature Reserve, then in 550 yards or so, bear right at a path junction and follow a clear path north-westwards for a full mile beside the Combe Haven stream across the Combe Haven Site of Special Scientific Interest, particularly noteworthy for its variety of dragonflies. Note that the path isn't marked as such on current OS maps. At length you meet the junction with the 1066 Country Walk (Bexhill Link) and turn right along it. There's now an overlap with this route for some 5 miles, and a fuller description of this overlap is provided in the 1066 Country Walk section. You shortly pass under the new A2690 Bexhill-Hastings link road then continue on excellent paths through **Crowhurst**, passing its fine church and ancient yew, then going on through Fore Wood, another nature reserve. A stretch of road walking ensues, as far as Powdermill Lane, and you then follow good clear paths through scrubland and along the edge of a broad sweep of rolling pasture, arriving in **Battle**, an almost obligatory stopping point. The SHT turns left onto Battle's High Street, but the station, about half a mile away, is reached by turning right along this street past the church, turning left at the fork junction along Marley Lane and then, just before the railway crossing, right along the footpath immediately adjoining the railway line for 250 yards.

At Battle the SHT leaves the 1066 Country Walk, heading initially northwards alongside the A2100 before veering just west of north along Netherfield Road. On joining this road you initially descend but then have a long slog up Netherfield Hill. Having followed Netherfield Road for a mile, you then strike out north-eastwards along a bridleway bordering the former Battle Golf Club, enjoying superb views. Soon, however, the SHT leaves the bridleway, heading north-westwards along an indistinct footpath across pasture before entering the lovely mixed woodland of Burnthouse Wood. You reach a path junction and bear right, northwards, through Goldspur Wood, then, having lost height, you ascend along clear paths to cross Eatenden Lane and then pass through Upper Hucksteep Wood, now heading north-eastwards. This is beautiful easy walking on an excellent path. Emerging from the woods briefly, the SHT crosses a meadow then strikes away north-westwards from the main path, passing through Lower Hucksteep Wood, crossing a road and then following a path sandwiched between a road on one side and quarry railway on the other. You cross the quarry railway and continue parallel with the Hastings-Tunbridge Wells line, soon passing over this and following a field edge northwards and uphill to **Mountfield**, described by Spence as "the quintessence of a forgotten Sussex village." The SHT turns right along a road eastwards past the superbly situated village church of All Saints which boasts a Norman nave and chancel. Leaving the road, the SHT then heads northwards along a driveway past the splendid early 18th century Mountfield Court. Beyond the house, the route is ill-defined and signage very poor, but the SHT drops down through a parkland landscape, passing the edge of woodland and descending to meadows, arriving at the Hastings-Tunbridge Wells line again and going underneath it. If you are fated to go off course, which is all too easily done between Mountfield Court and this point, it's better to err to the left where at least you will then pick up the railway, and can then follow beside it northwards to the point where the SHT passes underneath the line. Once you've passed under the railway, you enjoy much easier walking on a well-signed path that proceeds fractionally east of north more or less parallel with and just to the left of the railway. Your path kinks right to pass under the railway and reaches a road; you then have to turn left along the road, promptly passing under the railway again, bearing right almost immediately up a modern residential road to reach Brightling Road/Station Road. The SHT turns right then almost immediately left up a path continuing parallel with the railway, but by staying on the road you almost immediately reach Robertsbridge Station, and by continuing to the end of this road, Station Road, in 400 yards you reach **Robertsbridge** High Street. This is one of the most picturesque village streets in Sussex with many lovely brick and timbered houses.

Beyond Robertsbridge the SHT, as stated, stays initially parallel with and close to the railway heading just west of north on a good clear path, before striking out initially just south of west then north-westwards, climbing to pass two adjacent farms. Signage then becomes extremely poor and you will need to have the app directions as well as good map-reading/GPS skills, as you dip down into a valley, hopefully finding the all-important footbridge over a stream before climbing to Squibs Farm, enjoying good views to the valley of the East Sussex river Rother to your right. Indeed the sight of the valley and the sound of the trains on the railway which passes through the valley may be an invaluable navigational aid! Beyond Squibs Farm the going gets easier; don't be tempted onto the track heading westwards from the farm towards Ludpit Lane or the even more beguiling track that drops straight down to the valley north-eastwards. The SHT rather heads north-westwards through Gigmore Wood then descends to walk beside the Rother, the ground rising steeply to the left. You pass round the far side of the Lundsford Farm buildings then descend to cross a meadow, passing over the river Dudwell, a tributary of the Rother, and arriving at the A265 at **Etchingham**. The SHT turns left along the road but by detouring right you'll reach, in little over 100 yards, the station preceded by the magnificent 14th century church of The Assumption & St Nicholas. In front of the altar lies the headless monument of Sir William de Echyngham in chainmail, while other features of interest in the church include choirstalls with misericords and 15th century brasses. Etchingham is an important place as far as your progress on the SHT is concerned, as it is here that it reaches its most north-easterly point and from now on virtually all your walking will be in a westerly/south-westerly direction heading back to Chichester. You've actually passed the halfway point which was reached at Robertsbridge and as you head away from Etchingham you can now be said to have the end, proverbially if nothing else, in your sights. By Etchingham Church you've the option of a <u>detour D3</u> – requiring a full day – in order to visit the gardens at Pashley Manor and Merriments; Pashley Manor Gardens are described more fully in the Sussex Border Path section, while Merriments boasts magnificent displays of irises, peonies, primulas, foxgloves, geraniums and roses. If you've visited Pashley Manor on your Sussex Border Path adventure, a note to D3 also offers a simpler walk to Merriments only.

From Etchingham the SHT proceeds south-westwards firstly beside the A265 then along the metalled Borders Lane. After passing the Borders farm complex you strike out, still south-westwards, across fields to the splendidly-named buildings of Grandturzel, following the signage carefully round the complex – it's more awkward than the map suggests. You veer southwards and briefly south-eastwards past the buildings, then turn just north of west, heading for Burwash. Initially there's a drop down to the Dudwell valley, then having crossed the river you rise gently. This section is extremely confusing with lack of signage or properly defined paths, but the views across the valley are extensive – the trick, if you lose the route, is to avoid getting sucked down into the valley. If all is well you'll find yourself entering and passing through the churchyard of St Bartholomew's, **Burwash**. The views from here are superb, extending as far as the Brightling Needle, one of the Brightling follies, about which more below. The church is certainly worth exploring: it boasts a Norman west tower, a wide Early English chancel and, set into a wall at the end of the south aisle, a 14th century iron tomb slab, reputed to be one of the oldest of its kind in Sussex. The SHT continues along Burwash's attractive main street (A265), shortly passing Rampyndene, arguably the finest house along this street, dating from 1699 and concealing timber-framing beneath its brick façade. However the village street boasts many other lovely houses, several brick-faced and with many dating back to the 17th and 18th centuries. The village was an important centre of the iron industry three centuries ago when the Weald was England's main source of iron ore. The village sign, which shows a smith beating on his anvil, is testament to the ancient work of the Burwash smiths who used to celebrate the feast of their patron by hammering gunpowder on their anvils. From Burwash the SHT bears left by the village car park, southwards along a National Trust footpath leading out of the village and downhill to the Dudwell valley, turning right to join a road leading westwards to Bateman's, the sometime home of Rudyard Kipling. Bateman's is one of the highlights of the whole SHT journey. The house, now in possession of the National Trust, was originally built by an ironmaster in 1634; Kipling bought the house in 1902, it remained his home until his death in 1936, and his study remains just as it was when he was alive. During this period he wrote two of his most famous works, *Puck Of Pook's Hill* and the poem *If*. In the grounds of the house is a watermill which dates from 1750. You have to detour briefly along the road to the right to reach the public entrance.

From Bateman's the SHT heads very pleasantly south-westwards, and in 250 yards you reach a junction with a path heading to the right, aiming for Rye Green Farm. While the SHT bears right at this junction, there's a possibility of embarking here on a lengthy detour D4, which goes straight on. The detour takes you to Brightling, a delightful hilltop village, with spectacular Wealden views from the village centre and its surrounds. It boasts the beautiful 13th century church of St Thomas Becket, and in the churchyard is the 60ft high pyramid mausoleum of Jack Fuller, a local squire, ironmaster and sometime MP. The mausoleum was built in 1810; it's said that he's buried inside, seated, wearing a top hat and holding a bottle of claret! He is remembered particularly for his collection of follies in the vicinity of the village, and these will be visited by D4. I highly recommend it! However as stated the SHT bears right at the path junction, heading first south-westwards before veering north-westwards and then south-westwards again past Rye Green Farm, chiefly through meadows that are full of buttercups in the spring. The ground rises to provide splendid views on both sides, and passes Burnt House Farm which is most attractive with beautiful rhododendrons and camellias right by the path. Just before reaching the farm complex you in fact veer north-westwards, following a track to reach the A265 again. Having crossed it, you then have a pleasant but unremarkable field walk just south of west, sneaking round the north side of Burwash Weald, returning to the A265 and now following a minor road south of it, heading westwards through the straggling village of **Burwash Common**. Climbing away from it you continue westwards along an unclear and poorly signed path which does however provide superb views northwards across miles of Wealden countryside. Veering sharply northwards at a path junction, you return to the A265 yet again, crossing it again, and, heading north-westwards, you follow a minor road for roughly a mile. Now veering in a generally westerly direction, you go forward along a very undulating and twisting bridleway that rises, veers sharply north-westwards to drop steeply into woodland and then, veering south-westwards, rises to meet Pottens Mill Lane. The highlight of this section of walking is the tremendous view to the lovely village of Mayfield and in particular its church, and Argos Hill Windmill to its north-west. These are visited by a detour from the Sussex Border Path – please see the Sussex Border Path section for the description. Back on the SHT you follow Pottens Mill Lane south-westwards to reach Scotsford Road which you in turn follow southwards towards Broad Oak. There then follows an extremely messy and fiddly walk south-westwards through a mishmash of rough fields and often poorly defined paths, with numerous gates and stiles and little in the way of views! Skill with your map-reading or your navigation app is essential. You veer just north of west and continue to Newick Farm beside Newick Lane, beyond which the going gets much easier as you head westwards along clearer paths, with some pleasant woodland walking and alpacas to be seen in adjoining fields. There's then a steep and possibly muddy climb to Marklye Farm where you reach the top of Marklye Lane and cycle route 21. By bearing right along here and going forward along Newick Lane northwards you'll reach Mayfield in just under 3 miles. However the SHT turns left down Marklye Lane, soon arriving at the A265 once more, and you follow this westwards to shortly reach **Heathfield**, a small but busy town with excellent amenities including buses to the railheads of Polegate, Etchingham and Uckfield, and also to Mayfield if you want to visit this delightful village but fancy a break from walking!

The SHT exits Heathfield southwards by a straight overlap with the Cuckoo Trail via Station Road. You follow the course of this trail along the disused Heathfield-Polegate railway for just over half a mile, then just beyond the Ghyll Road crossing you leave the Cuckoo Trail and strike out south-westwards along a principally wooded path taking you to the A267 at Little London. Having crossed with great care, you then head westwards through the very pretty Church Wood, climbing steeply to Hanging Birch Lane and then heading just south of west along Whitehouse Lane, past a turning to the splendidly-named Ragged Dog Lane. Then, heading north-westwards, you proceed along woodland edges and across a succession of fields, the going pleasant rather than spectacular, although there is one particularly fine bluebell field in spring. You continue north-westwards along roads to Brittenden, here veering south-westwards along a very muddy bridleway taking you to Possingworth Lane. You head briefly north-westwards downhill along that lane, before what is, in spring, one of the highlights of the whole SHT, namely a path heading south-westwards through a magnificent bluebell wood. You then turn sharply north-westwards and climb steadily through further woodland, passing the imposing buildings of Dower House Farm, then enjoy a well-defined and well-signed walk westwards through Browning's Wood to meet the Vanguard Way. You overlap with the Vanguard Way up through Kiln Wood to arrive at **Blackboys** and its welcome pub, cross the B2192 and go forward to reach the B2102. There are buses from here to the railheads of Etchingham and Uckfield.

You turn briefly left alongside the B2102 then strike out north-westwards from it, initially losing the Vanguard Way, which prefers a more easterly course, then being reunited with it for the descent to Tickerage Wood and a most attractive mill with weir, a refreshing spot on a hot day. For a few yards, as you pass the mill, you're also overlapping with the Wealdway. You then part company from the Vanguard Way which heads north-westwards towards Pound Lane, but stay with the Wealdway and head westwards. This is lovely relaxing walking along an excellent path along the valley bottom, your route passing Tickerage Castle (which is not really a castle but an impressive house) and crossing Pound Lane, then heading in a more north-westerly direction alongside lakes and beside a stream through meadows, crossing Streele Lane. You should aim to walk this part of the SHT in spring, when you can enjoy the array of wild flowers and the brilliant whites of the waterside vegetation. Just under half a mile beyond the Streele Lane crossing the SHT leaves the Wealdway and the meadow, climbing steeply south-westwards through woods and arriving at Sandy Lane. You now have a straightforward walk north-westwards on to Uckfield, proceeding first along the tarmac of Sandy Lane then the rougher Hempstead Lane, going forward to cross the railway and soon arriving at Hempstead Mill, overlapping here very briefly with the Wealdway once more. Striking away from the Wealdway, the SHT heads south-westwards into the sprawl of Uckfield initially along Hempstead Lane, veering south-eastwards along an indistinct path through a park, and then veering south-westwards along a boardwalk through wooded wetlands in the valley of the river Uck. This brings you to the centre of **Uckfield**, the SHT emerging at the main street via the Waitrose car park with the station immediately adjacent to the left. Uckfield isn't the most attractive town in Sussex, its centre constantly choked with traffic, but by detouring up the main street to your right, you'll find a calmer and more villagey atmosphere. The town hit the headlines in 2000 when it was the victim of disastrous flooding.

The SHT's westward exit from Uckfield initially along the B2102 Bell Lane past the bus station (from which regular buses are available to Haywards Heath, Tunbridge Wells, Lewes and Brighton) is undistinguished to put it politely, although the McDonald's right by the route may be a blessing for some weary walkers! At McDonald's the SHT parts from the B2102 route, preferring the parallel road through an industrial park before returning to the B2102, and then there's a dangerous crossing of the A22 just by a busy roundabout junction. It's a relief to strike out south-westwards beyond the A22 along a path through open country taking you round the edge of what OS maps state to be a dismantled railway; in fact this was just a short spur off the now defunct Lewes-Uckfield line. The SHT heads south-westwards away from this spur across fields, then turns sharply right and ascends north-westwards to cross the Piltdown-Isfield road at Buckham Hill. Beyond the crossing, the SHT continues in similar direction through the most attractive grounds of Buckham Hill House; you do feel a little as though you're intruding, but you're then reassured by signage and then enjoy an excellent descent across a field to the valley of the river Ouse. The last time you saw the Ouse on the SHT was at Southease, many miles back! Once in the valley you veer south-westwards alongside a tributary stream then veer north-westwards again to cross the Ouse itself. Its flow and width are rather less impressive than at Southease but the surroundings are every bit as lovely. Note that there's no overlap here with the Sussex Ouse Valley Way which is in fact well away from the Ouse at this point. You climb gently out of the valley past Sharpsbridge Farm, and after crossing a road at Sharpsbridge you then enjoy a quite delightful walk westwards along the south fringes of woodland known as Sharp's Hanger, from which there are really fine views to the South Downs escarpment. You veer north-westwards before heading westwards along the north fringes of Founthill Wood. There follows a gentle but steady climb north-westwards then westwards over fields to pass the Norman church of St Mary, Newick, beyond which you cross **Church Road** and with it the Sussex Ouse Valley Way. The village of **Newick** is a quarter of a mile up Church Road to the right, but the SHT chooses, unlike the Sussex Ouse Valley Way, to avoid its centre altogether, using a footpath heading westwards to skirt its southern fringes with lovely views to the south. You arrive at the A272 and follow it westwards for just over a mile; thankfully there is a pavement! You cross back over the Greenwich Meridian Trail – although the actual Meridian is a little way to the east of the course of the trail at this point – and as you cross it you may now recall the last time you saw the Greenwich Meridian Trail, many miles back at Telscombe. Your roadside walk brings you, at a junction with the A275, to **North Chailey** which boasts a garage-cum-shop, café (at the time of writing) and good bus links.

You continue westwards along the A272 beyond the A275 junction, then strike out north-westwards, soon passing the lovely Chailey Windmill, a white smock mill with its four sails intact; it's stood here since 1864, although it was manufactured earlier in the 19th century. You then descend just west of north across Red House Common with its profusion of bracken, but you need to follow directions and signage carefully as there are so many paths and tracks. All being well, you'll pass just to the right of a pond then enter a completely different landscape, namely farmland fields, where you need to be prepared for inquisitive cattle! You pass Great Noven Farm then continue north-westwards through marshy fields and along the edge of Great Wood – a lake known as

Clear Water is just to the right – to arrive at Clearwater Lane. Now overlapping with the Sussex Border Path spur route, you follow the lane north-westwards then westwards uphill to **Scaynes Hill**, which offers refreshment and, again, bus connections. You've now passed back into West Sussex! You reach the A272 and turn right briefly along it, then bear right almost immediately right again, just east of north up Church Road past the fine church of St Augustine, with a very impressive altar tapestry and paintings devoted to the life of its patron saint. The SHT then leaves the road, striking out north-westwards into Costells Wood, soon being joined by the Sussex Ouse Valley Way coming in from the right. The SHT now overlaps with it all the way to Lindfield (albeit in a reverse direction from the description given in the Sussex Ouse Valley Way section). You descend through the trees on a wide track beside power cables, but need to watch for where the track narrows and dives into woodland, dropping steeply. You exit the wood and cross a wide field, passing the buildings of Nether Walstead and going forward to cross East Mascalls Lane. Pleasant walking follows along a clearly defined track north-westwards through farmland; your path turns sharply west at Hangman's Acre, then at the next path junction you head north-westwards again up a narrow path to reach **Lindfield**, here bidding a temporary farewell to the Sussex Ouse Valley Way. More information is provided about Lindfield in the Sussex Ouse Valley Way section. The SHT passes the church and arrives at the village street, turning left to follow it briefly, then bears right, south-westwards, along Hickman's Lane and right again, by the splendid Witch inn (with its "Good Stabling" sign) along Sunte Avenue. From here you go forward south-westwards along Gander Hill and College Road almost to the railway embankment. The SHT turns right here up Wickham Way but by following College Road to its end then turning left down Mill Green Road, you reach Haywards Heath Station in a quarter of a mile. The modern and frankly uninteresting centre of **Haywards Heath** is a good half mile south of the station via Perrymount Road then left along South Road.

The SHT leaves Haywards Heath northwards past suburban housing, turns right briefly to reach Wickham Farm then heads just east of north through woodland and beside Haywards Heath Golf Club, being joined again by the Sussex Ouse Valley Way and descending northwards through woodland to cross Copyhold

Lane. There's now an overlap with both the Sussex Ouse Valley Way and High Weald Landscape Trail for a mostly wooded walk just west of north, crossing the old Haywards Heath-Horsted Keynes railway, which is now only used by occasional freight trains between Haywards Heath and Ardingly. A gentle climb through River's Wood is followed by a drop to the valley, where by looking to the left you will see a section of the magnificent Ouse Valley Viaduct. Here you say another temporary farewell to the Sussex Ouse Valley Way but stay with the High Weald Landscape Trail, ascending sharply and arriving at Ardingly Reservoir. Here the High Weald Landscape Trail goes off towards Ardingly College, clearly visible on the hill to the right, but the SHT joins a path alongside Ardingly Reservoir, named the Kingfisher Trail. The reservoir not only supplies water but is used for watersports and enjoys a fine array of wildlife and plant life; trees to be found here include English oak, silver birch, ash, alder and Scots pine, among birds you may see are the kingfisher, great-crested grebe and green woodpecker, and plants you might find include the oxeye daisy and orchid. You now have a very easy and enjoyable walk predominantly northwards beside the reservoir. You reach **Balcombe Lane** coming from **Ardingly**, and you could detour up the road to the right to reach, in 1 mile, the attractive village of Ardingly with its pub and tempting Fellows bakery in the village centre. Roughly halfway there is the church of St Peter with its splendid timbered doorway, a fine 15th century tower, and, inside, some splendid brasses, most notably those to the Tudor Culpepers. However the SHT turns left at Balcombe Lane to cross the reservoir, beyond which you shortly bear left again to continue your waterside walk, heading first southwards then north-westwards. Near the northern tip of the reservoir you leave the path, joining Mill Lane then climbing very steeply through woods and negotiating a gentler field ascent south-westwards to reach Haywards Heath Road on the fringes of Balcombe. You turn briefly left beside the road then head westwards via Oldlands Avenue, a residential road at the south end of the village, to reach Balcombe Station from where there are regular trains to London and Brighton. The village centre of **Balcombe**, including (at the time of writing) a café, is just under half a mile north of the station via London Road.

The trail then heads briefly beside the B2036, and cuts south-westwards to cross Rocks Lane, then veers north-westwards along a path; having descended steeply it then climbs just as steeply up again to Westup Farm. Now really lovely walking follows as, enjoying fine views to the South Downs, you proceed in a generally south-westerly direction, firstly along a ridge on the south side of Bury Wood then steeply downhill into a narrow wooded valley in Northland Wood and up again the other side. You cross Brantridge Lane (along which you could detour right, uphill, for half a mile to visit, on the left, the fascinating World War 2-themed Wings Aviation Museum) then head westwards past the splendid red-brick Ditton Place beyond which, veering southwards into Sole's Coppice, there's a similar steep descent and climb. Pleasant field walking takes you past the buildings of Oldhouse, where you rejoin the Sussex Ouse Valley Way and then proceed just north of west through thick woodland where lakes and streams enhance the beauty of the landscape and there are several signed nature trails. There's then a stiff climb out of the woods past the buildings and gardens of Nymans (described, as is a detour from here to the gardens at High Beeches, more fully in the Sussex Ouse Valley Way section) into the centre of **Handcross**, where there are shops and regular buses to Crawley and Brighton. The trail, still overlapping with the Sussex Ouse Valley Way, crosses the B2114 in the village centre and uses the B2110 to cross south-westwards over the A23, then heads southwards down Park Road on a clear track to just short of **Slaugham**. This is a lovely village visited by both the High Weald Landscape Trail and Sussex Ouse Valley Way, and described in the Sussex Ouse Valley Way section. However the SHT, leaving the Sussex Ouse Valley Way and now overlapping with the High Weald Landscape Trail, turns right, westwards, 150 yards or so before the village and follows a clear path along woodland edges. In fact save for a very short stretch you'll be following the High Weald Landscape Trail all the way to Horsham. You cross Coos Lane then turn northwards to descend steeply to a dry valley and ascend equally steeply to meet the busy B2110. You have to follow this road for some 400 yards south-westwards, but then join Carterslodge – some OS mapping suggests it's Carters*ledge*! – Lane that strikes out north-westwards. You soon pass a charming pond and waterfall, then continue as clearly High Weald Landscape Trail-signed, descending to a ford (with footbridge). You turn briefly south-westwards and ascend, then veer north-westwards again, crossing Grouse Road then ascending to enter St Leonard's Forest. A steady descent is followed by another stiff climb to arrive at a clear wide forest track which you follow northwards, here briefly leaving the High Weald Landscape Trail to cut a corner. Soon returning to the High Weald Landscape Trail, the SHT descends most pleasantly just west of south through the woods, exiting them and then following field-edge paths to Stew Pond. Here you bear right and very shortly arrive at Hamper's Lane, heading left (westwards) to follow it; initially rural, it moves into suburbia as it enters the outskirts of **Horsham**. You reach and cross Comptons Lane and you then have an unexciting walk westwards along Depot Road to its end. You're now in the vicinity of Horsham Station with trains to Crawley, London and the coast. If you have a train ticket you can turn left along Station Road, soon bearing sharp right to enter the station via the barriers. Otherwise you need to turn right up Station Road then hard left along North Street to reach the main station entrance.

Just outside the main station entrance the trail crosses the roundabout and heads briefly north-westwards along Hurst Road, then bears left to pass through the congenial surroundings of Horsham Park, under the ring road and via Medwin Walk, South Street and West Street through the centre of the town. The SHT then turns left past the bus station and library, and strikes out south-westwards along the B2237 Worthing Road. As an alternative, requiring no extra mileage, you could explore the historic centre of Horsham, following the suggested route given from Horsham Station into the town centre as given in the West Sussex Literary Trail section, then turning left on reaching Worthing Road (B2237) to join the continuous route of the SHT. Once on the B2237 you shortly turn right, westwards, along Blackbridge Lane and south-westwards along Jockey Mead, going forward to cross the railway line and rising to the houses of Tower Hill. The SHT then negotiates a crude sideways M shape to avoid a road walk along Two Mile Ash Road, following paths to and then away from Parthings, returning to the road and following it south-westwards. Then, just beyond the A24 crossing, you bear right along Christ's Hospital Road, past the **Christ's Hospital** school buildings. The school was founded in London in 1553 and moved here in the 19th century, some ornamental sections being re-used from the original buildings; the present buildings are worth seeing more for their scale and size, and their ambience, rather than for their architectural merit. The road bends sharp left – the well-signed Christ's Hospital Station on the Arun Valley line is reached in 200 yards by turning right at this bend along Station Road – and becomes King Edward Road. Rather than cross the railway with the road, the SHT heads away south-westwards, overlapping with the Downs Link, then leaves the comparative comfort of this path; while the Downs Link veers south-eastwards, the SHT continues south-westwards along a clear path that follows immediately beside the existing Arun Valley railway all the way to Barns Green, switching to the right side of the railway just at the end. The SHT bears right along Two Mile Ash Road bringing you to the main street of **Barns Green** which you follow south-westwards, soon being joined by the West Sussex Literary Trail. You overlap with this route, soon heading away from the street past the ponds and through Vale Wood, crossing the road again and also the railway, and walking south-westwards on a clear bridleway. However in roughly half a mile beyond the railway crossing the SHT bears right off the bridleway, heading just north of east past Hook Farm to reach and cross the railway again. You walk westwards beside it, cross West Chiltington Lane (although here you're actually nowhere near West Chiltington!) and now proceed pleasantly westwards through fields before turning sharp left through an area of woodland beside a very active stream. You pass under the railway and enjoy a tree-shaded bridleway walk south-westwards to Fewhurst Farm, arriving at the A272; you cross this road then head westwards across fields, veering sharply northwards and then westwards to Daux Farm. It's quite a shock after the rural walking and the attractiveness of the farm buildings to then bear right along Daux Road and be faced with its lines of industrial units. You follow Daux Road to Billingshurst Station.

I recommend that to negotiate your way through **Billingshurst** you use a route variation V1 below: it's a more interesting walk which takes in the centre of the town. The SHT pefers a more suburban and less enjoyable journey, heading south-westwards from the station via Myrtle Lane to Natts Lane, turning right up this road to a T-junction, bearing right along the old A29 then left up Luxford Way, and then bearing right across a field going forward along a path to reach Newbridge Road East. Now reunited with V1 you turn left along Newbridge Road East and over the new A29, going on to reach the A272 Newbridge Road and turning left alongside it before turning sharply left alongside the B2133. Just past the welcoming (and welcome) Limeburners pub you bear right, westwards, towards Guildenhurst Manor, veering right (north-westwards) onto a path which drops sharply to cross the river Arun and then, a short way beyond, reaches the Wey & Arun Canal. Here you turn left along the Wey South Path which you'll overlap with (effectively in reverse), save for a few hundred yards around Coombelands Lane, all the way to Amberley; please refer to the Wey South Path section for a fuller description of this piece of walking. Turning south-westwards, the trail then enjoys a delightful walk through the meadows, the Arun meandering pleasantly to the left and the canal to the right, and at one point there's an attractive area of woodland where you squeeze between river and canal. You pass the beautifully restored Lordings Lock, described more fully (as is the canal itself) in the Wey South Path section, then cross the Arun and continue beside the canal south-westwards to the buildings of Haybarn. Leaving the canal, but never staying far from the Arun, your trail then follows first a farm lane then grassy bridleways, continuing south-westwards, crossing the Arun then veering westwards and rising above the valley to reach the Fittleworth-Wisborough Green road at **Westland.** You follow this road gently uphill into woodland then, swinging south-eastwards, descend through the woods along a path to recross the river and the canal at Pallingham Quay. In times of wet weather the path may flood, and I recall being very grateful for my wellies as I waded through floodwaters here in late winter. Proceeding in a predominantly south-easterly direction, you then move away from the watercourses, following a bridleway through pleasant low-lying farmland to meet a road, Coombelands Lane, at Pickhurst. You now head southwards along then beside the road (here losing the Wey South Path) past the Coombelands farm complex. There's a very horsey feel about this part of the walk! The SHT leaves the road to follow a field-edge path parallel with it, veering right to meet the road again. By detouring left here along **Coombelands Lane** you can proceed to **Pulborough**; see the Wey South Path section for more details including distances involved, there being a negligible difference between the distances shown there and from SHT. However the SHT crosses Coombelands Lane and heads south-westwards uphill to rejoin the Wey South Path, from here continuing south-westwards through most attractive woodland, with fine views opening up to the south. You descend to cross the A283 and walk on down to the White Hart at Stopham with its delightful bridge over the Arun, then bear left along the road to just short of the A283. Continuing along the Wey South Path, you head south-eastwards over the West Sussex river Rother then cross a meadow to reach the Hardham waterworks, going forward along the access road. The SHT bears right off the access road (C), following a track and then a small portion of the old Pulborough-Petersfield railway (described more fully in the Serpent Trail section) before bearing left across a field, crossing the extant Arun Valley railway and shortly then crossing the A29 and joining a path (D) heading just to the right of the private Hardham Priory. However by following the access road beyond (C) to its end, turning left alongside the A29 then forking first right, you'll reach the church at Hardham with its magnificent wall paintings. You can pick up the SHT again by retracing to the A29, backtracking alongside it and continuing for a quarter of a mile or so beyond the access road to point (D) above, here rejoining the SHT. This little variation adds half a mile to your journey.

Beyond the A29 the SHT, still following the Wey South Path, passes the buildings of Hardham Priory and follows a narrow path south-westwards in the shade of trees to Brook Lane just west of Greatham Bridge. You turn left to cross the bridge then bear right, southwards, initially close to the river Arun before striking out along a lane past houses then across the lovely wetlands of Amberley Wild Brooks. At length you arrive at the village of **Amberley**, briefly overlapping with the West Sussex Literary Trail as well as the Wey South Path. You turn left along Hog Lane then veer right to follow Amberley's main street southwards to reach the B2139; the delights of Amberley are more fully described in the West Sussex Literary Trail section. Cross over the B2139, walking uphill along Mill Lane to reach High Titten, then (here briefly overlapping with the South Downs Way) bear right down High Titten to return to the B2139. Turn left alongside the B2139, soon passing under the railway bridge; **Amberley Station** and Museum are reached by turning left up the slip road just before the bridge. Beyond the bridge, the SHT goes forward to cross the Arun at the delightful **Houghton Bridge**, here turning right along the left bank of the Arun (upstream) to meet the South Downs Way and follow it south-westwards to Houghton Lane. Leaving the South Downs Way, you turn left, south-eastwards, along the lane, walking back to the B2139 again! You arrive at this road by the George & Dragon at **Houghton**, famous for the fact that the future King Charles II stayed at this inn en route for Shoreham-by-Sea from Worcester in 1651. This, appropriately enough, is the start of your overlap with the Monarch's Way (again effectively in reverse), and the SHT now overlaps with it all the way to Eartham Wood on Stane Street. Please refer to the Monarch's Way section for more detail regarding this part of the walk. Heading very roughly parallel with the B2139, you now climb south-westwards on a clearly defined path, the views getting better all the time, to arrive at and cross the **A29**. (**Whiteways Lodge** café is just down the A29 to the left.) Observing the Monarch's Way signage, you now embark on a walk through Houghton Forest on excellent wide tracks. Right at the start of this walk beyond the A29 you need to take care to turn right rather than left, then follow signage carefully to join a path heading westwards through the forest. In roughly three quarters of a mile you reach a T-junction, turning right to head north-westwards, and the going is good and clear, through attractive woodland, climbing steadily but not too steeply and arriving on the Bignor Hill plateau. Now the trees relent to the left to provide absolutely superb views southwards to a broad stretch of coastline – the proximity of the sea being a sign that you're now not far from the end of your walk at Chichester. You veer just south of west, enjoying a tremendous ridge walk to Gumber Corner, and pass through another area of woodland then, emerging from it, you bear left for what is a fantastic walk south-westwards along Stane Street, a dead straight path heading confidently downhill with magnificent views throughout to Chichester Cathedral and beyond. You then dive into the trees of **Eartham Wood** and arrive at a road linking the A285 with Eartham. Here you leave the Monarch's Way but continue in a more or less straight line south-westwards along a much narrower path, downhill, which sometimes isn't well defined. You reach and follow the A285 downhill briefly then pick up another footpath section of Stane Street and climb, still heading south-westwards, to just south of Halnaker Windmill. It's worth detouring up the obvious path to the 18th century tower mill, from which there are stupendous views which extend as far as the Isle of Wight; the total detour is just three quarters of a mile. Returning to the route, you descend on a clear path south-westwards back to the A285 and now follow a path on its south side, still south-westwards. You turn right briefly along Tinwood Lane – by detouring left along here you reach, in little over 250 yards, the Tinwood Vineyard with its fne range of English sparkling wines – then bear left to continue along a path roughly parallel with the A285 and arrive at the A285 at **Halnaker**, the popular Anglesey Arms pub immediately to your right. The continuous SHT walk crosses the A285 and heads northwards up Park Lane. However, a detour southwards down The Street brings you, in just under half a mile, to the centre of **Boxgrove**, with its excellent shop/cafe; by detouring 200 yards along Church Lane more or less opposite the shop you arrive at Boxgrove Priory. The priory itself was founded around 1117 and fell victim to the Dissolution, but the stunning church remains. Particularly noteworthy is the early 16th century ceiling painting that consists of a rococo floral pattern including Tudor roses and De La Warr heraldry, while to the right of the nave is the De La Warr chantry of 1532, a mix of Gothic/classical style, painted and gilded with depictions of birds, flowers and human figures. By following the church path beyond the main door and on to the church car park, you can easily access the very impressive ruins of the priory itself. Having returned to the shop the same way you have the option of another detour, a further mile southwards, to visit Tangmere Military Aviation Museum, which celebrates the key role Tangmere Airfield played during World War 2. To visit the museum, continue down The Street, forking right as the road bends left and cross the footbridge over the A27. Turn right beside the A27 then immediately beyond the service station, turn left down Tangmere Road and follow it for three quarters of a mile, turning left into the complex just as the road bends right. Simply return the same way after your visit.

Although it's only three miles to Chichester from Halnaker as the crow flies, the route taken by the SHT is some three times that, but it truly is a grandstand finish to your journey. As stated you head northwards from Halnaker along Park Lane past the imposing ruins of Halnaker House to your right – the buildings date from medieval times, becoming ruined around 1800 – then follow a clear wide track through an area of woodland which boasts some extremely tall trees. Having followed the woodland track for just under a mile, you need to watch carefully for, and take, a narrower path heading north-westwards off the track, going quite steeply uphill through woodland, at length emerging from the trees and arriving at New Barn Hill. The SHT turns right to run beside this road, but a detour left here along the road takes you in half a mile to the fascinating Cass Sculpture Foundation. Dating from 1992, it's a huge outdoor gallery with works by both emerging and established sculptors, using a wide variety of materials including wood, bronze and marble. Almost 100 pieces are on display at any one time, all for sale (though you may have difficulty fitting one in your backpack), and replaced with new works as they are sold. As stated, though, the SHT bears right beside New Barn Hill, from which there are glorious views to Halnaker Windmill and down towards the sea, then heads north-westwards through another area of woodland, arriving at Selhurstpark Road. You're now reunited with the Monarch's Way as you head south-westwards beside the road past Goodwood Racecourse. At the end you cross Kennel Hill and now veer north-westwards steeply up onto The Trundle, a prehistoric hillfort and a fabulous viewpoint, with Chichester, the Manhood Peninsula and the Isle of Wight all visible on a clear day. As I've learnt the hard way, though, wet days can bring a blanket of mist down which blots out the view completely, combined with treacherously slippery going underfoot as you follow the ring round the plateau. Choose a good day! You're here overlapping with the New Lipchis Way, Monarch's Way and West Sussex Literary Trail but very soon you lose all three as having descended westwards to a multi-path junction the SHT heads south-westwards down Chalkpit Lane. Even though it's downhill all the way it will always take longer than you think it should, especially if you've undertaken the whole 200+-mile SHT journey in one go. On reaching the road you turn right along Pook Lane to immediately enter **East Lavant**, passing its Royal Oak pub (remembering to take your boots off before going in!) and going forward to its attractive green. Here you bear right along Sheepwash Lane parallel with the river Lavant which is usually dry in summer but can flow impressively in winter; in January 1994 it was too impressive, flooding the village green and adjacent Memorial Hall. You soon fork left off Sheepwash Lane along a path which rises gently to the Earl of March, another pub, crosses the A286 and goes forward via Meadow Close to the footpath/cycleway known as the Centurion Way, here reunited with the New Lipchis Way which will link hands with you until the end. It's now a lovely straightforward finish as you follow the Centurion Way southwards along what is the course of the old Chichester-Midhurst railway (a little more detail about which is given in the New Lipchis Way section) round the west side of Chichester. The Centurion Way ends by the extant Chichester-Havant railway, and here you turn eastwards and walk via Westgate and West Street into the centre of Chichester, turning right at the Cross down South Street and across Avenue de Chartres to return to **Chichester Station** – last seen over 200 miles back. Congratulations on completing the longest name path wholly within Sussex!

GOOD TO KNOW

Start and finish: Chichester Station.

Total mileage: 204.

Difficulty: Strenuous.

Stages: Hunston (RB) 2, Runcton (R) 4, Barnham (*RAB) 10, Arundel (*RAB) 15, Warningcamp 16, Patching (RA) 22, Goring-by-Sea (*RAB) 26, Durrington-on-Sea (*RAB) 28, West Worthing (*RAB) 29, Worthing (*RAB) 30, East Worthing (*RAB) 31, Lancing (*RAB) 32.5, Shoreham-by-Sea (*RAB) 35, Southwick (*RAB) 37, Hove (*RAB) 41, Brighton (*RAB) 42, Rottingdean (RAB) 46, Saltdean (RAB) 47, Lewes-Rodmell-Newhaven road for Rodmell (RA) 52.5, Southease (*R) 53, Firle Bostal 56.25, Alfriston (RAB) 60, Jevington (RA) 65, Eastbourne (*RAB) 69.5, Pevensey Bay (*RAB) 75, Normans Bay (*R) 78, Cooden Beach (*RAB) 80.5, Collington (*RAB) 82, Bexhill (*RAB) 83, West St Leonards (*RAB) 86, Crowhurst (*RA) 91, Battle (*RAB) 95, Mountfield 99.5, Robertsbridge (*RAB) 102, Etchingham (*RAB) 105, Burwash (RAB) 109, Burwash Common (RB) 112.5, Heathfield (RAB) 118, Blackboys (RAB) 123, Uckfield (*RAB) 128, Church Road for Newick (RAB) 132, North Chailey (RB) 134, Scaynes Hill (RAB) 136.5, Lindfield (RAB) 139, Haywards Heath (*RAB) 141, Balcombe Lane for Ardingly (RAB) 145, Balcombe (*R) 147, Handcross (RB) 151, Slaugham (RA) 152.25,

B2110 153.25, Horsham (*RAB) 159, Christ's Hospital (*) 162, Barns Green (RB) 164, Billingshurst (*RAB) 169, Westland 175, Coombelands Lane for Pulborough (*RAB) 178, Amberley (RA) 183, Amberley Station (*) 184, Houghton Bridge (R) 184.25, Houghton (RA) 184.75, A29 Whiteways Lodge (R) 186, Eartham Wood 191.25, Halnaker for Boxgrove (RAB) 194.25, East Lavant (RB) 200, Chichester Station (*RAB) 204.

OS: OL8, OL10, OL11, OL25,124, 136, 135, OL34.

D1 Walk up past the station and out of the village centre along Barnham Road, north-westwards. As you approach a pedestrian crossing, turn left immediately beyond Holmwood, No. 75, onto a narrow path. This shortly swings right to arrive at Elm Grove South. Don't join the road but bear left along a signed footpath immediately to the right of the entrance to St Philip Howard School. The path soon veers to the right, keeping the school buildings to the left, and strikes out north-westwards along the right-hand edge of open fields. The path bends right and reaches a T-junction with Church Lane, onto which you turn left. You pass Manor Farmhouse and the pretty church of St George, then continue along Church Lane past Eastergate School and the Wilkes Head pub, veering right and continuing to the end at the A29, with a shop to the left and A29/B2233 roundabout with war memorial to the right. Cross and now head north-eastwards from the roundabout alongside the A29 Fontwell Avenue, then in half a mile turn left along Level Mare Lane and in roughly 550 yards first right up Denmans Lane. The gardens are some 750 yards up on the right-hand side, just before the A27. Retrace to the A29, turning right and then in 275 yards left along Eastergate Lane. In roughly a third of a mile turn right along a signed footpath which emerges at the B2233. Turn left along this road to return to Barnham in three quarters of a mile. (Total detour 5 miles)

D2 Having turned left along the path, follow it to its end. Cross straight over the A259 and continue along an initially firm path which descends in a zigzag and peters out. Go straight on along the grass, keeping an area of bushes to the left and Adur Recreation Ground to your right, going forward to pass under the railway. Almost immediately beyond the railway, bear left, going forward along Cecil Pashley Way into an industrial estate. In some 400 yards you reach, on the right-hand side, the fine Shoreham Airport building, with an interesting visitor centre on the right. Return the same way. Note that at the time of writing the path from the start of the detour to the A259 was shut. In that case follow the parallel Beach Green, bearing right up Ormonde Way in roughly 400 yards, going forward up steps to the A259 and crossing to join the path on the other side. (Total detour 1.5 miles)

D3 (NOTE: YOU WILL NEED A FULL DAY FOR THIS DETOUR. SHOULD YOU SIMPLY WISH TO VISIT MERRIMENTS, HAVING VISITED PASHLEY MANOR ON THE SUSSEX BORDER PATH, SEE FURTHER NOTE AT END OF THIS DETOUR DESCRIPTION.) Follow the footpath along the right (north-eastern) side of the church, soon turning right onto Church Hill and following it to a T-junction of roads. Bear left here along Sheepstreet Lane, ignoring the first right bridleway turning, but, just under 300 yards further on, taking the next right bridleway/lane to Kitchingham Farm, forking left at the fork junction as you reach the buildings. Pass through the farm complex, forking right as signed beyond the buildings, then follow a lovely path uphill along the left edge of trees, with splendid views. At the end (E) you turn left onto the B2099, soon reaching Pashley Manor and gardens to the left. Return along the B2099, passing (E) and continuing past the impressive buildings of Little Boarzell which are to the left. You descend and at the bottom, just over half a mile from Pashley Manor, turn right along a bridleway/lane for Swiftsden Farm. Turn left onto a signed footpath immediately before the buildings, veering gently right to follow an initially clear path through the meadow, soon reaching a line of trees dividing the meadow in two. Go to the trees' right-hand side, crossing a footbridge and then veering right as the meadow continues, keeping a stream close to your right. As you approach the meadow end, veer left as signed into and steeply up through a field with woodland to your left. When the buildings of Bellhurst come into view straight ahead, strike out across the field away from the woods, aiming just to the right of the Bellhurst complex. As you reach the crest a sign reassures you; go forward along a clearer path and bear right onto a clear track, then in barely 50 yards left as path-signed, keeping a barn to your right and descending steeply to the edge of woodland. Go straight on over a footbridge, your path then veering a little to the left and crossing a mini-gully, before *veering more decisively right and ascending through the lovely Burgh Wood. You reach a T-junction of paths (unsigned, as most footpaths in Burgh Wood are), here turning left along a clear path which continues to rise and reaches another T-junction, where you again turn left. Ignoring a left fork you go forward to arrive at a five-path junction (F). Note, for later, the hard right-hand path (G).*

Go straight across at (F) along a woodland path, keeping the houses of Hurst Green to your right. *You pass the end of a residential street, Ridgeway, and continue along a clear walkway past the church to the A21. Cross and turn right alongside the road, then very shortly turn left along a plinth-signed path, actually a short lane, and on into a field by an outbuilding, turning left along the left-hand field edge. As you approach the corner, cut half-right across the field to the far right-hand edge of the woodland ahead, then bear left up a clear path keeping the woods to the left, the path soon being enclosed between fences. Reaching a driveway, follow it in the same direction, with one small right kink, to the A229, turning right alongside it to very shortly reach Merriments Gardens. Now retrace your steps to (F).

From (F) follow path (G) to a path T-junction, here turning left to reach the road; turn right down the road, Burgh Hill, to the A265, then turn right alongside the A265. You cross the railway just by Etchingham Station, arriving back at the church, which is on the right, about 150 yards beyond the crossing. (Total detour 7 miles)

FURTHER NOTE: To visit Merriments only, follow the A265 from Etchingham Church north-eastwards, crossing the railway, and 400 yards beyond the crossing turn left along Burgh Hill. You pass Fysie Lane going off left in just over a third of a mile; about 450 yards beyond Fysie Lane turn left up a footpath, and in 60 yards turn right and follow this path to the five-path junction referred to above. Working clockwise, take the third path round and follow it, keeping the houses of Hurst Green to your right. Now follow the directions to Merriments from the asterisk above. Having enjoyed the gardens, return exactly the same way to Etchingham. (Total detour 3 miles)

D4 (NOTE: THIS IS A VERY LONG STRENUOUS DETOUR FOR WHICH YOU SHOULD ALLOW AT LEAST HALF A DAY. IT CAN BE SHORTENED AND IT ALLOWS FOR A POSSIBLE RETURN TO BURWASH AT THE END. PLEASE READ THE WHOLE DESCRIPTION BEFORE FINALISING YOUR PLANS.) Instead of turning right with the SHT towards Rye Green Farm, continue straight on to Park Farm and pass through the farm complex; beyond it, follow the signage carefully as you leave the wider more tempting track but fork slightly left of it up a narrower path in the shade of trees, climbing quite steeply. You then enter woodland, keeping to the obvious track which ascends to a T-junction of tracks. Turn left here then almost immediately right, following the bridle track to a fork of tracks, unsigned at the time of writing. You need to take the left fork, following the track along the eastern edge of the wood, heading southwards then in some 330 yards veering right, south-westwards. It's straightforward walking now along a clear track that then dips down to arrive at a road. Turn left along this road which climbs steadily; as it levels out, you can enjoy quite magnificent views to the right, stretching all the way to the South Downs. To your left, in a field (but inaccessible), is the Brightling Needle, an unexplained obelisk, the first of the 5 follies of Jack Fuller. Shortly beyond the obelisk you reach a crossroads road junction. Here turn right and walk uphill to another folly, an observatory, originally housing a camera obscura. Now you have a choice. Immediately before the observatory is a signed footpath going left. You could if you wish take this path, walking initially along the field edge, then striking out across it north-eastwards, proceeding round the left side of buildings and continuing over tufty grass; on reaching a road you could turn right, eastwards, along it to a junction within 100 yards (H). For a longer walk from the observatory, visiting another folly, the Sugar Loaf, stay on the road and descend with it to a T-junction (I), turning right and, in roughly two thirds of a mile from the observatory, reaching Hook's Farm House on the right. Turn left immediately opposite along a driveway, then in a few yards turn right as signed up a woodland path signed Sugar Loaf. You emerge from the wood and continue across the grass to reach, just beyond a stile, the Sugar Loaf, a mock-up spire built by Fuller to win a bet. You can actually go inside it! A little further along is a trig point, and by walking the short distance on to the B2096 and following it to the right for 400 yards or so you reach the Swan inn at Wood's Corner, the only amenity on this detour. However the detour retraces from the Sugar Loaf all the way back to (I). Here you could go straight on along the same road to arrive at junction (H) above, but for better views I recommend you retrace to the observatory and take the footpath from it as described above, reaching the road and proceeding to (H) as stated; or simply stick to the road beyond the observatory, turning right at the crossroads junction and proceeding to (H). From (H) walk eastwards along the road towards Brightling. It's a superb ridgetop walk along the road, with magnificent views northwards to Burwash and the surrounding countryside. The road enters and passes through Brightling, where you should detour to visit the pretty church and Jack Fuller's pyramid-shaped grave in the churchyard.

Follow the road south-eastwards out of the village, using the road signed to Battle. In 550 yards from the church you pass Ox Lodge which is to your right, this being the closest the continuous detour comes to a fourth folly, a Grecian rotunda temple, in the private Brightling Park. (Note: by turning right down the Ox Lodge driveway, actually a bridleway, descending and kinking right, then left, you'll reach, 500 yards from the road, a junction with a footpath. By turning right up this path for 250 yards, where the path bends left, you'll get a much clearer view of the temple and in fact by going straight on at the bend rather than left, through a gate and uphill through the field, you'll reach the temple. However there's no right of way through this field.) In 50 yards down the Battle road beyond the Ox Lodge driveway, look out on your left for a stile. Cross the stile and walk up the field beyond – it is a footpath, albeit not very well defined – aiming for the left edge of the patch of wood at the top of the hill. Looking back the way you've come, westwards, you'll get great views back to the temple. Now walk to the edge of the wood and you'll see a clearer path entering and passing through the wood, very shortly going past the final folly, a 35ft viewing tower, not previously visible because of the thick woodland. There is a spiral staircase leading up the tower, which if it's accessible you tackle at your own risk! Continue along the path beyond the tower, then emerge from the woods and cross the stile in the field boundary immediately beyond. Pause here to enjoy an unbelievable view of the Sussex and Kent countryside to the north/north-east, with a particularly good view to the Darwell Reservoir. Then follow the field boundary beyond the stile steeply downhill to a path T-junction. Turn right here and descend quite steeply, turning right at the end down a driveway to reach a road at the hamlet of Hollingrove. Turn left and almost immediately reach a road junction by a converted chapel; take the left fork here, following the road to the hamlet of Oxley's Green, noting the old Jack Fuller inn sign on a house on the right here. Go straight over the crossroads and follow the Burwash-signed road downhill. As it bends sharply right in *just under half a mile, leave the road by forking left onto a signed bridle track. Ignoring a bridleway shortly signed left, follow what is a delightful track, soon passing two waterfalls and then ascending through attractive woodland to reach the buildings of Perryman's Farm. The bridleway peters out here; simply go forward into the complex, veering right to arrive at Perryman's Lane. Turn left along the road, soon reaching a road T-junction with Burwash signed as a mile away. Turn right and follow the Burwash road. Here you've another choice. You could simply follow this road all the way to Burwash and effectively re-walk the part of the SHT between the church, where the road reaches the main street, and Bateman's. Alternatively, in roughly 400 yards down the Burwash road at Kemland, turn left along a signed bridleway, initially through fields then diving into Park Wood, heading north-westwards and going straight over a crossing track. On emerging from the wood, descend heading northwards then veering sharply left westwards. Be careful here: the OS-mapped bridleway has been rerouted and heads more north of west than due west as the map suggests. Keeping well to the right of the oasthouse, you descend steeply through grass to a gate, beyond which is a path T-junction (which is signed on the gate). Turn right here and in barely 100 yards you'll reach the start of the detour, turning left along the Rye Green farm footpath to continue along the SHT. (Total detour 6 miles; add 2 miles for Sugar Loaf, add 1 mile for temple, and further 1 mile if returning to Burwash)*

V1 From Billingshurst Station instead of crossing the road and following Myrtle Lane, turn right up Station Road. In 550 yards look out for and turn right along a signed footpath, also signed for the parish church stated to be 7 minutes' walk away! Follow the path which leads you up to the church. Bear left to pass the west door – by following the path round the north side of the church you'll see the very pretty Churchgate Cottage – then follow the path downhill. At the fork, veer right to pass the lovely Botterels and timbered Tithe Cottage and reach the High Street.

Having enjoyed Billingshurst, walk southwards down the High Street and then right along West Street (A272). Follow this to the roundabout, here turning left alongside Newbridge Road East, veering right to cross a footbridge over the A29. You're now reunited with the SHT. (No extra mileage)

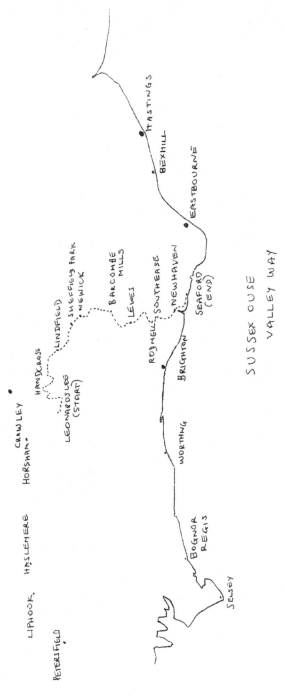

13 SUSSEX OUSE VALLEY WAY

The Sussex Ouse Valley Way (SOVW) is not, as the name might suggest, a straight riverside walk or even a walk that stays in the Ouse valley throughout. Certainly you will see a great deal of the river Ouse and follow it for a significant part of its length. But there's a good deal of up-and-down walking, a tremendous variety of landscapes and a great many really interesting places en route. It's a very fine walk indeed. The river Ouse is one of the great Sussex rivers; having been made navigable in the 19th century it was once an important means of transportation of goods and materials, the fast-flowing waters proved to be invaluable for milling, and at one time a series of mills along the river assisted in the manufacture of such diverse products as gunpowder, oil, paper and cloth. The most notable cargo was arguably the carriage of 11 million bricks for the construction of a railway viaduct, which opened in 1842 and is the most iconic sight on your SOVW journey. The growth in the road network and more sophisticated technology caused the river to decline in importance industrially, although Newhaven, at the mouth of the Ouse, remains a vibrant port to this day.

The SOVW rather tiresomely chooses to start well away from the nearest railhead which in this case is at Horsham. To reach the start your best bet is to get one of the Horsham-Brighton buses and hop out at **Leonardslee** where the A281 is met by the B2110, then walk 250 yards north up the B2110, Leechpond Hill, to the official start. Leonardslee Gardens just here used to be a major tourist attraction: started in 1801 by Charles Beauclerk, the gardens cover 240 acres with seven lakes, mature trees, a collection of rhododendrons (some nearly 200 years old), azaleas, camellias, magnolias and over 400 types of alpine plant. However they have been closed for some years with no date for reopening. The SOVW begins by heading eastwards, veering just south of east past the gardens and through a most attractive area of woodland, emerging into more open countryside but then descending through East Hanger Wood to a stream. From there, you have a brisk climb, bearing northwards and exiting the woods by Harvey's Farm, arriving at the B2115 Warninglid Lane. You turn right to follow this briefly, then bear left to join a path heading just east of north, climbing through fields.

This lovely path levels out and turns itself into a lane; continuing along the lane past a couple of houses you get your first view of the Ouse as you descend to cross it by means of a footbridge, although it is a very modest strip of water indeed at this point.

Beyond the crossing you go forward to a road which you follow briefly eastwards, passing the impressive Slaugham Furnace Pond which is on your left. You could then simply stick to the road eastwards into Slaugham, but the SOVW, apparently wanting to give you another fleeting glimpse of the infant Ouse, turns off southwards along the road towards Warninglid just beyond the pond, then shortly after crossing the Ouse, leaves the road and turns hard left along a path which goes back over the river. The SOVW then heads across or beside a succession of fields to rejoin the original road which it follows eastwards into **Slaugham**. Slaugham (pronounced Sluffham) is a very pretty village, with a particularly attractive Norman church that includes a 13th century tower and, in the south chapel, a superb monument to Richard Covert who died in 1579, while the churchyard holds the tomb of Catherine Matcham, the younger sister of Lord Nelson. If you've time you should detour from the churchyard to visit the impressive ruins of Slaugham Place, by following, from the far (south) side of the church, the signed path forking left, south-eastwards, and keeping on the path as far as the ruins. Built in 1591 and owned by Sir Walter Covert, Slaugham Place was one of the finest Tudor houses in Sussex, but sadly it fell into disrepair after Sir Walter's death. The total detour is about a third of a mile.

At the road junction opposite the church, the SOVW takes the road leading off to the left, northwards, here overlapping for a few yards with the High Weald Landscape Trail. That path soon strikes out to the left but you continue along the lane, now beginning an overlap with the Sussex Hospices Trail; as you follow the lane, you'll become very aware of the traffic on the nearby A23. You go forward along a slip road from the A23 to reach the B2110, turning right to cross the A23 and arrive at the centre of **Handcross**, where two of the best gardens in Sussex are within easy reach. The SOVW bears right and immediately left beside the entrance to the first of these gardens, Nymans. The gardens were begun in 1890 by Ludwig Messel, and consist of a historic collection of fine trees, shrubs and plants; features include sheets of white narcissi under sorbus trees, a circle of camellias round a lawn, sunken garden with stone loggia, a laurel walk, heather garden, rose garden and lovely herbaceous borders. Having visited these, you could walk straight on north-eastwards along Handcross' main street and continue alongside this road then soon bear right along the B2110 High Beeches Lane, following the road for just under a mile and a half to reach the gardens at High Beeches. The total round trip is 3.5 miles. Be warned there is no pavement and this road can be very busy. High Beeches was originally designed by Sir Edmund Loder in 1906, and has been described as a "garden of many seasons;" it boasts superb bluebells, rhododendrons, azaleas and magnolias, August gentian and autumn cyclamen as well as rare trees, unusual shrubs and wildflower meadows.

Beyond Handcross there's a very steep eastward descent along wide tracks through thick woodland; there are a number of signed nature trails and, at the bottom of the hill, there's a lake in a fine wooded setting. The SOVW veers from east to south, passing the lake and hauling itself out of the woods, for a pleasant walk along narrow metalled tracks and over the B2114 Handcross-Cuckfield road onto the green at **Staplefield Common**. Beside the green is the Victory inn, a useful watering hole, its name commemorating the hard-won legal battle by the landlord to convert it to a pub from grocer's shop. You cross the green and descend towards the Ouse, but then instead of going down to join it, you turn sharply eastwards, following a lane to reach the B2114 again. You follow this southwards, crossing the still very modest Ouse, then climb away from the valley and head eastwards again through pleasant woodland to Bigges Farm. There's now a delightful ridge walk, with lovely views to Ouse valley that lies to your left, and then a pleasant field-edge walk. You veer sharply left, northwards, and climb to the buildings of Sidnye Farm, here turning eastwards to enjoy another excellent ridge walk along a farm lane, veering south-east into Cherry Lane and reaching the B2036 Balcombe-Cuckfield road.

You cross the B2036 then continue predominantly eastwards, following a farm lane to just short of Great Bentley Farm, then strike out across a meadow that brings you to another crossing of the Ouse. From the meadow you rise to Ryelands Farm, and here you get your first really good view one of the highlights of the whole route, the Ouse Valley Viaduct. It was built in 1841 to carry the main London-Brighton railway across the Ouse valley; described as one of the wonders of the Victorian age, it has 37 arches, stands 96ft high and over a quarter of a mile long, and as stated in the introductory part of this section, required 11 million bricks, all of which were transported up the Ouse by barge! The SOVW passes underneath the viaduct and continues to Borde Hill Lane where you cross the Ouse once more and now, for the first time, have a proper Ouse-side walk, following a meadow with the river to your left. In roughly half a mile, though, you turn southwards, away from the river, now overlapping with the High Weald Landscape Trail and the Sussex Hospices Trail. There's then a determined climb through woodland, crossing the former Haywards Heath-Horsted Keynes railway, now only used for occasional freight trains between Haywards Heath and Ardingly. The SOVW then descends through a field, before another climb through woodland with a crossing of Copyhold Lane (where you lose the High Weald Landscape Trail), and then a walk south-eastwards across Haywards Heath golf course (where you say a temporary farewell to the Sussex Hospices Trail), arriving via Sandridge Lane at **High Beech Lane**. By turning right and following the road all the way to its end, then turning right along the B2028 and right at the roundabout along Sydney Road you reach the station at **Haywards Heath**, 1.5 miles from the SOVW.

The SOVW however turns left onto High Beech Lane and follows it steeply downhill – there's no pavement, so take care – then after 400 yards or so after joining High Beech Lane your route bears right onto the Kenwards Farm lane. Now proceeding south-eastwards you fork to the right of the farm, with views to the Ouse valley beyond, before a descent into woodland. You then rise again, reaching a further path junction where you turn just south of east onto an enclosed footpath, with houses and gardens to your right and extensive views to the Ouse valley to your left. From here you make your way through a gravelled courtyard to arrive at the main street at **Lindfield**, crossing the B2028 main street to enter the precincts of the fine 14th century church of All Saints. Lindfield, although effectively a suburb of Haywards Heath, is one of the prettiest villages in Sussex. It owes its prosperity to traditional industries including paper, gloves and candles, and its main street boasts many historic buildings with timber-framing, tile-hanging and elegant 18th century brickwork. A detour down the main street, reached pretty much at once, is almost obligatory! Among the best buildings of Lindfield, all of which face the main street, are the former Tiger Inn with its fine red-brick façade and timber-framed sides, the 15th/16th century timber-framed Barnlands, the early Georgian red-brick Malling Priory opposite, and, next to Barnlands, the excellent brick-built Nash House. At the very bottom of the village street, which offers lots of well-deserved refreshment opportunities, there's a lovely pond. Meanwhile, north of the church is the superb 16th century timber-framed Old Place with its massive roof of local Horsham slate; the house is effectively screened from the main street by the 15th century Thatched Cottage.

The SOVW passes the church of All Saints as stated then proceeds south-eastwards away from the village, initially downhill in the shade of trees then across pleasant low-lying farmland on excellent tracks, the Ouse some way away. You're now reunited with the Sussex Hospices Trail. You cross a road on Walstead Common then continue south-eastwards, crossing another tract of farmland before descending to enter Costells Wood. Following the signs carefully and avoiding any crossing tracks, you rise steadily through the woods with a line of raised power cables for company, then need to take care to fork left away from the trees, getting within sight of Nash Lane. Here, free of the Sussex Hospices Trail again, the SOVW turns sharply north-eastwards, enjoying lovely views northwards to the Ouse valley, crosses fields to reach the buildings of Pegden then drops down through the trees and past stud farm buildings to Freshfield Lane just south of the Sloop inn. The Freshfield Bridge crossing of the Ouse is situated immediately beyond to the left; as Terry Owen and Peter Anderson (authors of the definitive guide to the SOVW) point out, many a pint must have been consumed here by the bargees in the period between the opening of the adjacent Freshfield Lock in 1799 and its closure in 1868, the year in which operations on the so-called "Upper Navigation" of the Ouse came to an end. As you enjoy your pint, you may find yourself in the company of Sussex Border Path (spur route) and Greenwich Meridian Trail walkers, as both these routes meet the SOVW here. You can compare notes and decide who's got the best deal.

You turn right along Freshfield Lane then almost immediately left, proceeding in a predominantly south-easterly direction up through Hammer Wood, beyond which you lose the Sussex Border Path spur. After a short field interlude, you descend through Wapsbourne Wood – somehow you want to say *Wasps*-bourne! – and veer southwards. It's a lovely woodland walk along excellent tracks, where you may be fortunate enough to see roe deer. Emerging from the trees, and now having crossed from West Sussex to East Sussex, you have an easy field-edge walk eastwards to the fine Wapsbourne Manor House, where you part from the Greenwich Meridian Trail. Though it's believed there was a building on this site as long ago as Anglo-Saxon times, the fine brick and timber-framed building you see today dates from the start of the 17th century. You may well find yourself in the company of campers as this is a popular camp site known to regulars as "Wowo." There's then a south-eastward driveway walk to the busy A275 beside which (using the parallel field edge/verge) you walk north-eastwards to arrive at **Sheffield Park** and the entrance to Sheffield Park Station. By walking the 250 yards or so along the station approach road you reach the southern terminus of the Bluebell Railway, part of a line which linked Lewes with East Grinstead and which was opened in 1882. It became very popular and a total of 20 services were running each day by the start of the 20th century; as well as carrying passengers, the line conveyed freight including fruit, corn and milk. Sadly its usage declined and BR purported to close it in 1955. However the closure was challenged because allegedly certain legal formalities had not been completed, and as a result BR reopened it, disingenuously offering an extremely poor service, known as the "sulky service!" It finally closed legally, and apparently for good, in 1958, but almost immediately a preservation society was established, and the result was the steam railway that remains one of the most popular tourist attractions in Sussex. Trains on the reopened railway initially ran only as far as Horsted Keynes a few miles north, but since 2013 they have extended northwards all the way to East Grinstead. Even if you don't fancy a train ride, you can enjoy pottering around the station, which boasts pub/restaurant facilities and an excellent shop. The SOVW strikes out south-eastwards directly opposite the station approach road, but by walking north-eastwards up the A275 a little you reached a signed National Trust walking route to Sheffield Park Gardens. The round trip is just under a mile. These superb gardens are adjacent to the 18th century Sheffield Park House which was built for the 1st Earl of Sheffield by James Wyatt; the 120-acre landscaped garden and arboretum with its 2 lakes was created by Capability Brown for the Earl of Sheffield in 1776. Between 1909 and 1934, collections of trees and shrubs were planted that were notable for their autumn colours, and these, together with other fine specimens of trees, provide interest all the year round. The lakes boast fine water lilies, there are a number of fine varieties of azaleas, and in Queen's Walk there is amazing colour in the Chinese gentiana. The house itself is private and not open to visitors.

Back on the SOVW, you can now enjoy a bit more Ouse-side walking as your path heads south-eastwards through the meadow, keeping the river close by to the left. How close you choose to follow the meanders is a matter for you, but the marked route keeps a straight course, not following the Ouse's twists and turns. Eventually the path leaves the meadow and veers right, just east of south, uphill through Rotherfield Wood, then on reaching Mill Lane crosses pretty much straight over it along Newick Hill just east of Fletching Common. It's then a half-mile road walk, initially downhill then ascending quite steeply, to join the A272 at **Newick**. The SOVW follows beside this very busy road eastwards to the village centre, where you'll find two pubs, a charming green with village pump, a shop, and a bakery which at the time of writing did not only very tasty cakes but hot drinks too. There are also buses to Haywards Heath and Uckfield, so it's an ideal place to break your SOVW walk. A nice touch is the signpost showing mileages to Winchester and Canterbury, the west and east ends of the Pilgrims' Way. You'll see that you're not far off exactly halfway between the two! The SOVW strikes out southwards from the A272 along Church Road, past the impressively large Norman church of St Mary with magnificent sandstone tower; note the impressive timber-framed house beside it, and fine examples of topiary in the garden. It's by the church that you meet the Sussex Hospices Trail again and not for the last time! You then have an unremarkable road walk as far as a fork junction where you take the left fork and then shortly leave the road, taking a path heading south-eastwards away from it. And it's here that at last you're rewarded for your tarmac-crunching by what is one of the finest stretches of the SOVW so far (though there's even better to come) with glorious views northwards as you proceed along the top of the ridge on a clear path through fields. Having skirted an area of woodland you descend to cross a road then drop down gently to return to the Ouse valley just east of the lovely old buildings of Vuggles Farm. On reaching the valley floor you're signed right, southwards through the meadows, soon being joined by the Ouse as it comes in from your left.

It is now a walk of pure delight all the way to the so-called fish ladders of Barcombe Mills, roughly 4 miles away. The Ouse is always close by and you can enjoy watching it mature as it heads downstream, in a predominantly southerly direction, towards Lewes; it's particularly lovely in spring when the meadows are lush from the winter rains and the creamy white blossoms shine through the surrounding vegetation. Though the path through the meadows isn't always clear, excellent signage shows the direction to follow. Soon you pass close to a magnificent waterfall for which a short (and obvious) detour is necessary, but it's well worth the extra legwork. Shortly beyond the waterfall, you rise briefly to reach a track which you have to follow for 200 yards or so, then, continuing to keep the Ouse to your left, you enter another area of meadow from which there's a lovely view to Isfield Church. You now continue through the meadows, going forward to White Bridge, which you cross, then having crossed, turn right to switch to a meadow on the left bank of the river. However, by continuing straight on along the track beyond the bridge crossing there is the opportunity of a detour D1 to the church and railway station of Isfield, and, some three miles to the east, Bentley House. The church contains tombs of the Shurley family, and the chapel still has 16th century linenfold panelling and pews. Note however that the church is usually locked so you may need to make advance arrangements via the keyholders to view it. The old railway station is on the now defunct Lewes-Uckfield line which opened in 1858 and shut in 1969. In 1983, however, the station was purchased by the Millham family and restored, adjacent track was relaid, and trains began to run along an all too small stretch of line towards Uckfield. It continues to flourish today as the Lavender Line, after the coal merchants A.E. Lavender who used to operate from the station yard. The fine Palladian Bentley House boasts a magnificent collection of wildfowl and a display of vintage cars and motorbikes while the grounds contain mixed woodland dotted with sculptures.

From White Bridge it's now a very straightforward and enjoyable walk through the meadow to the left of the Ouse as far as the Anchor inn. You pass under a bridge which used to carry the Lewes-Uckfield line; in recent years there have been calls to resurrect the whole of this line so who knows, you may see trains on it when you walk this section! At the Anchor, an even more photogenic riverside pub than the Sloop, you switch to the right bank of the river and are forced briefly away from it, but then soon return and cross once more to the left bank. There's a short but delightful section of path which passes between the main Ouse to your right, and an eastern "arm" of the river coming in from the left; then, however, the arms join and you remain on the left bank as far as Barcombe Mills. The main Ouse veers a little right and you remain beside a narrower channel which you will notice incorporates so-called "fish ladders," a series of mini-weirs separated by level stretches of water enabling elvers to effectively travel upstream. Your riverside walking comes to a temporary end at the fine old Pikes Bridge, grooves in the parapet of which were cut by ropes that were used to haul barges. You cross over Pikes Bridge and now follow the road over the main Ouse channel, perhaps pausing to be amused by the table of tolls that are still exhibited by the bridge. Beyond the bridge the lane swings sharp left and goes forward to a T-junction with **Barcombe Mills Road**. You follow this road briefly westwards – the village of **Barcombe Cross** is just under a mile further along this road – passing the site of Barcombe Mills' old station which sadly, at the time of writing, had been developed in such a way as to provide little indication of its former usage. Previously it used to be a delightful café where you could sit and pretend to be waiting for a train. Now the SOVW heads south-westwards away from the road, keeping a considerable distance from the Ouse, initially passing just to the left to the village of Barcombe and its beautifully situated church of St Mary. To detour to it you could turn right off the SOVW to join the signed Greenwich Meridian Trail which has come in to rejoin you after taking a rather shorter and less circuitous route from Wapsbourne where you last saw it. Beyond Barcombe the SOVW, overlapping with the Greenwich Meridian Trail throughout, continues south-westwards for the next 2 miles or so across a succession of fields. It's easy walking, with excellent signage, and there are fine views to Cliffe Hill just east of Lewes, but it's a shame to have "lost" the river. The SOVW then goes forward along a narrower track in the shade of trees to a road which it then follows southwards to Hamsey. This is a straggling village, its chief glory being its magnificently sited hilltop Norman church just south of the village, albeit at the time of writing it is shut for major restoration work. If you wish to detour to it, simply turn left immediately opposite the junction with Ivors Lane and follow the road uphill. The detour is a half-mile round trip.

From Hamsey the SOVW now continues south-westwards along a path beside a cut of the Ouse, the "proper" river describing an extravagant meander just east of the church. Not long after the two channels meet up, you arrive at the bank of the main London-Lewes railway line – to your right is the point where the Lewes-Uckfield branch left the main line until 1868 when the branch was rerouted out of Lewes – then, just short of the railway embankment, the river and your riverside path swing south-eastwards. The SOVW now simply follows the right bank of the Ouse towards Lewes, entering and passing through the outskirts of the town. It's delightfully easy walking, and progress is fast. In just under a mile from the swing south-eastwards mentioned above, you reach a footbridge; by detouring right here for roughly 200 yards you reach Pells Pool, which, built in 1861, is thought to be the oldest freshwater open-air swimming pool in the country. If you detoured further, kinking left at Pelham Terrace and right up St John's Hill you'd reach the fine Victorian church of St John-sub-Castro, a quarter of a mile from the river. However, the SOVW turns left over the footbridge and switches to the left bank of the Ouse along a metalled path. You proceed past Tesco and under the A277 then away from the river to reach the pretty High Street of Cliffe, immediately east of Lewes. The SOVW turns right along this street but by turning left, eastwards, there is at this point the possibility of a substantial and strenuous <u>detour D2</u> to visit the eastern part of Cliffe High Street, Mount Caburn, Glynde Place and adjoining church, and Glyndebourne. All are worth visiting. Cliffe High Street has a lovely mix of architecture and shops, and on the left, the very pretty flint church of St Thomas Becket with 14th century arcades. Mount Caburn has a nature reserve and the summit is the site of an Iron Age habitation and hillfort, from which there's a fantastic view to the Ouse valley, Lewes, the South Downs and the sea. The 16th century flint-built Glynde Place boasts impressive Tudor flint gables and a fine set of paintings from overseas, while the grounds enjoy a splendid situation with further superb views eastwards towards Arlington Reservoir, and the 18th century flint church just beyond is particularly noteworthy for its hessian-covered walls and box pews. The part-timbered house at Glyndebourne dates back to pre-Elizabethan times but is more famous now for its opera house which opened in 1934 and which now hosts the world-famous summer Glyndebourne Festival of Opera, described in *The Rough Guide To Kent, Sussex & Surrey* as "an indispensable part of the high-society calendar."

Having turned right along Cliffe High Street, the SOVW passes the 19th century Harvey's Brewery which is to the right, then crosses the bridge over the Ouse and shortly turns left along Railway Lane. To access the delightful old centre of **Lewes** and its excellent bus and rail links, you go straight on, crossing Eastgate Street. The bus station is immediately to your right here, while the railway station, just over a quarter of a mile from the SOVW, is reached by turning left, walking up to the crossroads and turning left down Station Road. To proceed to the centre of Lewes you walk straight up the hill beyond Eastgate Street, arriving in roughly 400 yards from the SOVW at the main traffic-light-controlled junction by the information office. The section devoted to the Greenwich Meridian Trail describes the highlights of Lewes west of this junction, and they are all well worth a detour. However on the near (east) side of this junction you can turn right along Fisher Street past the Town Hall and right again along Market Lane to visit the Needlemakers, previously a Victorian industrial building and now a complex of shops and café, then rejoin the lane via the café. You could then follow Market Lane to its end and here turn right along Market Street past the late 18th century red-brick Market Tower which incorporates a bell cast in 1555, bearing left at the end down the High Street, retracing your steps to the Railway Lane turning. As you set off from here, it's worth casting your mind back to 2000 when the Ouse in Lewes made national headline news: after weeks of heavy rain, it burst its banks and caused flooding which devastated houses and businesses in this area.

As stated, the SOVW proceeds away from Cliffe High Street along Railway Lane, skirting the Lewes Railway Land nature reserve; this, as the name suggests, is on or around the course of the rerouted rail exit from Lewes on the Lewes-Uckfield railway, the course of which you've met a few times now on your SOVW walk. Shortly you're reunited with the Ouse and continue along the embankment path, passing under the railway bridge and shortly under the A27 Lewes bypass. It's very easy going for a while now, and very pleasant walking: from your riverside path you can enjoy lovely downland views both to your right and to the left, and follow with your eyes the respective courses of the Eastbourne and Seaford railway lines. There's one section of riverside path which can get extremely muddy, so be patient and don't get too close to the edge! Roughly 2.5 miles from Cliffe High Street, the SOVW leaves the river and heads west/south-westwards along a track through fields to reach **Rodmell**. You join the village street and soon reach Monk's House, where the novelist Virginia Woolf had her country retreat between 1919 and her death (by drowning herself in the Ouse) in 1941. The house, furnished in similar style to that of nearby Charleston Farmhouse where Virginia Woolf's artist sister Vanessa Bell lived, is now owned by the National Trust.

Just past the house you turn left up an alleyway to pass the pretty village church then veer south-westwards again up a path taking you to a junction (A) with a busy road linking Newhaven with Kingston near Lewes. The mapped and signed route turns left and follows beside this road then overlaps with the South Downs Way and Sussex Hospices Trail for a parallel roadside path going uphill to the Southease road; you then cross the main road to join the Southease road. However it's far better – there's no extra mileage involved – to turn left immediately before reaching (A), and join a permissive Southease-signed path, which offers lovely views across the Ouse valley to Mount Caburn. Whichever route you take, you arrive at and follow the Southease road downhill, just south of east, passing the exceptionally lovely Norman church of St Peter at **Southease,** which has a stunning setting above a green; the church is briefly described in the South Downs Way section. You continue on down to the Ouse, here leaving the South Downs Way and Sussex Hospices Trail and turning right to rejoin the right bank of the river. (Note that Southease Station is 275 yards further on along the South Downs Way, with refreshments, when available, just beyond the station.) You continue on along the bank for roughly a mile and are then forced away from it, being signed over the road and away, south-westwards, towards the sprawling settlement of Telscombe Cliffs, before then turning hard left, eastwards, over a hillside and back down to the road which you cross to reach Piddinghoe. Piddinghoe is a most attractive and tranquil village of flint-built cottages grouped round two small greens, but it was once an extremely busy workaday place. It used to contain a forge and malt house, bricks were manufactured here, and indeed the quayside adjacent to the church of St John was used for unloading cargo well into the 20th century. The church itself, also flint-built and dating back to the 12th century, has one of the only 3 Norman round towers in Sussex; it is topped by a shingle spire with a golden fish-shaped weather vane, described by Kipling as a "begilded dolphin."

The SOVW bears to the left of the church to join a path that then rejoins the embankment, and you now follow this on to Newhaven, becoming, as you walk, increasingly aware of the more industrial and less pastoral surroundings. The highlight of this part of the SOVW for me was the sight of two women swimming in the river – on a grey damp 14th January! The Ouse is now impressively wide, in contrast to its modest trickle back near Slaugham when you first saw it. Your journey now gets disappointingly messy as you find yourself leaving the main river course and instead following the right bank of a subsidiary arm of the river. At the time of writing this area is being redeveloped and signage was diverting walkers off the embankment and along a cycle path, ending in an untidy area of suburban housing and industrial works. SOVW signage was poor and unless and until it improves with the redevelopment I suggest the easiest course is to aim for the Jolly Boatman pub, and turn left just before it along Elphick Road to arrive at the A259 ring road. Bear left along the parallel footpath/cycle path and follow it round, aiming for the big swing bridge over the Ouse. The SOVW crosses the swing bridge using the walkway on its south side but by walking on beyond the bridge (before crossing it) to the adjacent pedestrian crossing you can conveniently detour into **Newhaven**, as described in the England Coast Path section.

Having crossed the swing bridge the SOVW immediately forks right down the slip road which passes beside Newhaven Town Station on the Brighton-Lewes-Seaford line. Beyond the station the SOVW overlaps, via **Newhaven Harbour Station** and **Bishopstone,** almost exactly with the England Coast Path as far as its end at Seaford, staying well east of the mouth of the Ouse. Please therefore refer to the England Coast Path section for a description of what are the final, it has to be said, underwhelming two miles or so of the SOVW; if you've walked the England Coast Path from Newhaven to Seaford you could end your walk at Newhaven with a clear conscience! The Vanguard Way, which starts roughly half a mile south of Newhaven Town Station, overlaps in the same way. The SOVW would appear to officially end just beyond the sailing club building referred to in the England Coast Path description, but I recommend you stick to the promenade as far as Dane Road as described in the England Coast Path section then bear left up Dane Road, turning left at the end to immediately reach **Seaford Station**, or right for Seaford town centre. For a grandstand view of the mouth of the Ouse, either instead of or as well as taking the SOVW to Seaford, stay on (or return to) the western side of the swing bridge at Newhaven and follow the described England Coast Path walk, heading back along the west bank of the Ouse then along Fort Road, bearing right to ascend past the Newhaven Fort complex to the clifftop. The total round trip is 2 miles from Newhaven. On a clear day you'll get a superb panorama from the cliffs – a much more fitting and satisfying finale to your SOVW journey.

GOOD TO KNOW
Start: Leonardslee, Lower Beeding. Finish: Seaford Station.
Total mileage: 43.5.
Difficulty: Mostly easy.
Stages: Slaugham (RA) 4, Handcross (RB) 5.25, Staplefield Common (R) 7, High Beech Lane for Haywards Heath (*RAB) 13, Lindfield (RAB) 14.5, Sheffield Park (R) 20, Newick (RAB) 21.5, Barcombe Mills Road for Barcombe Cross (RB) 27.5, Lewes (*RAB) 31.5, Rodmell (RA) 35, Southease (*R) 35.5, Newhaven (*RAB) 39.5, Newhaven Harbour Station (*) 40, Bishopstone (*RAB) 42, Seaford Station (*RAB) 43.5.
OS: OL34, 135, OL11.

D1 NOTE: THIS IS A SUBSTANTIAL DETOUR! However there

are pubs at Isfield and Rose Hill and regular buses to/from Rose Hill. Follow the track just north of east from White Bridge and in about 400 yards just after a bend to the right, you reach a stile on the left (B). Here you could detour to Isfield Church by going over the stile and following the clear field path for just over 250 yards, just east of north past the village hall to Station Road. Turn left along it then just round the next bend beyond Quarry Barn South/North bear left along a path heading north-westwards, crossing a footbridge; follow the left side of the hedge beyond it as signed, then veer left beyond a second footbridge to reach a road and the church on the far side of it. Return to (B) to continue. Follow the track south-eastwards from (B) to reach Station Road, turning right alongside it to pass (or visit!) the pub and old station. Go past the old level crossing gates to a T-junction. By turning left you immediately reach bus stops on the Brighton-Tunbridge Wells route but your detour turns right along Lewes Road. In a few yards immediately before Birches Farm turn left along a path which soon veers right, and in 50 yards beyond the right bend, turn left to cross a stile and follow a signed path. Initially you follow the left-hand edge of a meadow of rough grass, then in 80 yards or so reach a gap in the hedge to your left with a large tree in the middle of the gap. Switch here to follow the right-hand edge of the adjacent meadow; don't be tempted away left. You cross a footbridge in a thicket then go forward eastwards along a right-hand field edge, going on into the next field and veering right to reach the buildings of Brook Lodge Farm, aiming for the stile to the right of the little gate. Go forward to the farm driveway, turning right along it, veering immediately left and following it to the A26. Turn left alongside it for 50 yards then cross and follow a signed path heading eastwards through trees just north of Plashett Park. The path is well signed but often very rough and ill-defined. In just under half a mile you're signed left, north-eastwards, up a much wider track. (Ignore a track which then strikes shortly out to the left.) You veer gently left and climb to exit the trees, following as arrow-signed north-eastwards across the field to reach a road. Turn right along it past the fine brick buildings including oasthouse at Brockwells. Shortly beyond these buildings fork right along Harvey's Lane, soon bearing right again and following the road on for just over a quarter of a mile to reach, at a sharp right bend, the gates of Bentley House. Now turn left to follow the driveway to the public entrance. This is the far end of the detour! Having enjoyed the house return to the road and now follow it on south-westwards for half a mile. There's a sharp ascent to Mount Farm, and opposite the farm you turn right along a signed bridleway north-westwards, first through woods, then along a left-hand field edge, then through an open field keeping the lovely brick Moatpark Farm to your right. Beyond the farm you pass the edge of woodland, the going quite juicy here, and reach a farm lane; turn left here as signed and follow it all the way to the A26 at Rose Hill. Cross and turn right alongside the road then in 110 yards turn left, north-westwards, down a signed path. Initially it's a well-defined driveway but as this peters out within sight of a barn you need to transfer to a grassy path passing to the right of the barn and hen coops. A clear enclosed grassy path continues north-westwards to a path junction in the trees; here turn right and walk through a field, going forward through trees and veering left to return to Lewes Road at Isfield. Turn right along Lewes Road then very shortly left along Station Road past the crossing gates, station approach and pub. Continue along Station Road, forking left opposite the smart village sign along a farm track which returns you to White Bridge. Turn left just before the bridge to resume your SOVW walk. (Total detour 7.25 miles; 6 miles if detour to church at Isfield omitted)

D2 NOTE: THIS IS ANOTHER SUBSTANTIAL, AND ALSO STRENUOUS, DETOUR. THE ONLY AMENITIES ARE AT GLYNDE, 3 MILES FROM THE START OF THE DETOUR (AND OFF THE DETOUR ROUTE!). Turn left along Cliffe High Street and follow it past the lovely flint-built church of St Thomas Becket which is on the left. At the crossroads at the far end cross straight over onto Chapel Hill, rising steeply and joining a parallel path, soon getting superb views to Lewes and the Ouse valley. As the road ends at the golf clubhouse, bear right as footpath-signed through the gate into a field, then follow the left-hand field edge, going forward along a clear green path which soon becomes obvious beyond the clubhouse. In about 400 yards, at a wooden post leave the "main" path and go straight on along a narrower path, dropping downhill and passing through a gate in a fence to descend to the valley bottom. Proceed as signed along the valley bottom, then very shortly after veering sharp left with the valley, you reach on the right a sign by the fence welcoming you to Mount Caburn Nature Reserve, and a clear green *path rising beyond. Turn right to follow this path steeply uphill all the way to the top. Cross the stile in the fence at the top (C) and turn right, beside the fence, to reach the summit of Mount Caburn, Return to the stile at (C) but now carry on northwards beside the fence until you shortly reach a signed permissive path going off to the right (D). You now have a choice. If you're pushed for time, to omit the Glynde attractions simply continue northwards, passing through a gate/stile and continuing in the same direction, reaching another stile and going forward along a chalk track, descending as far as the escarpment edge by a gate (E). However, to visit Glynde Place, its adjacent church and Glyndebourne, turn right at (D) along a path that's indistinct at first but becomes obvious. You pass through some trees and emerge to enjoy a superb view ahead. Now descend steadily, taking care where you reach a gate within sight of the road ahead to veer left with the path and shortly reach the road. Turn right to follow the road which in less than 200 yards brings you to Glynde Place and church beyond. (The village of Glynde with its café, railway station and pub, is just down the hill; the station is on the same road half a mile from Glynde Place.) Now retrace your steps but this time continue along the road – there's no pavement, so take care – and after a mile or so you reach Glyndebourne with its opera house. Turn left off the road more or less opposite the house up a signed path which climbs steeply south-westwards and passes the edge of trees. Beyond them bear right to reach the gate at (E) and rejoin the shorter route. Now turning hard left and following a clear path you head uphill, south-westwards, keeping to the escarpment edge and enjoying superb northward views; you pass the left-hand edge of a plantation then continue along the hilltop, reaching a fence where there's an access land sign and Southerham Nature Reserve information board. Go straight on into the reserve along the path, contouring the hillside and reaching another fence and gate. DON'T be tempted along the main path beyond the fence but take the narrower right-hand forking path, continuing to a third fence. Leave the access land here, keeping along the path across Lewes golf course; initially the going is clear, but you then do need to follow the wooden posts with the yellow arrow signs. If you're unfortunate enough to lose the thread, veer down to the 14th tee and work uphill northwards (directly away from the Ouse river valley) and shortly, looking left, you'll see the next post. As the buildings of Lewes come into view, the path veers very gently right. Keep following the wooden* posts, aiming for Lewes Castle ahead. At length you pass over a practice fairway and enter an area of trees, descending steeply – steps are provided at one point – and reaching Chapel Hill; turn right to follow it to the crossroads junction at the bottom, and go straight over along Cliffe High Street to rejoin the main SOVW route. (Total detour 7 miles; 5 miles if Glynde and Glyndebourne omitted)

14 1066 COUNTRY WALK

The 1066 Country Walk (TCW) commemorates the key places and people around the Norman invasion of that year, and in doing so provides a walking route linking a number of places of huge historic interest, including Pevensey, Battle, Winchelsea and Rye. The route is generally across lowland terrain and lacks the variety and drama of many of the other name paths in Sussex, but there is plenty to see and enjoy along the way including some magnificent castles, fine churches, old oasthouses and windmills, and you'll enjoy some great views as well as some beautiful waterside walking. What makes this path particularly curious, and potentially confusing for those looking at the mapping of the route for the first time, is that besides the main route, starting at Pevensey and ending in Rye, there are three "link" routes – the South Downs Link which joins the main route at Pevensey or Rickney, the Bexhill Link which joins the main route at Battle, and the Hastings Link which joins the main route at Doleham. These links get the green diamond treatment on OS maps as though they were part of the TCW, and the same waymarking logo is used for both the main route and link route. Accordingly, it is only right to include a description of all three links within this section. There is no ideal place to insert the links but in order to promote consistency and avoid breaks in continuity I have decided to describe all three link routes at the end, while making it clear at what point each link route joins the main route.

So then to the main route. To reach the start of the main route from **Pevensey & Westham Station**, I suggest you turn right from the station briefly along the B2191 Eastbourne Road, then shortly right onto Westham High Street, passing two really fine timber-framed houses and also St Mary's Church, possibly the first Norman church in England, with its particularly impressive 14th century tower. As the main street veers left, continue straight on along a path, reaching and passing through a gate giving entry to the castle grounds. This should be regarded as the start of the main route, and the place where I suggest the South Downs Link should meet with it (though OS mapping may indicate otherwise – see the South Downs Link description below). Now you proceed through the

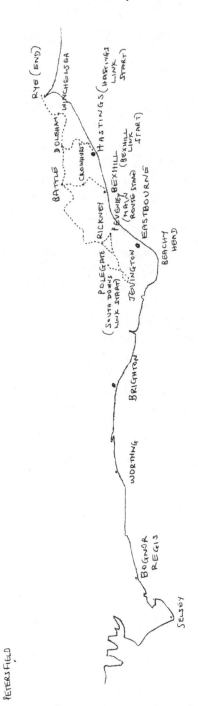

1066 COUNTRY WALK

precincts of Pevensey Castle, built by the Normans but previously the site of the great Roman fortress of Anderida; garrisoned until the 14th century, it was refortified during the Spanish Armada and World War 2. The inner ward, which carries an admission charge, is easily accessed to the right. The TCW exits the castle precinct to immediately reach Castle Road. By going straight ahead you'd find yourself on Pevensey's High Street, with its tile-hung 14th century Mint House and Court House Museum; by turning right off the High Street along Gaol Lane, you reach the 13th century church of St Nicholas. However you need to turn left along Castle Road, crossing it and soon passing a hotel/café, just beyond which you turn right down a clearly signed track. You shortly cross the A27 then veer left, north-westwards, along the path/bridleway down to the channel known as Pevensey Haven. It's now a lovely waterside walk north-westwards of just under 2 miles as far as Rickney, keeping the channel to your right. As you approach the pylons close to Rickney the path veers a little away from the bank, and you then go forward along a path with farm buildings to your right, arriving at a metalled road at **Rickney** itself. Coming in from the left here is the South Downs Link route variation V2, described below. The TCW turns right along the road, immediately reaching a road T-junction; you turn right along the road and cross the channel then immediately bear left along a path, keeping the channel to your left. You're in the heart of Pevensey Levels, an extensive marshland area and an important site for flowering water plants, aquatic beetles, damselflies and dragonflies. You follow the bank for about 2 miles then just before the channel bends sharp left, you reach a conspicuous line of bushes at right-angles to the bank; here you leave the channel and walk eastwards across the grass to a gate. Now you follow a winding but clear path in a predominantly easterly direction with excellent views towards Herstmonceux. You bear left, north-eastwards, onto a track which takes you uphill past the buildings of Church Farm to the road; the TCW immediately turns right, eastwards, but I recommend you walk a few steps further up the road to view, on the left, the part-12th century church of All Saints, Herstmonceux, with its superb monuments, most notably to Thomas Lord Dacre and his son Sir Thomas Fiennes. A highly recommended <u>detour D1</u> from the church takes you north to the mill at Windmill Hill, built around 1814 and the largest post mill in

Sussex. However as stated the TCW heads eastwards from the road along a path which descends, with lovely views to Herstmonceux Castle on your left; if you're not planning to visit the castle this is the best view of it that you'll get from the TCW. You then ascend just north of east through woodland to Wartling Road, along which the TCW turns right, but immediately to your left here is the access driveway for **Herstmonceux Castle and Science Centre**. Originally built in 1440, Herstmonceux Castle was one of England's first and largest brick buildings, and the original battlements and turrets still remain, making it one of the most photogenic castles in Sussex; the grounds contain a lake full of waterlilies and populated by kingfishers and dragonflies, while the walled garden boasts rhododendrons and azaleas. The Science Centre, with its domes and telescopes, is part of the former home of the Royal Greenwich Observatory and provides more than 100 interactive exhibits.

Having turned right along Wartling Road – **Wartling** village is just under half a mile further in this direction – you turn left in roughly 200 yards, just before The Well House, along a path that proceeds north-eastwards along the right-hand edge of firstly a field and then a wood, dropping down to a narrow road. You cross and walk parallel with it, then veer left, initially parallel with Boreham Lane then striking out across a succession of fields, just west of north, rising steadily. You skirt a small wood, veering just east of north and arriving via a further field at the A271. You cross and turn right along this road through the ridgetop village of **Boreham Street** then just beyond the village turn left, northwards, as signed. You plunge steeply down a hillside, enjoying the views to the broad valley ahead, then proceed along the valley floor, crossing the charming Blackstock Bridge and after a short woodland walk, picking up a farm track which you follow past Gardners Farm. Look left for a charming lake hereabouts; this is really the only highlight of what is a rather nondescript lowland landscape, though the signage is good and clear. Keeping to the farm track and veering just west of north, you arrive at a road, Henley's Hill, turning right to follow it initially downhill, then up again, heading for Brownbread Street. After three quarters of a mile, heading north-eastwards, you reach a road heading to the right, signed Ninfield. From here you can take a detour D2 to Ashburnham, whose magnificent Gothic church of St Peter boasts superb monuments to the Ashburnham family, a blue ceiling, cream walls, box pews, gallery and panelled pulpit; the adjacent Ashburnham Place complex, which includes an excellent café, dates back to Georgian times. Whether you've detoured or not, carry on just east of north along the road which soon reaches the deliciously-named village of Brownbread Street with pretty houses and a pub.

You follow the road on northwards beyond Brownbread Street, but in just over a quarter of a mile bear right along a field-edge path which takes you to another road. You turn left then almost immediately right along a further road, heading predominantly north-eastwards. The road plunges downhill, crosses a weir and then begins to climb, almost at once coming to a sharp right-hand bend. The TCW forks right, away from the road, just beyond the bend, but by detouring along the road for half a mile you reach Penhurst (not to be confused with Penshurst in Kent!), bearing left at the junction to reach, almost at once, the beautiful village church with its old box pews, Jacobean pulpit, 15th century oak screen and heraldic glass in the east window. Penhurst village itself is like something from a 1930's film set – a beautifully tranquil and remote spot. However as stated above the TCW forks right off the road, striking out across fields and descending steeply south-eastwards. This is lovely walking and makes a nice change from the tarmac! You plunge down to the valley bottom, crossing two footbridges in the shade of trees, then climb very steeply onto Tent Hill; this is the most strenuous section of the whole TCW main route, but you're rewarded with magnificent views back to the downland above Eastbourne. You veer very subtly eastwards at the top, proceeding across a very broad field past a pond and wooded hillock then skirting an area of woodland before yet another climb past a further pond. The views remain superb as you proceed to meet the A271 again at Steven's Crouch. Now the going gets much easier as having crossed the A271 you follow a very clear track south-eastwards through woodland downhill, all the way to **Catsfield** and the B2204. Don't be fooled into trying to visit the impressive-looking church just along the street east of this road: it's now converted into dwellings and you will not be welcome! The TCW turns left, north-eastwards (your direction of travel all the way to Battle) alongside the B2204 up the village street, then cuts a corner, forking left to cross a field before shortly returning to the road. Turning left you follow the road briefly then strike out north-eastwards past Starcroft Farm and then over a field and through the pretty Hoathybank Wood. You need to look out carefully for a left turn in the wood along a path that brings you down to a bridleway; the TCW turns right along the bridleway, passing Farthings Farm then keeping woodland to the right. You then rise quite steeply through a parkland landscape, in due course being joined by the Bexhill Link from the right. You then follow an obvious path in the shade of trees, going forward along a metalled path that passes Battle Abbey and arrives at Battle's main street.

Battle is an almost obligatory stopping place on your journey. Battle Abbey, arguably its focal point and its most popular attraction, was built by William the Conqueror on the very place where Harold fell; the gatehouse was built in 1338 and in the various arches there are examples of Norman, Gothic and early Renaissance architecture. You can take an interactive audio tour of the Abbey as you explore the atmospheric ruins and historic battlefield. Although the TCW turns right along the High Street it's well worth detouring left to enjoy the town more fully. I suggest that having turned left you walk up the left-hand side of the High Street, passing, among many historic buildings, the magnificent half-timbered Pilgrims Rest of 1420, the 17th century Bull Hotel built of ashlar masonry from the Abbey kitchen, the timber-framed 1642 Friar House, and the 15th century timber-framed Almonry, where you'll also find the Battle Museum of Local History and lovely gardens. I suggest you then cross and return down the High Street, shortly turning left up Mount Street. There's a remarkable variety of buildings on the left of this street including the weatherboarded Bayeux Cottage, the robust Victorian red-brick Roman Catholic church and Zion Chapel, both 19th century, and the red-brick Old Court House. You should then continue along the same street up Caldbec Hill, and just beyond Providence Cottage bear left up a driveway, almost immediately reaching the superbly restored 1810 Kings Mead smock mill. Then walk back down Caldbec Hill (going forward into Mount Street) following the left-hand side and passing a magnificent group of timber-framed cottages; as you get near the High Street, you reach the superb 15th century King's Head, a masterpiece of tile-hanging. Now turn left down the High Street, past the impressive originally 16th century Langton House, to return to the TCW route. This detour will add roughly a mile to your walk.

Now back on the TCW, follow the High Street south-eastwards past the Norman church of St Mary the Virgin with a fine 15th century west tower, then at the roundabout junction go straight on along Marley Lane and over the railway crossing. Battle Station can be reached by turning right along a path for 250 yards immediately before the crossing. Continue along Marley Lane beyond the railway crossing but as the built-up area ends, some 550 yards after the level crossing, you turn right along an excellent path which heads eastwards in a dead straight line through Great Wood. This wood is very popular with dog walkers and signage is excellent. There's a significant descent roughly three quarters of a mile from where you left Marley Lane, your trusty path dropping to a path crossroads with a seat on the other side of the crossing path. You go straight over this crossroads and very shortly there's a path forking left and then a few yards beyond that another forking right. The right fork is the route of the main TCW walk but the left fork offers a detour D3 to Sedlescombe by way of the well-signed Sedlescombe Walk off the main TCW route – note the logo for this signed walk is essentially the same as the TCW logo. Sedlescombe is one of the prettiest villages in Sussex, with a wide sloping green on either side of which are brick and tile-hung cottages, and among many particularly fine houses are the magnificent Queen's Head pub, the Old Thatched House and the superb timber-framed Manor. Half a mile north of the village is the attractive 14th century church of St John the Baptist, with 15th century tower. Having rejoined the main route you fork right, as stated, along another woodland path which exits south-eastwards from the wood and you're now signed eastwards across Sedlescombe golf course then north-eastwards on a farm lane taking you to the A21.

Cross the A21, a very busy road, with care, turning left beside it and then right to continue the TCW as signed. There now follows pleasant rather than spectacular walking, along narrow but clear and very well-signed paths through fields beside a stream heading just north of east. The only real highlight is the splendid late 17th century (Grade II listed) Spraysbridge Farm to your right just before the next road crossing. The TCW crosses more or less straight over this (Westfield-Sedlescombe) road and continues briefly by the stream. You pass through a small wood and emerge into a delightful more open landscape, dropping down to the so-called

Forge Stream heading north-south; the TCW bears right to follow beside it southwards along the edge of a wood. Veering round the far side of the wood the TCW heads steeply uphill north-eastwards through trees to arrive at the village of **Westfield**. At the houses at the top of the rise the route turns east along a lane, New Cut, then, beyond the next bend, veers just south of east along a path between houses that emerges at Cottage Lane; a short path walk east of there brings you to Westfield's main street on the busy A28 Hastings-Tenterden road, the village centre less than 100 yards to the right. There are regular buses from here to Hastings.

The TCW however crosses the A28 and heads north-eastwards initially along a lane, then a woodland path, passing a cricket pitch and following another lane past Downoak Farm, before striking out eastwards along field paths. There's a nice open feel to the walking and the houses and traffic of Westfield seem a long way back. You pick up another farm track and veer right to pass Pattleton's Farm then again strike out eastwards across a field beside the farm buildings and a much wider field beyond. This is some of the best walking on the TCW with glorious views towards North's Seat and Fairlight above Hastings, and north-eastwards towards the Brede valley. There's then a delightful descent through the field to arrive at Doleham Ditch and the meeting of the TCW and the Hastings Link.

You now climb quite steeply through woodland, crossing the single-track Rye-Hastings railway and continuing uphill through open pasture to reach Fourteen Acre Lane, **Doleham**. By turning right along this road and right at the end along Butcher's Lane you reach Three Oaks Station (roughly 1.5 miles from the TCW) with direct if infrequent trains to Hastings and Rye. However the TCW turns left, north-eastwards, along Fourteen Acre Lane, soon passing a left turn down Doleham Hill which leads in 275 yards to Doleham Station from which the train service is even more infrequent, and for much of the day non-existent! The road bends right to pass Lidham Hill Farm and just beyond the farm the TCW turns left off the road and heads north-eastwards. A track takes you past Lower Lidham Hill Farm and the TCW now drops down steeply to walk across part of Brede Level, an area of meadows and marshes round the river Brede. Signage is thankfully very good, and it's enjoyable walking in very peaceful surroundings, the only noise likely to come from trains on the Rye-Hastings line. As you approach the imposing buildings of Lower Snailham on the hill above you, you're signed sharply right, just south of east, across what can be an extremely juicy area of grass. You then veer north-eastwards again to ascend to and pass the Lower Snailham buildings, then keep on a track heading south of east, gently rising and enjoying lovely views westwards. You pass the Snaylham (sic) Farm complex then, staying on farm lanes, are signed hard left and right past Brook Farm, dropping steeply back to Brede Level.

Still heading just south of east, the TCW proceeds pleasantly across fields, aiming just to the right of a very prominent green hill ahead. You then climb to the shoulder of this hill; it's quite a shock to ascend so steeply after so much gentle walking! You then need to follow the left edge of the plateau, the path poorly defined here, before following a clear track along the edge of **Icklesham** village with houses immediately to your right. The TCW veers right to cross the A259 at the eastern end of the village, then follows Workhouse Lane briefly southwards and strikes out eastwards to pass the church of All Saints, Icklesham. This is one of the more impressive churches on the TCW, boasting late 12th century arcades, finely carved Victorian roof corbels in the form of flowers and fruit, a number of Norman windows in the south aisle, and a north tower that dates from early Norman times and which rises in three successive steps. The TCW then veers south-eastwards past Manor Farm and along an excellent field-edge path arriving back at Workhouse Lane and bearing left along it. However, the TCW leaves it almost at once, turning left and going uphill, eastwards, through a field past Hog Hill Windmill, a post mill with four sails; built in 1781, it was moved here in 1790 and stopped working in 1920. Beyond the mill, at the top of the rise, there's a delightful and unexpected surprise in the form of a wonderful view to the sea and Pett Level in front of it. From here you dip down to Wickham Rock Lane.

The TCW turns left to follow the road briefly then joins a footpath heading in the same (eastward) direction while the road bends left. This is glorious walking with splendid sea views and an excellent path. You return to the road but almost immediately fork left, north-eastwards – your direction of travel all the way to Winchelsea – along a path which follows roughly parallel with and left of the road, soon passing the splendid Wickham Manor buildings, which date from the 16th century and are now owned by the National Trust. To your right there's a great view to New Gate, one of the medieval gateways guarding Winchelsea, although nowhere near the town itself; its isolated setting is consequently at once quirkily incongruous and delightful. You drop down to a stream known as Town Ditch then ascend steeply beyond, passing a ruin which is actually a remnant of the old St John's Hospital. You then bear right along a road, Monks' Walk, and shortly veer left with it, now heading northwards into **Winchelsea**. This is one of the loveliest old towns in Sussex and you could spend a good half day pottering round the old streets of weatherboarded and tile-hung cottages, many decorated with climbing roses and wisteria. Following a storm in 1287, which washed most of the old town away, a new town was built, its grid pattern making it effectively England's first piece of town planning, and its grid pattern can still be seen today. The TCW, entering the town, passes the superb church of St Thomas with its marbled effigies, canopies and pinnacled tombs that are some 700 years old, and, close by, the Wesley Tree where the preacher John Wesley delivered his last open-air sermon in October 1790. Reaching the New Inn, you should detour right down High Street, passing the Court Hall (now a museum), believed to date back to the first days of the "new" town, and walk on down past Tower Cottage, the sometime home of actress Ellen Terry, to another medieval gateway, Strand Gate, enjoying fine views towards the sea. Returning up High Street you should detour first right up Barrack Square to see the fine Old Cambric Factory, then, returning to High Street, detour second right up Castle Street to view the Town Well and adjacent 14th century Armoury. Then return to the crossroads junction by the New Inn. Beyond the New Inn the TCW continues northwards along Hiham Green but you should detour westwards by the New Inn along a continuation of High Street, crossing the A259 to immediately reach the ruins of the 14th century monastic (possibly Dominican) house Blackfriars – noting the Wesley Chapel directly opposite. Now returning to the New Inn, head north along Hiham Green. The TCW turns first left, westwards, along Mill Road but by detouring on to the T-junction with North Street and turning left down this street you reach the third of the Winchelsea town gates, known as Pipewell Gate. As stated however the TCW heads westwards along Mill Road, crossing the A259 and going forward to a trig point and a magnificent viewpoint, from which there are sweeping views across Brede Level as well as back to the Hog Hill Windmill and Icklesham Church.

Beyond the trig point, the TCW descends steeply north-westwards along a sunken grassy path, then veers right to head briefly north-eastwards, keeping a steep embankment to the right, before veering just south of east to meet the A259 again at its junction with Station Road. Notice the hairpin bend which A259 users must negotiate! Here the TCW turns left along Station Road, passing the station (from which again trains are infrequent – you may be better off going on into Rye for your train) in just under a mile, and continuing to a road T-junction. You turn right here along Winchelsea Lane but then as the road bends sharply left the TCW continues north-eastwards along a bridleway below Cadborough Cliff. It's also a designated cycle route so watch out for bikes! The excellent path proceeds pleasantly for a mile or so, arriving at the B2089 via West Undercliff, and entering **Rye**. You turn right to follow the B2089 briefly then just beyond Ashenden Avenue you turn right along a car park approach road, soon veering left along a metalled path that brings you to the right bank of the river Tillingham. Noting the reconstructed 19th century smock mill on the other side of the river, you then follow the bank of the Tillingham to reach the A259 and the end of the trail. Coincidentally the High Weald Landscape Trail starts and ends immediately across the river at this point, and you here also meet the England Coast Path and Royal Military Canal Path! I suggest you turn left alongside the A259 (just here overlapping with the England Coast Path and Royal Military Canal Path) then when it shortly veers right, go straight on along Wish Street, going forward into Cinque Ports Street, as far as the crossroads junction with Station Approach and Market Road. If you wish to explore Rye, please refer to the England Coast Path section which contains a suggested described walk starting and ending at this crossroads junction. By turning left down Station Approach you reach the bus stands and **Rye Station**.

South Downs Link

To access the South Downs Link (SDL) from **Polegate Station**, turn left out of the main station exit and head southwards from the railway along High Street past the church. By turning left just beyond the church down Church Road you can undertake a route variation V1 to Polegate Windmill, a tower mill dating back to 1817 with its four sails intact. However the SDL goes straight on along High Street and over the A2270 along Wannock Road (V1 joining you once you're over the A2270). In just over half a mile the road bends sharply to the right. Follow the road round this bend then in 250 yards on your left look out carefully for, and follow, a plinth-signed "Footpath to the Downs," initially up a driveway then on along a footpath heading south-eastwards. Don't be tempted to veer right towards the hillside but stay with the bottom path through a field, keeping houses fairly close by to the left. You go through a patch of woodland then on through another field to reach a signed crossroads of paths by a cemetery, here seeing the TCW (SDL) logo on a sign for the first time. This is effectively the start of the SDL. It does seem a strange place to begin; with respect, I suggest Polegate Station would have been a more logical start point!

The first section of the SDL consists of a climb towards Butts Brow and then a loop route. Almost all of it overlaps either with the South Downs Way (bridlepath route) or Wealdway, and if you've walked these routes you may decide to give this section a miss, turning left at the signed crossroads to head towards Pevensey, descending past a cemetery that's to your left. However, if you wish to walk this first section, turn right and begin with a steep climb uphill along the right-hand field edge, keeping woodland to your right, then continue along the woodland edge, veering sharp right and more gently left. In roughly 250 yards from where you veered sharp right you strike out south-westwards away from the woodland edge and climb very steeply up the hillside through an area of trees; you then veer right, aiming for a fence (A) incorporating a large new gate on the left. Here the loop route begins. Pass through the gate and now proceed southwards along an excellent path which climbs onto the Butts Brow ridge. You then enjoy a splendid walk, continuing southwards along the ridgetop, passing a car park and a mast; look out for the so-called Liberator Memorial, dedicated to the crew of an American aircraft which crashed here in 1944. You need to keep to the path – avoiding being tempted onto one of the many paths to the left – and rise with it, enjoying superb views, soon reaching a signed junction with the South Downs Way.

The SDL now turns right along the South Downs Way, heading westwards downhill. As the path drops into the shade of trees on the approach to **Jevington** (which the South Downs Way reaches in barely 125 yards), you leave the South Downs Way, forking right, plunging steeply downhill to a dry valley bottom and rising less steeply up the other side, proceeding through an area of vegetation. Now heading resolutely north-eastwards you make a steady ascent, your narrow path twisting through some trees, emerging to link with the Wealdway and climb towards Combe Hill. Aiming for the highest ground ahead, you shortly regain the ridgetop and enjoy a magnificent high level walk to the tumuli on top of Combe Hill, the site of a Neolithic camp. Just by the tumuli you leave the Wealdway, dropping steeply down to the fence marked at (A) above. You've completed the loop! From here you retrace your steps all the way back to the official start of the SDL.

Now reunited with those who gave this first section a miss, go straight on downhill, keeping the cemetery to your left. At the end turn right along Gorringe Valley Road and at the end of that, left, northwards, alongside the busy A2270 Eastbourne Road at **Willingdon** for some 550 yards. Just before the road bends left you fork right, north-eastwards; as you approach Mornings Mill Farm, you fork right again and continue along field edges – it's all very well signed – north-eastwards to reach and cross the railway. Carry on in the same direction as signed to a footbridge and straight on beyond that to pass between clumps of vegetation and reach a large field with pylons running through. Signage is bad here; you need to follow the left-hand field edge (it would be very easy to be sucked away to the right) and continue in the same direction, keeping vegetation to the left. This is pretty tame walking, a sad anticlimax after the joys of Butts Brow, and indeed the view back to Butts Brow is just about the only saving grace of this part of the walk. At length you reach and cross the metalled Cuckoo Trail (watching and listening for speedy cyclists!) then descend steps to cross the busy A22, climbing up again and following a path through trees, crossing the course of the long defunct Eastbourne bypass rail route. You emerge and now proceed confidently just east of north along a field edge to reach Ditton's Road along which you turn right, soon reaching a stile and signed footpath going left (B).

You're now just over 2 miles from the main route and you can choose to proceed to Pevensey where the main route begins, or to take a short cut from (B) to Rickney to pick up the main route there, saving yourself a couple of miles overall but missing Stone Cross Windmill and Pevensey. You would have to be in a huge hurry to do the latter, and although it's an official SDL alternative I don't recommend it, so I treat it as no more than a route variation V2 below. To proceed to Pevensey, you stay on Ditton's Road, in just under half a mile crossing the junction with the B2104 at the church at **Stone Cross**, then immediately beyond the church turn left up the narrow but metalled Peelings Lane. By detouring along Ditton's Road a bit further you'll soon reach the splendid Stone Cross Windmill, a tower mill that was completed in 1876 and remained operational until the 1930's. Whether you've detoured or not, now follow Peelings Lane in a generally easterly direction, staying close to and roughly parallel with the noisy A27 that's to your left. Roughly a mile from the church at Stone Cross you cross Gallows Lane and continue eastwards along what is a wider road. Roughly half a mile beyond the crossroads look out for and take a path half-left over a stile, aiming for the buildings of Castle Farm, the route sneaking between the buildings. Walk through the farmyard and follow the signed route – footpath signs rather than SDL signs – eastwards through meadows, emerging at the B2191 between Westham and Pevensey. To reach the amenities of Westham and also Pevensey & Westham Station, turn right along the B2191 to arrive at Westham almost at once; follow the road and then bear left at the junction to reach the station. If you're continuing on, OS mapping suggests the SDL turns left along the B2191, but much to be preferred is to cross straight over the road and follow a lane, keeping the **Pevensey Castle** walls to your left, to reach the gate leading into the castle precinct. This gate should be regarded as effectively the start of the main route.

Bexhill Link

To join the Bexhill Link (BL) I recommend the following route from **Bexhill Station**. Head northwards up the main road, Upper Sea Road, beyond the station into Bexhill Old Town, veering sharp right along De La Warr Road at the junction with High Street. Just by the right bend look out on the left for the superb timber-framed Forge House, the excellent Quakersmill building, and Church Street, with its attractive brick and weatherboarded houses, the highlight being the hall house to the right of the church. The Norman church of St Peter here contains a tower from 1070, but its most famous relic is the Bexhill Stone, an 8th century sandstone slab, thought to be the lid of a reliquary containing the bones of a saint. On the right-hand side of the main road are the lovely colourful Manor Gardens, within which are the remains of a 13th century manor house. Having veered sharp right along De La Warr Road, you then shortly fork left along Hastings Road, now officially on the BL. (Again it seems a very random place to begin even a link route to a Great Walk. What was wrong with starting it at Bexhill Station?) You go forward to cross a footbridge over the A259 and continue along Hastings Road on the other side; shortly you bear left along a signed path then turn right as signed along a suburban alleyway, reaching and crossing the A2036. You then strike out north-eastwards along a right-hand field edge, then cross diagonally over the next field past Upper Worsham Farm, turning left onto a farm track. The BL now follows the track sharply round to the right, before turning left by Little Worsham Farm and joining a well-signed path heading northwards and soon crossing the old Crowhurst-Bexhill railway. The line, which opened in June 1902, was intended to provide a short cut to Bexhill off the London-Hastings railway and at one time was very popular but became less so following electrification of the Hastings-Eastbourne line, and shut in June 1964. Beyond the railway you continue along a field edge then through an area of marshland that's very popular with dog walkers. You're joined here by the Sussex Hospices Trail with which you'll overlap as far as Battle. Clear signage takes you beneath the new Bexhill-Hastings bypass and on along an excellent path which skirts a lake, then proceeds picturesquely along field edges, still heading northwards and arriving via Woodland Way at **Crowhurst**. The BL turns right along Chapel Hill then left along the bottom edge of a field, veering sharp left over a footbridge and across a meadow to rejoin the road; you turn right along it, passing the part-13th century church of St George. Its churchyard boasts a massive yew tree and fine views to the ruins of the adjoining late 13th century Manor House. By turning right off the road, more or less opposite the church, up Station Road, you reach Crowhurst Station in half a mile.

The BL follows the road round to the left then as the road bends right you leave the tarmac and go straight on north-westwards, past houses and through a field down to a thin patch of woodland. You soon emerge and pass through another field then enter Fore Wood which is also a nature reserve. The reserve, with a fine variety of birds and butterflies, is particularly noteworthy for its steep-sided ravines and is host to a number of rare ferns, as well as early purple orchids and profusions of wood anemone and bluebells in spring. The BL, always well signed, follows a clear path north-westwards then northwards through the wood, veering left to emerge and cross another field. You turn right onto a track which rises steeply northwards through another area of wood, then continue northwards as signed on a clear track, kinking and descending to Peppering Eye Farm, with its very striking tile-hung buildings and a tastefully converted oasthouse. At the end of the track the BL turns left along Telham Lane, soon reaching a junction with the busy B2095 Powdermill Lane. The BL crosses this road then bears right to follow parallel with it on a clear woodland path. As the main road veers away right, you go straight on as clearly signed, following an obvious path downhill, then start to rise through a very attractive parkland landscape to be united with the main TCW route coming in from the left. From here it's less than half a mile along the path into **Battle**.

Hastings Link

To reach the Hastings Link (HL) from Hastings Station I suggest the following route. Exit **Hastings Station** and walk via Station Approach straight ahead down Havelock Road to the town centre. At the main junction turn left – not hard left – along Wellington Place and follow beneath the underpass to reach the Breeds Place roundabout. Turn left, eastwards, here alongside the A259 and now follow the England Coast Path route all the way up onto East Hill. Now head north-eastwards along the grassy plateau, effectively taking (for the time being) the alternative Ecclesbourne-Glen-avoiding England Coast Path route, gently rising and following signs for the Fish Trail; at the very top end of the plateau aim for the left corner where you'll see an information board. Pass beyond the board onto a track, going forward along Rocklands Lane and now officially on the HL.

The HL (soon losing the England Coast Path alternative) follows Rocklands Lane north-eastwards to a T-junction with Barley Lane, turning right to follow Barley Lane in the same direction past the caravan park to the road's end at a road T-junction. At the time of writing, signing was misleading here: the HL actually turns left up the road to a T-junction with Fairlight Road, now in Hastings Country Park which is described more fully in the England Coast Path section. You cross Fairlight Road and head just north of west through a field and into a wood where there's a path junction. Here you could detour onwards for 150 yards or so to the North's Seat viewpoint with a really excellent panorama, the eastward views particularly good. However, the HL, now heading away from Hastings Country Park, strikes out north-eastwards from the path junction; the going is initially excellent, your route crossing Martineau Lane, then following a right-hand field edge and keeping The Hall, a splendid building, on your right. Unfortunately, things then become fiddly and potentially confusing. Initially you veer sharp left to join a left-hand field edge followed by a right-hand one, then drop down to a wood before rising through a succession of fields. Don't be tempted to remain on the lower slopes: you need, unaided by signage which is poor hereabouts, to veer half-left to the tops of the fields. There's then a sharp descent to the road at Friar's Hill – the road is also called Friar's Hill! The HL bears right along the road briefly then turns left and immediately right along a path through the pretty Glebe Wood; having crossed Church Lane your route heads eastwards, before turning sharply northwards to enter and pass through the delightful Guestling Wood. Signage is excellent through the wood. The HL turns left, north-westwards, in the wood, exiting it and now climbing through a field to reach the very pretty and photogenic church of St Laurence, **Guestling**, which boasts a Norman west tower and west window.

Beyond the church the HL heads westwards along a narrow path parallel with the church approach road to reach the A259 then turns right to follow beside the A259 northwards – thankfully there is a pavement. You then strike out north-westwards through another wood on an excellent track, emerging to follow clear field-edge paths then veering westwards across a field to the village of **Three Oaks**, turning left onto the main street, Butcher's Lane, but in 100 yards or so turning right, off the street. Three Oaks Sation is some 550 yards on along this street although, as intimated above, trains from the station are infrequent. As stated, however, the HL soon leaves the street, bearing right and heading westwards along a residential lane then going forward along a path; veering north-westwards, it then proceeds clearly through one large field and then smaller fields to cross the Rye-Hastings railway by a footbridge. Almost immediately beyond the railway the HL turns right onto a track leading down to the buildings of Great Maxfield. You bear right off the track, and follow this through the meadows heading north-westwards; you cross Sailor's Stream at its meeting with Doleham Ditch then veer north-eastwards, keeping Doleham Ditch to the right. This is delightful walking along a good clear green path, the ground rising most picturesquely to the left. In roughly three quarters of a mile from Great Maxfield you arrive at the clearly signed junction with the main TCW route close to **Doleham**.

GOOD TO KNOW

Main route start: Pevensey & Westham Station. Main route finish: Rye Station.

South Downs Link start: Polegate Station. Link ends: Pevensey Castle.

Bexhill Link start: Bexhill Station. Link ends: Battle.

Hastings Link start; Hastings Station. Link ends: Doleham.

Main route total mileage: 32 miles.

South Downs Link mileage (to join at Pevensey): 12 miles.

Bexhill Link mileage (to join at Battle): 7 miles.

Hastings Link mileage (to join at Doleham): 7.5 miles

Difficulty: Moderate.

Main route stages: Rickney 2.5, Herstmonceux Castle and Science Centre for Wartling (R) 7, Boreham Street (RA) 8.25, Catsfield (RB) 14, Battle (*RAB) 17, Westfield (RAB) 21.25, Doleham (*) 22.75, Icklesham (RAB) 26.25, Winchelsea (*RAB) 29.25, Rye Station (*RAB) 32.

South Downs Link stages: Jevington (RA) 4.25, Willingdon (RAB) 8.25, Stone Cross (RB) 9.75, Pevensey Castle (join with main route) (*RAB) 12.

Bexhill Link stages: Crowhurst (*RA) 3.5, Battle (join with main route) (*RAB) 7.

Hastings Link stages: Guestling (church) 5.25, Three Oaks (*R)

6.25, Doleham (join with main route) 7.5.
OS: OL25, 124.

D1 Continue briefly up the road beyond Herstmonceux Church but in 200 yards or so, just opposite the house called Church Meadow, fork right along a bridleway heading northwards through woods, ignoring crossing paths. You emerge from the wood and carry straight on downhill through a field on a thin path, reaching a path T-junction. Turn right along a clear path, ignoring a bridleway going off to the right, and head northwards uphill on a left-hand field edge, enjoying good views to the brick-built Herstmonceux Place to the left and across the Pevensey Levels beyond. Beyond the field you join a clear path in the shade of trees, going forward along Comphurst Lane, now heading north-eastwards and passing the fine buildings of Comphurst. You arrive at a small green with a pub to the right. Veer left round the top of the green to reach the A271. Turn left alongside the A271, crossing to reach the Windmill Hill mill; the entrance driveway is just beyond the mill itself. Return the same way. (Total detour 2.75 miles)

D2 Follow the Ninfield-signed road eastwards for just over half a mile, reaching a road T-junction (C). The quickest way to Ashburnham – although see Note 1 below – is to go straight over along a track, then after 550 yards, immediately beyond Garden Cottage, bear right along a driveway to the buildings of Ashburnham. The church, Ashburnham Place and café are all off this main driveway to the left. Simply then retrace your steps to the TCW – although see Note 2 below. (Total detour 2 miles)

NOTE 1: You should be aware there's no official right of way along this detour route from the T-junction and although there are no obstructions or "keep out" notices, you take this route at your own risk. The much longer alternative to Ashburnham would entail your turning right at the T-junction along the road, bearing left on reaching the A271 and bearing shortly left again down the Ashburnham complex main driveway. This will double the length of the detour!

NOTE 2: On returning to the road T-junction at (C), instead of crossing straight over to return to the TCW the way you came, you could turn right and follow the road northwards to meet the TCW coming in from the left, about a mile and a half from the T-junction.

This will save you about half a mile but you will miss the lovely hamlet of Brownbread Street.

D3 Having forked left, follow a clear woodland path which then veers left and right, reaching a gate where you exit the wood. Beyond the gate go straight ahead along the right-hand field edge, keeping a ditch to your right and then veering right to pass a pond, which is also to your right. You then veer left, still on the right-hand field edge, going forward along a rough track to a T-junction of tracks just to the right of the Beanford Farm buildings. Turn left to pass the buildings then shortly right as signed, passing through a gate and following a good path north-eastwards past Horsmans Farm to reach the A21. Cross with care, straight over, and keeping the same line, follow a clear path downhill through a field. At the end go forward over a footbridge and then along a narrow but clear path, crossing 3 further footbridges. Just beyond the last you reach a path junction, turning right over another footbridge with a weir to the left as you cross. Beyond the footbridge continue on a clear path to reach the bottom of Sedlescombe's main street, turning left to follow it to the village centre. To reach the church simply follow the main village street uphill, continuing alongside the same road, the B2244, for just over half a mile, the parallel footpath drifting away from the road to pass Coach House. Just beyond that, turn right as plinth-signed up to the church. To return to the main TCW, retrace your steps exactly, remembering to turn right off Sedlescombe's main street just beyond the converted garage; bear left at the path junction beyond the footbridge by the weir, then beyond the A21 crossing and the Horsmans Farm path, left and then right at Beanford Farm, following the left-hand field edge all the way to the gate, then the signed woodland path. Turn left at the end to rejoin the TCW then immediately fork right to continue. (Total detour 3 miles; add 1 mile for round trip to church)

V1 Follow Church Road, veering right to reach the A2270 Eastbourne Road. Cross over and turn left, walking briefly beside the A2270, then go first right into Clement Lane, immediately left into The Thatchings, and right again into Park Croft, soon reaching the windmill which is on the left. By turning left again just past the mill, opposite Windmill Place, and following the lane, you reach the mill entrance. Retrace your steps to the A2270 and now walk beside this *road to the junction with Wannock Road, turning left along Wannock Road to rejoin the main route as described above. (Extra half a mile)*

V2 The route from (B) to Rickney is as follows. Cross the stile and follow the grassy path which goes down to the A27. Cross with great care as indicated then follow the obvious farm track north-eastwards as signed, rising to and crossing straight over the B2104. Having crossed, continue north-eastwards, passing Sharnfold Cottages then following the right-hand field edge downhill. You then rise again through a field, passing under pylons, then dip down to a hollow and, veering right, follow a path through trees uphill, going forward along a driveway leading you to Hankham Street. Turn left along the road then in just over a quarter of a mile fork right along the Rickney-signed road; just before the end, as it veers sharply left to reach a T-junction, the main route comes in from the right. This variation will save you 2.5 miles but you will miss the amenities at Pevensey.

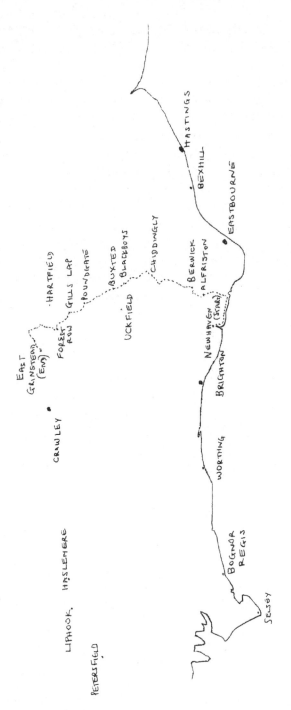

15 VANGUARD WAY

Unlike the majority of the Great Walks covered in this book, the Vanguard Way (VGW) does not have a particular theme, nor does it follow a particular feature through its journey. It was conceived by the Vanguards Rambling Club (hence the path's name) as just a jolly good walk linking the London suburbs and the Sussex coast via the North and South Downs, with no particular magic in the choice of route. The club's name has a somewhat whimsical origin: one day in 1965 a group of ramblers found themselves on a train so packed that they were forced to occupy the guard's van, and they began their own club which therefore they decided to call the Vanguards!

The VGW has more than a little in common with the Wealdway in that both run through East Sussex across sections of the Low and High Weald and Ashdown Forest, both extend to (or from) the Sussex coast, both extend outside Sussex, the VGW having its start (or finish) in East Croydon, and both have their sections that are uninteresting and/or hard to follow at times although in fairness both offer some great walking too. Because I have chosen to describe the Wealdway in a seaward direction, and because the VGW is a natural continuation of the Sussex Ouse Valley Way (the first 2.5 miles of the VGW being the last 2.5 miles of the Sussex Ouse Valley Way) I've decided to describe the VGW from the coast heading towards London. Signage is in any case equally good, or bad, in both directions, with a clear black-on-yellow/blue VGW waymark providing a striking logo. Certain sections are indeed better signed than others, and you need to be aware that the waymarking across Ashdown Forest – all the way between the A26 crossing at Poundgate and the centre of Forest Row – is, owing to signage restrictions imposed by the Forest authorities, pretty much non-existent. You will definitely need your maps and/or your technology!

The VGW could hardly have a more undistinguished start. I recommend you explore Newhaven first – its attractions are described in the England Coast Path section – then start at **Newhaven Town Station**, heading south from the station on its east side along B2109 Railway Road, going forward along Clifton

Road and then Beach Road to a clear signed path forking right (south-eastwards). This fork is the official start of the VGW. You could actually save yourself just under half a mile by getting off the train at **Newhaven Harbour Station**, walking east from the down platform exit to hit Beach Road, and turning right along it to reach the start of the VGW. However Newhaven Harbour Station has to be one of the most, if not *the* most, depressing railway halts in Sussex, and it frankly is a ghastly place to begin your journey. It can only, and does, get better! It should be remembered, of course, that the VGW overlaps with the England Coast Path all the way from Newhaven to Cuckmere Haven and with the Sussex Ouse Valley Way from Newhaven as far as **Bishopstone** on the outskirts of **Seaford**, so if you've walked either or both of those routes you could pick the VGW up in more congenial surroundings with a crystal-clear conscience! Given the exact overlap of the VGW with the England Coast Path as far as Cuckmere Haven, this route being fully described in the England Coast Path section, no further description is necessary here. On reaching Cuckmere Haven the VGW, unlike the England Coast Path, doesn't in fact go all the way to the river, but bears left up a clear wide grassy track that proceeds pleasantly along the valley floor, reaching the A259 at the Cuckmere Inn (formerly the Golden Galleon).

Rejoining the England Coast Path the VGW turns right, eastwards, to follow the A259 across the Cuckmere river and past the visitor centre at **Exceat** as far as the bus stop, where you meet the South Downs Way footpath section which links Alfriston with Eastbourne via Beachy Head. Here you turn left to join the South Downs Way and will in fact be following it (in reverse direction to that described in the South Downs Way section) all the way to Alfriston; the South Downs Way signage is so good you can put the map or technology away, but don't forget where it is as you'll certainly need it when you get further on! You begin with a sharp little climb up a grassy hillside, enjoying one final view of Cuckmere Haven from the top, then drop down steeply along a stepped path through woods to the gorgeous village of Westdean, described more fully in the South Downs Way section. You then climb through the woods of Friston Forest, taking care to turn left as signed along an excellent forest track heading north-westwards, descending to skirt the grounds of the imposing Charleston Manor. The VGW, still with the South Downs Way, branches off the track, veering just east of north and ascending to get an excellent view of the Hindover White Horse which is to the left, and Alfriston Church ahead. You descend to the pretty village of Litlington (a 200-yard detour up the road bringing you to the tea garden and pretty Norman church), and, veering first north-westwards and then north-eastwards, you follow the bank of the Cuckmere to **Alfriston**. This, arguably the loveliest village on the VGW, is described more fully in the South Downs Way section. You also cross, but don't overlap with, the Sussex Hospices Trail in the village.

The VGW now parts from the South Downs Way. Your route heads resolutely along a road heading north-westwards from the village centre then, as the road veers sharply eastwards, you continue northwards on a field path. You veer just east of north, dipping and rising to pass immediately to the east of the sensational 13th century church of St Michael & All Angels, Berwick, with its stunning paintings on the pulpit and nave wall – the work of Duncan Grant, Vanessa Bell and Quentin Bell in 1942/43. Returning to the VGW after visiting the church, you pass through trees and go through a kissing gate to enter a large field. As you enter it there's the possibility of a <u>route variation V1</u> to visit the lovely village of Alciston. It boasts some fine old timber-framed houses and Norman church, but its two most remarkable features are the ruined medieval dovecote and 170ft tithe barn, one of the country's biggest; its roof contains around 50,000 tiles! If you're omitting V1, the VGW goes straight down through the field and on along a narrow path past buildings and a pond to reach the main street of the village of **Berwick** with its attractive pub, the Cricketers Arms. The VGW turns right onto the road here (V1 joining you here too), and goes down to the A27 which you cross with immense care, there being no bridge, pedestrian crossing or even island. Assuming you've got over in one piece, you now head north-westwards across a succession of fields, crossing Common Lane and rising gently to Stonery Farm, veering sharply eastwards along a clear green track that takes you to **Berwick Station**. Here there are hourly direct trains to Lewes, Brighton, Eastbourne and Hastings and there's a pub if you find you're in for a long wait! The VGW crosses the railway line with the road and in what is a rerouting of the original (and currently still mapped) route, immediately turns left along a path first running beside the railway then veering right, through the trees – beware stinging nettles! – and along a field edge, reaching, and turning left along, a lane to Ludlay Farm. However you may wish to take a route variation V2 to Arlington Reservoir, which is reunited with the VGW as you join the Ludlay Farm lane. The reservoir, which opened in the 1960's, not only supplies water to the nearby area but is a nature reserve with over 170 recorded species of birds including migrating ospreys and egrets, and you may also see such species as the great-crested grebe, swallow, mallard, pied wagtail and cormorant.

Back on the VGW you'll be aware that the character of the walk has now changed. You've left the chalk South Downs behind – although initially you can enjoy good views back to them – and for the next 20 miles or so, all the way to Ashdown Forest, your walking is through the Low Weald and its landscape of rolling farmland, pockets of woodland, serpentine streams, ponds and clay soil. There's none of the drama of the Seaford-Westdean section, and some segments are frankly uninteresting. The VGW follows the lane on to Ludlay Farm, rises to Mays Farm, where the views to the South Downs escarpment are certainly very good – do make the most of them! – then descends north-westwards through fields, and follows a road heading north-eastwards to the edge of the village of Chalvington. Here your route strikes out, still heading north-eastwards, along a really delightful byway in the shade of trees, particularly attractive in spring when you'll find a profusion of wild flowers. Beyond the byway you keep on along a charming traffic-free narrow road still in the shade of trees, with lovely views through the trees towards the South Downs and Mount Caburn. Again this lane is at its best on a sunny day in the spring. At Marnhull Farm you're signed left, north-westwards, away from the road; you pass the gorgeous brick-built Limekiln Farm, one of the unsung gems of the VGW, and follow a driveway to reach another road. Field walking, unexciting but thankfully very well signed, then takes you north-westwards past Brickfield Farm Mohair Centre beyond which you cross, in quick succession, the B2124 then the **A22** at Holmes's Hill just over a quarter of a mile west (left) of the amenities of **Golden Cross**. Having crossed the A22 with great care, you strike out north-eastwards, initially in the shade of Kiln Wood (one of two Kiln Woods on the VGW) then across a succession of fields and through another pretty patch of woodland with a wide stream crossed by a footbridge. From here you have a straightforward ascent through fields to the village of **Chiddingly**, passing just to the left of the church with its fine monuments to the Jeffray family. The Wealdway section gives a little more information about the church. There's a very brief meeting with the Wealdway, which could hardly be called an overlap, in the village centre. A detour from the church to Farley Farm, sometime home of the artist Lee Miller, is available, and more information about Farley Farm and a description of the detour itself is given in the Wealdway section.

Field walking dominates on the VGW beyond Chiddingly, signage very unclear in places; you begin with a descent to a rather soggy meadow then gain height and veer from north-eastwards to north-westwards along clearer paths. Now the walking improves dramatically. After a brief road walk between farms there's a fine high level field-edge march along firm pasture with Broomfield Wood to the right, your progress confident and easy. Beyond a track crossing you pass through the top edge of Gray Wood, a gorgeous area of woodland in fact, with bluebells that are sensational in springtime. Emerging from the wood, you veer north-eastwards along a road, Graywood Lane, and in fact you now have a good mile of road walking, first quite steeply downhill, veering just west of north to cross the East Hoathly-Waldron road at Scallow Bridge, then uphill, northwards, along Moat Lane. Just before the prominent Moat Farm you head westwards away from the road, descending through trees, emerging for a sharp field climb then field-edge walking round Wenhams Farm. When I walked this section the signage hereabouts was particularly poor, and there are precious few landmarks to indicate the correct route. It's not one of the most enjoyable or fulfilling pieces of long-distance walking in Sussex, and sad to say, your route beyond Wenhams Farm remains for a while both itty-bitty and largely uninteresting. First you walk briefly south-westwards along a road skirting the southern edge of the woods of Hawkhurst Common, then strike out north-westwards along a path keeping the woods to the right, arriving at another road. You follow that briefly northwards then head westwards along a path leading to a segment of Bushbury Lane; from here you strike out just north of east along a path taking you to Hollow Lane, which you follow north-westwards. Now at last there's an improvement as you reach the attractive Kiln Wood (the second wood of that name on the VGW) where you begin a brief overlap with the Sussex Hospices Trail, and a north-westward climb through Kiln Wood takes you to **Blackboys**. The peculiar name of the village is derived from Richard Blakeboy, whose home it was in 1398, although local tradition likes to derive the name from the "black boys" or charcoal handlers who after a day at the iron foundries hereabouts would come to the village inn for a well-earned drink.

The heart of Blackboys, including the pub, is sandwiched between two B roads, which you cross in turn: firstly you cross the B2192 Lewes-Heathfield road, then the B2102 Uckfield-Heathfield road. Beyond the B2102 crossing you head north-westwards from the village, passing some allotments and parting briefly from the route of the Sussex Hospices Trail. You then descend north-westwards along clear tracks and paths, being rejoined by the Sussex Hospices Trail and arriving at Tickerage Mill with its beautiful waterfall where again there's a short overlap with the Wealdway. You then say farewell both to the Wealdway and the Sussex Hospices Trail and things are straightforward initially, as you follow a well-defined bridleway heading north-westwards and have a short road walk along Pound Lane. From here, there's a descent to the messy Scantlings complex, a real anticlimax after the beauty of the Tickerage Mill area, and you need to follow signage carefully. Following a sharp right turn here you proceed in a predominantly northerly direction, with firstly a meadow stroll and then a climb away from the valley, joining a clear and pleasant path through woodland which brings you to a road, now on the edge of **Buxted**. The VGW now follows the road north-eastwards. It's tame stuff, this, and if after a long day's walk you're planning to stop at Buxted, the first settlement of any size since Alfriston, this road walk will feel longer than it is. At length, having been carried by the road seemingly away from Buxted, you're then signed left along a narrow path that brings you to the A272 at the north-eastern edge of the village. The VGW eschews the village and proceeds more or less straight on down Redbrook Lane, but you may wish to turn left, and walk for three quarters of a mile, alongside the A272 to the centre of Buxted where there's a railway station on the London-Uckfield line adjoining the main road. It's only a short rail journey to Uckfield, from which there are plenty of buses to Tunbridge Wells, Lewes and Brighton.

From the A272 the VGW proceeds north-westwards down Redbrook Lane as stated then continues forward across rough pasture, passing underneath the London-Uckfield railway and through lovely woodland which again is at its best in spring. You then climb along a field edge and through further trees, heading northwards; you cross Fowly Lane and then strike out north-westwards down through two fields and on to Holders Farm. Progress is now very easy as you proceed along farm lanes, then, after a short road walk, continue along a narrow path threading through trees and thereafter descending through more open country to arrive at the 19th century church of the Holy Trinity at High Hurstwood. The setting of this church is beautifully rural. To quote Nikolaus Pevsner: "Next to the dell with rhododendrons of the parsonage garden, Arcadia indeed." As you reach the church you bear left onto a lane and descend to a T-junction with a road, Chillies Lane (A). The mapped and official VGW turns right up this road, heading northwards, then leaves the road and heads north-westwards again, first passing the very pretty cottage at Woodpeckers and crossing a bridge over a mini-gorge. From here you ascend steadily in a north-westward direction, firstly along an enclosed path then through a succession of fields; veering westwards, you ascend sharply (following the signage carefully – it's easy to go wrong here) to reach a path T-junction (B) just south of the Stroods farm complex. However at the time of writing the bridge over the mini-gorge referred to above is shut indefinitely. If it remains shut, as seems sadly likely, you need to turn right at (A) as per the mapped route but then turn almost immediately left along a well-signed path which, heading westwards, goes initially through trees then uphill through fields to Perrymans Lane; turn right onto the road and in a few yards turn right along another well-signed footpath which heads through Quarry Wood and then on uphill, northwards, to reach point (B) above. The diversion adds a quarter of a mile to your walk. The VGW now follows a clear path northwards past Stroods then through woodland beyond the farm, veering north-eastwards and passing the buildings of Newnham Park Farm to arrive at the A26 at Poundgate. You're now 620ft above sea level compared with just 112ft at Tickerage Mill. There's a pub at

Poundgate and there are also bus stops with excellent services, as at Uckfield, to Tunbridge Wells, Lewes and Brighton.

The character of your walk now changes completely and very much for the better as after crossing the A26 and walking briefly westwards alongside it, you strike out north-westwards across Ashdown Forest. Gone, thankfully, is the fiddly field/farmland Low Weald walking as you follow a splendid wide unmistakeable track which firstly heads steadily downhill then climbs, with the extensive views improving all the time. This part of the VGW is best walked in late summer when the heather turns a beautiful purple, complementing the yellow of the gorse. "Forest" seems a bit of a misnomer for the surroundings as there aren't many trees around, but there is an explanation. This area, equidistant between the North and South Downs, was indeed once part of the great forest of Anderida that covered south-east England. However, the great trees were cut down, many for fuel to heat the ironmasters' forges; although there are pockets of woodland here and there, it is now predominantly open heathland dotted with bushes, comprising some 6,500 acres in total. It was once a royal hunting ground, favoured by sportsmen for its large deer population, although the deer had gone completely by the middle of the 17th century. Long before the hunters and ironmasters arrived, prehistoric man had created trackways over it, hence the splendid network of paths that make the forest so attractive to visitors today. You should thus thank your ancestors for what is a lovely fast piece of VGW walking, your wide track not signed but very easy to follow. On that subject, please note that footpath signage generally is very sparse on Ashdown Forest, not because of vandalism or lack of funding but as part of a policy on the part of the authorities to restrict any man-made structures across the forest. As you gain height you need to take care to follow the main track which veers left to the cluster of trees at **Kings Standing Clump**. Signage does reassure you as you cross a car park and reach a junction of the B2188 and the B2026, the VGW following very roughly parallel with the latter towards Hartfield, heading north-westwards, and the path in turn maturing into an excellent wide track. It rises steadily, and at the very top of the rise you get a superb view ahead as the ground begins to fall away. Here, at the top of the rise, you could detour briefly left, crossing the road to reach the car park, just beyond which is a topograph marking the so-called Four Counties viewpoint (150 yards from the VGW). Although there are good views to the south-west, there are in truth far better viewpoints on Ashdown Forest; you'll come to one of them shortly, and there are others on the Wealdway, described in the Wealdway section of this book. The VGW however continues north-westwards along the wide track, descending to cross the B2026 and going forward along what becomes a clear path that proceeds uphill to the trees of Gills Lap, keeping them to your right. The OS-mapped VGW here turns left – by continuing straight on for 250 yards or so you reach the memorial stone for Pooh's creator A.A. Milne, the view from here much better than at Four Counties viewpoint – and having turned left, darts away downhill on a very steep narrow path, continuing to a crossroads of tracks. Beyond this crossroads the VGW follows a wide track which sweeps on downhill, veering left and right, and plunging into the trees to arrive at a minor road at Newbridge.

The next section, to the edge of Forest Row, is not properly signed at all, for reasons I've stated, and your map-reading/GPS skills need to be at their sharpest. The VGW essentially heads north-westwards from Newbridge along a succession of forest paths heading uphill, passing round the edge of sports fields, crossing Sandy Lane and, shortly thereafter, crossing Colemans Hatch Road; beyond the road, the VGW continues downhill, and soon you have Royal Ashdown Forest Golf Club to your left. This is one of the most prestigious golf clubs in southern England, and is unusual in that it is a totally natural golf course without a single bunker. The famous South African golfer Bobby Locke, four times Open Champion, played the course in 1936 and completed every hole in four strokes. The trick as you proceed is simply to keep the golf course immediately to your left and the trees to your right, using the obvious albeit unsigned tracks and keeping a watchful eye out for golfers in play. You'll find yourself veering left, westwards, and at length arriving at a metalled road, now on the outskirts of Forest Row. You follow the metalled road north-westwards then head westwards along Primrose Lane before negotiating another path section with the golf course to your left – there certainly is a lot of golf course – and then after a rise you descend via Chapel Lane to the B2110 which you follow north-westwards into the centre of **Forest Row**, described more fully in the Worth Way section. Here you can heave a sigh of relief as the trickiest part of the VGW is behind you! Also there's an excellent range of amenities including buses to Tunbridge Wells, East Grinstead and Crawley.

The VGW leaves the village centre by bearing right along Station Road, going forward to cross the course of the old East Grinstead-Tunbridge Wells railway and with it the course of the High Weald Landscape Trail and the Worth/Forest Way. You're now entering the so-called High Weald, characterised by its rolling sandstone hills and woodlands, with more elevated ground and generally much better views than the Low Weald. Having crossed the old railway you continue along a path heading just east of north, and the going now becomes extremely easy and quick. Initially you climb steadily along an excellent if narrow path through the trees to reach and join Cansiron Lane, maintaining your northerly direction. In fact northwards is your predominant direction of travel all the way to the border with Surrey. Taking care to go straight on rather than swing westwards with the lane, you continue along a lane past Grove Farm, and, aided by very good signage, keep to a metalled lane that passes the imposing buildings of Thornhill and veers north-eastwards to another very fine old house at the edge of the trees. Here you leave the tarmac and proceed along a lovely bridleway downhill to cross a stream then rise steadily, proceeding northwards through the beautiful Wet Wood. Roughly 275 yards beyond Wet Wood the VGW turns left off the bridleway, but instead of turning left you could take a <u>route variation V3</u> to the stone-built Hammerwood House. Built by Benjamin Latrobe around 1793, it was one of the first houses in England to be constructed in Grecian Revival style and has been superbly restored in the last 30 years. However the VGW takes the left turn as stated, along a path that takes you to a lane onto which you turn right, following it to the busy **A264**.

Cross with care and, now rejoined by V3, go straight on north-westwards along Shepherdsgrove Lane past Gotwick Manor Farm to cross another stream. This marks the Sussex/Surrey border – out in the middle of nowhere! The VGW continues on through Surrey to end its journey in the outskirts of London but we will shortly leave it. The quickest way back to civilisation if you're without a lift would be to return to the A264 then turn right to follow it for around 3.5 miles to East Grinstead on foot – there being no buses available – but I don't recommend it. Instead I suggest this route to

East Grinstead. Continue along Shepherdsgrove Lane, ignoring the road in 170 yards going to the right (which conveys the VGW so now's the time to wave it goodbye). In just over 250 yards beyond this turning you negotiate a sharp left bend then ascend, passing a row of cottages, and bend less starkly right. In 400 yards beyond this right bend, as you continue to ascend, you reach a lodge to the left, and here you've 2 options. Option 1 is to proceed up the road beyond the lodge, and 200 yards past the lodge turn left along the Sussex Border Path. Option 2 (preferable and 200 yards shorter) is to turn left at the lodge along a signed path, following a driveway briefly. Just before the first house on the right, 200 yards beyond the lodge, the continuous route takes a signed fork to the right, off the driveway, but by detouring along the driveway you almost immediately reach, on your left, the superb buildings of Lullenden, a Tudor manor once owned by Churchill but not open to the public. If you've detoured return to the fork and take it, and now enjoy a lovely open field walk just south of west, with fine views, aiming for a pylon. At that pylon you cross a stile and bear left to join the Sussex Border Path, linking with Option 1. Whichever option you've followed, you now continue along the Sussex Border Path south-westwards, and indeed you'll be following the Sussex Border Path all the way back to East Grinstead. You descend to arrive at a T-junction of tracks, turning left and walking down to a fork junction, forking right to very soon reach the magnificent timber-framed Old Surrey Hall, which is described more fully in the Sussex Border Path section. Bear right here along the signed footpath (actually a driveway here) and continue straight on along a track just north of west into Blockfield Wood, taking care to fork left as signed. You emerge from the wood and are shortly signed right, off the track, across a very long field, dropping down to pass between trees and enter another very long field! At the end of that, good signage takes you between trees then steeply uphill to reach and cross the A264. Turn left and immediately right along a signed path, actually a lane, then in 300 yards, just before Fairlight Cottage, turn right to enter Ashplats Wood. You now follow the obvious and well-signed path downhill along the left edge of the woods with housing to your left. Ignore right-hand turns into the heart of the woods or left turns into the housing areas! You're frequently reassured by fencing to the left. Momentarily the path stops at an area of green, but you continue as signed, shortly rising along a very narrow and possibly muddy path, at length arriving at and passing the beautiful timber-framed Estcots Farmhouse. You go forward along a lane to arrive at College Lane. Turn left along College Lane to its end, bearing right along High Street leading into the centre of East Grinstead. For information about the town and access to **East Grinstead Station**, please see the Worth/Forest Way section.

GOOD TO KNOW
Start: Newhaven Town Station. Finish: East Grinstead Station.
Total mileage: 44.5.
Difficulty: Strenuous in places.
Stages: Newhaven Harbour Station (*) 0.5, Bishopstone (*RAB) 2.5, Seaford (*RAB) 3.5, Exceat (RB) 6.5, Alfriston (RAB) 9, Berwick (RB) 10, Berwick Station (*RA) 11.5, A22 for Golden Cross (RB) 16, Chiddingly (R) 17.25, Blackboys (RAB) 22.5, Buxted (*R) 25.75, Poundgate (RB) 29.5, Kings Standing Clump 31, Forest Row (RAB) 37, A264 40, East Grinstead Station (*RAB) 44.5
OS: OL25, 135, 147.

V1 At the field beyond the kissing gate bear left, aiming for the far left corner of the field where you cross over a stile and go forward along a gravel track to reach a T-junction with the road leading to Badgers. Turn right here and immediately reach a T-junction with a road, turning left. Follow the road which becomes a farm track and, ignoring the left fork to Church Barn, go on uphill past Church Farm, and forward along a grassy field-edge path heading downhill. At the far end bear left and then in 130 yards turn right along a right-hand field edge path; at the top end, turn right and then immediately left over a stile to approach Alciston. Walking alongside the churchyard, reach and cross another stile by the church gate then walk up the church path to Alciston's main street. By turning left you'll soon pass the ruined medieval dovecote and huge tithe barn. There's a lovely thatched cottage opposite the barn and some fine old houses up the street beyond. Retrace your steps then continue past the church path and enjoy some stunning old houses of timber and thatch, and the pretty Rose Cottage Inn. Return to the church path once more and go back to Berwick the way you came, but this time, having passed the Church Farm buildings and gone forward along the farm lane, continue on the metalled road which veers sharp left and continues to the Cricketers Arms to rejoin the VGW. (Extra 1.75 miles)

V2 Instead of turning left up the path immediately beyond the railway crossing at Berwick Station, go on alongside the road – actually the original route of the VGW and shown on OS maps as the current route – and in just under half a mile you reach the signed entrance to Arlington Reservoir, turning right and walking via the car park to the reservoir-side path. Having enjoyed the reservoir, retrace your steps for just under 300 yards, turn right up a lane past the village hall and continue on towards Ludlay Farm, the signed VGW shortly coming in from the left. (Extra three quarters of a mile)

V3 Instead of turning left here with the VGW continue straight on along the bridleway, following the left-hand field edge round, then turn left up a path northwards through the trees to the A264. Turn right to follow beside it briefly, then shortly right as signed to Hammerwood; follow the driveway down to a pond, noting in particular the superb timber-framed Bower House on the right, then by the pond veer left and soon climb, bearing right as signed to reach Hammerwood House. Retrace your steps to the A264 and turn left, westwards, alongside it for around 500 metres – there's no pavement but there is a reasonable verge – then turn right along Shepherdsgrove Lane, now back on the VGW. (Extra 2 miles)

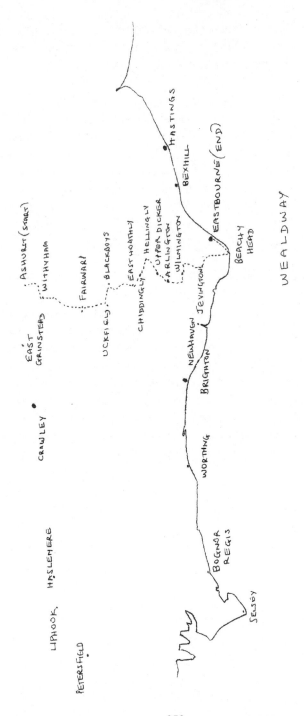

16 WEALDWAY

The Wealdway (WW), which was inaugurated in August 1981, has much in common with the Vanguard Way. It is a walk with one end on the Sussex coast, and the other end outside Sussex altogether; it crosses the High Weald, the Low Weald and the South Downs; although there is no particular significance in the choice of route, it incorporates some splendid scenery and many places of architectural and historic importance; and signage varies greatly, some sections being well signed and others very poorly signed. Having described the Vanguard Way from the coast northwards, I have chosen to describe the WW seawards. It begins impressively with a traverse of Ashdown Forest; the ensuing walk across the Low Weald to Horsebridge is very pleasant if unspectacular; the journey from Horsebridge to Michelham Priory is disappointingly dull; but from Michelham Priory onwards the route becomes extremely rewarding again, with a really fine climax.

The WW starts at Tonbridge in Kent, proceeding across an area of High Weald – see the Vanguard Way section for a brief description of the geography of the High Weald and Low Weald – but we shall pick the WW route up just before it enters Sussex. My suggestion is you find your way to **Ashurst Station** on the London-Uckfield line, and immediately join the Sussex Border Path, turning right out of the station exit, soon forking left and then bearing right, southwards, along a path past Jessup's Farm. Shortly beyond the farm you bear left and ascend, then turn right at the top, and sticking to the Sussex Border Path, follow a good hillside path south-eastwards, dropping to reach the WW coming in from the left. You turn right, south-westwards, at the path junction and descend to pass under the railway, bearing left beyond the railway across a meadow, and cross a stream which marks the border between Kent and East Sussex. Still heading south-westwards you continue across the meadow to a path crossroads where the Sussex Border Path strikes out to the left and you bear right. You now head just north of west, and shortly cross another waterway. This may seem like just another strip of water but it is in fact the infant river Medway which will shortly flow into Kent and mature into one of the widest estuaries in the south-east, emptying into the Thames at Sheerness. Beyond the Medway crossing the meadow theme continues, the WW veering south-westwards along an obvious path to reach and cross a road just north of Balls Green. You follow a clearly signed track past Summerford Farm, the ground rising significantly to your right, then, veering just north of west, you ascend a little before veering south-westwards again, descending to walk just beside the Medway and across the meadow to arrive at and cross the Forest Way. A clear path heads southwards from here through meadows to arrive at the **B2110** along which you turn left. In 150 yards or so the WW turns shortly right, southwards, away from it, but by carrying on beside the B2110 for a futher 250 yards into **Withyham** you reach the Dorset Arms pub and nearby bus stop where there are buses to Tunbridge Wells, East Grinstead, Three Bridges and Crawley. However as stated the WW strikes southwards away from the B2110 along a metalled lane which very soon passes a path leading up to the 17th century church, of St Michael, Withyham. The church was rebuilt after the original church was struck by lightning, and is particularly noteworthy for its astonishing chapel with most impressive memorial effigies to the Sackville family. There are also some excellent Italian paintings in the south aisle depicting scenes from Christ's life.

Beyond the church the WW continues southwards along the metalled lane, overlapping here with the High Weald Landscape Trail; that trail soon goes away to the right but you keep to the lane all the way to its end by Buckhurst Farm, leaving the tarmac to follow a parallel path before entering the so-called Five Hundred Acre Wood. If that sounds familiar, it's because it features in the Winnie the Pooh books of A.A. Milne, so keep a look out for Christopher Robin, Eeyore and stray Heffalumps! Excellent signage now directs you westwards, along clear forest tracks; roughly half a mile after entering the wood you're then signed sharp left, southwards, at a path junction, and you now rise steadily on a lovely woodland path, veering just west of south. Careful attention to directions is essential as you continue to climb through the woods, with two right forks to be taken. Do not allow yourself to be sucked away to the left into what is a very extensive area of forest indeed. All being well you'll find yourself emerging from the woods and skirting the edge of them along a clear track with the glorious open heathland of Ashdown Forest (described in more detail in the Vanguard Way section) just to your right, and magnificent views beyond. It's an astonishing contrast to the tame meadow scenery you were walking through five miles back. I walked this section on the hottest day of 2016, with temperatures in excess of 30 degrees Celsius; often extreme heat can create a murky haze which is hateful to walk in, but on this Tuesday morning in July, there was an awesome clarity, not even a wisp of cloud daring to clutter the majesty of the sky. The prospect of the heat had clearly lured other would-be visitors away to the beach, and the result was a landscape that seemed, for a while at least, mine and mine alone.

Progress continues to be very straightforward as you follow the track in a predominantly south-westerly direction, being reassured by the proximity of the B2188 which follows a roughly parallel course to your left. You're now crossing the great central plateau of Ashdown Forest and while in the summer heat I had this all to myself, you can generally expect to meet a goodly number of walkers, riders and cyclists enjoying this remarkable landscape of heather, gorse and occasional clumps of trees. You cross the Vanguard Way which you'll see again a little further on, then very shortly afterwards cross the B2026. The roads may seem a little intrusive but they're invaluable landmarks so don't moan about them too much! Beyond this crossing the WW follows an initially narrow then wide path heading just east of south, maintaining height and staying parallel with the B2026. It's glorious walking, with the perfect combination of clear track, firm surface and magnificent views. Just when you thought this walking couldn't get any better, it does: the path veers south-westwards and rises to reach Camp Hill Clump, a group of tall coniferous trees 650ft above sea level. It's not the highest point on Ashdown Forest but it's a superb landmark and a lovely shady spot on a hot day. The WW, veering sharply south-eastwards, proceeds anticlockwise round the far side of the trees past some benches and a plaque commemorating the opening of the WW in 1981, and continues on to the trig point beyond the clump. The views on a clear day are stunning, extending all the way to the South Downs.

It's here that I strongly recommend your leaving the WW and taking an alternative route onwards to Oldlands Hill. Beyond the trig point the official mapped route of the WW drops to and crosses the B2026, and suddenly the picture changes: gone at a stroke is the lovely high-level open walking on clear paths, as the WW now follows an extremely fiddly course along often very narrow, indistinct, and, worse, unsigned paths taking you from Ashdown Forest into the pleasant but less dramatic Low Weald. Not only is this very tame stuff and a real anticlimax after Camp Hill Clump but the lack of signposting hereabouts – see the Vanguard Way description for the reason for this – presents many opportunities to get badly lost. Much to be preferred is a route variation V1 from Camp Hill Clump to a point just west of Fairwarp, this point referred to at (A) below. This variation includes three, or with a detour four, features of real interest. The first is the lovely duet of pools known as Ellison's Pond (singular) which are reminiscent of Lake District tarns with their still waters and lofty settings. The second is Nutley Windmill, a mill with four sails which is believed to date back to 1817 and thus thought to be the oldest post mill standing in Sussex. The third is Airman's Grave, a beautifully kept memorial to six RAF pilots who lost their lives when their plane crashed here in July 1941 – although they are not actually buried here. Finally, Christ Church at Fairwarp, built in 1881, is a charming village church in an isolated setting on the very edge of the forest. As an extra incentive to take this route, you'll also pass the Foresters Arms in the village of Fairwarp. If you prefer to stick to the mapped WW from Camp Hill Clump and trig point you first head south-eastwards, crossing the B2026 and joining a field path. You then follow a track through bracken and, beyond Crest Farm, continue along woodland paths which take you southwards, downhill, to the house at Brown's Brook and along the driveway beyond the house. The mapped route then turns right off the driveway – don't bother looking for a signpost for the turning, because there isn't one – and continues in a predominantly southerly direction along a tree-shaded track, before turning off along a wooded track eastwards to arrive back at the driveway again. You turn right along it to reach a road, **Oldlands Hill**; by turning left along it you reach, in half a mile, the A26 at **Heron's Ghyll** where buses are available to Tunbridge Wells and Brighton. However the WW turns right along Oldlands Hill. In just under a quarter of a mile a WW signpost (A) – better late than never – directs you left into the trees. By carrying on along this road you reach **Fairwarp** and the Foresters Arms pub in roughly 500 yards from the WW.

South of Oldlands Hill, things get a great deal easier, the path well marked as it heads southwards through woods, with one particularly steep climb, then emerges and veers south-eastwards, skirting the buildings of Hendall Manor Farm. Excellent signage now leads you downhill through fields and into the lovely Hendall Wood where there's another big climb; emerging from the woods you enjoy a field descent and a woodland path walk parallel with the A26, crossing Cobdown Lane, and arriving at and crossing the busy A26 at **Five Ash Down** at a road junction. There are frequent and regular buses from here to Uckfield, Lewes and Tunbridge Wells if you've had enough for today. Once over the A26, still heading south-eastwards, you strike out away from the traffic noise and buildings of Five Ash Down, joining a lovely path heading downhill along the edge of trees and going forward to a road which you follow to the A272. You have to walk alongside this very busy road eastwards for just over a quarter of a mile before crossing it and turning right along the Buxted Park approach road, heading just west of south towards Uckfield. You now walk through Buxted Park, soon passing the lovely albeit much restored 13th century church of St Margaret the Queen – a water tap here is a most helpful amenity – and then a splendid luxury hotel. This building had its origins in the 18th century and in 1931 was bought by the architect Basil Ionides who altered it considerably and made it what has been described as a "magpie's nest" of bits from other houses that were being demolished or had been blitzed in World War 2. You continue beyond the hotel along a delightful path that drops down into woodland; just by a footbridge you turn hard left, eastwards, climbing and emerging to walk through rough grass. You then veer south-westwards along an attractive path beside the river Uck (a tributary of the Sussex Ouse), going forward along a lane to the lovely 18th century **Hempstead Mill**, a Grade II listed building, where you meet the Sussex Hospices Trail. Here the WW turns left to head towards Blackboys but the town of **Uckfield**, with its wide range of amenities including excellent bus links, is just a mile and a quarter away to the right, most pleasantly reached via the Sussex Hospices Trail. A route description for this link is given in the Sussex Hospices Trail section.

Almost immediately after turning left towards Blackboys there's a potential problem. The official route of the WW turns left again

(B) initially along a narrow path then strikes out in a generally easterly direction across the fields around Hempstead Farm Stud, over the London-Uckfield railway, and across a field and through trees to a road. However at the time of writing the railway crossing was shut with no date for its reopening; the alternative is to go straight on rather than left at (B), over the level crossing, on along Hempstead Lane beside Hempstead Wood, then left at the first left road turning and left at the T-junction along a road which at a sharp right bend is met by the mapped WW route. This diversion will add three quarters of a mile to your journey. Not what you want at the start of a day's walk.

You now continue eastwards along the road, descending to a valley, then turn right to head southwards across a meadow. Now keeping a lovely stream close by to your left, and with the Sussex Hospices Trail (which varies from the WW between Hempstead Mill and here) rejoining you from the right, you veer left, south-eastwards, for a very pleasant and well-signed walk through the meadows, the stream to your left a constant and delightful feature. You cross two minor roads, Streele Lane then Pound Lane, and pass some delightful ponds and fine old buildings including, just beyond the Pound Lane crossing, the imposing 17th century, Grade II listed, Tickerage Castle (which incidentally has never been a castle). It's a shame to reach the end of this stretch of WW, but at length you reach a lane by Tickerage Mill and must now bear right along the lane, overlapping briefly with the Vanguard Way. However this overlap and indeed that with the Sussex Hospices Trail ends as you strike out southwards, climbing steeply through the trees to cross the **B2102**. At this crossing there's an opportunity for a detour to the pub at **Blackboys**, by walking 550 yards eastwards to the village then southwards down School Lane. Vanguard Way and Sussex Hospices Trail walkers do better as the pub is right beside the course of those routes!

Now the walking gets a bit fiddly albeit with better signage than on that infamous section south of Camp Hill Clump. A narrow overgrown path takes you southwards to Stonebridge Lane, which you follow briefly to the left. You then strike out south-westwards, downhill; you skirt the attractive Newplace Wood then veer westwards through delightful parkland to the fine buildings of Newplace Farm, going forward to Pump Lane and bearing left.

Then, striking out left again from this lane almost at once, you head just south of east in a straight line through fields all the way to the B2192 Ringmer-Blackboys road. Turning left briefly along it you then bear right along Bushbury Lane but soon head away south-eastwards along a field path incorporating a sharp drop to a wooded valley and a sharp climb back up into open fields. You cross Beechy Road and it's then a repeat performance: a descent to a narrow wooded valley and stream, then another short stiff ascent. It's very typical Low Weald scenery, with its combination of field, woods and water – never particularly dramatic but pleasantly undulating. In the first field after negotiating this second wooded valley you turn south-westwards, at what is a path junction in the field. It wasn't properly signed when I explored it but if in doubt just turn right shortly before the end of the field! This next bit of walking is lovely, as you head south-westwards along a clearly defined path through elevated fields then on through the very pretty Great Wood before following a superb path downhill to the buildings of Old Whyly, with tremendous views to the South Downs escarpment, Mount Caburn, Cliffe Hill and the Glyndebourne wind turbine above Ringmer. Beyond Old Whyly you continue southwards along woodland edges, cross a road linking the A22 with East Hoathly, then, after following a succession of field/woodland edge paths south-eastwards, arrive at the chiefly 19th century East Hoathly Church, its finest features arguably being its altar and 15th century so-called Pelham Tower, built by the Pelham family. The church has a somewhat unusual setting, on the edge of an area of modern development and away from the heart of the old village. The WW heads north-eastwards beyond the church up **East Hoathly** High Street to reach the delightful old village centre with regular buses and, at the time of writing, a cosy café.

The WW turns right off High Street along Buttsfield Lane, though I suggest you take the next right turn along Cider House Lane, which has the prettier houses, then bear left along Buttsfield Lane. The WW continues just south of east from Buttsfield Lane, soon leaving the houses behind and following a pleasant course, keeping a parallel bridleway to the left; shortly the paths join forces and head resolutely south-eastwards, crossing Graywood Lane and continuing through attractive meadows past Frith's Farm. It's relaxing, uncomplicated walking and there's even better to come.

Beyond the farm you go forward to Highlands Lane along which you turn left. You pass the imposing Chiddingly Place Farmhouse, which incorporates remnants of a Tudor mansion, and soon reach **Chiddingly**, a lovely place to pause on your WW walk, with pretty cottages and a refreshment opportunity at the Six Bells pub. In the pub you may meet Vanguard Way walkers, as the Vanguard Way crosses the WW in the village. There's a real 1930's feel about the village centre, with its olde-worlde inn sign on the Six Bells, and the (now defunct) general store which has retained its old signs. The church boasts a 130ft high spire dating from the 15th century, box pews, canopied pulpit and superb 16th and 17th century memorial effigies to the Jeffray family. From the church there's the opportunity of a <u>detour D1</u> to the beautiful red-brick Farley Farm House in the village of Muddles Green. The house, kept largely as it was after World War 2, was home to the British surrealist painter Roland Penrose and his wife Lee Miller; the house contains examples of Penrose's work and also a tile painted by Picasso (himself a guest here), the garden is filled with sculpture, and the gallery in an adjacent complex holds regular art exhibitions. As there's a shop/café just across the car park from the gallery, you've an added incentive to make the detour!

Beyond Chiddingly the WW heads pleasantly eastwards through the heart of the Low Weald, beginning with a lovely field walk and a woodland stream crossing. After going over Scraper's Hill you've then a gentle descent past a campsite to a lovely meeting of trees, water and lush vegetation, and a climb along field edges to Gun Hill. A 250-yard (each way) detour to the left up the road here brings you to the Gun pub, but the WW, following a metalled lane then a rougher track, drops gently just south of east to the twin farms of West Street and Rock Harbour. There's a quick climb away from the complex followed by a pleasant walk south-eastwards, initially through a succession of fields then through an area of woodland, with a sharp drop and ascent to the buildings of Lealands; descending again, you join North Street which takes you to the busy A267 Tunbridge Wells-Eastbourne road. Having crossed the A267 you follow a field edge to cut a road corner, beyond which you enjoy an easy road walk southwards along Church Lane. This brings you to the pretty village of Hellingly, past the late 12th century church of St Peter & St Paul which has a particularly fine chancel full of late

Norman detail; it's believed the churchyard dates back to the 8ᵗʰ century as it's in the form of a circular mound that was typical in the early days of Saxon Christianity. Adjoining the churchyard there are some particularly lovely tile-hung cottages. You pass through the churchyard to reach New Road which you follow eastwards, then having crossed the Cuckmere river you turn southwards along a path, and pass the quite magnificent timber-framed Horselunges Manor, one of the highlights of the whole WW walk. Substantially restored in around 1925, it actually dates from 1475, being built on an older site; its bizarre name is a corruption of the names of two owners of a previous house here, Herst and Lyngyver. Sadly the house is not open to the public but you can marvel at the exterior of the house, the moat that guards it, and its superb setting.

The section of WW between here and Upper Dicker is one of the most disappointing sections of any of the Great Walks of Sussex, being both scenically dull and hard to follow in places. It's only redeemed by Michelham Priory which in any case is off route. Beyond Horselunges Manor you continue southwards through a meadow, keeping the Cuckmere to your right and chalets ahead. You arrive at the **A271** and follow it briefly westwards, then bear left into Cuckmere Close. Where this road bends right, bear left again as WW-signed, going forward into a cul-de-sac, Sheppey Walk, and then, opposite No.24, turning right along a narrow grassy bridleway between houses, crossing Shetland Close and Lundy Walk. The route on the current OS Explorer map is misleading: the mapping suggests you skirt an area of housing then emerge into the country. In fact a brand new housing estate covers this previously rural area and the WW passes right through it. The signage is excellent and you shouldn't have any problems. From the Lundy Walk crossing you go forward along a gravel track, descending to a stream where your track swings sharp right and then sharp left, forming a reverse S. Shortly beyond the left bend you bear right (NOT first right but second right as WW-signed) and head uphill to reach Brunel Drive. Turn right along it then as Brunel Drive veers right, turn left as WW-signed along another gravel track, keeping houses to the left, then opposite 79 Hedley Way (helpfully very clearly marked) you turn right across a green area, going forward over a stile to the A22. Having crossed the A22, with immense care, you turn left alongside it briefly until you reach a stile. You then turn right to head initially westwards from the road then veer south-westwards along a narrow and often very overgrown path beside and then through woods; barely adequate signage then directs you across a succession of fields (with no views) culminating in one very large field. Having crossed this one you veer due west, keeping the woods of Bramble Grove to your left, then veer gently left and gently right, joining a track and veering more sharply left (still with no views). Just short of a complex of buildings you strike away to the right (westwards) from the track and rise gently to a path fork junction. The WW forks right but by forking left you can embark on a <u>route variation V2</u> to Michelham Priory, one of the best features on or close to the WW. The priory dates back to 1229 when Augustinian canons arrived, taking over the site of a moated Norman manor house, and it was dissolved in 1536; the Tudor rooms boast an excellent collection of Dutch paintings, Flemish tapestries and Old English furniture. The garden is packed with colour and variety including exotic waterside plants and sweeping herbaceous borders. If you decide to omit the Priory, the WW route having taken the right fork follows an ill-defined path north-westwards through the grounds of St Bede's School. On emerging from the grounds the route becomes clearer and you proceed more confidently to reach Coldharbour Road in **Upper Dicker**, turning left to follow the road past the village shop/café to a crossroads junction where V2 ends. The crossroads marks the end also of this poor section of the route. Much better things lie ahead.

Now maintaining a fairly clear south-westerly course, you head away from the centre of Upper Dicker, passing the pub and then leaving the road to climb along the edge of a golf course; at the top there are magnificent views to the South Downs which will rarely be out of sight between here and Wilmington. You descend, keeping Park Wood to your left, and it's now a very straightforward well-signed walk south-westwards (your direction of travel all the way from Upper Dicker to beyond Arlington) through a succession of fields and across a fine footbridge over a tributary of the Cuckmere river. You reach a path junction, bearing left to cross the Cuckmere then right to negotiate a stiff ascent, for which you're rewarded with further excellent views towards the South Downs and the unmistakeable Long Man of Wilmington. A field-edge descent brings you into the precincts of the church of St Pancras, Arlington, and you proceed through the churchyard past the very pretty flint-built part-Saxon church, with a Saxon window in the south wall and also some medieval wall paintings. The WW goes straight to the lychgate by the road, and here by turning left along the road you'll reach, in roughly 150 yards, the pretty Old Oak Inn in the village of **Arlington**; however the WW turns right along the road from the lychgate. When the road ends you go straight on through a field down to a footbridge and a **path junction** (C) beyond. Here there's the possibility of a route variation V3 to Arlington Reservoir, the reservoir described more fully in the Vanguard Way section; this is also the recommended means of access to **Berwick Station** for trains to Lewes and Eastbourne. The WW however continues south-westwards, initially across pasture then going forward along a track to reach the **Arlington-Berwick road** crossing, where V3 ends. The WW goes more or less straight over it, but by turning right here there's another opportunity here to access Berwick Station on the Lewes-Eastbourne line, one mile away. To do this, turn right along the road. In roughly half a mile the road bends left towards a railway overbridge. Now you have a choice. You could simply follow the road to its end and then turn right up Station Road to shortly reach the station. However there is, just beyond the left bend, a signed path through a metalled gate, which passes to the left of a waterworks. You could take this path then, beyond the works, carry straight on through the field aiming for a gate just to the right of a stone enclosure ahead. Pass through this gate then aim for another gate between the houses, walking up to and through it and arriving at Station Road, turning left for the station. Unfortunately this path, which will save you about 550 yards, is very poorly defined and its original course no longer exists. If you have problems it's best to return (and stick) to the road!

Beyond the Arlington-Berwick road crossing the WW initially follows beside the Cuckmere then swings away from it to the left and shortly heads southwards through or beside low-lying fields, the field sequence interrupted by a railway crossing. Picking up a track at the Milton Gate complex you then proceed briefly along it to the A27, the last unpleasant main road crossing of the WW. There have been a few! Crossing straight over you follow the Milton Street road briefly then turn left along a path initially in the shade of trees then along field edges, striking out south-eastwards and picking up a clear path to **Wilmington.** The village's amenities are down the attractive village street to the left but the WW turns right up the street, with its cottages of brick, flint, timber and thatch, and soon passes the pretty village church of St Mary & St Peter, in the churchyard of which is a magnificent yew. Like the church itself, the yew is believed to date back to Norman times. Just beyond the church are the ruins of a Benedictine priory founded by the half-brother of William the Conqueror, Robert de Mortain, soon after the Norman Conquest, although what you see today is chiefly 13th/14th century; at one time the priory was connected to the church by a cloister. Note that the buildings aren't open to the public. The WW continues past the priory and just opposite the adjacent car park you join a parallel path beside the road, then at the bottom of the dip you turn left, southwards, along a clear path heading uphill to the Long Man. This featureless chalk hill figure, 226ft high – some say 237ft, but it's still some 40 times a human's average height – is the largest hill carving in Britain, and has intrigued and baffled generations of archaeologists. Some attribute it to the Romans, while others say it is a pagan god or Saxon cult figure. The irony is that although you've had it in your sights for so many miles and no doubt anticipated the pleasure and satisfaction of reaching it, the Long Man does, as the adjoining information board says, look better from a distance!

You turn left by the information board along a clear path just north of east, contouring the hillside. The views, especially northwards across the Low Weald, are magnificent, and are arguably the finest on the WW so far. You reach an area of trees and a T-junction of tracks, here turning right along a byway which you follow firstly south-eastwards then predominantly southwards, avoiding turnings-off, all the way to the edge of Jevington, just under 3 miles away. It's a most pleasant and straightforward walk in the shade of the South Downs, the only landmark en route being the very picturesque flint church of St Peter at Folkington. At length you reach a T-junction and turn left to shortly reach Jevington Road, turning right along it into **Jevington** itself. Just by the Eight Bells pub which is on the right, you turn left, eastwards, up a clear WW-signed path, climbing steeply. As the gradient slackens you enter an area of access land and are joined by the 1066 Country Walk (South Downs Link) coming in from the right. You now climb up onto Combe Hill, and clear signage takes you just north of east along an obvious path which passes the site of a Neolithic camp. This is splendid walking and gets even better as you arrive at the Butts Brow ridge, ascending and bearing south-westwards along a lovely ridgetop path, with sensational views eastwards to Eastbourne, to Hastings and, on a clear day, to Dungeness. The field tramping between Hailsham and Michelham is now a distant memory, and the sea is clearly in your sights! Though the signage is unclear, the WW follows the ridgetop path heading southwards, passes straight through the car park and by the Liberator Memorial – see the 1066 Country Walk section for more information about the memorial – then follows the track along the right-hand edge of the ridge, keeping the mast to the left. There are numerous path options beyond the mast; I suggest you keep to the one nearest to the right edge of the ridge, enjoying fantastic views not only to Jevington with its very photogenic church, but also to a massive area of countryside including the Arlington Reservoir, the complete Jevington-Butts Brow walk you've just done, and the Sussex coast westwards to well beyond Brighton.

Soon the South Downs Way bridleway route from Alfriston comes in from the right and, while the 1066 Country Walk dives off down towards Jevington, you now bear left, seawards, along the same route as the South Downs Way, shortly passing the Willingdon Hill trig point, where the eastward views are magnificent. It's now a very straightforward walk south-eastwards along the South Downs Way, all the way to the A259 crossing, just under 2 miles from the trig point. You cross more or less straight over the A259, staying with the South Downs Way, and after a fine hilltop march, you reach a fork of paths just short of the conspicuous Warren Hill trig point. Here you bear right, downhill, passing the trig point and a pond, soon reaching the top edge of woodland. Staying with the clearly signed South Downs Way you follow the top of the woodland, reaching the B2103 by a junction. You cross the B2103 just to the left of this junction, going uphill to a path crossroads (D) where the South Downs Way bears left. If you were in a hurry (and signage suggests this is a legitimate alternative route) you could follow the South Downs Way downhill from here, once again meeting the B2103 (which here is Duke's Drive). From here it's a straightforward walk on along the WW into Eastbourne.

However, I recommend you take the longer route (by about 2 miles), shown on current OS maps as the official course of the WW albeit not signed as such. To do this, don't turn left with the South Downs Way at (D) but go straight on at the crossroads. You can see a road ahead – which leads from the B2103 to Beachy Head – and in about 140 yards, almost exactly halfway between the path crossroads and the road, you fork left along a clear but unsigned path heading south-westwards down the hillside and meeting a path carrying the South Downs Way coastal footpath alternative from Alfriston at a South Downs Way sign. Turn right onto the path by the sign, shortly veering left to enter the vegetation. You now enjoy a superb high-level walk through the vegetation, aiming for Beachy Head, with glorious views out to sea. Emerging from the vegetation you reach a flight of steps going down to the left, and the WW takes those steps. However although it means a slight detour, roughly 250 yards each way, I recommend you pass the steps and continue along the signed South Downs Way all the way up to the red-brick shelter marking the top of **Beachy Head**, then head back the same way, making a short detour this time to the splendidly sited war memorial from which there are great views to the lighthouse below the cliffs. Retrace back along the South Downs Way towards the vegetation again, but this time look out carefully after a few yards for the steps to the right, and use these steps to descend to, and go forward along, an obvious wide green path heading for and reaching the edge of the cliff. You now turn left to follow the cliff path. The path goes forward to a track and you continue along it, rising then falling to meet the road at Duke's Drive and the start/ end of both the South Downs Way bridleway and coastal footpath routes.

Whether you've decided on the shorter signed walk or the longer mapped walk, the WW turns seawards down Duke's Drive. There's now a straight overlap with the England Coast Path into Eastbourne, described more fully in that section. According to OS maps, the official end of the WW is at Terminus Road, a left turn off the coast road shortly before the pier, although there's no sign to mark this or acclaim your efforts! To reach **Eastbourne Station**, turn left along Terminus Road and veer left with it as it arrives at the main shopping area, going forward to the station. Of course, if you've already walked the England Coast Path – or the Sussex Hospices Trail which overlaps with it through Eastbourne – you could, with a clear conscience, leave the WW just beyond the Lifeboat Museum, obtaining quicker access to Eastbourne's centre via Lascelles Terrace as described in the England Coast Path section.

GOOD TO KNOW
Start: Ashurst Station. Finish: Eastbourne Station.
Total mileage: 46.5.
Difficulty: Moderate, strenuous in places.
Stages: B2110 for Withyham (RAB) 3.75, Oldlands Hill for Heron's Ghyll (B) and Fairwarp (R) 9.5, Five Ash Down (RB) 12, Hempstead Mill for Uckfield (*RAB) 14, B2102 for Blackboys (RAB) 16.5, East Hoathly (RAB) 20.5, Chiddingly (R) 22, A271 26, Upper Dicker (RA) 28.5, Arlington (R) 30, Path junction for Berwick Station (*RA) 30.25, Arlington-Berwick road 31, Wilmington (RA) 34, Jevington (RA) 37, Beachy Head (R) 43, Eastbourne Station (*RAB) 46.5.
OS: 135, OL25.

D1 Make your way to the south side of the church and beyond it walk down through the cricket field aiming for the very bottom left corner. There you'll see a signed path heading southwards. Follow this path which then veers left (south-eastwards) and follows a clear course through fields and alongside Belt Wood to arrive at a road, Scraper's Hill. Turn right onto it then almost immediately right at the T-junction and you'll see the imposing red-brick Farley Farm House straight in front of you. The car park with gallery and shop/café is just a few yards further down the street. Return the same way to Chiddingly. (Total detour 1.5 miles)

V1 Return from the trig point to the bench in front of the WW opening plaque with a dedication on the bench to Anthony Field. Immediately in front of you, facing out from the bench, are two forking green tracks. Take the left-hand one and follow it downhill to reach two delightful pools, known as Ellison's Pond, one pool on either side of the path. Just beyond the left pool, at the narrowest point between the pools, the continuous route forks left, aiming for a bench; there is however the option here of a further detour to Nutley Windmill (described below). If you omit the detour, walk directly to the bench and go straight on to Crowborough Road, crossing over and aiming for a footpath fingerpost. Go past it and turn left to join the signed path but almost immediately turn right down a green path; don't veer right alongside the bottom end of the car park, but keep straight on, veering very slightly left and now enjoying a lovely walk on a clear wide path downhill with sensational views to the South Downs which on a clear day will extend from Firle Beacon to Chanctonbury Ring. As you lose height you pass Airman's Grave. At the very bottom of the valley you reach a multi-path junction and streams; as you get to this point, look carefully left to identify and cross a narrow plank bridge which takes you to two forking paths heading left from the path you've just followed. Take the near (left-hand) one of these, climbing away from the valley. Look out for a barn to your right; just beyond the barn and gate you reach two forking paths going ahead. Take the left of these and follow it, keeping a prominent white house not far to your left, and going straight over a crossing path to arrive at the B2026. Cross straight over and turn immediately right along the wide grass verge downhill – note the grass is thinnest on the far side of the verge – going forward via a crude pavement to the gates of Fairwarp Church. Go through the gates and up the path to the door; to continue, turn right opposite the door and follow the path to the car park. Walk half-right across the car park to join a path which goes downhill to reach a driveway, which you follow on to a road. Turn left to pass through the village of Fairwarp and perhaps enjoy the Foresters Arms. Stay on the road and a couple of hundred yards beyond the village you reach (A) as described in the main body of the text. Turn right here to rejoin the WW. (Extra 2.5 miles)

To visit Nutley Windmill, instead of turning left just past the left-hand pool at Ellison's Pond, follow the path on, veering right immediately beyond the right-hand pool. Your path goes through trees and emerges to pass a car park that's to the left. Immediately beyond the car park turn right off the main track onto another track that contours the hillside then veers left and drops to a path crossroads. Turn left, steeply uphill, then as this wide path veers left, go straight on up a rather indistinct path that enters the trees and reaches a junction (E) with a path and a fence behind. Turn right and in a few yards you'll find the entrance to the Nutley Windmill area. Having enjoyed the mill, return to (E) but this time carry on along the top path, keeping the fence to the right. Go forward to exit the trees and rejoin the wide path, going straight on along it in the same direction (just south of east) ignoring the signed footpath to the right. The views across Ashdown Forest, especially the so-called Old Lodge away to the left, are fantastic. Keep on the wide path which then drops steeply, passes the car park and goes through the woods to arrive back at the pools. At the narrowest point between them turn hard right, aiming for the seat, to rejoin the continuous "preferred" WW route. (Extra 1.75 miles on top of continuous route variation)

V2 Having taken the left fork, follow the field edge and shortly reach a road, turning left to shortly reach the entrance to Michelham Priory. Having visited the priory retrace your steps up the road but this time carry on along the road to reach the crossroads in the centre of Upper Dicker. To continue along the WW turn left here. By detouring right at the crossroads along Coldharbour Road you'll find the village shop/café. (Negligible extra mileage)

V3 At (C) turn right onto a signed path following right-hand field edges and going forward to cross the Cuckmere by an impressive footbridge. From here aim for the plank bridge ahead then, reassured by a signpost, proceed north-westwards uphill on an excellent path. As you reach the top of the hill you veer left to a stile, here reaching Arlington Reservoir. Turn left to follow the reservoir round, enjoying tremendous views back to Arlington and forward to the South Downs. At the bottom (south) corner where the reservoir-side path ends, pass through a kissing gate and turn left onto a bridleway. In 80 yards you reach a gate (F) and path going off left, downhill. To return to the WW, follow this path, aiming for the tallest evergreen at 11 o'clock to the bridleway. Your path then becomes clear alongside a fence, keeping the evergreen immediately to the right. You pass through a thicket (G) then beyond a stile continue through a marshy field aiming for a stile at the far end. Beyond the stile you reach the Arlington-Berwick road; turn left along it and, just beyond the sharp right bend, you arrive back at the WW. If you wanted to incorporate Berwick Station into this variation, don't turn left at (F) but follow the bridleway on for about 50 yards then turn right as path-signed, heading uphill along a left-hand field edge. Continue as signed downhill then, keeping the same westerly direction, climb gently through fields and go forward to pass between buildings and reach Station Road. Follow the path accordingly to arrive at this road. Turn left, and shortly right to arrive at Berwick Station. To return to the WW from Berwick Station, retrace to the bridleway. This time turn right along it then turn almost immediately left onto a signed path beside a house. You feel as though you might be trespassing but you're not! This path takes you to a footpath T-junction. Turn right to follow it via the thicket described at (G) above and on as described above via the marshy field and stile to the Arlington-Berwick road, turning left along it to shortly arrive back at the WW. (Extra 2 miles with Berwick Station included, extra 1 mile with it excluded)

17 WEST SUSSEX LITERARY TRAIL

The name West Sussex Literary Trail (WSLT) suggests a literary tour of West Sussex, following in the footsteps of all the great authors at one time connected with the county, visiting the houses they lived in and seeing the rooms where they wrote their immortal prose and verse. The reality is somewhat different. Although you will pass through a number of places that are linked with great writers of the past, the connections are often rather loose and the walk goes nowhere near the West Sussex homes of arguably the county's most famous author residents, namely H.G. Wells (who lived for a while at Uppark and in Midhurst – see respectively the South Downs Way and New Lipchis Way sections) and William Blake (who lived for some years in Felpham – see the England Coast Path section). That said, it is a fine walk blessed with some very splendid villages, towns and historic buildings, not to mention two of the finest vineyards in the south of England, and there's a good variety of walking, with gentle riverside strolling complemented by more energetic walking over the South Downs. You need to allow time to enjoy the many features of interest on this walk, although it has to be said that overall the second half of the walk offers very much more than the first.

The walk starts bang in the centre of Horsham. To access the official start of the route (A) from **Horsham Station**, I recommend a slightly roundabout route which incorporates some of the more historic sights of the town (although I also offer a quicker alternative if you're anxious to get going on the WSLT). I suggest you turn left out of Horsham's main station exit along the station side of North Street past the splendid timber-framed 17th century North Chapel. Cross North Street by the next pedestrian crossing and continue down North Street, forking right into Chart Way, and go past the impressive RSA atrium, a glass-clad structure with fine window decoration depicting Sussex scenes, and boasting a magnificent chandelier inside. Go on past the preserved spire of the 1840 church of St Mark which stood till recently on this site, and descend via the steps/slipway, then walk straight on, keeping the bandstand to your right, as far as the junction with Middle Street (to your right) and East Street (to your left). To cut straight to (A),

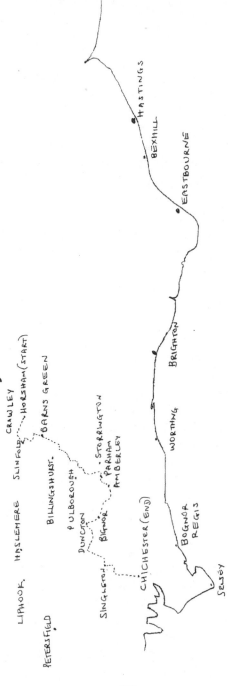

saving no more than about a third of a mile, go right down Middle Street and forward along West Street, following all the way to the crossroads junction at the end (A). Otherwise cross straight over (though a detour left up East Street, as far as the splendid medieval house on the left, is recommended first) noting the former Inland Revenue office labelled AD 1401, and then passing round the left side of the Old Town Hall which looks like a castle – it was built by the Duke of Norfolk in 1812. You're now on Market Square. Easily missed to the left just here but also well worth detouring to see is Talbot Lane via a narrow twitten, at the entrance to which is the Old Posting Box, an early collection point for London mail; there are some fine timber-framed buildings down this lane.

Returning to Market Square, walk on down Causeway, arguably Horsham's finest street. You pass the town museum, and keeping the Manor House to the right, continue past some really excellent buildings to the left including the stunning pink timber-framed No.12. There's another lovely alley, Morth Gardens, just beyond, while No.18 was the home of author Hammond Innes from 1919 to 1924. Just beyond the beautiful 1615 house Flagstones is the mainly 13th century church of St Mary, which boasts a magnificent spire; pass round the church's right-hand side, continuing along the path. You cross a bridge over a stream then approach a bridge over a wider watercourse. Just before this second bridge turn right along a lovely (signed) riverside path to the fine old red-brick Provender Mill and adjacent pill box, then continue along the signed riverside path as far as Worthing Road (B2237). The Sussex Hospices Trail goes left along this road but for the WSLT, bear right along the road as far as the roundabout. Cross straight over and follow the left side of the street, shortly passing the fine 1786 Quakers' Meeting House and the Unitarian church, built as a Baptist church in 1721 and set in lovely gardens. Go forward to the pedestrianized area, reaching a junction with the main West Street shopping area going away to the right. At this junction you're at point (A). If you're a High Weald Landscape Trail walker visiting Horsham as an appetiser, I suggest you turn right up West Street and go on up Middle Street to the Town Hall, retracing from there to the station to start that walk!

You're now ready to begin your WSLT journey. Here, (A), is the site of the 1966 water sculpture, Rising Universe, built in honour of the lyric Romantic poet Percy Bysshe Shelley, born at Field Place,

Warnham, just outside the town in 1792. Even though he only lived 30 years his output was prodigious and the current *Chambers Dictionary of Great Quotations* contains over 100 entries by him from such works as *To A Skylark* and *Prometheus Unbound*. The sculpture, which used to incorporate an ingenious water feature, has now been dismantled and 16 silver birch trees have been planted on a mound in its place. You walk from here up West Street, then bear left along South Street past the top edge of the Swan Walk shopping centre and go forward via Medwin Walk to pass under the inner ring road. You then enter and pass through the attractive Horsham Park, close to the police station and hospital, before exiting the town in a north-westerly direction via Milnwood Road, Newlands Road, Kempshott Road and Spencers Place, crossing Redford Avenue and continuing along a track beside a golf course. It's only after you pass under the A24 that the surroundings become more rural, a short section of walking westwards along Robin Hood Lane being followed by a delightful north-westward stroll across parkland to the 14th century Balling Hill Farm, a stud deer farm supporting a herd of 70 breeding hinds. You cross Balling Hill itself, which links Warnham and Broadbridge Heath, and after a stiff field climb heading north-westwards you then veer south-westwards, crossing two roads and enjoying a mixture of woodland and high-level field walking with excellent southward views. The trail passes the school at Strood Green, crosses the **A281** and now, maintaining its broadly south-westerly course, follows farm lanes and tracks, dropping suddenly then rising quite steeply to pass Rowfold Farm and descend to **Slinfold**, the first settlement of any size on the route since Horsham. Slinfold is an attractive village with a gently curving village street and houses of a variety of styles, including some fine Georgian buildings, and being the first settlement out of Horsham it's your first chance of on-route rest and refreshment. The church of St Peter is 19th century but contains some much earlier monuments and tablets, and there is not one but two lychgates, each with a stone roof.

Having joined and followed Slinfold's main street southwards you strike out left, westwards through the outskirts of the village then head briefly southwards away from the village to arrive at the Downs Link. Here you turn left, overlapping with this path along the course of the old Christ's Hospital-Guildford railway described more fully in the Downs Link section. This is lovely easy level walking; by contrast, after leaving it in 550 yards or so, you then have quite a steady slog along right-hand field edges, maintaining a fairly straight south-westerly course. Traffic noise announces the A264 crossing where care must be taken to join the path signed half-left across the road, not the more tempting one going right. This section of the A264 is known as Toat Hill and it was hereabouts that the Regency and detective novelist Georgette Heyer rented Blackthorns, one of a number of properties rented by her in Sussex between 1930 and 1942. The house is not accessible to the public but one may assume she gained inspiration for her books from the surrounding countryside. She was born in 1902 and died in 1974 and wrote a total of over 50 novels. The WSLT heads south-eastwards away from the A264 then veers south-westwards to Lower Toat Farm before heading south-eastwards again, crossing Bashurst Hill. You emerge from the shade of trees to enjoy a splendid high-level field walk, then a plunging descent and another woodland walk brings you to the lovely hamlet of **Itchingfield** with its timber-framed houses and Norman church of St Nicholas, dating from around 1125. Its most remarkable feature is its 600-year-old belfry tower made entirely of huge beams held together by oak pegs. When the interior of the church was being restored a skull was found on one of the beams; it was said to be the head of Sir Hector Maclean who was executed for his part in the rising of the Old Pretender in 1715. It's suggested that as the vicar at the time was a friend of Maclean, he put the skull on the beam for safe keeping. In the churchyard is the tiny half-timbered Priest's House, dating from the 15th century and described by Nikolaus Pevsner as a "rare and lovable survival…just like a toy." It was intended as an overnight lodging for the priest who rode over from Sele Priory not far from Steyning to collect church dues, and in the 19th century it was used as an almshouse.

Thus far the trail has described a crude semi-circle round Horsham, and despite being a good half a day's walk from the start, you're still no further from the town centre than at Strood Green. Now, however, the WSLT adopts a more resolutely south-westerly course. You head south-westwards from Itchingfield to reach a driveway, although by following the road left, bearing left at the end along Westons Hill and then in 275 yards going right along Christ's Hospital Road for 1100 yards, veering left along King Edward

Road and forking along Station Road you reach **Christ's Hospital Station**, 1.25 miles from the WSLT. The WSLT, however, follows the driveway which passes the buildings of Muntham House, a neo-Tudor building dating from 1887 and now a school, and then drops down through trees, turning sharply south-eastwards to reach **Barns Green** and begin a brief overlap with the Sussex Hospices Trail which has followed a more direct route from Horsham. Of Victorian origin, the village is now quite sprawling and principally a dormitory village for Horsham (and the commute from there into London) but there's an unspoilt pub, the Queen's Head of 17th century origin, and a fine timber-framed house called Bennetts. You bear right along the village street then strike out south-westwards again to pass the Sumners Pond campsite and fishing lakes, where anglers can fish for roach, carp, chub, perch and tench among others, and there's an agreeable stroll through Vale Wood beyond. You then cross the railway – the so-called Arun Valley line linking Chichester, Arundel and Billingshurst with Horsham, Crawley and London – taking care to observe the warning lights. Now the character of the walk changes, the rather stop-start walking along a variety of different paths, roads and lanes giving way to a bridleway that continues in a generally south-westerly direction right down to the A272. The going is initially straightforward on a firm surface but then the bridleway continues as a path through fields, rises to pass Emmets Farm and then uses farm tracks and field edges all the way to the A272. It's not difficult or demanding walking but lacks any features of historic or scenic interest, the surroundings remaining largely unremarkable, and you may feel as though you're marking time, waiting for something more interesting to happen. The countryside hereabouts, part of the Low Weald, was once densely forested and abounding with ponds and streams with wet woodlands of willow and alder; bird life includes nuthatch and tree creeper, and deer and badgers are common.

In due course you reach the A272, which stretches all the way from Winchester in Hampshire to near Heathfield in East Sussex. A whole book has been written about it by Pieter and Rita Boogaart, subtitled *Ode To A Road,* so it's eminently appropriate that the WSLT, celebrating the written word as it does, should meet and follow the road that forms the subject of it! There's a not too exciting walk of around 550 yards just north of west beside it, then the WSLT turns left, southwards, along Old House Lane, arriving at one of the most impressive and iconic sights on the trail, the **Blue Idol**. This is a superb timber-framed Elizabethan farmhouse, part of which was converted into a Quaker meeting house in 1691, at a time when Quakers were struggling to find acceptance in society notwithstanding the Toleration Act of 1689 which had granted freedom of worship to Nonconformists. William Penn, best known for being the founder of the state of Pennsylvania in North America, lived at nearby Warminghurst and had actively encouraged the establishment of a Quaker meeting house locally; he used to walk here to worship from Warminghurst while his wife and children came in an ox-drawn coach. He was also an author and is the third well-known writer on your journey to be associated with the course of the WSLT. He was a man of deep Christian convictions, in contrast to the avowed sceptic Shelley, whom we met at the start of the walk; he wrote a number of Christian works, and indeed his book *No Cross, No Crown* has become a Christian classic. The unusual name for the house is thought to be derived from the fact that when during the 19th century it was not in use, therefore idle, it was colour-washed in blue and therefore known as the "blue idle meeting house." It is however in use today as a Quaker meeting house and in recent years has been superbly restored, the impressiveness of its exterior complemented splendidly by its attractive gardens which make an ideal picnic spot.

The going is now straightforward but unremarkable, the metalled road petering out and the trail continuing down Old House Lane along what is an often muddy path, maintaining a southerly/south-westerly course through the trees with no views. It all seems a bit of an anticlimax after the Blue Idol and during or after heavy rain the mud could well prove a bit demoralising. I walked this during a particularly wet September and the experience wasn't a pleasurable one. The trail crosses the B2133 – half a mile north-west of here up the B2133 is Broadford Bridge, where "fracking" has been and at the time of writing remains a hugely controversial issue – and continues to follow often muddy but easy-to-follow woodland paths, arriving at Willetts Farm and another road crossing, this time of Broadford Bridge Road. You now begin more enjoyable walking, westwards then southwards, through the trees of Woodshill Copse and there's then a gentle field-edge climb to another patch of woodland, involving a stiffer climb. However the reward is a magnificent view to the west and then a terrific high-level march, the best walking of the trail so far, before a descent, this time southwards then westwards, round the edge of the Nyetimber vineyard. Nyetimber was the first producer of English sparkling wine to exclusively grow three celebrated grape varieties, Pinot Noir, Pinot Meunier and Chardonnay; the first vines were planted in 1988 and Nyetimber is now reputed to be one of the finest sparkling wines in the country. The walking is suddenly so much better – perhaps it's the thought of a glass or two at the next pub – and with the South Downs escarpment clearly within your sights ahead for the first time on the WSLT, you'll find the spring returning to your step! Beyond the vines there's a drop to the Nyetimber complex and a path crossroads, OS ref TQ084195 (B), and you here have a choice, involving no difference in mileage. The mapped route turns left, southwards, along a lane to Lower Jordans, veering right and reaching a point (C) where the WSLT joins a parallel path above the lane. Much to be preferred (and seemingly confirmed by later signage) is to go straight over at (B) along the complex approach road, then veer just left of the road on a signed path keeping the vines to the left. Simply follow the signed path round the vines, veering sharply south then, at the bottom of the field, east, to reach point (C). The WSLT then heads westwards parallel with the lane before turning southwards to walk parallel with and immediately above Gay Street. At the point where the path veers sharp left (D) the WSLT descends steps to cross Gay Street (OS TQ082187), turning sharply westwards towards Nutbourne vineyard.

However if at (D) rather than descend the steps you veer left and continue along the footpath there is a detour D1, providing a circular tour that includes the lovely villages of West Chiltington and Thakeham and the church at Warminghurst. West Chiltington has some attractive cottages in Church Street and a smock windmill, dating from around 1800 and now part of a private dwelling, with two surviving sails; opposite the mill is the fine 17th century Friar's House. The village's chief highlight is the church of St Mary, with nave and chancel walls dating back to the 11th century, a large number of wall paintings some of which date back to the 12th century, and an unusually – Pevsner says "fantastically" – long squint to the chancel through a thickened chancel wall. Thakeham has an Early English church, again dedicated to St Mary, with an unusual "henhouse" roof on top and an impressive collection of monuments to the Apsley family. Close to the church is the lovely timbered Church House and a spot called Thakeham Halt which might from its name alone be thought to be the site of an old railway station but which in fact is a lovely area of green and, on a fine day, a perfect picnic place. At Warminghurst there is the 13ᵗʰ century church of the Holy Sepulchre, boasting a neat tile-hung belfry, magnificent Queen Anne screen, fine arched roof, 18ᵗʰ century box pews – some facing backwards – and a memorial brass to Edward Shelley, an ancestor of the poet. It's a remarkable building in such an isolated location. Warminghurst Place was the home of William Penn whom we met earlier at Blue Idol, but his house has long since been pulled down.

The WSLT route, as stated above, heads down the steps from (D) and across Gay Street, heading westwards to pass Nutbourne vineyard. Vines were first planted here in 1980 and the vineyard is considered one of the premier wine producers in south-east England with its range of still and sparkling wines, grapes including Schonburger, Pinot Blanc, Bacchus and Reichensteiner. At the 19ᵗʰ century tower windmill to the right it's possible to sample and buy the produce. From here it's a short walk to the stunning Mill House, the WSLT turning hard left and left again, passing between this house and the old mill before a pleasant waterside walk heading just east of south. You then veer westwards between fields before veering right and then left, dropping down to the main street at **Nutbourne**. A route variation V1 offers an alternative to the walk from Mill House to the main street, passing the converted mill with wooden mill wheel and millpond, the stunning 14ᵗʰ century thatched and timber-framed Ebbsworth, and the Rising Sun pub. Confusingly Nutbourne is one of two villages in West Sussex that is so named, but this one is certainly prettier than its namesake further south with many attractive old houses on its main street including the fine timber-framed Drovers.

There's now a section of road walking through and beyond Nutbourne southwards along The Street and Nutbourne Road. By staying with this road, bearing right along West Chiltington Road and right again alongside the A283 you reach **Pulborough** in 1 mile and its station in 2 miles. However the WSLT forks left off Nutbourne Road and ascends south-westwards along a lane and then a very narrow path onto Nutbourne Common where a sign warns one to beware of adders. The trail turns left along the surprisingly busy West Chiltington Road for about 150 yards then turns right away from the road, and after a short stream-side walk ascends through the trees, still south-westwards, to arrive at and cross a couple of fairways of the exclusive and very picturesque West Sussex Golf Club, one of the finest golf courses in the whole of Sussex. The sand, heather and pine course, opened in 1931, has some truly tremendous holes including the 6th with a 200+-yard carry over a lake from an elevated tee. On arrival at a tarmac lane, Golf Club Lane, beyond the fairway crossings, the WSLT turns left, south-eastwards. However by turning right along Golf Club Lane you can embark on a route variation V2, which is much better, I suggest, than the WSLT route. This variation proceeds to Parham via Wiggonholt, Pulborough Brooks Nature Reserve and, if you wish, Greatham. Wiggonholt boasts what is almost the epitome of an English country church, a simple 13th century building on a hillside, while Pulborough Brooks is one of the most important wetland habitats in south-east England, supporting many species of insects, mammals, birds and butterflies, and providing a home to large numbers of swans, ducks and geese in winter and dragonflies, owls, nightjars and butterflies in summer. Deer and Highland cattle are to be found here throughout the year. Greatham, meanwhile, has a lovely unrestored church, probably 12th century, and a part-17th century manor house. If despite the attractions of V2 you decide to stick to the WSLT, you turn left as stated along Golf Club Lane towards and past the golf clubhouse. Beyond the clubhouse the WSLT continues south-eastwards to Hurston Place Farm, veers south-westwards along Hurston Lane, then embarks on a roughly semi-circular walk, first south-eastwards then veering south-westwards. Initially you follow field edges then proceed through woodland round the edge of Parham Airfield – home of the Southdown Gliding Club, founded in 1930 – to reach the A283 at **Cootham**. By turning left (eastwards) beside this road you reach in just over half a mile the centre of **Storrington**, a small town with ample amenities. However the WSLT turns right, westwards beside the A283, then continues along the driveway heading for Parham House, passing a lodge. The footpath is signed off the driveway and passes to the right of the house, while to visit the house (when it's open) you continue along the driveway for half a mile then have to return to pick up the path again afterwards. Parham House, arguably the finest stately home in Sussex, was the work of Thomas Palmer. It dates from 1577 and the house's interiors are mostly of the late 16th and early 17th centuries. The Great Hall has a ceiling with heavy pendants and huge windows; the adjacent parlour boasts a lovely set of portraits by John Fawcett, manager of Covent Garden Theatre; the Great Chamber and West Room both have magnificent flame-stitch embroidery; the ante-room has an exquisite Coromandel cabinet and walls of Hungarian needlework; the Green Room is dedicated to the voyages of discovery of the 18th century with globes, prints of yachts and Reynolds' painting *Portrait Of Omai*; and on the 2nd floor is the Long Gallery, with beautiful views out to the South Downs as well as some more fantastic embroidery. Indeed the house has the best collection of historic needlework outside London. The 18th century gardens include a 4-acre walled garden with opulent mixed borders, and also a 19th century church with box pews of yew wood and a 14th century lead font, but the gardens' arguably most delightful feature is a 2-storey Wendy house, a child-scale house set into a brick wall. Even if the house is shut, the footpath walk past the house and through its grounds is still most rewarding.

The WSLT continues along the estate road to the far end (V2 meeting the WSLT here), turns left along Rackham Street briefly then strikes out westwards at Rackham, passing a very conspicuous sandstone outcrop on leaving the road. After an enjoyable stroll along a lane westwards below woodland, the WSLT joins a footpath heading south-westwards, soon passing Rackham Mill, a watermill built in the 18th century but closing in 1925. You continue through trees then ascend through a field to Rackham Road, turning right, westwards, along it and going forward along East Street – the same road, in effect. This brings you to **Amberley**, without doubt the most picturesque village visited by the WSLT. Enjoying a lovely setting immediately beneath the South Downs, it boasts a splendid castle with Norman features, a part-Norman church, a popular shop, a lovely tea room, and a large number of historic houses of thatch, brick and timber. The square-towered castle, not open to the public (though the outer walls can be seen and marvelled at) was built by Bishop Rede in the 1370's to defend the upper reaches of the Arun valley but in due course it became a summer retreat for bishops and never saw military action. It is believed the future Charles II stayed in the castle in October 1651 in the course of his flight to France. Much of the village church of St Michael dates from just after the Norman Conquest, and was the work of Bishop Luffa who founded Chichester Cathedral; among its most notable features are the 12th century wall paintings of Christ In Majesty and The Resurrection. I suggest that you follow the WSLT as it veers southwards off East Street down High Street then detour right along Church Street which takes you past the church to the viewable parts of the castle. The detour is half a mile each way. Beyond High Street the WSLT, overlapping with the Wey South Path here, goes southwards along School Road to the B2139. You cross this road and climb steeply up Mill Lane where there's another literary link, this time with John Wyndham's classic sci-fi novel *The Day Of The Triffids*: it can be inferred from the text that the eponymous antiheroes made the very same ascent while on the rampage! At the top the WSLT meets the South Downs Way, here turning right down High Titten, crossing back over the B2139 – at this point parting company from the South Downs Way – and following beside it south/south-westwards to reach the station approach road just before the railway bridge. **Amberley Station** is just a few yards up this road. Next to the station is Amberley Museum, a 36-acre open air museum with a tremendous rage of exhibits devoted to crafts and industries of yesteryear such as those of blacksmith, wood turner, claypipe maker, wheelwright and potter; there are stationary engines, old buses and a working narrow-gauge railway as well as a print workshop and telecommunications display. As far as literary connections are concerned, there are quite a few hereabouts. The poet Eleanor Farjeon, who wrote *Morning Has Broken*, lived for a while at Houghton, just a little further along the B2139 beyond Houghton Bridge; the children's author Noel Streatfeild, author of *Ballet Shoes*, was born in Amberley; the last home of the *Flower Fairy* book illustrator Cicely Baker was in Amberley; and the author Arnold Bennett, famous for his work *Clayhanger*, rented a house in Amberley – Boxwood, in Church Street – for 8 weeks, completing his novel *The Strange Vanguard* while staying in the village.

Beyond the station the trail continues briefly beside the B2139, going under the railway bridge, but then a few yards beyond the bridge turns right, heading for the right bank of the river Arun.

Veering north-westwards, the WSLT soon reaches and follows the right bank of the Arun, then uses a bridge – also used by the South Downs Way – to cross to and follow the left bank of the river as far as the very picturesque village of Bury, once linked to Amberley by a ferry which closed in 1955. Bury is the first of four villages which the WSLT will visit in close succession, being followed by West Burton, Bignor and Sutton. This part of the WSLT thereby retraces, very roughly, the fictional path taken by the eponymous heroes of Sussex author Hilaire Belloc's novel *The Four Men* as part of a "secular pilgrimage" from Robertsbridge to Harting. The complete route was traced by Bob Copper, author of works including *A Song For Every Season* and *Early To Rise*, in his book *Across Sussex With Belloc* which was published in 1994 when Copper was 79. You leave the river at **Bury,** bearing left to join Church Lane (noting the superb timbered Jessamine Cottage on the left) but soon being diverted away from the road to pass immediately in front of the church of St John the Evangelist; the church, which has Norman features, is one of the most photogenic in Sussex. You return to the road and ascend to the crossroads junction with The Street. Here you turn right, up The Street, but by going straight over you reach, in roughly 100 yards on the left, the magnificent Bury House where John Galsworthy, author of *The Forsyte Saga* and Nobel Prize winner for literature in 1932, lived for 7 years up to his death in 1933. As stated however the WSLT goes northwards up The Street, passing the magnificent thatched and timbered Fogdens Barn, one of many beautiful old houses in the village. You're signed left by the thatched brick-built Kesters Cottage along a driveway then down a path to cross the A29. Beyond the crossing you proceed predominantly north-westwards across fields, interspersed with a short woodland walk, to the scattered but beautifully situated West Burton. Here you join a road heading westwards and another heading southwards through the village, and from there it's a straightforward field walk north-westwards immediately beneath the South Downs escarpment, going forward along a road to **Bignor.** On reaching the village you bear right up the main street, soon reaching a path going right which takes you the half a mile to Bignor Roman Villa. The villa's existence was discovered in July 1811 when a ploughman struck a large stone thought to have been a piscina. Beginning as a simple farmstead about 190 AD, it developed into a palatial governor's house with 65 rooms which formed a complete square around a central courtyard. It boasts one of the longest mosaics on display in Britain at 24 metres, the mosaic floors depicting the seasons and the heads of legendary figures such as the Medusa and the Ganymede. Beside Bignor's main street itself is the tremendous 15th century thatched Yeoman's House with its flint, brick and timber exterior, and continuing along the main street, veering left with it, you reach the pretty part-Norman church of the Holy Cross, guarded by an ornate lychgate and two massive yews. The 18th century novelist Charlotte Smith spent her childhood at nearby Bignor Park. The WSLT turns left at the road junction by the church, then hard right along a woodland path beside Bignor Mill. There follows a stiff field climb north-westwards to the last of this village quartet, **Sutton**. You turn right along The Street, past the White Horse pub and, a little further up, the church of St John with a nave that dates from the 11th century. The Street has a nice mixture of sandstone, brick, half-timbered and flint houses.

In order to avoid some road walking the WSLT describes a crude semi-circle, striking out north-eastwards from the road then veering north-westwards through pleasant but unremarkable farmland, skirting Winters Copse at the top of the arc, to return to the road. You follow the road briefly past the buildings of Sutton End, now overlapping with the Serpent Trail, then head north-westwards on a woodland path. You reach a road, following it briefly westwards past Crouch Farm, then continue north-westwards along a possibly muddy path that passes between Burton Mill and Chingford Ponds. Chingford Pond, to your left, is a 16th century hammer pond, built in order to power an ironworks, and together with Burton Mill Pond, to the right, is now a Site of Nature Conservation Importance, particularly noteworthy for its varieties of dragonflies in summer. You continue north-westwards past the Lodge Green complex of buildings, then at a path crossroads you turn left, parting from the Serpent Trail. Now heading south-westwards you soon reach Burton Park, and bear left onto a driveway to immediately reach the estate church which became dedicated to St Richard of Chichester in 2003. It boasts a Norman nave and chancel and, described by Pevsner as "a lovable, unrestored building, one of the mellowest in Sussex," contains a superb range of memorials for such a small church including effigies and brasses, many to the Goring family and their descendants. Taking care to fork right off the driveway and enjoying a fine view (to the left) of the main house of Burton Park, built in 1831, you continue south-westwards through the park then through a short piece of woodland, and arrive at **Duncton**. Duncton is far from being the prettiest village in West Sussex, having the misfortune to be split by the busy A285, and its 19th century church is unremarkable. However it boasts a fine 16th century pub, the Cricketers (on the A285, just yards beyond where the WSLT turns away towards Duncton Mill). At one time it was owned by the cricketer James Dean who played over 100 times for Sussex across 25 years in the 19th century, and who gave the pub its present name; it was previously called The Swan.

Having turned left alongside the A285 to follow it briefly, the WSLT turns left along the bridleway-signed road for Duncton Mill. The road veers right to pass some lakes then the early 19th century watermill and its pond – note all the large fish! The waters provide excellent fishing for rainbow trout and brown trout. Beyond the mill you go forward to a road, turning right along it and returning to the A285, then leaving it to enter woodland and ascend very steeply, zig-zagging in places. William Cobbett, the late 18th/early 19th century writer and author of *Rural Rides*, is known to have ascended this hillside, known appropriately enough as Duncton Hill, albeit using a different route. The WSLT heads initially eastwards then sharply turns south-westwards, continuing to climb, albeit not so steeply, as it proceeds through the woods. However you're then rewarded for your efforts when you emerge from the woods to enjoy a superb high-level field path providing glorious views northwards. Yet again you find yourself back at the **A285, crossing** this road and now following a driveway then a byway, This provides yet more climbing, initially going through woodland before emerging into more open land, still heading south-westwards. You continue to climb until at last you reach a junction with the South Downs Way at Crown Tegleaze (the name meaning "sheep pasture"). You're very close here to the highest point on the whole of the South Downs at 830ft. As you might expect, the views from here are magnificent, but you need to make the most of them as your walk along the ridge which follows is largely in the shade of trees. You now follow the ridge north-westwards, overlapping with the South Downs Way throughout, for just under 2 miles, then leave the South Downs

Way and turn left, south-westwards, to undertake a lengthy descent through the woods on a clear path. This is Charlton Forest, famous for the Charlton Hunt founded in the 17th century and regarded as the most fashionable hunt in the country. Roughly a mile and a half from leaving the South Downs Way you emerge from the woods and descend, again on a clear path; you cross over North Down before descending steeply to hit the valley and join a road, North Lane, turning left along it to reach **Charlton** at Charlton Road. Charlton is a pretty village of flint cottages with a popular pub, the Fox Goes Free (about 250 yards along Charlton Road to the left), which in 1915 saw the first ever formal meeting of a Women's Institute. A mile to the east of Charlton is East Dean, for many years home of the playwright Christopher Fry who was born in 1907 and died in 2005, and is best known for his play *The Lady's Not For Burning*. After crossing Charlton Road the WSLT heads westwards from Charlton and proceeds over fields through the valley of the river Lavant, a winterbourne stream that rises close to East Dean. You'll see a lot more of the Lavant as you approach Chichester. Soon you arrive at **Singleton**, the path wending its way through an area of housing and a park to reach the pretty village church, described more fully in the New Lipchis Way section. Corner Cottage in the village was the home of the children's writer Ian Serraillier whose novel *The Silver Sword* was dramatized for television in the 1960's. Coincidentally, he and Eleanor Farjeon, whom I referred to earlier in this section as having lived at Houghton near Amberley, were part of a quartet of children's poets who contributed to the anthology *The Puffin Quartet Of Poets*, published in 1958. It's at Singleton, visited by William Cobbett on the same day he (Cobbett) ascended Duncton Hill, that the WSLT meets the New Lipchis Way which has descended from Levin Down; the section devoted to the New Lipchis Way describes a detour from the Partridge inn to the nearby and fascinating Weald & Downland Open Air Museum, again more fully described in that section. To reach the Partridge, rather than turn left with the WSLT at the north-west corner of the churchyard, turn right to almost immediately arrive at the road with the Partridge facing you, and turn left for the detour. Instead, or as well, you could cross over this road and walk the 100 yards up to Singleton's charming village green with its pond and flint cottages.

Beyond Singleton the WSLT overlaps with the New Lipchis

Way, ascending steeply southwards up a clear field-edge path, then after a short road walk climbs to the topmost ring of the site of the massive Iron Age Trundle hillfort. Overlapping briefly here with the Monarch's Way and Sussex Hospices Trail as well as the New Lipchis Way, you turn left to follow the ring round, enjoying quite magnificent views to a wide coastal strip. Your route veers towards the hilltop mast, then leaves the ring and descends south-westwards to a multi-signed road/track junction (where the Sussex Hospices Trail leaves you), continuing just south of west on along a lovely hilltop path. Here the Monarch's Way leaves you, but you (and the New Lipchis Way) keep straight on, enjoying fine views towards the Kingley Vale Nature Reserve, then descend to a path crossroads. Here the New Lipchis Way goes straight on but the WSLT bears left to follow a footpath southwards to East Lavant; it's a nice grassy path in the valley of the river Lavant. In due course you reach Sheepwash Lane, crossing the river. Rising at East Dean and emptying into Chichester Harbour, it's a remarkable river, celebrated in book form by Ken Newbury; in drier periods it's liable to be waterless but after concerted heavy winter rains it can be spectacular and indeed caused major disruption when it burst its banks during exceptional rainfall in 1994. When it is in full flow but behaving itself, it hugely enhances the beauty of the surroundings, complemented as it is by lovely old flint bridges.

You follow Sheepwash Lane beside the pretty **East Lavant** village green then turn left to cross the river again and pass the red-brick church of St Mary, which contains a 12th century nave and west doorway and impressive 17th century brick tower. More or less opposite the church path the WSLT bears right along Fordwater Road briefly (although by detouring straight on here for 100 yards or so you reach the popular Royal Oak inn). Having joined Fordwater Road you soon leave it, bearing right, southwards towards Chichester, but by carrying straight on along the road for just over a mile and turning left at the roundabout, you reach in roughly 400 yards the entrance to Goodwood House. The house is late 17th century in origin, but was substantially enlarged during the following century and boasts a magnificent interior containing art works by van Dyck, Canaletto and Stubbs. Among the best rooms are the front hall, with a fine collection of Stubbs' paintings, the music room with its fireplace by William Kent, and the wonderfully restored Egyptian dining room with furniture of mahogany and ebony. It's best to check before you make this detour that the house is open: it's an awfully long way to detour – nearly 4 miles' round trip, including the walk up the driveway from the road – only to find you can't get in!

The WSLT however proceeds Chichester-wards from Fordwater Road as stated, to follow a succession of fields, crossing the river Lavant for the final time, and after a short field-edge path walk you enter Summersdale, a suburb of Chichester, your arrival here being an indication of your nearness to the end of the walk. You follow a continuation of Fordwater Road southwards, going forward down Summersdale Road. The WSLT then kinks left and right to wend pleasantly on southwards through a park, then kinks right and left, over College Lane and down through Oaklands Park between the rugby fields and the buildings, to the Chichester Festival Theatre complex. The theatre was opened in 1962 and has seen a huge number of very famous faces perform there including Sir Laurence Olivier, Sir Peter Ustinov and Dame Maggie Smith. You walk between the main theatre and its smaller sister the Minerva Theatre then having negotiated a large car park and ring road system you enter North Street, now in the heart of Chichester. Having followed North Street briefly you bear right to walk along the city walls, and arrive at West Street. Here you turn left, heading eastwards along West Street to the cathedral, which is described more fully, as are all the historic highlights of the city, in the Sussex Hospices Trail section. The WSLT turns right just before the bell tower to follow the walkway past the cathedral entrance, turning left to proceed to and enter the cloister and then right and right again down St Richard's Walk to Canon Lane, turning left here to reach South Street. Here the trail officially ends, although there are no signs to tell you so. To reach **Chichester Station**, turn right down South Street and at its end carry straight on across Avenue de Chartres and along Stockbridge Road. A circular tour of the historic centre of Chichester, starting and finishing at the station, and including the walls and cathedral precinct – both already of course visited by the WSLT – is given at the start of the Sussex Hospices Trail section.

It is fitting that the WSLT should end in Chichester, for the city has a large number of literary connections. It has (admittedly rather tenuous) links with two particularly famous writers: William

Blake was tried here for sedition in 1804 in the Guildhall in Priory Park, and John Keats began writing his poem *The Eve Of St Agnes* in Chichester in 1819. The poet and biographer William Hayley was born in Chichester in 1745 and spent a good deal of his life in the locality, while the grammarian John Bullokar (credited with the first book of grammar to be published in England) lived in Chichester in the 16th century and his lexicographer son William was born there. Canon Victor Whitechurch, a prolific novelist, was born in Chichester in 1864 and studied at the theological college there, while the 18th century poet William Collins, who has a marble memorial in Chichester Cathedral, was born in the city. Other literary figures associated with Chichester are Anna Sewell who wrote *Black Beauty*, and whose father was a bank manager here at the time of the Crimean War; Daniel Defoe, who wrote *Robinson Crusoe*, visited both Chichester and the area around Goodwood; and there is evidence of visits to Chichester by traveller and writer Celia Fiennes in around 1694, the naturalist W.H. Hudson some two centuries later, and Samuel Johnson in the late 18th century. And we should not forget the contemporary and highly successful novelist Kate Mosse who was born in the city and raised in Fishbourne, just outside it. But, as stated, to see where arguably the most famous authors with West Sussex connections, William Blake and H.G. Wells, lived, it's another day and another walk.

GOOD TO KNOW

Start: Horsham Station. Finish: Chichester Station.

Total mileage: 54.5.

Difficulty: Moderate, one or two strenuous climbs.

Stages: A281 5.5, Slinfold (RAB) 7, Itchingfield for Christ's Hospital Station (*) 10.25, Barns Green (RB) 11.5, Blue Idol 15, Nutbourne (R) for Pulborough (*RAB) 20.5, Cootham (R) for Storrington (RAB) 24.75, Amberley (RA) 28, Amberley Station (*) 29, Bury (RA) 31.5, Bignor (RA) 34, Sutton (RA) 35, Duncton (RAB) 38, A285 crossing 39.5, Charlton (RB) 46.5, Singleton (RAB) 47, East Lavant (RB) 51, Chichester Station (*RAB) 54.5. OS 134, 121, OL8.

D1 NOTE: THIS IS A SUBSTANTIAL DETOUR. *Head just south of east along the footpath from Gay Street as stated and descend, then ascend through an area of vineyard and continue in the same direction until the path T-junction at the end. Here turn right and descend to the road, turning left along it to enter West Chiltington. At the shop just past the pub, turn right down Church Street, past the church of St Mary; veer sharp left with the tarmac along Juggs Lane and at the end of Juggs Lane, go left along Sinnocks. Opposite the complex of buildings reached in some 140 yards on the left, turn right along a signed track. At the T-junction with a bridleway at the end, just beyond the trees, turn right along the right-hand field edge, then very shortly bear left as signed along a clear bridleway; this is superb open walking with tremendous views to the South Downs. Go forward through a gate and along a clear path through the trees. At the end turn left to reach the buildings of Town House Farm, veering right onto the farm approach road and going forward to the B2139 (Duke's Hill). Cross more or less straight over, climbing the steps to a field. Walk across it as signed then in obedience to the sign cross into the next field and immediately turn right to follow the right-hand field edge. At the end you enter trees, briefly emerging into another field with rougher grass, again following the right-hand field edge. At the path T-junction at the end, turn right onto a track and follow it as it veers left, downhill to reach the road at the little green signed Thakeham Halt. Turn right along the road for a few yards then at the junction bear left. Follow the lane down then just beyond the cattle grid at a signed path crossroads turn left (beyond the hedge) along a path that proceeds pleasantly north-eastwards through pasture, veering right as signed to descend to a footbridge. Now bear left up to Mill Copse and gently right to ascend through the copse and emerge to follow a right-hand field edge. The views northwards are magnificent, stretching to Leith Hill in Surrey on a clear day. You drop down to a dirt track and turn right to follow it to Warminghurst, passing Warminghurst House and going forward to the church of the Holy Sepulchre. Retrace roughly 50 yards from the church and now turn left, westwards, along a lovely green track. You veer gently right with the track, going forward along a lane past the fine Thakeham Place to return to Thakeham. This time go straight on up Thakeham's main street, past the White Lion pub (the last refreshment opportunity on this detour, with still just over 2 miles to go) and all the way to the B2139.*

Turn right along the B2139 then in 220 yards left as path-signed to retrace through the Town House Farm complex, veering left as signed and then shortly right, still retracing. You enter the trees, but this time in 140 yards fork left along a narrow signed path. Beware stinging nettles! You emerge from the trees and now head very pleasantly downhill, just north of west, aiming for the buildings of Southlands Farm straight ahead. As you reach the farm buildings you need to veer left, then right, then left again through the complex before veering right along a lane that brings you to a road. Cross straight over, entering a mini-industrial estate, heading in the same direction and soon reassured by a path arrow. This directs you alongside a large greenhouse. You're then signed left along a narrow grassy path and then follow round the edge of another area of vineyard, taking care to exit the field – don't follow it round to the right – and reaching a T-junction of paths. Here turn right uphill, and at the next signed path junction turn left along a clear path just north of west, the church at West Chiltington clearly visible to your right. At the path T-junction you bear left then almost immediately right, still heading just north of west, descending to pass the windmill and arrive at Mill Road. Turn right along it then almost immediately left along Stream Lane, ignoring the bridleway going north from the junction. In just a few yards along Stream Lane bear right up a half-hidden signed path through the trees, emerging into what feels like a private garden! Keeping in the same direction, follow the right-hand edge of the green area keeping the tennis court immediately to your right, and aiming for a footpath sign beyond. At the sign turn right along a field edge, arriving at another area of vineyard. Veer left (north-westwards) here as signed, keeping the vines to your right, and drop down to the metalled Gay Street. Turn right and shortly reach TQ082187 at the bottom of the steps coming down from point (D), turning left here to rejoin the WSLT. (Total detour 6 miles)

V1 Instead of turning left to pass round the side of the Mill House, remain on the wide track, keeping the garage to your right, then turn left to pass between the site of the old mill and millpond. You go on past Ebbsworth, which is to your right, and veer gently left to reach the top of Nutbourne's main street. Turn left to follow it downhill, soon passing the Rising Sun pub which is on your right and being reunited with the WSLT soon coming in from the left. (Negligible extra mileage)

V2 Turn right along Golf Club Lane as stated to reach the A283. Bear left alongside it for just under a quarter of a mile then turn right along Church Lane to view the delightful unspoilt church of Wiggonholt. Opposite the church notice board at the end of the metalled lane, turn left over a stile to join a grassy path downhill. Having reached the valley bottom you then ascend to the Pulborough Brooks RSPB reserve car park; the visitor centre is just to the right. Following the signage, go straight on then right along a lovely woodland path, reaching a T-junction with a bridleway. Turn right here and follow a clear wide path to its end at Greatham Street. Here you've a choice. The shorter route goes straight over down Rackham Street for a mile, past Sparrite Farm, to reach a gateway and driveway for Parham House, the WSLT coming to meet you along this road. However, to visit Greatham Church, turn right along Greatham Street until you reach, in just under a mile, a metalled gate and signed footpath to the right. This takes you across rough grass to the beautiful unrestored Greatham Church and adjoining manor house. (The best views of the manor are from a path going left just before the churchyard, but this isn't a public right of way.) Retrace back down the road for some 550 yards, then at Washingham, at the edge of the trees, turn right along a signed bridleway, initially a driveway then veering left and becoming rougher. The bridleway reaches Rackham Street and you're here reunited with the shorter route. You now turn right and proceed to the Parham House gateway/driveway as described above, meeting the WSLT here. The through route goes straight on along the road. However if you want to visit Parham House turn left here and continue (effectively walking the reverse way along the WSLT) until you meet the public access road for the house. (The straight variation saves 1.25 miles but the Greatham mini-variation adds 750 yards, the backtrack to Parham 1.5 miles.)

18 WEY SOUTH PATH

The Wey South Path (WSP), created in the early 1970's by one Aeneas Mackintosh, is certainly the closest any of the big inland walks of Sussex comes to being a truly waterside walk. It centres on the Wey & Arun Canal, and though other waterways are visited en route, the canal is very much the main attraction. Besides the canal it also follows sections of the river Arun and the river Wey, although the Wey-side walking, bringing the WSP to an end in Guildford, is in Surrey and outside the scope of this book (albeit we will in fact be following the WSP as far as Cranleigh, just over the border into Surrey). Being essentially lowland in character, it's certainly not the most exciting of the Great Walks of Sussex, and there are one or two sections that may seem a little ordinary in comparison with, say, the South Downs Way, but it's a delightfully peaceful and relaxing walk in unspoilt countryside, and thanks to the restoration work on the canal sections, it's a great chance to revisit an important aspect of our industrial heritage. The first part of the walk stays close to the Arun, one of the classic rivers of Sussex, rising close to Horsham and meandering its way to the sea via Pulborough, Amberley and of course the lovely town of Arundel. Then in due course you'll reach the Wey & Arun Canal, consisting of two parts, the northern part of the Arun Navigation and the Wey & Arun Junction Canal, and we'll learn more about it, and the work of the Wey & Arun Canal Trust in restoring both the canal and its paraphernalia, as we go. The route is generally very well waymarked and easy to follow, and most walkers will easily complete the walk from the start of the route, near Amberley, to Cranleigh in two days. It should be noted that there is a substantial overlap between the WSP and the Sussex Hospices Trail from Amberley all the way to just short of the A272 crossing at Newbridge (albeit my description of the overlapping part in the Sussex Hospices Trail section is from the reverse direction) so if some of this walk seems familiar you'll realise why!

It's not totally clear from OS mapping or signage where the WSP really starts, but it seems convenient to start at **Amberley Station** and follow beside the B2139 to meet the South Downs Way, then overlap with it to turn right off the road and head just north of east

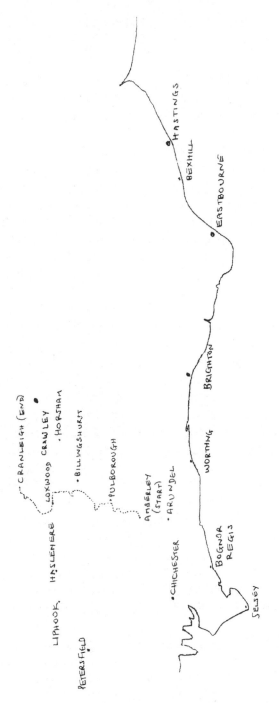

up another road, High Titten, away from the valley. At the top –
where the official guidebook states the WSP should actually start
– you leave the South Downs Way and promptly bear left down
Mill Lane, crossing the B2139 again! You pass through **Amberley**,
a quite delightful village described more fully in the West Sussex
Literary Trail section; from the B2139 crossing you need to walk
straight up the High Street (detouring left up Church Street for
Amberley's best bits) past the tea room and shop to the old pub at
the far north end of the village, turning left (west) along Hog Lane,
then as this lane veers left you bear right to head northwards out of
the village. You're now properly on your way.

The WSP, now overlapping with the Sussex Hospices Trail (as it
will do all the way to just short of Newbridge), proceeds away from
Amberley by following a wide track northwards (your predominant
direction of travel as far as Greatham Bridge) through the fields
of the Arun valley, the river Arun close by to your left and lovely
views across the valley towards the spire of the church at Bury. This
area, known as Amberley Wild Brooks, is used as a flood plain
for the Arun, being crossed by numerous drainage ditches, and is
home to a large number of wetland species of plants and birds. You
enter an area of much thicker vegetation, the path narrower and
boardwalked in places, but always clear, continuing in the same
northerly direction. I walked this section on one of the hottest July
days on record in Sussex, and there was something soothing and
refreshing about this lush wetland landscape. But in winter after
sustained and heavy rainfall, you can suddenly feel quite vulnerable
in this remote-feeling landscape with so much water around you,
and your boots are unlikely to stay dry! You emerge from the
thicker vegetation and follow firstly a field-edge path, then a track
past houses and after that a grassy path beside the river Arun to
reach a junction with a road at Greatham Bridge. This is one of
the most impressive bridge crossings of the Arun; it was originally
built around 1294, was reconstructed five hundred years later and
was an important strategic point during the English Civil War. The
WSP turns left along the road over the bridge and follows the road
briefly westwards, then bears right onto a narrow but clear path
north-eastwards through the trees, towards the busy A29. As you
approach the main road, look to the right to see the fine farmhouse
of Hardham Priory. The Priory, a small house of Augustinian

canons, was founded in 1248 and dissolved in 1534, and the little that remains – just the walls of the refectory and the roofless Chapter House – is not open to the public. The modern farmhouse, into which the refectory has been incorporated, is a Grade I listed building. You then shortly arrive at the A29 which the WSP crosses and continues over the railway. However by turning right alongside the A29, following it for just under half a mile and forking right along the metalled road by the sign for Moseley's Barn you reach the lovely church at Hardham, with its superb wall paintings that date back to 1100. You can either retrace to where you left the WSP, or, for a short cut back to it, having retraced your steps to the A29, crossed over and turned left along the pavement, you take the first signed right turn to join the waterworks access road, almost immediately crossing the railway and going forward to be met by the WSP 80 yards or so beyond the railway. If you do the detour but with a "short cut" back to the WSP it'll add about half a mile to your journey; the straight out-and-back detour will add 1.25 miles.

As stated, though, the WSP, heading north-westwards (the predominant direction of travel as far as Stopham) crosses straight over the A29 onto a path which soon goes over the extant Arun valley railway (linking Horsham with Bognor Regis and Chichester) and crosses over a meadow to reach the course of the former Pulborough-Petworth-Petersfield railway, described more fully in the Serpent Trail section. The WSP turns right to follow the old trackbed briefly, crossing the site of the so-called Hardham Tunnel which was part of a now long defunct extension of the Arun Navigation canal; the tunnel was 375 yards long and had an internal height of just 13ft. Just before reaching the extant railway the WSP leaves the old railway and proceeds along tracks to reach and turn left along a road near the Hardham waterworks (now reunited with the short cut route from the church at Hardham), going forward past the pumping station to cross the West Sussex river Rother, the longest and widest river in West Sussex which doesn't flow into the sea. In fact it ends its journey at its confluence with the Arun only a mile or so to the east of this point. There's a pleasant meadow walk and a crossing of the Arun beside an old aqueduct, and it's a short hop beyond there to Stopham with its impressive bridge over the Arun dating back to 1403, and White Hart pub, a lovely place to stop especially on a hot day. By the pub you join a signed bridleway which must be one of the shortest such paths in the country, taking you almost immediately to the A283. The WSP crosses the A283 and proceeds north-eastwards along a lovely woodland-edge path high above the Arun, with superb views from here to the South Downs escarpment, then after leaving the woods your route descends to a signed path junction immediately north of Park Farm. The WSP turns left and descends along a muddy farm lane to **Coombelands Lane.** However by going straight on eastwards along a signed path you could access the amenities of **Pulborough** by means of a detour D1, the detour then returning you to the WSP at the junction of the muddy farm lane with Coombelands Lane. Pulborough, although offering refreshment and rail services, isn't a hugely interesting place; its best secular buildings are around the A29 crossing immediately east of the church of St Mary which itself boasts a particularly fine nave and early 15th century tower.

The WSP, on reaching Coombelands Lane, now continues either along or parallel with it, heading northwards. This is very horsey country, with gallops on both sides and racing stables in the main Coombelands complex on your left. You climb steadily, enjoying great views back to Pulborough, then descend to the hamlet of Pickhurst; on your descent there's a fine view ahead to the distinctive castellated octagonal tower of the hilltop Toat Monument, 40ft high and built in 1823 as a memorial to a Samual Drinkald who, poor fellow, died as a result of falling from his horse. Don't bother to try detouring to it as there's no public access. From Pickhurst you branch off north-westwards along a lane towards Sheepwash, then veer northwards and soon westwards at a T-junction of paths to cross Pallingham Bridge, restored by the Wey & Arun Canal Trust and opened in 1976. It was hereabouts that a canal route known as the northern part of the Arun Navigation opened in 1787, connecting Pallingham with Newbridge further north, and becoming part of what was to be the complete Wey & Arun Canal. The area just south of Pallingham Bridge was known as Pallingham Docks and created for the building and repair of barges. You continue westwards and cross the Arun, then pass the buildings of Pallingham Quay Farm; I walked this section on a winter's day after a comparatively dry January but it had rained hard the day before and as I passed the farm buildings I found myself almost knee-deep in flood water. Sometimes wellies, which I was fortunate to have on then, can be the best option. Beyond the farm you temporarily leave the valley, climbing westwards into woodland along a track then, veering north-eastwards, descending via a road to…return to the valley! The explanation is simple: the track leading upstream from Pallingham Quay Farm to Pallingham Manor Farm is private and there are no rights of way available, hence a semi-circular negotiation of this obstruction.

Once normal valley service is resumed, you leave the road at **Westland** and it's most pleasant field walking initially eastwards, veering north-eastwards past the buildings of Furnacepond – near which is the site of an iron works – and crossing in close succession Pallingham Lane, the course of the old canal, and the Arun. The surroundings are totally unspoilt, and there are lovely views back to the wooded hills you've just negotiated. You pick your way through a complex of barns beyond which you soon reach, and cross, Haybarn Bridge, installed by the Wey & Arun Canal Trust in 2004/05 but formerly in use on the Leeds & Liverpool Canal. Now you begin what will be the chief characteristic of the walk from now on – canalside walking – as, proceeding north-eastwards, you join and follow the canal's left bank, switching to the right bank over a fine restored bridge, and soon reaching Lording's Lock. This is one of 26 locks that were originally built on the Wey & Arun Canal, and a number of them, this being one, have been restored by volunteers of the Wey & Arun Canal Trust since 1970. This part of the canal is all the more interesting because close by Lording's Lock is the site of an aqueduct with waterwheel built into it. Your route follows the course of the aqueduct and you can admire the waterwheel which is in fact a 21st century reconstruction by Winston Harwood. The surroundings are quite unspoilt and timeless and it's easy to imagine the days when the canal was fully operational and barges would be negotiating this stretch of water.

Beyond the lock you leave the canal, crossing a stile in trees and following clear paths north-eastwards through the meadows, the river Arun never very far away on your right, and indeed there's one very pleasant interlude in which you walk beside the river Arun in the shade of trees. Be aware, however, that the Arun may flood after sustained rainfall and you may have to be somewhat creative in negotiating the flood waters! Roughly one mile beyond Lording's Lock, pretty much level with the splendid **Guildenhurst Manor** above you to your right, you reach a signed **path crossroads** – the only such crossroads between the lock and the A272 crossing at Newbridge. This marks the end of the overlap of the WSP with the Sussex Hospices Trail, the WSP going straight on north-eastwards and the Sussex Hospices Trail bearing right. If you wish to visit **Billingshurst,** and/or access the station there, turn right with the Sussex Hospices Trail to begin a <u>detour D2</u>. Billingshurst isn't the most attractive town in Sussex, but it has plenty of shops and cafes for the hungry walker, and given the total absence of amenities between Pulborough and this point, a detour may be more than welcome! The town's hillside church of St Mary boasts a prominent spire and features dating from the 13th century; adjacent to the church is the lovely redbrick Churchgate Cottage; and there's a delightful row of cottages leading from the church to the main street including Botterels and the beautiful timbered Tithe Cottage.

However as stated the WSP goes over the path crossroads, carrying on through the meadow, veering to the right of Guildenhurst Farm as signed but keeping the same general direction and going forward to reaching the A272 at Newbridge. It was at Newbridge that the so-called Wey & Arun Junction Canal, which ran as far as Shalford near Guildford in Surrey, opened in 1816, thereby forming a complete canal link between the rivers Wey and Arun. The complete Wey & Arun Canal saw little freight traffic and was abandoned in 1871 – although there is a record of a barge travelling between Pallingham and Newbridge in 1888 – but since 1970 the Wey & Arun Canal Trust have worked hard to restore parts of the canal to navigable standard and the aim is that one day it should all be navigable once more. Work is continuing at the time of writing and as you proceed you may see a good deal more fully restored sections of canal than I saw when I did the WSP walk!

The WSP crosses over the A272 and continues very pleasantly indeed northwards along a path which follows the canal for about a mile. You pass the Northlands Lift Bridge, provided by the Wey & Arun Canal Trust in 1979/80, and arrive at a crossing bridleway just short of pylons at the impressive Rowner Lock; this was the scene of the Wey & Arun Canal Trust's first working party in March 1971, the lock being restored by the Trust between then and 1982. Beyond Rowner Lock the WSP continues northwards beside the canal as far as the brick Loves Bridge, rebuilt by the Trust in the mid-1970's.

This is a delightfully peaceful and timeless spot, and on a fine day will provide one of the highlights of the whole walk. Here the WSP sadly leaves the canal, heading westwards, crossing the bridge and ascending from the canal by means of a pretty woodland path, then climbing through fields past Loves Farm. From here you descend south-westwards by way of a track to the B2133 at Newpound Common, turning right to walk north-westwards alongside this road. It's not a hugely enjoyable interlude. Thankfully on a sharp left bend you're able to join a parallel bridleway, then strike out north-eastwards through woodlands. Having emerged from the woods, you then enjoy pleasant and straightforward farmland walking, predominantly northwards, along farm lanes and footpaths past the extensive Malham Farm complex. You proceed northwards from Malham Farm through or beside fields, and after pausing to enjoy superb views back the way you came, you then enter further woods that take you to the somewhat unglamorous sounding Drungewick Lane. The WSP turns right along the lane, following it for about half a mile and arriving back at the canal.

Just before the bridge crossing, rebuilt in 2000/01, you turn left along the towpath which you'll follow westwards (but with some long meanders) all the way to Loxwood, and you'll see what a tremendous restoration job has been done in respect of this part of the canal. This is a beautiful walk of about a mile and a half, the towpath superbly maintained throughout, the canal waters and mainly wooded scenery quite delightful and unspoilt. You soon pass the stunning Drungewick Aqueduct, rebuilt in 2002, and the walk beyond the aqueduct passes two locks, Baldwin's Knob Lock and then Brewhurst Lock, again beautifully restored and in delightful settings, as well as fine brick bridges over the canal. This section is navigable so you may well see some narrow boats and indeed match them for speed! A little before Brewhurst Lock, it's worth detouring left to the lovely white weatherboarded Brewhurst Mill – a water-powered corn mill originally built in the 18th century – and the superb tile-hung/timber-framed buildings of Brewhurst. Returning to the towpath, not far beyond the second lock you reach the excellent canal visitor centre and, immediately beyond, the **Onslow Arms**. This was built as a coaching inn in the early 17th century, and today is an obvious and ideal place for refreshment. After your drink you could, at weekends and on bank holidays, enjoy a canal boat trip if you fancy enjoying the canal in comfort! Even if you decide against that, you can enjoy the sight of the narrow boats parked up on the water. The village of **Loxwood**, which boasts some fine tile-hung and timber-framed houses as well as a charming pond, is reached in just under half a mile, most pleasantly by going up the slipway and turning right beside the B2133, continuing over the canal, forking very shortly right up the signed footpath, going forward to Station Road, bearing left along Station Road, then at the end turning left alongside the B2133 to return to the WSP. The total round trip is just over half a mile. However the WSP uses a tunnel under the B2133 to continue its journey. This tunnel is arguably the biggest achievement of the Wey & Arun Canal Trust; there was insufficient height between the canal and the road crossing to enable boats to proceed, and so the canal was actually lowered here and a brand new tunnel built. This necessitated the building of a further lock immediately beyond the road crossing. This was done in 2005/06 and the tunnel was opened in 2009.

The WSP continues westwards beyond the Onslow Arms along the canal's left bank past the new lock referred to above. It's now a very easy walk along the bank, your path veering right, north-westwards, and passing two more locks. Roughly a mile and a half from Loxwood you cross the Sussex Border Path and, keeping the canal to your right, you continue through the woods, entering Surrey 250 yards or so beyond the Sussex Border Path crossing. It's hardly convenient or practicable to stop your walk here; you could of course retrace your steps to Loxwood for a lift or taxi (there being no buses to speak of) or you could join the Sussex Border Path and follow it to Rudgwick, 3.5 miles to the east, to pick up a bus to Guildford or Horsham. I recommend you do neither of these things but continue along the WSP for a further 7 miles as far as Cranleigh, a satisfying place to finish and again offering good public transport. To do this, keep on the path through the woods, the canal to your right; you cross over a road then, maintaining a north-westerly course, enter the delightful Sidney Wood, once a base for charcoal burners and home to a flourishing glass industry. You follow an obvious forest track for just under half a mile, and it's then vitally important not to miss a right turn onto another good path which follows beside the canal course in the woods. It's lovely walking, with a very remote and peaceful feel, your path following the meanders of the canal with two or three quite pronounced bends. At length, now veering in a predominantly north-easterly direction – which you'll maintain much of the rest of the way – you leave the course of the canal to follow a path and then a metalled track through the woods to the Dunsfold-Alfold road. There's then a rather dull road walk to Laker's Green, where at least there's the consolation of the **Three Compasses** pub; you're walking roughly parallel with the canal but some distance from it.

Beyond the Three Compasses you continue north-eastwards along a narrow grassy path then forward along a good clear field path which at the end meets and goes parallel with, and up close to, the canal. You cross the busy A281, joining and following Alfold Road. Just beyond the Holdhurst Farm turning on the right, the WSP bears left along a lane bringing you to the superb timber-framed Great Garsons from which it's a rather fiddly field walk westwards returning you to the canal. Once there, you're able to bear right along the right bank of the canal for roughly a quarter of a mile; it's most pleasant walking, with woodland to your right. As the woods relent you then leave the canal for the final time, striking out north-eastwards round the near side of Uttworth Manor and then heading eastwards along a lane returning you to Alfold Road. You turn left to follow this again briefly as far as the start of an industrial estate that's to your left. At this point we leave the WSP. The WSP will shortly bear left and return to the canal, then will continue close to the canal or the river Wey as far as Guildford. However for Cranleigh, turn right at a gateway, almost opposite the entrance to the industrial estate, along a lovely field path which heads eastwards past the buildings of Knowle Park above you to the right. In half a mile you reach Knowle Lane; turn left up the lane, shortly crossing the Downs Link, and soon arriving at **Cranleigh High Street**.

GOOD TO KNOW
Start: Amberley Station. Finish: Cranleigh High Street.
Total mileage: 27.5.
Difficulty: Easy.
Stages: Amberley (RA) 1, Coombelands Lane for Pulborough (*RAB) 6, Westland 9, Guildenhurst Manor path crossroads for Billinghurst (*RAB) 12.5, A272 13, Onslow Arms (R) for

Loxwood (R) 19, Three Compasses (R) 24, Cranleigh High Street (RAB) 27.5.
OS OL10, OL34.

D1 Having joined the signed path eastwards, follow it, enjoying excellent views to the South Downs, then descending with it to Coombelands Lane. Turn right along it, soon passing the splendid 15th century Old Place which is to the left, and crossing the railway bridge. To reach Pulborough Station turn right along the path immediately beyond the bridge, descending along the path to soon arrive at the station. The centre of Pulborough is reached by then walking down the slip road to the A283 Station Road, turning left alongside it to a roundabout, crossing straight over and continuing eastwards along Lower Street. To reach the centre of Pulborough avoiding the station, continue beyond the aforementioned railway bridge along what was Coombelands Lane and becomes Church Place, soon passing the church of St Mary and crossing straight over the A29. Beyond the crossing walk eastwards along Old Rectory Lane, soon arriving at a green open space to the right. In 140 yards beyond the A29 crossing, bear right along a metalled path which descends across the green space to reach Lower Street (A283) opposite Allfreys Wharf (the marker should you wish to walk back this way), turning left along it to reach Pulborough's village centre. To access the station from the centre, follow Lower Street westwards, passing the spot where you joined it; cross the A29 and follow Station Road westwards, then bear right up the slip road just before the railway bridge. Finally, to return to the WSP from the station, take the footpath running north-eastwards parallel with the railway, starting on the far side of the bike racks, to arrive back at Coombelands Lane. Whichever route you've used to get back to Coombelands Lane, retrace westwards, passing the point at which you joined it, picking up the WSP as the lane bends very sharply right. (Detour to Pulborough centre only: total 1.75 miles. Detour to Pulborough and then back via station (or vice versa!): total 2 miles. Detour to Pulborough Station only: total 1.25 miles.)

D2 Having turned right at the crossroads, follow the signed path over the meadow across the Arun, then ascend the hillside on the obvious signed path, keeping Guildenhurst Manor to the right. You then head for and join the manor approach road, turning left along it and arriving at the B2133. Turn left alongside it past the Limeburners pub then just before the T-junction with the A272 turn right along the footpath which then proceeds alongside the A272. Keep to the footpath which then veers a little to the right of the A272, beside a metalled road with houses to the right. Go forward to walk alongside Newbridge Road East, then veer just to the left of the dead end to cross a footbridge over the A29. Keep on the path, following the road ahead as it bends gently left and keep beside it to the roundabout by a superstore. Turn right at this roundabout and walk alongside what is the A272 West Street. At its end you can access Billingshurst town centre by going left, north-eastwards, up the High Street. The church of St Mary and Churchgate Cottage adjoining it can be reached by bearing right up a walkway some 275 yards up High Street, and returning from the church you can fork right to pass Botterels and Tithe Cottage, this fork bringing you back to High Street. However, to get to the station (coming from West Street), at the junction of West Street and High Street turn right, south-westwards, along Alicks Hill, then in just under 200 yards turn left down Station Road, the station just under half a mile down the hill. To return to the WSP, rather than simply retrace your steps (although that is an option) I recommend you use the Sussex Hospices Trail route via Myrtle Lane, or, if you've not detoured to the town centre, the Sussex Hospices Trail route variation via the church of St Mary. Please refer to the Sussex Hospices Trail section for the relevant instructions. (Straight detour to Billingshurst centre only: total 4.5 miles. Straight detour to station only: total 5 miles. Walk from Billingshurst centre to station: 0.75 miles. Round trip incorporating town centre and station using recommended route: total 5 miles.)

19 WORTH WAY/FOREST WAY

A gain here we have two paths for the price of one. The Worth Way and Forest Way not only join up but their nature and character are so similar that it makes sense to marry them up to form a single "Great Walk." (I abbreviate the single walk to WFW below.) That said, there's no reason why you shouldn't split them at East Grinstead where one ends and the other starts.

This is another name route in Sussex, like the Downs Link and the Cuckoo Trail, where the course of old railway lines has been used to create a really fine walk. But although you shouldn't expect any hill climbing or hilltop panoramas, there are some delightful views all the way along the route. The Worth Way section traces the old line that linked Three Bridges with East Grinstead, and the Forest Way follows the course of a line that proceeded from East Grinstead to Tunbridge Wells, although, just to confuse, I need to add that the Forest Way ends at Groombridge, some way short of Tunbridge Wells. The section of old railway between Three Bridges and East Grinstead was built by the East Grinstead Railway Company and opened on 9th July 1855; the London, Brighton & South Coast Railway operated it and duly acquired it from the East Grinstead Railway Company. It was then local enterprise, in the form of the East Grinstead, Groombridge & Tunbridge Wells Railway Company that led to what was effectively the extension of the line on to Tunbridge Wells which opened on 1st October 1866. There had been a number of delays in the commencement of services on the line, and the press eventually got so tired of waiting that they failed to report the actual opening! In 1890 there were 5 through services between Three Bridges and Tunbridge Wells each weekday (with 2 on Sundays), plus a couple of trains from Three Bridges to East Grinstead with the possibility of going forward to Tunbridge Wells on a train leaving 40-45 minutes later. However, the line grew in popularity and usage, and by 1955, the section of line between Three Bridges and East Grinstead had 17 weekly and 10 Sunday return journeys. Being a cross-country connection or lateral line, not a route in and out of London, it was an obvious candidate for Dr Beeching's hit list, and the part of the route between Three Bridges and Groombridge closed on 1st January 1967. The remainder of the

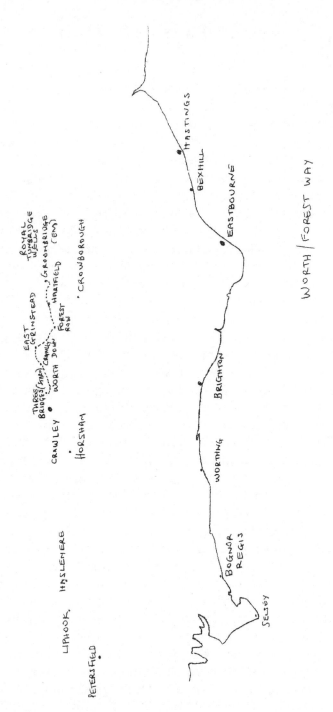

line, to Tunbridge Wells, survived until July 1985 when it was closed but then reopened as part of the Spa Valley Railway. Ironically East Grinstead was Dr Beeching's home town for many years and on what was the old line there is now a street in East Grinstead called Beeching Way!

The start of the Worth Way part of the WFW is very easily accessed from **Three Bridges Station**, by turning right out of the station exit, right again at the A2220 to pass under the railway, immediately right up Station Hill (which becomes Billinton Drive), and then left as signed in just over a quarter of a mile from where you joined Station Hill. You begin by following a section of old line south-eastwards, veering just north of east, in distinctly suburban surroundings, then roughly three quarters of a mile after joining the WFW off Billinton Drive you pass under the B2036 Balcombe Road. Just beyond the B2036 overbridge you turn hard right, off the old line, following route 21, signed to East Grinstead and Worth. You ascend gently then turn hard left to follow parallel with and above the old line, before bearing right (southwards) along Church Road. In about 375 yards you turn left, eastwards, along a road actually called Worth Way to reach one of the architectural highlights of the whole route, the church of St Nicholas, Worth. Founded by Edward the Confessor, it's one of the finest surviving Saxon churches in England; moreover, the chancel arch at 22ft high and 14ft wide is one of the largest Saxon arches in the country. Entering the church at the west door, look out for two blocked-in Saxon arches opposite each other facing the nave. They were said to be for knights on horseback to ride through and pay their respects without dismounting! You continue eastwards on what is an excellent footpath over the M23 then north-eastwards past Worth Lodge Farm to arrive at Turners Hill Road. Just before the road there's a stile from which there's a possible <u>detour D1</u> to Worth Abbey, a modern Benedictine community of Catholic monks, the Abbey church being built in the 1960's. Also on the complex is a magnificent grey-stone Tudor-style country house, built in the 1860's and known as Paddockhurst; after the owner's death in 1927 the site was acquired by monks from Somerset who established a school here. The house remains a school today, known as Worth School. There are tremendous views from the grounds to the surrounding countryside and the complex as a whole is a fascinating mix of old and new. The trail heads very briefly northwards beside Turners Hill Road, then heads eastwards away from it, back on the course of the old railway, and the going is now delightfully rural. In less than a mile you cross Wallage Lane and pass the former station of Rowfant. The site of the station seems quite remote, and you may wonder why it is here at all. The answer is that it was opened in the days when land was given to a new railway company in return for the provision of a station on the estate. The land through which the line passed here was given by an American fur trader named Curtis Miranda Lampson and the station was given to Lampson in return, including a shelter for Lampson's coachmen! It's a short detour, roughly 300 yards each way, to the left along Wallage Lane to Rowfant House, described in the Sussex Border Path section, and indeed if you wanted to "short cut" back from Rowfant House to the WFW, avoiding doing two sides of a triangle (saving all of 400 yards!), you could follow Sussex Border Path signage from the house to rejoin the Worth Way with which the Sussex Border Path overlaps as far as Crawley Down. From Wallage Lane to Crawley Down the going is straightforward and really delightful, the route remaining either on or immediately next to the course of the old line throughout. Shortly you arrive in **Crawley Down** which despite its name is some distance from the modern town of Crawley and there is no downland to speak of! It may be welcome for walkers because of its parade of shops and its very frequent buses on the East Grinstead-Crawley route. There was another station on the old line here, known as Grange Road For Crawley Down And Turners Hill – quite a mouthful for station announcers in days gone by – which opened in 1860, but there's no trace of it left today.

You now part from the Sussex Border Path and have a bit of a suburban trudge. You follow Burleigh Way north-eastwards from the village centre, bearing right to follow Woodland Drive briefly before heading left, just north of east along Hazel Way. You then fork right along Cob Close, going forward along a footpath that in turn goes forward to rejoin the course of the old railway. Now it's a very easy and delightful 2-mile walk to East Grinstead through unspoilt countryside, heading just north of east, with a mixture of woodland and open fields around you, and the Sussex Border Path rejoining you briefly as well. You then enter East Grinstead and, crossing the existing railway, descend to the forecourt area of the mainline railway station. You can now go straight on along what is the Forest Way but if you've time you may want to detour down past the station to the very well-signed northern terminus of the Bluebell Railway. This preserved steam railway line, part of the former line linking East Grinstead with Lewes, runs as far as Sheffield Park where the headquarters of the railway are situated. For more information about the Bluebell Railway, please refer to the section of this book devoted to the Sussex Ouse Valley Way, which passes right by the Sheffield Park station approach road.

You've now reached the end of the Worth Way but can carry straight on along the Forest Way part of the WFW. Walk from the mainline station forecourt, keeping Sainsbury's to the right, to a roundabout; cross straight over up Railway Approach and then turn right along London Road and left along **East Grinstead** High Street. There's a brief overlap here with not only the Sussex Border Path but the High Weald Landscape Trail and Greenwich Meridian Trail. Truly a spaghetti junction of name routes in Sussex! East Grinstead isn't the prettiest town in Sussex, and is hardly a tourist honeypot; in fact it is mercilessly ridiculed in Alan Ayckbourn's *Norman Conquests* trilogy as a most unlikely place for a clandestine romantic weekend. That said, there is plenty of interest on both sides of the High Street. On the right (very close to the junction with London Road) is the splendid timber-framed late 16th century Clarendon House and several attractive shops (including great bookshop!) as well as Middle Row beyond, followed by the 18th century Dorset Arms then the superb half-timbered 12th century Cromwell House. On the left there's a detour possible via Cantelupe Road to the town museum (100 yards or so along the road), then further along the High Street is the sandstone church of St Swithun, built two centuries ago and boasting eight bells, the largest peal in Sussex. Then you reach the fine stone-built Sackville College, dating from the early 17th century, and often open to the public. Beyond the college on the left and Cromwell House on the right the Forest Way continues away from the town, forking onto a clearly signed path, heading downhill and now rejoining the course of the Three Bridges-Tunbridge Wells railway line.

Your excellent path soon leaves the suburbs of East Grinstead behind and you now head south-eastwards into open countryside, enjoying really excellent views, particularly to the right, where woodland dominates the skyline. You're here overlapping briefly with the Sussex Border Path spur section as well as the High Weald Landscape Trail. As you approach the A22 and Forest Row, just over 2 miles from East Grinstead, there's a well-marked crossing of Brambletye Lane, where a right turn and a walk of just 250 yards each way brings you to the ruins of Brambletye House, built in Elizabethan-Jacobean style in 1631 but soon afterwards destroyed in the English Civil War. The ruins do make a highly impressive sight and give a clear impression of how the house would have looked externally had it survived. In 2.5 miles from East Grinstead the Forest Way crosses the A22, but a quarter of a mile (each way) detour to the right alongside this road brings you to the pretty village of **Forest Row**. Forest Row is cited by Keith Spence as one of the few villages where the main hostelry – in this case the tile-hung Chequers Inn Hotel, a former coaching inn, established around 1452 – is older than the parish church, which wasn't built till 1836. A stone in the wall of the 19th century village hall commemorates the visit of President Kennedy. Nowadays the village is sadly spoilt by the volume of noise and fumes from motorists negotiating the A22, but as the village's name suggests, it lies right on the edge of Ashdown Forest and it's not far from the bustling village centre into the forest itself. If you've walked the Vanguard Way you'll remember that that trail passes through Forest Row, and you may have particular cause to recall the village if you've lost your way in the forest (which is very easily done) and staggered into Forest Row several hours behind schedule and desperate for a drink! When the railway line between Three Bridges and Groombridge was operational, this was the busiest of the intermediate stations on the route; indeed, in the final years of the line, a number of London commuters were using this station, and some trains from London to East Grinstead were in fact extended to terminate here. Beyond the A22 the WFW follows a metalled lane which rises and then forks right, crossing the Vanguard Way and saying farewell to the High Weald Landscape Trail.

You now enjoy a straightforward 4-mile walk to Hartfield along the course of the old line. Initially you continue south-eastwards, but having shaken off the built-up area on the eastern side of Forest Row, you begin to head north-eastwards, enjoying excellent views to the fine Ashdown House which lies on the left (north) side of the old line. Ashdown House, now a school, is a Grade II listed building that dates from 1794; it was designed by Sussex-born Benjamin Latrobe, who also designed nearby Hammerwood House close to the Vanguard Way as well as the front portico of the White House in Washington. The countryside on both sides of your route is quite delightful. You can see why the Forest Way gets its name as the fringes of Ashdown Forest are clearly visible to your right, and you also have lovely views to meadows to your left. This section of route, in which you actually cross back over the High Weald Landscape Trail (which has taken a more circuitous route to get here from Forest Row) is particularly popular with cyclists as well as walkers, so do not expect to be on your own! You pass underneath the **B2026** Maresfield-Edenbridge road, but by joining this road (reached via the slipway to the right, just beyond the bridge, and then the station approach road) you can detour just a quarter of a mile southwards to **Hartfield**, which together with a further detour to Poohsticks Bridge is described more fully in the High Weald Landscape Trail section. The station building, just to the left down the station approach road, survives and boasts an impressive frontage. Despite the modest size of the community it served, the old station at Hartfield boasted a goods yard loop that could hold 13 wagons.

Back on the WFW the walk, just north of east, from Hartfield along the old line is delightfully fast and easy in lovely surroundings, crossing the Wealdway in a little under a mile. A detour along the Wealdway to the right brings you in about half a mile to the delightful Withyham Church, described more fully in the Wealdway section. The WFW however continues past the rather inelegantly named village of Balls Green and the site of the old station at Withyham, which also boasted a goods yard during its lifetime. Very roughly parallel and to your left is the infant river Medway, which rises between Crawley and East Grinstead and goes on to become a major river in Kent, emptying into the Thames and being crossed by major motorway and rail bridges. There's little hint of that just here! You veer in a more north-easterly direction for a while, but then turn south-eastwards, crossing the B2110 and for a very short distance beyond it overlapping with the Sussex Border Path. The latter soon veers away right and heads towards Mott's Mill, but you stick to the old line, shortly aware of the extant London-Uckfield railway coming in from the left. You veer right to cross the B2188 and continue on beside the extant railway, then veer left to pass under the railway and right, eastwards, to go forward to Corseley Road where the Forest Way part of the WFW ends.

To complete your walk I suggest you turn left up Corseley Road, here overlapping with the High Weald Landscape Trail as far as the school (and also, for the whole of this road walk, the Tunbridge Wells Circular Walk), then dropping down along the road to **Groombridge**, arriving at Station Road and turning left along it to reach the **B2110** where the buses stop. The best bits of Groombridge, including the fine Groombridge Place, are less than a quarter of a mile across the border in Kent and most conveniently reached by turning right beside the B2110 or, for slightly quicker access to Groombridge Place, a footpath leading away to the east of the village car park which is immediately opposite the Corseley Road/ Station Road junction, this path veering north to Groombridge Place. However the Sussex part of Groombridge contains a station on the preserved Spa Valley Railway (a full journey along which is available from the High Weald Landscape Trail; see the High Weald Landscape Trail section). To access Groombridge Station, turn right off Corseley Road along Springfield Road (some 375 yards beyond the school) then right again up Station Road. As stated in the High Weald Landscape Trail section, it's worth riding the railway to the remarkable sandstone rock outcrops at High Rocks, which has its own station (the next one up the line from Groombridge). You could then continue from High Rocks by train to Tunbridge Wells where there are excellent bus and train connections.

GOOD TO KNOW
Start: Three Bridges Station. Finish: B2110 Groombridge.
Total mileage: 17.
Difficulty: Easy.
Stages: Crawley Down (RB) 4, East Grinstead (*RAB) 7,
Forest Row (RAB) 9.5, B2026 for Hartfield (RAB) 13.5, B2110
Groombridge (RAB) 17.
OS 134,135.

D1 Cross the stile and follow, beyond the stile, a signed path through Worthlodge Forest on a clear very well-signed woodland track, Standinghall Lane, ignoring crossing tracks (most of which are clearly signed as private, so it would take a genius to stray!). In just over 1.25 miles you reach the B2110 Paddockhurst Road. Cross the road and turn left, walking uphill to soon reach the signed entrance to Worth Abbey. There are excellent views from above the abbey including to the grey bulk of Worth School. Now retrace back down the B2110 the way you came. You could now do another short walk to get a closer view of the school still, but it comes with a caveat. To do this walk, shortly beyond the school entrance (and more or less opposite the footpath you used to get to the B2110 in the first place) turn left, south-eastwards, along the signed footpath and in 250 yards or so climb a little wooden staircase to the left and continue briefly south-eastwards to view the school to the left. Here's the caveat: technically by leaving the path you're on private land but as long as you don't stray any closer to the school you should avoid any difficulty. Then retrace to the B2110. Now, whether you've done this further detour along the footpath or not, recross the B2110 and return to the start of the full detour the same way. (Total detour 3.75 miles; 3.5 miles if footpath south-east of B2110 omitted)

DIAMOND WAY

The Diamond Way (DW) isn't a waymarked route and therefore technically doesn't belong in this book. However it's right to mention it because it clearly does resonate with many Sussex walkers; it was conceived to commemorate the 60th birthday of the Sussex Ramblers, and its west to east course across the Low Weald is, appropriately enough, 60 miles. Beginning at Midhurst it pulls away across Cowdray Park and through Lodsworth, climbs to Pitshill and descends past vineyards to Tillington and Petworth. Beyond Petworth the DW continues through the woods of Flexham Park and on to follow the Wey & Arun Canal and pass round the south of Billingshurst. There's then classic Low Weald walking along field tracks interspersed with some woodland, the DW crossing the A24 and the Downs Link near Southwater. The terrain becomes more wooded as the DW passes Bolney and arrives at Cuckfield. Fiddly, chiefly suburban walking takes you past Haywards Heath and Lindfield, then Low Weald farmland takes over again, bringing the DW to the pretty Heaven Farm complex. A potentially confusing traverse of Sheffield Wood is followed by a walk through Ashdown Forest, and expert navigation skills are essential to negotiate the forest and the woodland round Fairwarp. The DW crosses the A26 then normal Low Weald service resumes with a mixture of field and woodland tracks, points of interest being the splendid red-brick viaduct carrying the Uckfield-London railway, the fine views south to the valley of the river Uck, and the trees of Broadreed Wood. Beyond Five Ashes there are further good views to Mayfield and there follow a number of quite demanding climbs and descents, mainly wooded, the DW veering south-eastwards to end at Heathfield.

I have walked the route in full over four days and did enjoy it for the most part. That said, there are no particular scenic or historic highlights unique to the DW. There is one potentially highly dangerous road crossing (A24), there's an unpleasant piece of pavement-less B-road walking (B2133), and the lack of waymarking can be a real problem even with maps and technology to hand. Moreover, sadly the DW guidebook advertised online is out of print. But the fact that it avoids traditional "honeypots" is

414

a point in its favour, and indeed much of the countryside through which it passes is most pleasant and unspoilt, while amenities are never too far away. Perhaps a new generation of Sussex Ramblers will be instrumental in turning it into the twentieth Great Walk of Sussex!

THEMATIC INDEX

All of the walks listed in this book pass through or close to many features of great interest. And through completing not only the walks themselves but also the detours and route variations I've described, you will have the opportunity to see the best of everything Sussex has to offer: scenery, architecture, history and much more besides. The purpose of this index is to enable you, quickly and easily, to locate the best features of Sussex, listed by theme rather than simply alphabetically. By cross-referring to the text where these features are described, and noting in which walk and at which point in that walk they come, you can plan your visits to them accordingly, possibly including a number of such features in a single walk.

There is obviously an element of subjectivity about my nominations for "best features." I have been guided to a large degree by the inclusion of these features in standard reference works as included in the bibliography and suggestions for further reading. Some features, such as the Royal Pavilion in Brighton, Chichester Cathedral or Bodiam Castle, can be guaranteed to appear in any such work, but *all* the features listed below constitute in my view the best examples of their type in Sussex. Please note that I have decided to omit, under Visitor Attractions, those attractions primarily aimed at families with young children such as animal, adventure and fun parks. They are in any case not generally referred to in the route descriptions.

I have had to be particularly selective about historic churches, as Sussex has so many! In order to ensure consistency, I have in the body of the text confined myself to churches that are of historic interest and that are on or within a quarter of a mile EITHER of the route itself OR a recommended detour/variation off the route that contains other features of interest. Those self-imposed restrictions won't have applied if the church in question is listed in Simon Jenkins' *England's Thousand Best Churches,* or in Tim Locke's *Slow Travel Sussex* which in my view is the best contemporary guide to Sussex currently available. I have kept my list below simply to the churches listed in those two guides, and you should make every effort to include them in your itinerary, but other churches besides those listed below may have been described in the text.

Please note that some of the features listed below carry admission charges, which can be substantial. Common sense will generally tell you when you're likely to have to pay to enter a particular place, but if in doubt, check before you visit. Please note also that opening times of some of the features are very restricted. Many windmills, for instance, may only open on the occasional Sunday afternoon, while some buildings listed below don't open to the public at all, and walkers may have to be content with viewing their exteriors only. Even some churches may regrettably be locked at certain times. In all cases, it's best to check the relevant website and/or telephone ahead to avoid disappointment!

Please note that this index doesn't include features of interest on parts of the routes described in this book that are outside Sussex.

HISTORIC VILLAGES

HISTORIC TOWNS/CITIES

INDEX OF CENTRES

In this index I list all the significant centres in Sussex, indicating which Great Walks (using the abbreviations as stated in the text) or variations, pass through them as well as the page(s) in the text in which reference to them may be found. If no Great Walk, or variation, passes through a centre mentioned below I state the nearest place at which a Great Walk, or variation, may be located, and the page or pages in which reference to that place may be found.

Southwater – DL 19
Steyning – DL, MW 15-6,23-4,145
Storrington – WSLT variation 380
Uckfield – SHT, WW 279,357
Winchelsea – RMC, TCW 170-1,326-7
Worthing – ECP, SHT 49,51,93-4,267

BIBLIOGRAPHY & SUGGESTIONS FOR FURTHER READING

Please note that many of these books are sadly now out of print and unavailable in bookshops, and to obtain a copy you may need to order online or visit one of the Sussex public libraries.

AA Book Of British Villages, Drive Publications

Anderson, Peter & McKenna, Keith: *West Sussex Literary Trail*, Per-Rambulations

Antill, Trevor: *Monarch's Way Part 3*, Meridian Publications

Bathurst, David: *Sussex Station Walks*, SB Publications

Bathurst, David: *Walking The Coastline Of Sussex*, SB Publications (2012 ed)

Bathurst, David: *Walking The Disused Railways Of Sussex & Surrey*, SB Publications

Bathurst, David: *Walking The Sussex Border Path*, SB Publications

Cowan, Bea: *Saxon Shore Way*, Aurum Press

Cuckoo Trail – A 14-Mile Trail For Walkers, Cyclists And Horseriders (local authority publication in leaflet form, available online)

Downs Link – A Six-Stage Route Guide (local authority booklet, available online)

Harrison, David: *Vanguard Way*, SB Publications

Heap, Graham & Heap, Hilda: *Greenwich Meridian Trail Book 1*, New Generation Publishing

Jenkins, Simon: *England's Thousand Best Churches*, Allen Lane

Jenner, Lorna & Lawton, Eila: *Along And Around The High Weald Landscape Trail*, High Weald Forum

King, Geoffrey: *Wealdway*, Ramblers Association

Locke, Tim: *Slow Travel Sussex, South Downs, Weald & Coast*, Bradt Travel Guide (Edition 2)

Millmore, Paul: *South Downs Way National Trail Guide*, Aurum Press (2016 ed)

Morgan, Julian, Nash, Lynn & Perks, Geoff: *Wey South Path*, W & A Enterprises Limited

New Lipchis Way (Footprints Of Sussex publication in leaflet form, available online)

Owen, Terry & Anderson, Peter: *Sussex Ouse Valley Way*, Per-Rambulations

Pevsner, Nikolaus & Nairn, Ian: *Sussex*, Buildings of England series, Penguin Books

Rough Guide To Kent, Sussex & Surrey, Rough Guides (2017 ed)

Serpent Trail Official Guide (obtainable from the South Downs Centre, Midhurst)

Smailes, Brian: *1066 Country Walk Official Guide*, Challenge Publications

Spence, Keith: *The Companion Guide To Kent and Sussex*, Companion Guides

Worth Way/Forest Way (local authority publications in leaflet form, available online)